SCIENCE IN THE SNAKEPIT

SCIENCE IN THE SNAKEPIT

Tales of the often eccentric people who have studied serpents over the centuries and sometimes paid with their lives

RICK SHINE

NH

Carpet Pythons (*Morelia variegata*) are abundant across much of Australia, even in the highly modified habitats of suburbia. ALANA DE LAIVE

Contents

Acknowledgements

In writing this book, my greatest debt is to my fellow researchers both past and present. I especially thank the colleagues, students, collaborators, snake keepers and friends who have helped me learn about the ecology of snakes.

For comments on drafts of this book, I am grateful to Aaron Bauer, Greg Brown, Sean Graham, Chris Jolly, Bill Lamar, Kevin Markwell, Rich Seigel and Georgia Ward-Fear. Graham Alexander and Dave Barker also helped me clarify my thinking. Alana De Laive allowed me to use her beautiful illustrations. For stunning photographs, I thank the people whose work graces these pages. I've never even met many of those photographers, and I am gobsmacked by their generosity. My research assistant for the last 30 years, Melanie Elphick, helped with proof-reading. She deserves sainthood, as does my wife Terri who processed the photographs. For support over many years, I thank Terri, my sons and daughters-in-law and our grandchildren. I respectfully acknowledge firm supervision over a 40-year period by West Highland White Terriers.

The author face-to-face with one of his long-term study species – a Water Python (*Liasis fuscus*) from tropical Australia.

Foreword

Men have been writing nonsense about snakes for centuries, but the first truly informative 'popular' book on snake biology was authored by an Englishwoman named Catherine Cooper Hopley. Her 1882 book, *Snakes: Curiosities and Wonders of Serpent Life*, summarised scientific understanding of the time, enlivened by her own first-hand observations of live snakes.

Born and raised in England, Hopley travelled to Richmond, Virginia, in 1860 to work as governess to a plantation-owning family. The American Civil War broke out in 1861 and Richmond became the capital of the Confederacy. But warfare didn't faze the intrepid Ms Hopley, who travelled extensively across North America – even to the frontline of battle in Baltimore. The passport that she obtained (under a false name) to make that journey describes her as "4 feet, 11 inches tall [about 1.5 m]; complexion florid; hair carroty; eyes hazel; build robust." By any standards, Hopley was extraordinary. As governess, she taught French, piano, singing, drawing and painting, Latin, mathematics and algebra. Suspected of spying for the British, she was imprisoned in the USA for several months. After her return to England, she developed a strong interest in snakes, and her 1882 book was the result.

In her foreword to that book, Hopley wrote: "To the many friends who have repeatedly asked me; 'What could induce you to take up such a horrid subject as snakes?' a few words of explanation must be offered. ... The little history will be a sort of OPHIDIANA, or gossip about snakes... Whatever of romance or sensation attaches to it, is due to the marvellous powers of the creatures who fill its pages, and whose true nature I have laboured to comprehend." In a society where snakes were shunned, Catherine Hopley took on the daunting job of serpent public relations.

Hopley's inspirational efforts have been followed by many others, including people who devoted their lives – and sometimes, ended their lives – in pursuit of knowledge about the world of serpents. Over the course of my own research on the ecology of snakes, I became fascinated by the complicated, error-ridden and dynamic process by which human beings have come to understand snakes – and especially, to understand the private lives of those mysterious animals. The scientists who forged that understanding were (and are) a strange mix of personalities, united only by their curiosity about peculiar creatures. Some of those scientists contributed tiny snippets of information. Others devoted decades to rigorous research on snakes, at the cost of being regarded as odd by almost everyone they met.

Progress from ignorance to enlightenment has sometimes moved forward in great bounds, and at other times has crept along by millimetres. The early practitioners included some

Author of a groundbreaking 1882 book on snake biology, Englishwoman Catherine Cooper Hopley is pictured here holding a newly hatched tortoise.

amazing personalities, whose discoveries set the foundations for our current views. But the most extraordinary phase in snake research has been the most recent one. Our understanding of snakes – and especially, of their ecology and behaviour – has been transformed over the last 50 years.

Before 1980, our knowledge of snake ecology was fragmentary and was mostly based on a few species from Europe and North America. That situation has changed dramatically. Ecological, experimental and behavioural studies have now been conducted on hundreds of snake species, and those studies have asked new questions, developed new methods, and generated new insights. I had the good fortune to be part of that modern snake-ecology revolution.

In the following pages, I explore how ecologists, behaviourists and evolutionary biologists developed an understanding of their secretive and sometimes deadly study animals. I talk about the pioneering scientists, and the impacts of their discoveries. I look at new methods that were developed, and how they evolved. I document the upsurge in snake research, and how that effort expanded to encompass more diverse kinds of snakes, from more diverse places, and with contributions from an increasingly diverse array of people.

To really appreciate the feelings and attitudes of early workers, though, you need to read their own words. So I've added a section at the end of each chapter for pioneering snake ecologists to express their opinions.

To keep the book accessible to readers with no professional training in science, I've only added scientific (Latin) names of snakes to the text in cases where common names are hopelessly ambiguous. If you want to know the Latin name of a species I refer to in the text, just check the Index entry for that common name.

And lastly, I don't pretend that this is an objective overview. Other researchers will have different opinions concerning the growth of our understanding about the secret lives of serpents. This book tells the story of the snake-ecology revolution from my own personal perspective.

The giant Nawaran, or Oenpelli Python (*Nyctophilopython oenpelliensis*), is a rarely encountered denizen of sandstone outcrops in tropical Australia. ALANA DE LAIVE

PART 1

CHARTING A REVOLUTION

Scientific understanding does not progress smoothly from ignorance to enlightenment. Instead, it moves in irregular fits and starts. A field of enquiry lies dormant for decades, then leaps into prominence and reveals new dimensions. Almost overnight, researchers begin to ask new types of questions, discover new types of answers, and overthrow conventional mythology.

To tease apart the processes at work in that tangled transition, we can begin by asking about the earliest contributions to snake ecology, and then move to the timing of the Great Leap Forward. Why did the modern revolution in snake ecology research begin in the latter part of the 20th century rather than earlier or later? What factors delayed its onset? What changed to overcome those obstacles?

Chapter 1

Emerging from the Dark Ages

Homo sapiens evolved at least two hundred thousand years ago, and curiosity is a defining aspect of our species. Nonetheless, scientific research is a recent invention. The earliest people created narratives, but for most of human history our 'explanations' were rooted in myth. A scientific approach based on evidence and logic arose more recently, and now coexists uncomfortably with older ways of thinking.

The idea of science as a profession – of people employed to gather and interpret information – is newer still. The notion of paying someone to conduct research arose about two hundred years ago. Until then, exploring the natural world was an option only if you were rich (like Charles Darwin) or could conduct your investigations while doing other work. For example, the co-inventor of the theory of natural selection, British naturalist Alfred Russel Wallace, made his living by collecting exotic animals for European museums. Until the latter half of the 19th century, professional scientists were as scarce as rocking-horse droppings. The word 'scientist' was only coined in 1834. Until then, researchers were called 'natural philosophers'. To visualise the degree to which research is a modern-day phenomenon, consider this statistic: 90 per cent of all scientists who ever lived are alive today.

But although they lacked academic credentials, our early ancestors understood a lot about the natural world. Living in nature, there was a strong pay-off to avoiding danger – and at the top of the list of 'dangers to be avoided' were snakes. Even before our forebears came down from the trees to wander the African savannahs four million years ago, we encountered snakes that were big enough to eat us (pythons) or venomous enough to kill us (such as mambas and Puff Adders). That threat changed the course of human evolution. Some of our potential ancestors never contributed to the modern-day gene pool because they fell by the wayside, in the coils of a python or with venom coursing through their veins. The survivors were the people most adept at seeing a half-hidden scaly body in the grass or among the branches. Some researchers believe that the risk posed by snakes explains why humans have better eyesight than most other animals.

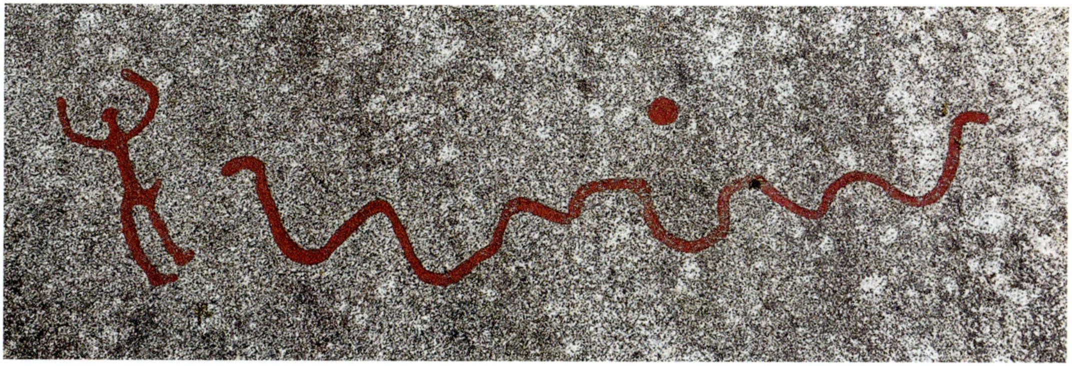

A fear of snakes has been a perennial theme of human culture, as shown by this Bronze-Age petroglyph photographed by the author on rocks near Tanum in Sweden. The gentleman involved appears to be excited as well as frightened.

The ability to detect a half-hidden snake would be useful, but even better would be the ability to predict the habits of snakes. Correctly guessing where and when you were likely to encounter snakes might make the difference between life and death. For millions of years, our ancestors paid attention to snakes and taught their children how to avoid becoming snakebite statistics.

Those lessons took the form of stories, because a tale of misadventure is easier to remember than a dry list of instructions. Many anecdotes would have been quite specific – for example, about the death of a person foolish enough to walk around in bare feet after sunset. But much of the early literature about snakes seems designed to simply scare the hell out of the reader, warning them to remain vigilant against this unpredictable menace. As a result, the strongest themes in snake folklore are the mysterious nature of the beast, its trickery, and its magical links to immortality. The oldest living cultures today (the First Nations people of Australia) have snakes as their central creation being – the mighty Rainbow Serpent, world creator, river maker, God-like but chaotic when angry. A story to teach children about the dangers of snakes, but also about their importance.

In some cultures, though, snakes have been revered rather than feared or despised. In one small village in West Bengal, India, for example, local people have tolerated cobras for hundreds of years – and as a result, the local cobras also tolerate people. The highly venomous snakes serve as rat-catchers and are venerated as demi-gods – the earthly embodiments of the goddess Jhankswari. Known as 'old ladies' to the villagers, the cobras are so revered that only Brahmin priests are permitted to touch them. The docility of the snakes is as impressive as the forebearance of the villagers.

Snakes attract awe and veneration as well as fear. This image shows Thai men ceremonially carrying a snake effigy. PIXABAY.

Such peaceful coexistence is scarce in Western societies. For people raised in the Judeo-Christian tradition, the best-known story is the one in Genesis. Satan takes the form of a snake in the Garden of Eden, convinces Eve to transgress, and sets the human race on a path towards sin and depravity. Scholars trace the Garden of Eden story back to the legend of Gilgamesh from more than a thousand years earlier, when a snake stole a magic herb that could restore youth. Snakes have been cast in the role of sly arch villains for a long time. Such stories taught your children to be watchful; snakes appear when you least expect them, and they behave in unpredictable ways.

The supernatural powers of snakes percolate through many early fables, including a famous Greek tragedy that centres on sex-shifting. The story begins when a man named Tiresias encounters two mating snakes on the sacred slopes of Mount Cyllene, and he kills the female snake. Hera, formidable wife of the god Zeus, is horrified by this persecution of females. To enforce a new perspective on life, she transforms Tiresias into a woman. Seven years later, Tiresias encounters another pair of copulating snakes and kills one – but this time it is the male. Delighted at the shift in sexual targets, Hera transforms Tiresias back into a man.

Sadly, however, that gender fluidity proves dangerous when the marriage of the Gods hits a roadbump. When Hera accuses her husband of extramarital affairs, Zeus downplays the issue by claiming that men obtain less pleasure from physical love than do women. That's a difficult proposition to test, but Hera recalls that Tiresias has experienced life from the viewpoint of both sexes. When Tiresias agrees with Zeus, Hera retaliates by blinding him – but as compensation, Zeus gives Tiresias the gifts of prophecy and longevity.

The story of Tiresias's snake-killing exploits is puzzling on many levels, but hinges on an ability to distinguish between a male snake and a female. And unless Tiresias was more observant than my students, that challenge is formidable. In mammals and birds, males differ from females in traits such as size, shape, and (in most mammals) external genitals. A rooster versus a hen. A stallion versus a mare. It's far more difficult to distinguish a male snake from a female – rendering Tiresias's punishment unfair. But the Greek gods were renowned for their arbitrary exercise of power.

As civilisation progressed, myths about snakes gave way to pseudo-rational explanations. Most of these were based on observations from nature, but it can be difficult to see exactly how. For example, in his fifth-century tome *Inquiries*, Herodotus wrote: "So it is also with the vipers... when they are mating in couples and the male is in the very act of emitting his seed, the female… seizes him by the neck and, hanging on, never lets go till she has bitten the neck through. This is how the male dies; but the female pays a kind of recompense, too, to the male. For the children, while still in the womb, take vengeance for their male parent by eating through their mother's insides and so make their entry into the world after eating up her womb." The narrative is a bold attempt to incorporate three observations. First, European vipers are venomous. Second, they bear live young rather than laying eggs. And third, adult males are active only during the mating season. When the springtime hi-jinks conclude the males go into hiding, so it seems as if they have died. With a creative leap, Herodotus interpreted those natural-history observations as evidence that God had created a system to keep viper abundance in check.

Up until the Middle Ages, people had a wide range of supernatural entities to be frightened of. Devil-spirits still lurk around the campfire at night for many First Nations cultures. But Western societies have changed. As science eroded belief in demons, storytellers needing an antihero turned to real animals. Trolls and dragons vanished but snakes still occupy a special place – a very dark place – in the recesses of the human mind.

As time went by, nonsensical tales about snakes found their way into the emerging literature of professional science. Research papers in the 19th century earnestly describe female snakes swallowing their offspring to protect them, and snakes creeping up to nurse from sleeping women.

European vipers – especially Eurasian Adders (*Vipera berus*) – have attracted scientific attention for at least 15 centuries. In this image, the author is assisting Belgian biologist Katja Claus in her long-running field study on this pugnacious little serpent. TERRI SHINE

Present-day fables mostly are about snakes that attack people without provocation; or venoms so potent that a bitten person collapses instantly. A venom-laden snake fang impaled in a boot, killing people who later pull on that boot. Snakes that can outrun a galloping horse. A lovesick male snake intent on revenge after its mate is killed. And the underlying message is cautionary: BEWARE! By terrifying your children, you teach them to avoid these dangerous creatures.

Indeed, some myths about aggressive snakes may have been created to control the behaviour of unruly children. My friend Steve Wilson tells a great story about the terror that sea kraits inspire among village children in the Solomon Islands near New Guinea. Despite possessing toxic venom, these black-and-white banded sea snakes are incredibly tolerant; native people in other Indo-Pacific regions handle them with impunity. But villagers in the Morovo Lagoon area call this snake the *noki nungunu nungunu peri*, which translates as 'up-your-bum snake' – because the snake is thought to take refuge inside the anus of an unwary person. That's nonsense of course, and the adults probably don't believe it, but it's a great way to get the kids out of the water when you're trying to call them for dinner. Steve reckons that "Look out, here comes *noki nungunu nungunu peri*" was a virtual guarantee of having a bunch of screaming kids hurtling up onto the beach.

Given the lethal firepower of venomous snakes, you might expect serpents to be among the most-frequently studied types of animals. But they aren't. In 1962, South African biologist Walter Rose wrote that: "No animal has had to bear such a load of exaggeration, misrepresentation and unparalleled nonsense, spoken and written, from Genesis to yesterday's newspaper, as have members of this unfortunate tribe … it may be said that a person's fear of snakes varies inversely with his knowledge of them; the greater the ignorance the greater the fear."

In fact, there were no detailed studies of any snakes until midway though the 20th century. Instead, most wildlife research focused on mammals and birds – especially, species that are attractive to look at, fun to kill, or good to eat. Generations of students have peered into the details of those species' lives. University libraries have shelf after shelf of books about Great Tits and Red Deer, but you won't find equivalent shelves of books about snakes. Researchers ignored these mysterious animals.

Why did snakes attract so little research? There were several reasons, and below I'll talk about each of those in turn.

'The only good snake is a dead snake'

The sight of a python basking in the sunlight fills me with joy, but it fills my neighbour with an overwhelming desire to thump that animal on the head. Why? In every Western country, many more people are killed each year by dogs than by snakes – but if a Cocker Spaniel wanders into the front yard, we don't bash it with a shovel. Deep within our psyche, snakes arouse a special terror. It's primal. Even in countries that lack venomous snakes, fear of serpents is the norm. In 1893, the English fungus enthusiast Mordecai Cubitt Cooke wrote: "Everybody shudders at the name of a snake. Very few possess courage enough to attempt … staying to count the number of scales on its head."

These images from 1950s Australia capture the unthinking hostility that people felt for snakes...
Two proud men pose with a slaughtered Tiger Snake (*Notechis scutatus*) in front of admiring schoolchildren in Railston, Tasmania.
THE ADVOCATE NEWSPAPER
Two young Aussies after a day spent murdering the same species in South Australia. STATE LIBRARY OF SOUTH AUSTRALIA

That terror is a formidable obstacle for a young researcher who wants to study snakes. A university-based scientist is likely to be unpopular when one or more serpents escape from their cages and find their way into the offices of colleagues. This seems an appropriate time for me to apologise to Bob Winokur, my office-mate who one day opened his desk drawer, reached in, and put his hand on a large venomous snake. Indeed, snakes are legally embargoed from many workplaces, and even from entire countries such as New Zealand. A study organism that horrifies your department manager is a poor career choice for an ambitious young researcher.

American boy scouts with reptiles and amphibians in the 1950s. LIBRARY OF VIRGINIA

Even today, anti-snake sentiments can be powerful enough to curtail research. But in an historical context, the modern antipathy towards serpents is a pale shadow of the universal paranoia that once existed. For a modern environmentally enlightened citizen, it's difficult to understand the passionate hatred towards snakes – all snakes – that was so prevalent just a few generations ago. In British-controlled India in the 1880s, villagers killed around half a million venomous snakes a year to obtain a financial reward from the Raj. In 1890, British lawyer George William Vidal (1845–1907, better known for popularising the sport of badminton than for his zoological interests) noted approvingly that Indian villagers brought in more than

100,000 snakes within an eight-day period after a reward was introduced. A North American writer in 1889 summarised people's attitudes to snakes as follows: "However innocent, or even useful, a snake in the popular creed is 'a varmint with no right to live'." Those attitudes persisted into the 20th century. A 1906 book on snakes of Pennsylvania by H.A. Surface decribed the inoffensive American Copperhead as "treacherous, despicable and dangerous." Also in the USA, 1930s boy scouts were awarded 'conservation medals' for killing water snakes to protect trout populations. In 1970s Australia, national parks rangers routinely killed snakes in reserves where 'wildlife' was stringently protected.

In today's world, where many people would share Richard Williams's enthusiasm for this recently captured Eastern Kingsnake (*Lampropeltis getula*), it's difficult to imagine the unreasoning hatred that snakes attracted just a few decades ago. NOAH K. FIELDS

From a modern perspective, many statements in early scientific literature seem callous. The early writers take it for granted that venomous snakes should be exterminated. In 1887, American author and fossil enthusiast Oliver Perry Hay (1846–1930) laments the decline of the massasauga (a small rattlesnake) by noting: "Some 25 or 30 years ago this species was excessively abundant on the then sparsely-settled prairies of Northern Illinois; and among the farmers' boys of that day the slaughter of these snakes furnished a means of establishing a reputation for courage and enterprise."

Snake slaughter was an international recreational pastime. On the Bass Strait islands off southern Australia in 1891, the Bishop of Tasmania (Henry Hutchinson Montgomery, 1847–1932; the father of Field Marshall Montgomery, a renowned soldier in both World Wars) wrote: "The young men spend Sunday morning sometimes in killing snakes. Two parties the other day started out to see how many they could get – one party brought in 100, the other 70. Nor did anyone in the islands to whom I mentioned this think it an extraordinary case." In 1964 the pioneering French snake biologist Hubert Saint Girons (1926–2000) wrote of finding a pile of dead New Caledonian Sea Kraits on a small coral-reef island in the Indo-Pacific, which had been massacred by tourists. Fuelled by fear, ignorance and machismo, the persecution was worldwide.

Even today, snakes strike terror into the hearts of many people. Surveys list snakes as the Number 1 'extreme fear' for 25 per cent of Americans. US poet Emily Dickinson (1830–1886) beautifully captured the feelings that rise up when a snake crosses your path: "But never met this fellow/Attended or alone/Without a tighter breathing/And zero at the bone." Judging by their reactions, many other species – including monkeys, dogs and horses – share Emily's response. Even when the risk is zero, the sight of a snake can induce a moment of full-blown panic. In 1872 Charles Darwin (1809–1882) wrote: "I put my face close to the thick plate-glass in front of a puff-adder in the zoological gardens, with the firm determination of not starting back if the snake struck at me; but as soon as the blow was struck, my resolution went for nothing, and I jumped a yard or two backwards with astonishing rapidity. My will and reason were powerless against the imagination of a danger …"

A typical example of early attitudes to snakes is nicely summarised by the title of a chapter in one of the first books ever written about snakes. Charles Owen (d.1746) was a Presbyterian minister in Lancashire, England, known more for his controversial political statements than for his biological interests. But he wrote a book about snakes in 1742, and my favourite chapter title reads: "Upon the Adoration of Different Kinds of Beasts by the Egyptians, with Instances of the Same Stupidity in Other Nations."

Fortunately for these long-persecuted reptiles, that mindless fear is slowly evaporating. Negative vibes towards serpents have become less extreme. Society's view of 'wildlife' underwent a seismic shift as an increasingly urban population moved away from seeing wild animals as either useful (sources of meat and leather) or candidates for extermination (dangerous or ugly). As ecosystems worldwide were degraded by deforestation, pollution and excessive offtake, a new generation began to view wild animals as worthy of respect. The public's insatiable appetite for wildlife documentaries on TV spawned shows about more diverse types of animals. And science broadened its scope as well; the historical emphasis on mammals and birds began to fade. Simplistic ideas about some animals being 'good' and others 'bad' no longer resonated with an educated and secular population. Children began to see wild animals as living beings rather than resources: creatures to learn about rather than to demonise and kill.

In Western societies, increasing social acceptance of snakes through time brought other forces into play. Pragmatically, a researcher needs money to buy equipment and employ assistants – and as society began to view snakes as animals not demons, research funds became available. Conservation organisations widened their priorities to include reptiles as well as mammals and birds. For example, government committees provided funding to study a small kind of rattlesnake – the Eastern Massasauga – that was declining across eastern North America. Another target for funding was the Concho Water Snake, which was imperilled by reservoir construction in Texas. My own research in the Australian tropics was kick-started by government funds to investigate if Arafura File Snakes were under threat from uranium mining.

One of the first snake species to attract widespread conservation concern was a small North American rattlesnake named the Eastern Massasauga. The closely related Western Massasauga (*Sistrurus tergeminus*) – pictured here – is also threatened. NOAH K. FIELDS

Conflict among research groups played a role as well. Perhaps because snakes were so difficult to study, and so few people wanted to study them, competition was non-existent. Most snake researchers were supportive of each other. Information, methods and ideas were freely exchanged. Rivalry among groups was reduced by the availability of many as-yet-unstudied species, reducing overlap among studies and thus, the potential for competition when it came time to publish our results. I assumed that kind of positivity was the norm in science until I visited the USA for the first time. At the conferences I attended, competition was sometimes ferocious among researchers working on frogs, lizards and freshwater turtles. By contrast, the snake biologists were a mellow and co-operative bunch.

'Natural history is old-fashioned science'

A second impediment to studying the ecology of snakes involved the low scientific status of field-based ecological research. There are fads within any human activity, and natural history fell out of favour in the 1960s. It was seen as outdated compared to the emerging powerhouse of molecular genetics. Modern biology was done in the laboratory, by people in white coats who investigated genes or conducted detailed physiological investigations. Research focused on 'model species' such as white rats and fruit flies. Wandering around a swamp in muddy boots, clutching a field notebook, was yesterday's approach. Natural historians were creatures of the 19th century, at the bottom of the list when it was time to hand out grants, jobs or promotions. The stigma was especially great for 'peculiar' animals such as snakes. Birdwatching was OK, but snakewatching was for losers.

Beginning in the late 1960s, the low status of natural history was transformed by new ways of thinking. Visionary biologists encouraged scientists to study natural selection in the field as well as the laboratory. According to Charles Darwin's ideas, small differences among individuals within a population affect the trajectory of evolution. Those differences could involve behaviour and ecology as well as size, shape and colour. Some behaviours enable their bearers to survive and reproduce successfully; other behaviours doom their bearers to a celibate life or an early grave. If offspring inherit their parents' traits, behaviours that enhance survival and reproduction will become more common. The same is true of life-history traits such as growth rates, ages at maturity, and reproductive output. That's 'natural selection', pure and simple.

Perhaps the most compelling stimulus for a resurrection of natural history came from a curmudgeonly American named George C. Williams (1926–2010), a professor at the State University of New York at Stony Brook. This pioneering savant was also a lifelong fan of Icelandic sagas, even writing a long novel about the topic. But in his professional role, George pointed out that we could test evolutionary hypotheses about behavioural and ecological traits

A renaissance of interest in natural history encouraged biologists to go into the field to study snakes. In this image, Bill Lamar is admiring 'the ultimate pit viper' – a large Bushmaster (*Lachesis muta*) from Peru.

just as powerfully as earlier workers had tested ideas about the sizes and shapes of animals. Rather than just speculating, we could rigorously examine Darwin's propositions. And to conduct such analyses, we had to gather our data in the field not the laboratory. These were intoxicating ideas, transforming natural history into a modern science.

The interface between evolution and natural history took on a new name – 'evolutionary ecology' – and a new respectability. The first studies were based on creatures that are easy to observe. Before long, the private lives of birds and insects were being revealed in unprecedented detail. The stigma of field studies evaporated. Inspirational researcher Jane Goodall documented the private lives of free-living Chimpanzees, and young biologists took up the same challenge for their own favourite organisms. Snakes remained a challenge, but field-based studies on snakes were no longer academic suicide.

'Snakes are too difficult to study'

The next impediment to the great revolution in snake ecology was practical. Snakes are diabolically difficult to study – unlike exhibitionist creatures such as birds. The feathered denizens of my suburban backyard behave like stars in a TV soap opera. Magpies forage for insects on the lawn. Parrots engage in raucous domestic disputes on my balcony. But snakes are shy, and they want to be left alone. If I see a snake in my backyard, it flees. Snakes and people don't mix. Snakes don't give up their secrets easily.

To understand that situation, imagine that you are a space alien visiting Earth. Your task is to find out about the day-to-day lives of human beings. It's challenging! Humans are abundant but they flee from your spaceship. And even if you blast a few with your death-ray, then dissect them, you end up with incomplete evidence. You can discover what they eat, what parasites they carry, and broad patterns of their distribution in space and time ('human beings are most common in cities, are active primarily by day, and are often found in aggregations of mixed sexes and ages that appear to be family units'). But those scattered facts don't coalesce into a well-rounded understanding of what humans do, or why they do it.

A snake ecologist faces the same quandary. For example, to discover what kinds of prey are eaten we can look inside the stomach of a preserved serpent, or gently squeeze a newly captured snake so that it regurgitates its meal. That's useful (and fun, especially if you have a poor sense of smell), but it's putting the story together after the fact. It's a poor substitute for watching a snake find, catch and subdue its prey. To really understand the interaction between predator and prey, we need to watch snakes feeding. And to know *why* a snake eats what it does, we need to see how it responds to cues from its potential meal (scent, sight, warmth, and so on). And doing this once or twice wouldn't be enough. To answer those questions, we need to

Most snakes are secretive and feed infrequently, so it's rare to find one having a meal. In this case it's a Barnes' Cat Snake (*Boiga barnesii*) from Sri Lanka snacking on a day gecko (*Cnemaspis* sp.). RUCHIRA SOMAWEERA

observe many individuals. Ditto for every other aspect of snake life, ranging from movements to reproduction. And sadly, it's a lot easier to watch birds feeding, courting, fighting and mating than it is to watch snakes doing those same things.

That poses huge obstacles for an intending researcher. In 1929, pioneering Australian snake biologist and museum curator James Roy Kinghorn (1891–1983) wrote: "The study of the habits of snakes in their natural surroundings is … practically impossible, on account of the extreme caution they display. It would need weeks of undivided attention ... to observe the habits of any of our snakes, and as very few people are able to find the time necessary for this work, our knowledge of the habits of all but the commoner snakes remains practically where it was many years ago." Kinghorn's pessimism about fieldwork on snakes partly reflected his own mobility issues; he was severely wounded in the knee during military duties in Egypt during World War I. But nonetheless, fieldwork on snakes remained firmly in the 'too difficult' basket even for his able-bodied compatriots. Kinghorn's summary of our ignorance remained true until the 1950s in Europe and North America, and until the 1970s in most other parts of the world.

The obvious way to overcome some of those problems is to catch your snake and put it in a cage where you can observe it – but early snake-enthusiasts found it difficult to keep captive snakes alive. The snakes were stressed, and they refused to eat. In 1863, Brazilian researcher Otho Wucherer (1820–1873) complained: "I have repeatedly tried to keep live specimens in confinement, but they all soon perished, after incessant disquietude, without ever taking food of any kind."

If snakes are so difficult to study, why bother? Most ecologists focus on easier species such as birds, lizards or frogs. If serpent-focused research is impossible, get over it. Move on. We will never understand snakes in as much detail as birds. Some animals – such as snakes, deep-sea fishes, man-eating Tigers, and insects at the tops of rainforest trees – are impossible to study. Maybe we should forget about snakes, and focus instead on animals that provide a better return per unit effort?

That's a compelling argument. Most scientific research focuses on 'model organisms' that are easy to work with, using tried and true methods. But knowing all about white rats is not enough. If we want to understand the natural world, we can't ignore 99.999 per cent of the species within it, including the ones that are difficult to study.

When I talked with my fellow snake-scientists at conferences in the 1970s and 1980s, we bemoaned the difficulties of doing cutting-edge research on snakes. Observing snake behaviour

Although large and highly venomous snakes such as this Australian Tiger Snake (*Notechis scutatus*) have always attracted intense public interest, conducting research on such a beast is a logistical nightmare. JULES FARQUHAR

in the field seemed to be impossible. Experiments on free-ranging animals, or studies on hundreds of animals from a single population, were not feasible. Instead, we had to chip away at the edges of interesting questions, borrowing ideas from studies on user-friendly creatures such as lizards and birds. My American colleague Rich Seigel coined the term 'lizard envy', advising snake biologists to stop complaining about how difficult it is to study snakes compared to other types of animals. Instead of grumbling, he argued, we need to somehow overcome the logistical hurdles to snake research.

Technology came to our rescue when electronics engineers developed radio transmitters small enough to be implanted surgically into a snake's body. That made it possible to gather data on rare and secretive animals, because you could relocate the same individual time and again. Hey presto, snakes could run but they couldn't hide. And snakes of many species are big enough to carry a powerful transmitter. There's more room for a transmitter inside a python than inside a small frog, lizard or bird.

Researchers still had to catch their snakes, but progress was happening there as well. Quietly working away at a small forest in Kansas farmland, an American named Henry Fitch (1909–2009) developed funnel-traps that were very effective at capturing snakes. Simple wire-mesh

Non-venomous snakes can make terrific pets, as evidenced by the gleam in this boy's eyes as he holds a Common Garter Snake (*Thamnophis sirtalis*). SHERI RYSTRA

cylinders with a funnel at one or both ends, so that a snake who slithered into a trap couldn't find its way back out again. The traps could be left in place for months at a time, re-catching individuals again and again.

And scientists weren't the only people devising new methods. A rapidly expanding range of domestic pets soon saw snake keeping come into its own. Dedicated snake keepers overcame problems that had plagued early attempts to maintain captive snakes. Many species of snakes proved to be excellent pets – thriving, growing and breeding in small cages, on a diet of defrosted white mice. It became apparent that snakes could survive on remarkably little food; but would eat far more if given the opportunity. Hence, snakes were ideal subjects for experimental studies on the impact of food supply on an organism's life history. For example, how does variation in feeding rate modify a snake's allocation of energy between growth and reproduction? Scientists exploited the hard-won expertise of pet-keepers, spawning experimental studies on ecological flexibility.

'Snakes are too far away'

Another impediment to research on snake ecology was geographic. Put simply, snakes and researchers lived in different places. Most kinds of snakes live in the tropics, whereas most of the researchers – especially prior to 1980 – lived in northern Europe and North America. Tight budgets and heavy teaching responsibilities kept university-based researchers close to home. As a result, research was focused on snakes that lived near Northern-Hemisphere universities. And those sites were hidden beneath snowdrifts for much of the year, curtailing opportunities for field research.

But cheap air travel changed the world. In 1960, a flight from New York to London cost around ten times as much as it does today. Far too expensive for a snake researcher. But in 1978, US President Jimmy Carter signed the Airline Deregulation Act, allowing open competition between carriers. Ticket prices went into free-fall. Researchers from Western countries could travel widely for fieldwork, and students from tropical countries could enrol in research-intensive universities in other parts of the world. When those people returned home, some of them began research on the local snake fauna. And, in many cases, friendships they had forged with Western scientists encouraged collaborative studies in new locations.

'Research on deadly snakes is a profession for young white males'

Most cultures define certain activities as appropriate for some people but not others. Individuals who don't fit the stereotype are excluded from those pursuits either through regulations or customs.

Even if they try to bite, most species of snakes are harmless to people. This Scarlet Kingsnake (*Lampropeltis elapsoides*) is an enthusiastic but ineffective retaliator. NOAH K. FIELDS

Wrestling venomous snakes in remote jungles was viewed as macho science, suitable only for university-trained alpha-males at the height of their powers. No room for 'outsiders' such as women, or gay men, or elderly or disabled people, or mere mortals who lacked a university degree. Or, heaven forbid, foreigners.

But over the decades, such stereotypes weakened. Photographs from scientific conferences in the first part of the 20th century reveal a sea of white male faces. But women slowly penetrated that world and the macho culture surrounding field-based research on venomous animals began to crumble.

In summary, research on the ecology of snakes had been unpopular for millenia, but the barriers to its acceptance were breaking down. As scientific research exploded in the second half of the 20th century, snakes were left behind at first … but it wasn't long before that gap was filled by pioneering researchers.

IN THEIR OWN WORDS

Many early books talk of the mystery of snakes. For example:

"Now the serpent was more subtil than any beast of the field." OLD TESTAMENT, GENESIS 3.1

And some of those books emphasise the long history of curiosity about snakes:

"An acquaintance with reptiles may be traced backwards to a very remote period. The Sacred Scriptures ... have numerous passages alluding to them ... and the ancient monuments of the Egyptians prove that ... the serpents ... were well known to that people. These forms of animal life must, therefore, have attracted attention from the earliest times; while a natural desire to ascertain which of them were dangerous, and which innocuous, must have led to particular inquiry, in order to solve the doubt. It is evident, moreover, from the ancient writings ... that notions not merely vague but precise were entertained respecting many species." *CASSELL'S POPULAR NATURAL HISTORY*, 1881

And frequently complain about the paucity of knowledge:

"Less is understood about them [snakes] than almost any other natural group of animals." CATHERINE COOPER HOPLEY, 1882

Catherine's more verbose contemporary Arthur Stradling expands on her sentiments:

"The study of reptiles 'at home' – of their nature, habits, peculiarities, mode of life, of everything, in fact, beyond their mere anatomical characteristics – seems to have deferred until the entire animal creation, exclusive of the unpopular class, should have received the attention of practical naturalists. Pet fish were recognised attractions in ornamental garden ponds and greenhouse tanks a hundred years ago, and until a comparatively recent date the word 'aquarium' suggested the idea of crystal prisons for gold and silver carp, adapted to the hall table or conservatory, rather than that of mammoth music saloons. Bees have been 'kept' for pleasure and profit, saccharine and scientific, from time immemorial; the ant has been honoured with a long line of distinguished observers, from Solomon to Sir John Lubbock; while wasps, worms, spiders, beetles and fleas have all in turn been commended to public notice by learned men. Moreover, the allusions to many of these creatures in ancient aphorisms betrays a close acquaintance with their manners and customs, such as could only be gained by watchful curiosity. But with regard to reptiles – snakes in particular – it must be confessed that all proverbial philosophy which has come down to us concerning them is nothing more or less than an epitome of the gross and common errors which still hold their ground. Even in the days when the wondrous chain of animated nature was being patiently and laboriously followed out, link by link, by those earnest minds who may be said to have founded our system of zoology, for a man to have done anything with a snake except kill it would have pointed irrefragably to demoniacal possession, and the luckless conservator might very likely have incurred penalties awarded to those who practised the black arts. We do not burn ophiologists now, certainly; and a person may even have living serpents in his house without being considered mad or morbidly desirous of a reputation for eccentricity, as he would have been not long ago. And further, captive snakes are now preserved for higher purposes than to be stared at as monsters, and too often teased or tortured to death." ARTHUR STRADLING, 1882

Realising the difficulty of snake eradication by direct killing, some early writers suggested using the snakes' natural enemies for biocontrol. In 1837, German biologist Hermann Schlegel (1804–1884) suggested:

"By transplanting ... the enemies of serpents into countries infested by them, we might perhaps prevent the too great multiplication of these dangerous reptiles."

In Oregon, colonists liberated pigs to eradicate rattlesnakes. In the Caribbean, sugar-cane farmers brought in the mongoose from India. Such ill-advised translocations caused environmental mayhem, as immigrants that were supposed to eradicate snakes instead feasted on 'useful' native wildlife. But in the 1800s, before that lesson was learned, importing snake-killers was viewed as a clever new approach to snake control.

Less often, snakes were the species being transported rather than the targets of control. They could be both, because many snakes eat other snakes – but the risks with introducing snakes to control other snakes argued against such initiatives. Nonetheless, the idea of releasing predators to wipe out venomous snakes was so popular that in 1876 one eminent authority, Edward Drinker Cope (1840–1897), felt the need to recommend against using deadly snakes (King Cobras) for this purpose.

The only published report I've found of large-scale introduction of snakes to a new area is likely mythical. Australia-based biologist Edgar Waite (1866–1928) wrote about hordes of harmless North American snakes being shipped to Ireland to control agricultural pests. I suspect that the story arose from a modest translocation (of six European Grass Snakes, *Natrix natrix*) from England to Ireland in 1831. The English zoologist Thomas Bell (1792–1880) told that story in 1849 as follows, based on a report by a gentleman named James Clealand:

"Being curious to ascertain whether the climate of Ireland was destructive to that class of reptiles, about six years ago I purchased half a dozen of them in Covent Garden Market in London; they had been taken some time, and were quite tame and familiar. I turned them out in my garden; they immediately rambled away; one of them was killed at Milecross, three miles distant, in about a week after its liberation; and three others were shortly afterwards killed within that distance of the place where they were turned out; and it is highly probable that the remaining two met with a similar fate, falling victims to a reward which it appears was offered for their destruction."

It thus seems that snakes were brought to Ireland not to control 'pests' (it's difficult to imagine how these frog-eating serpents would aid agricultural production) but to satisfy a gentleman's curiosity – in particular, to test the belief that Irish air was instantly fatal to snakes (as claimed in Bede's *Ecclesiastical History*, AD 731).

Chapter 2

A disorderly revolution

If your only contact with professional science comes from public media, the world of scientific discovery may seem orderly. Respectable people wearing white lab coats, applying cold logic to some clear-cut problem, and moving step by careful step towards the right answer. Like jigsaw zealots who solve a puzzle by first separating out pieces with straight edges, pieces with a dash of a specific colour and so forth. Then building up different components of the larger puzzle, then combining those components. Piece by piece, highly organised. The reality of scientific research is dramatically different. The path towards insight is riddled with red herrings, wrong directions and changes in focus driven as much by human foibles as by academic merit. The great physicist Albert Einstein is supposed to have once said: "If we knew what we were doing, it wouldn't be called research, would it?" A great quote, although I can't find any evidence that the world-famous scientist ever said it.

Discovering the chaotic nature of scientific research surprised and alarmed me when I was a graduate student. My high-school classes had talked about 'the scientific method' and attributed the progress of knowledge to a well-organised set of procedures. I assumed that, with suitable training, two scientists faced with the same question would go about solving it in the same way. But as the years went by, I realised that science is far more subjective than that. A person's interests, abilities and opportunities fashion their approach. Some topics give less room for straying off the beaten path – for example, if you want to establish evolutionary relationships among species using genetic tools. But if your aim is to elucidate the ecology of snakes, especially in the wild, the options are endless.

So if you take two people with identical backgrounds, abilities and resources, and ask them to conduct a research project on snake ecology, the resulting studies will be massively different. Some individuals love precision and detail, whereas others adore simplicity and generality. Some crave collaborators, whereas others are lone wolves. And tiny accidents can drive the entire trajectory of a major program – some apparently trivial observation of a snake doing something might trigger a new idea that suggests a whole new explanation. A conversation with a farmer in the local pub might identify the perfect study area, or some unexpected seasonal pattern, or a new hypothesis. The end result of a research program may look well organised and sensible, but only in hindsight. The completed jigsaw is elegant, but the trial-and-error process of fitting those pieces together was a blend of serendipity and mayhem.

Scientists try to appear logical when they present their results in a paper or a press conference, but it's a façade. Research scientists are passionate. Seduced by mysteries of the natural world, they hurl themselves at the unknown with ferocity and flexibility, adapting questions and approaches that work and abandoning those that do not. Collaborations introduce another layer of complexity, because the mix of people with diverse backgrounds generates important interactions. You can't dissect a cake and identify exactly how each ingredient has affected the final product. Likewise with a scientific collaboration.

Snake ecologists tend to be informal. Most conferences for scientists to discuss reptile research are relaxed affairs, such as this meeting of the Australian Society of Herpetologists in tropical Queensland.

A piece of science is like a piece of art or music, dependent in intricate ways upon the personalities of the people who have created it; and there can be just as much disagreement about the worth of a scientific paper as about a modern art installation. One of the great myths of research is that we can objectively judge the quality of a scientific paper. If so, reviewers of journal articles would agree with each other about papers they are evaluating – but in practice, they don't. Any editor can recount a hundred instances where the same paper has attracted laudatory comments from some reviewers and scathing contempt from others. Many papers now widely regarded as inspirational milestones were rejected for publication several times before they were finally accepted. And some of those papers languished unappreciated and uncited for decades before changing scientific fashions brought them to prominence.

Snakes that inhabit cold climates reproduce by bearing live young rather than by laying eggs. In Australia, most species of the genus *Pseudechis*, including the King Brown Snake (*Pseudechis australis*), live in warm climates and lay eggs; but the distribution of one species, the Red-bellied Black Snake (*Pseudechis porphyriacus*), extends into cooler climates and it bears live young. PHOTOGRAPHS: JULES FARQUHAR

Given the chaotic and subjective nature of research, then, we wouldn't expect the history of a research field to be any more organised and predictable than the history of art or music. But in all fields, we can identify periods of stability punctuated by stunning upheavals. Revolutions, where the dramatic overthrow of an older perspective opened the floodgates for a new approach. For example, publication of *On the Origin of Species* by Charles Darwin in 1859 threw a hand grenade into biological thought, consigning older ideas to the dustbin of history. Although a few scholars clung tenaciously to religious explanations, Darwin's idea of 'natural selection' provided a compelling explanation for the diversity of life, and it suggested new approaches and topics for study. No matter how you look at it, *On the Origin of Species* kick-started a revolution.

Other revolutions begin gradually, with little fanfare. The first step forward for the revolution in snake research was the slow accumulation of knowledge about where different types of snakes are found, as well as on 'ecological' traits such as growth rates, ages at maturity, diets and reproductive biology. The new information arrived in small fragments – a rare kind of viper found where it wasn't expected; a pet python producing a clutch of eggs; a serendipitous encounter with a rattlesnake swallowing a rabbit in the Everglades. Anyone could make such observations; no training was required. The amount of information in each anecdote was small, but those short notes built up into a cascade, and then a flood. The international tsunami kept building, and it hasn't slowed down. Information on snake ecology was scarce in 1980, and now we are drowning in it. And as new methods emerge, the types of data are expanding as well.

But information is only a first step. A spreadsheet with 10,000 lines of data doesn't tell us anything until somebody works out what it means. That's where scientific training comes in. Students learn to tackle data using methods such as statistics and modelling, to extract general patterns out of a bewildering pile of raw observations. For example, knowing the geographic distributions and modes of reproduction of hundreds of snake species doesn't get you very far. All you have is a pile of numbers. But hidden within those data is a general pattern: live-bearing snakes live in colder climates than do egg layers. As soon as you detect that pattern, you're on the way to insight.

So, the revolution in snake ecology wasn't just about accumulating information. Some of the most influential studies described patterns rather than providing case studies. For example, pioneers such as Henry Fitch in the USA and Hubert Saint Girons in France looked for consistent differences in reproductive biology between snakes from warm climates compared to those in colder areas. That integrative approach evolved through the generations, with increasing power as data sets expanded. When my modern-day colleagues look for general patterns in snake reproduction, they have access to thousands of data points and a sophisticated arsenal of statistical approaches.

After you identify broad patterns in the data, you can ask why those patterns occur. In other words, you can develop hypotheses about evolutionary advantages and disadvantages. With luck, your ideas will predict specific trends – finescale correlations and the like – and you can test your new hypothesis by exploring those predictions. Often, the broad pattern immediately suggests an adaptive explanation.

In the case of live-bearers in cool climates, three people independently noticed that correlation in the 1930s. One of those people was the exuberant German schoolmaster Rudolf Mell (1878–1930), who established a school in south-eastern China and financed his own exploring trips in search of reptiles in that region. The second was the brilliant but tragically short-lived Alexei Sergeev (1912–1943) in Russia, who made major breakthroughs as a student. The outbreak of World War I ended Alexei's research career and eventually his life. He joined the Russian army in 1941 but was captured by German troops in the Ukraine. Although he was later rescued, the Soviet Army was paranoid about prisoners of war collaborating with their German captors and Sergeev was sentenced to a slave-labour gulag where (ill with dysentery and despair) he hanged himself in 1943 at the age of 31.

The third pioneer of reptile viviparity also faced huge obstacles, in this case driven by her gender. Claire Weekes (1903–1990) conducted research on reproduction in Australian reptiles early in her career before abandoning science to sing professionally in Europe, and then switching professions again to become a high-profile authority on dealing with anxiety. Her books on that subject changed lives and made her a household name. But Weekes faced extraordinary challenges in a chauvinistic society. When she returned to Australia after her singing career, the main Sydney newspaper reported: "Miss Claire Weekes, D.Sc, . . . has an appreciative eye for smart frocks and accessories. Among her belongings when she returned from a two years' tour abroad last week was this smart wet-weather outfit, which she bought in Paris. The swagger coat with a Peter Pan collar is of navy spotted rainproof..." (*Sydney Morning Herald*, Thursday 21 January 1937, p. 24). Claire's formidable scientific accomplishments did not rate a mention.

Remarkably, all three of those pioneers hit on the same explanation for why live-bearing reptiles thrive in cool climates: a pregnant snake can keep her developing babies warm by basking in the sun, so live bearing works even in places where the soil is too cold for eggs to develop in an external nest. With that hypothesis in mind, you can look in more detail – for example, if egg layers evolve live bearing because of cold conditions, we'd expect to see that transition when a warm-climate lineage of reptiles extends into cooler areas, or when global climates shift towards cooler conditions. And we can test the hypothesis in other ways as well. For example, we can measure thermal regimes within nests compared to within the oviducts of reproductive females; and we can incubate eggs at cool versus warm temperatures, to see if colder nests produce inferior hatchlings. Also, we can look in detail at apparent exceptions – for example, how can an egg-laying species such as the European Grass Snake reproduce in frigid Scandinavian climates? The answer involves hot-spots in a cold landscape: piles of cow manure that are heated by bacterial decomposition. All of those studies show the patterns we expect, supporting the idea that live bearing evolves when warm nest sites are scarce.

It's even more exciting if the process works in the reverse direction. First, you develop a new idea. That idea predicts a pattern in the data, so then you can check your prediction. That's what happened when I began to wonder why males grow larger than females in some snake species but not others. I thought it might relate to whether or not the males physically battle each other for access to the females. Larger males defeat smaller ones in combat, providing mating opportunities. In contrast, size may not matter if males don't fight each other. Under that hypothesis, we expect males to grow larger than females if (and only if) males engage in combat bouts with each other. That's the pattern I found when I assembled the data. Male snakes grow larger than females only if males fight with each other.

These two male Lesser Black Whipsnakes (*Demansia vestigiata*) are engaged in a combat bout, with each male trying to push down the head of his rival. Bigger combatants usually win such contests, so they obtain more matings. That consistent advantage over evolutionary time explains why male whipsnakes grow larger than females. DAVID NELSON

In summary, then, the revolution in snake ecology was three revolutions in one: gathering data, identifying patterns, and finding reasons for those patterns. Disagreements were common. Some observations were flawed; some apparent patterns were due to sampling bias or overactive imaginations; and many explanations proved to be incorrect. But those disagreements were just roadbumps on the route to insight. The tidal wave of new information and new perspectives showed which routes on that superhighway were dead ends, and which led to further discoveries.

Why study snakes?

Two important problems attracted the attention of early snake biologists. The first was snakebite. Efforts to mitigate the toll of fatalities began early and continue to the present. Much of that research has focused on ways to cull snakes, as for programs targeted at the Habu in Okinawa.

Another approach to reduce rates of snakebite involves education to change human behaviour. For such a campaign, we need to understand when, where and why people encounter deadly snakes; and why snakes sometimes bite people. For example, João Alves-Nunes and his Brazilian colleagues studied the responses of Jararaca Lanceheads, large and deadly pit vipers from South America. Wearing safety boots, the investigators stepped on or near-captive snakes in enclosures, as well as during encounters with free-ranging snakes. Whether or not one of these formidable snakes launched a defensive strike was affected by factors such as the snake's sex and body size, the time of day and the temperature – and also, by interactions between those factors. The same variables were correlated with rates of snakebite in rural Brazil, enabling João and his team to identify why people get bitten – and so, what we might do to reduce that risk. Until you understand why snakes bite people, it's difficult to frame management tactics. Sometimes, the answer is simple. For example, Australian marine biologist Tim Lynch showed that 'attacks' on scuba divers by Olive Sea Snakes were due to mistaken identity: male snakes looking for mates. If a diver allows the snake to approach closely, the lustful male realises that the object in question isn't a female of his own species – and so he loses interest.

A second focus for snake research arose later, driven by the senseless killing of snakes by members of the public. Hatred of rattlesnakes in the western USA was especially intense; even Laurence Klauber (1883–1968), an electrical engineer who kept snakes in his basement and wrote several books about these iconic tail-shakers, reluctantly endorsed the massacre of his favourite animals. Although slaughter of snakes by people was the initial concern, biologists soon became aware of other threats such as habitat degradation. Spurred by a nosedive in global biodiversity, conservation became a growing aim of research.

Some populations of snakes are declining so rapidly that they will disappear unless we protect them and their habitats. So at the same time as managers in Guam and Okinawa are culling snakes, researchers elsewhere are trying to conserve them. Such studies receive a major impetus if imperilled snakes find their way onto official lists of endangered species, because those lists affect funding priorities.

An inquisitive Blue-lipped Sea Krait (*Laticauda laticaudata*) approaches a diver (in this case, Margaux Bonnet), but he is motivated by curiosity or misplaced lust rather than aggression. XAVIER BONNET

Resources for snake research can also come from concerns about over-harvesting. In China, the unsustainable culling of Shedao Pit Vipers for traditional medicine led to stringent protection of the species in 1980 and initiated intensive research. Likewise, the widespread collection of pythons across Asia resulted in calls to ban the skin trade. Faced with that threat to their livelihoods, the skin traders supported research on hitherto-unknown Asian species to evaluate the sustainability of the harvest.

The stage was set. A gradual shift in social attitudes towards wildlife; a scientific revolution in theoretical biology, transforming fieldwork from descriptions and anecdotes through to hypothesis-testing; new methods that overcame the logistical hurdles of studying snakes; and increasing representation of female as well as male researchers, including from biodiverse tropical countries.

Progress was also stimulated by competition to name new species – and especially, by the way that European countries viewed scientific knowledge as a benefit of their colonial adventures. Any collector who sent tropical specimens back to European museums was likely to be honoured by having the new species named after them. National pride was at stake. In 1882, English writer Catherine Cooper Hopley (1817–1911) complained that: "We must admit that as a nation we English have followed, not taken, the lead as naturalists… The French outstrip us in nice observations. First by their numerous clergy; … Secondly by gentlemen accompanying these religious missions, sent out to explore and make discoveries and to keep strict journals, which duly were handed over to science."

Filling in the knowledge gaps

The diaspora of European armies and colonists to snake-rich continents such as Africa, Asia, South America and Australia initially focused on species descriptions. But often, someone describing a new type of snake included brief notes on where and when the animal was found, what it was doing at the time, and so forth. Bit by bit, information accumulated on the day-to-day lives of these mysterious animals. A dread of snakebite encouraged herculean efforts to collect and identify snakes from remote regions, and to work out where these fearsome beasts were most likely to be encountered.

Pioneering reptile biologist Joseph Batty and snakes in Mexico in 1904. AMERICAN MUSEUM OF NATURAL HISTORY

The result was an explosion of information about snakes. Similar great leaps forward occur in every field of research – periods of stagnation followed by sudden surges in activity. But some leaps are bigger than others, and the growth in information about snakes was a giant step. The day-to-day lives of many mammals and birds were already well known, but it needed a revolution to give us the first real insights into the behaviour and ecology of secretive animals such as snakes. The species most affected by the surge in knowledge were the organisms that had previously been neglected. Snakes were near the top of that list.

The easiest way to highlight how little we know about snakes is to look at the rate at which new species are being formally described by science – that is, given their own scientific name. Most types of birds and mammals were described long ago. It's big news if somebody discovers a new kind of mammal. But for snakes, we are still in the midst of that process. We don't know how many species of snakes occur on Earth, because the rate at which new species of snakes is being described has been increasing rather than decreasing over recent decades.

The graph shows this pattern. If we were getting close to some final number, that curve should be flattening through time, and we could guess what the final number might be. The graph shows that we are not even close to that point. From around 3,000 recognised snake species in 1980, we have now gone past 4,000. And if you don't know a species exists, you won't know about its biology.

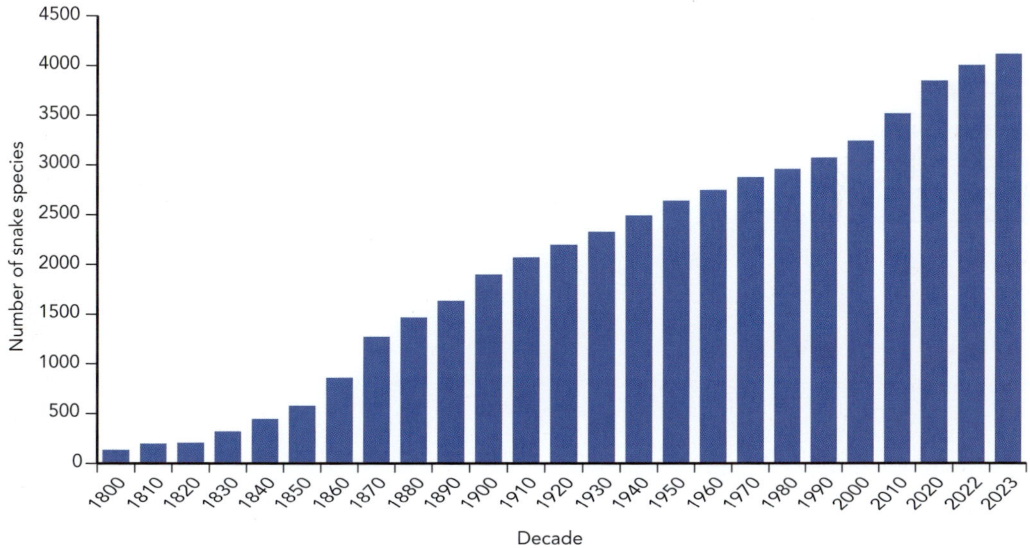

The number of snake species scientifically described continues to increase rapidly though time.
DATA COURTESY OF PETER UETZ, FROM THE REPTILE DATABASE

Misleading descriptions

Many early snippets of snake-ecology information were embedded in formal descriptions of species thought to be new to science. Most of the paper would focus on describing the specimens at hand, with just a paragraph or two devoted to notes from the wild. The number of 'new' species described was astronomical, reflecting a mad scramble among Europeans living in tropical countries to discover species and name them after the describer's colleagues and friends. Those taxonomic contributions typically were based on a few poorly preserved animals from unknown localities, and often were slipshod efforts.

For example, early workers often erroneously described snakes of different sexes or ages as separate 'species'. In my favourite example, pioneering Australian herpetologist Gerard Krefft (1830–1881) described two species of Turtle-headed Sea Snakes, one after another on the same page of a scientific journal in 1869. In this species, females are smooth-scaled whereas males are rugose. And sure enough, Krefft described the two sexes as two separate species: *Emydocephalus*

Cobras and snake-charmers being admired by Australian soldiers in Kolkata, India, in 1945. STATE LIBRARY OF NEW SOUTH WALES

annulatus for the smooth-scaled females and *Emydocephalus tuberculata* for the keeled-scaled males. At least he put them in the same genus.

The same problem crops up in cases where a snake changes its colour as it grows older; and this time we can give Krefft credit for recognising that two 'species' of Australian banded snakes – one small and banded and the other large and uniformly brown – were juveniles of the widespread Eastern Brown Snake.

With no access to the specimens examined by other workers, early researchers gave multiple names to widely distributed species. That was especially true if local populations differed from each other in size or colour. As a result, many of the 'new species' proudly named in these early papers ended up as long-forgotten footnotes in later taxonomic revisions. Few of those names are still used.

But over-enthusiastic taxonomists made the reverse error as well, combining several different kinds of animals into a single 'species'. With sublime arrogance, India-based Englishman and wine merchant Herbert Musgrave Phipson (1850–1936) wrote in 1887: "*Naja tripudians*, the cobra, is too well known to need description. It is found all over India up to 8,000 feet in the Himalayas. There are a great number of varieties, differing in colour and markings... The natives, who give separate names to these varieties, maintain that they are distinct species, and that they differ considerably, not only in appearance, but in habits. The natives are, I need hardly say, profoundly ignorant in such matters". We now know that at least 10 species of cobra occur across Asia, suggesting that Phipson was the 'profoundly ignorant' participant in that early debate. But let's not be too harsh on Herbert; thoughout his long life he was a fervent supporter of worthy issues ranging from Indian zoology to women's health.

Myths about snake ecology

Reading 19th-century papers about snake ecology is fascinating. It's difficult to know whether to be more impressed by the persistence of myths or the tantalising hints of behaviours that we still don't understand. Some myths proved remarkably resistant to change, with authors such as German biologist Hermann Schlegel (in 1837) and Englishwoman Catherine Hopley (in 1888) despairing of the continued popularity of bizarre stories. Indeed, that persistence of myth was a major motivator for Hopley to pen the first 'popular' book on snakes: "After a time I proposed to write a book about snakes, starting with the stereotyped ideas that they all 'stung' in some incomprehensible way; that the larger kinds crushed up horses and cattle like wisps of straw; and that all, having viciously taken the life of the victim, proceeded with epicurean gusto to lick it all over and smear it with saliva, that it might glide down their throat like an oyster! There are those who to this day believe the same."

Nonsensical stories about the ecology and behaviour of snakes are so alluring that they persist through generations. Indeed, some of the earliest tales are still alive today. For example, one persistent myth involves the supposed ability of female snakes to protect their young by swallowing them. Papers in the 1800s earnestly recount eye-witness descriptions of young snakes taking refuge inside their mother's mouth. Those stories doubtless arose from the difficulty of watching a snake in the wild, combined with the discovery of full-term embryos inside a mother's uterus (likely revealed when the mother's body was smashed open by a stick). The babies were mistakenly inferred to have entered mum's body through her mouth rather than being ready to exit her body through the other end. But how could a snake scientist in the early 1800s challenge this myth without antagonising those gullible 'eyewitnesses'? Accusing a fellow scientist of falsehoods might lead to ugly scenes. By the 1830s the Europeans had concluded (correctly) that those stories were bunkum, but the Americans believed the myth for decades longer.

Explanations as well as observations from the early naturalists are intriguing. For example, the function of the rattlesnake's rattle has long been a subject of debate. The earliest explanations invoked divine benevolence. In 1676, American colonist Thomas Glover wrote that: "The rattlesnake is ... about the bigness of a man's legg, and for the most part a yard and a half long. He hath a rattle at the end of his tail, wherewith he maketh a noise when any one approacheth nigh him: which seemeth to be a peculiar providence of God to warn people to avoid the danger; for this creature is so venomous that the bite of it is of most dangerous consequence."

The front and rear ends of a Mexican West Coast Rattlesnake (*Crotalus basiliscus*). MATTHIEU BERRONEAU

That biblically-inspired explanation fell out of favour as new ideas emerged. For example, creationists used the rattle as an example to attack Charles Darwin's theory of natural selection, on the grounds that the rattle evolved to warn other individuals rather than benefitting the snake itself (as would be expected under natural selection). Darwin countered by suggesting that the loud buzzing from a rattlesnake's tail discouraged large animals such as Bison from stepping on the serpent (an encounter unlikely to end well for the snake or the Bison). But the Americans were sceptical. Some writers continued to believe that the rattle was provided by God to warn people of the snake's presence, whereas other biologists looked for prosaic benefits to the snake. A debate erupted in the pages of *The American Naturalist* in 1872, with correspondents suggesting that the rattle attracts birds to the snake by imitating the sound of cicadas; or by bringing the sexes together for mating; or to call for help when attacked; or to frighten prey into submission. Observations of captive snakes striking prey without rattling were the kiss of death for the 'dinner-bell theory'. Darwin's explanation eventually won the day, although some modern workers have suggested a new explanation: that the rattle may have evolved initially as an insect-mimicking visual lure.

Other mistakes in the early scientific literature were simple misinterpretations. For example, the eminent Albert Günther (1830–1914) reported in 1864 that the aquatic Tentacled Snake from Asia eats aquatic plants as well as tadpoles and fishes. No modern scientist believes in vegetarian serpents, and Günther's report doubtless reflects a case where he looked inside the stomach of a snake that had eaten tadpoles or fishes wrapped in water weeds. I think we can forgive Albert for the occasional mistake; he described 340 new species and made many major discoveries. For example, he was the man who realised that the Tuatara (a strange lizard-like reptile that clings to existence on windswept New Zealand islands) is the last representative of a once-great reptile lineage. His obituary in *The Times* not only praised his "well-directed energy, laborious research and unflagging zeal" but commented that "Dr Günther was … also an accomplished field naturalist, equally at home in park and covert, or by lake and river. In his earlier days he was remarkably agile and hardy, and used to say he gained as much knowledge of natural history in the field as in the closet." I'm less confident about the observational powers of early American naturalist H.A. Brons, who in 1882 described a Hognose Snake grabbing hold of a Box Turtle's hindfoot and digesting it slowly as the snake was being dragged along behind the turtle. Unlikely, methinks.

Hidden gems within the early literature

But early writers reported some fascinating observations as well, that anticipated mainstream research by many decades. As an example of 'observations before their time', a 1901 paper by

Sri-Lankan-born physician Frank Wall (1868–1950) and his colleague George Evans describes the foraging behaviour of Asian Bockadams (or water snakes) in detail, including this story: "Sometimes they practice a curious and interesting manoeuvre as follows: Lying perfectly still for an interval with their length parallel to the run of the ditch, they cautiously make a sweeping movement with the caudal extremity of their body across the drain, first on one side and then on the other, thus driving any creatures within reach, forwards into their sight and sometimes within their grasp." That's a remarkable trick – shepherding prey with your tail – and it sounds plausible. But there's a problem. If it works for bockadams we might expect similar tactics in other water-dwelling snakes. Surely, if water snakes were catching prey in this way, somebody would report it? Well, no. It took more than a century for the next description of this behaviour. In 2023 Lucas Machado Botelho and his Brazilian colleagues watched a Military Ground Snake flush fish out of hiding places in a small tidal pool by sinuous sweeping movements of the body and tail. Other Brazilian snakes also poke their tails into crevices to flush out prey. Australian researcher John Scanlon has spent much of his professional life excavating and describing dinosaur fossils, but he keeps an eye out for live reptiles as well. In 1998 he suggested that land-dwelling snakes twitch their tails to frighten lizards towards the snake's jaws. So, snakes all over the world are scaring prey with their tails so they can seize a confused fish, frog or lizard as it watches the snake's tail or runs away from it. The fact that scientists didn't notice that behaviour for 100 years after the first description says more about us than about snakes. Sadly, watching snakes is neither an easy nor a popular activity.

Reading those early accounts can be humbling. For example, English surgeon and zoologist Thomas Rymer Jones (1810–1880) wrote in 1845 that: "In many of the reptiles which lay eggs,

African Rock Python (*Python natalensis*) consuming a small antelope called a Common Duiker (*Sylvicapra grimmia*). Observing the events leading up to such a capture is extremely difficult. BRYAN MARITZ

especially the Colubri (colubrine snakes), the young one is already formed and considerably advanced in the egg at the moment when the mother lays it." A few years later, Catherine Hopley wrote: "At whatever period a snake's egg is examined, whether it has been laid or not, the embryo will be found more or less advanced. Sometimes in an egg just deposited, a perfectly formed fetus will be found." When I wrote a paper in 1983 pointing out that snake and lizard eggs contained well-developed embryos at the time of laying, I thought I was the first person to notice this fact. In truth, I was more than 100 years behind the times.

I wasn't alone in failing to appreciate the rich heritage of information hidden away in early publications. Much of that information was difficult to access, because it was written in a diverse array of languages, often in small publications that were hard to locate. And in the days before the digital revolution, finding information was far more difficult than it is today. When I wrote reviews of published knowledge about a topic, I had to rely on librarians to search out arcane references and copy them for me. Most of that early literature is still not digitised and thus is invisible to modern researchers who, by and large, restrict their literature searches to digital databases and never visit a library. I have no doubt that the coming years will see triumphant announcements of more 'new discoveries' about snake biology that were in fact foreshadowed a century ago.

The changing focus of snake research

Another way to document progress in our understanding of snake biology is to look at the numbers and topics of scientific papers written about these animals. Some of the papers are short notes, just one paragraph long, whereas others are massive reviews running to hundreds of pages. But regardless of their size, all scientific papers – at least over the last several decades – have had to undergo anonymous peer review before they were accepted for publication. That's a tough hurdle, so tough that many hopeful authors have had their hopes dashed by critical assessors and journal editors. High-ranking journals reject most of the papers that they are offered by aspiring authors. That attrition means that many interesting ideas and observations never make it into a scientific publication – a loss that is balanced by the fact that if a paper does make it through the review process, it's likely to be robust and accurate. Scientific papers are the building blocks of knowledge, and we need those building blocks to be reliable.

Details about the titles of scientific papers are accessible in online repositories of data such as the Web of Science, so I asked my hard-working research assistant Melanie Elphick to pore through those datasets. The graphs show the results of Mel's efforts. She found more than 27,000 papers on snake ecology – not every paper, I'm sure, but more than enough to reveal major patterns.

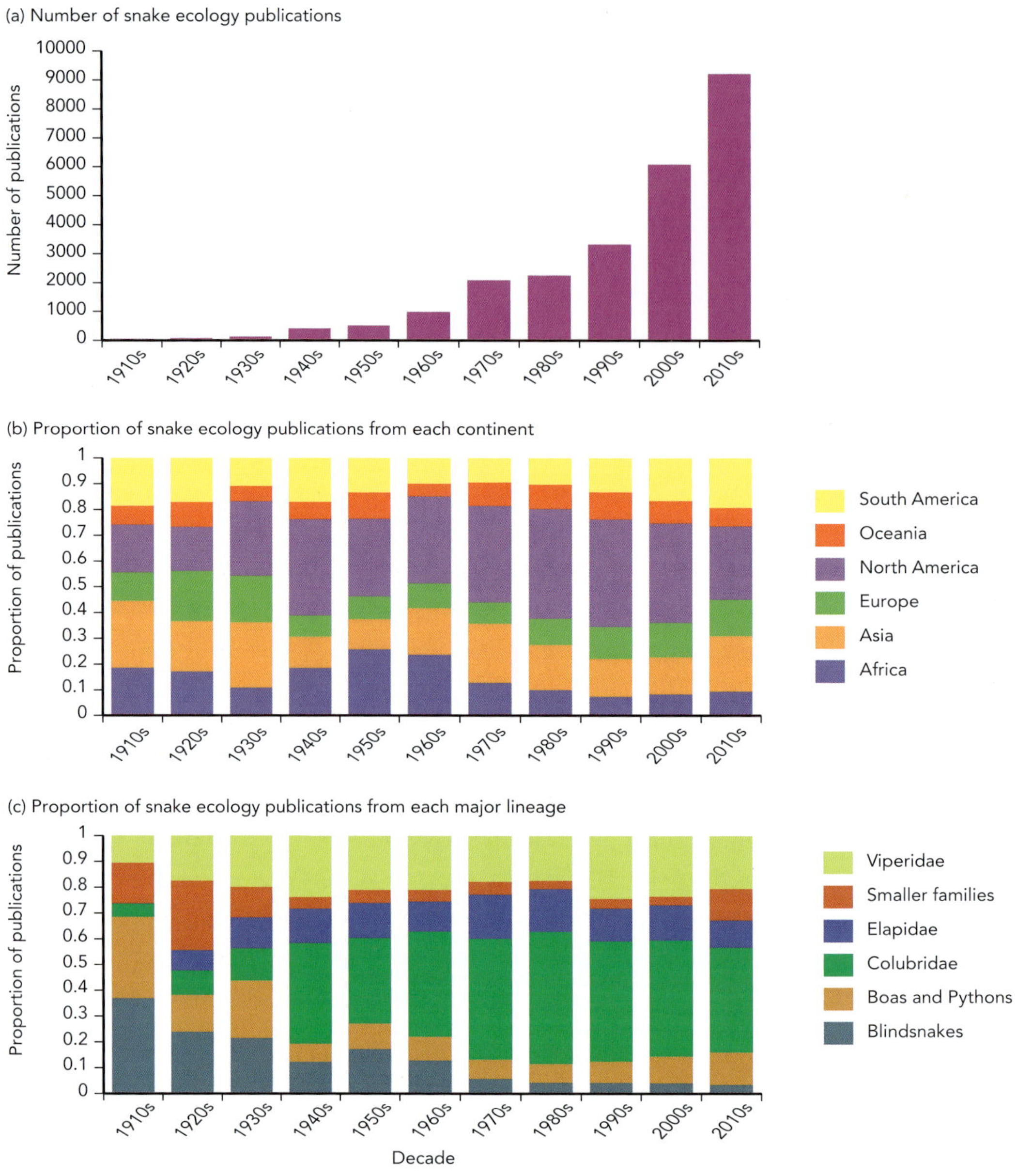

The trajectory of research effort into snake ecology across decades from 1910 to 2020. The upper graph (a) shows that the number of scientific papers written has increased dramatically with each decade. The middle graph (b) shows that ecological studies since the 1940s have been dominated by North American snakes. The lower graph (c) shows that the kinds of snakes being studied have changed through time – for example, colubrids and vipers have become increasingly popular subjects for study.

The first result that leaps out and smacks you in the forehead is the pace of the revolution. Up until 1960, the Web of Science lists less than 7,000 papers on snakes overall, and only 1,000 on snake ecology. But fast-forward to 2020 and those totals have zoomed up to 118,000 and 27,000 respectively. That's a spectacular increase over 50 years – about 16-fold for total papers on snakes, and 30-fold for papers on snake ecology.

Different topics have waxed and waned in importance. Early research on snakes was dominated by taxonomy (classification of species) and geographic distributions. You can't understand a group of animals if you don't know how to tell the difference between one species and another; and once you've worked that out, the next important question is where each species is found. Venom emerged as a central theme in the 1920s, as new methods for antivenom production emerged. But other motivations are important as well, and there have always been people who study snakes because of interest, not just because some of them are deadly. Compared to other types of research on snakes, ecological studies have increased dramatically through time.

What kinds of snakes have attracted the least scientific study?

How has research effort been divided among snakes from different parts of the world? If we look at overall numbers, a snake species that lives in Europe or North America has attracted more attention than a snake that lives in the Sahara or Mongolia. Europe has only 85 snake species, but Mel's online search discovered 2,414 papers about their ecology. That's an average of 28 papers per species. North America has a lot more snakes (181 species) but also a lot more papers (6,359); so the average is similar to that of the Europeans (about 23 papers per species). In contrast, the incredible snake biodiversity in Africa (898 species), Asia (1,339 species) and South America (1,772 species) has attracted far less attention. With 1,809 snake-ecology papers from Africa, 3,363 from Asia and 3,033 from South America, the average number of papers per species is down around two. That is, around two papers per snake species; less than a tenth as much research per species in tropical countries compared to cooler habitats in North America and Europe. That pattern doubtless reflects the long history of snake research in North America and Europe, plus the large number of research institutions in those regions, and the availability of research funds. Also, cool-climate snakes are easier to study because they emerge from their hiding-places to bask in the sunshine whereas tropical serpents remain hidden. Those explanations also fit with Oceania (including Australia) averaging about midway between those two extremes – that is, about 8 papers per species (1,541 papers for 181 species).

Unsurprisingly, some of the snakes that have attracted the least scientific study are species that are too small for radio telemetry, or that live underground or high in trees, or that live in areas that are difficult or dangerous for researchers to access. But even among snakes that don't fit these criteria, some kinds have been ignored.

Perhaps the most striking examples of abundant but understudied serpents are the snakes of tropical Asia. Many of these species, from giant pythons to small water snakes, have been intensively harvested for skins, meat and medicines for hundreds of years – and so, you might think, would be relatively easy animals for ecologists to study. Just pop along to the village marketplace or snake slaughterhouse and take some data on the unfortunate reptiles on display. Nonetheless, detailed ecological research on the snakes of tropical Asia didn't happen until the late 1990s.

The best illustrations of this neglect are the homalopsid mud snakes. Containing more than 50 species, snakes of this lineage inhabit the fringes of waterbodies in tropical Asia – all the way from India to Papua New Guinea and Australia.

A homalopsid mud snake with its dinner. This photograph shows a Schneider's Bockadam (*Cerberus schneideri*) swallowing a fish.
RUCHIRA SOMAWEERA

The abundance of homalopsids can defy the imagination. For example, in 1990, ornithologist Wim Giesen and his colleagues were counting waterbirds on Paluk Bakung, a mangrove-fringed island off the coast of Sumatra. As the tide fell, their boat became stranded in deep mud – and when the evening light faded, hundreds of Schneider's Bockadams (also known as Dog-faced Water Snakes) emerged from their burrows to hunt for mudskippers. Wim estimated the density of foraging snakes at around 670 per hectare (an area of 100 m x 100 m) – that is, around 67,000 snakes per square kilometre (173,500 snakes per square mile). Multiply that number by the total area of muddy mangroves around the coasts of tropical Asia, and the overall population of bockadams must be astronomical.

But homalopsids don't just hide away in remote places – they thrive in some of the most densely populated parts of the planet, in canals that run through Asian villages. American biologists John Murphy and Daryl Karns recorded one adult Rainbow Mud Snake for every two metres of shoreline. Once again, if we multiply that number by the kilometres of canal edge and lakeshore in tropical Asia, there must be millions of homalopsids in that habitat alone. Add in paddyfields flooded for rice cultivation and the numbers become mind-blowing. Indonesian researcher Mirza Kusrini and colleagues estimated that Java contains hundreds of millions of Masked Water Snakes. English researcher Sharon Brooks calculated that villagers harvest almost four million mud snakes per annum from a single lake in Cambodia. Yet with the striking exception of John Murphy and his American and Cambodian colleagues, who began working on these mysterious serpents in the 1990s, ecologists ignored these snakes.

As Murphy eloquently noted: "There is a good reason why homalopsid snakes have remained relatively unknown for the last 300 years ... The one common factor most homalopsid habitats share is mud. ... Few people would consider a recreational swim in silt-laden water, a casual stroll across a mud flat, or a nocturnal hike through a muddy mangrove forest at low tide. ... It is much more pleasant to search for snakes by walking through a forest or grassland, or swimming along a coral reef, than it is to wade through liquid or sticky mud." Homalopsid mud snakes have been ignored because they live in places that are squelchy and smelly to work in.

'Boom and bust' species

Some of the largest and most spectacular animals attracted very little research for a different reason. A snake's ecology affects the ease with which specimens can be collected – and thus, how soon they are formally described (given a scientific name), and how rapidly their distinctive features are recognised. A species known from very few specimens is likely to be misclassified; and with only limited material to go on, researchers can make mistakes about the distinctions between different types of animals.

Some kinds of snakes are difficult to collect because they are rare or they occupy inaccessible habitats, but another problem involves species whose abundance shifts dramatically through time. Even an expert collector can spend years in the right habitat and never see one; and then a few years later the snakes are briefly common before disappearing once again.

Taipans (genus *Oxyuranus*) are a good example of that problem, and how it has affected scientific knowledge. The genus contains three species of large deadly snakes, found over a massive area of Australia from rainforests to deserts. You might expect such snakes to be among the first animal species to be scientifically described, because identifying the snake that bit you is key to predicting how much trouble you are in, and how you should treat the bite. As a result, scientists of the 19th century put more effort into describing large venomous snakes than they did into describing small harmless species. Nonetheless, two of the three currently recognised taipan species were mistaken for other kinds of snakes for many decades, and the third species escaped the attention of science until recently.

The first Coastal Taipan was described (as *Pseudechis scutellatus*) in 1867 by the German biologist and explorer Wilhelm Peters (1815–1883). Peters never visited Australia himself; his fieldwork had been mostly in Africa. But while visiting the Godeffroy Museum in Hamburg he saw a huge elapid snake on display and recognised that it belonged to an as-yet-undescribed species. The museum was a short-lived venture (1861 to 1885) to display specimens collected by employees of its founder, the shipping magnate Johann Cesar Godeffroy VI (1813–1885).

The giant snake had been obtained in 1866 by 42-year-old single mother Konkordie Amalie Dietrich (1821–1891), the only woman that Godeffroy ever employed as a collector. Leaving her daughter in a boarding school, Dietrich set sail for tropical Australia in 1863. A friend described Dietrich as having "a crooked back, a face full of wrinkles, with real bush-man habits, but still with a fresh energetic spirit; she was regarded in Hamburg as a personality as well as a scholar." She returned to Hamburg to work at the Godeffroy Museum in 1872, five years after Peters had described 'her' snake as new to science. Dietrich never published anything under her own name but she collected vast numbers of plants and animals.

It's difficult to know what to think of Amalie Dietrich. Undoubtedly possessed of incredible tenacity and fiery independence of spirit, her contributions to science were remarkable. Capturing a taipan says it all. Unsurprisingly, Dietrich has been celebrated as an inspiring example of a single mother who triumphed against both social and physical challenges. A laudatory biography by her daughter – much of it fictional – transformed Dietrich into such a celebrity in Germany that her image still adorns bottles of a popular brand of herb-flavoured liquor. But there's a dark side to Dietrich's reputation as well: she has been accused of desecrating Aboriginal graves to obtain bones for the Godeffroy museum. Skulls of Indigenous

The first specimen of a Coastal Taipan (*Oxyuranus scutellatus*) known to Western science was collected by Amalie Dietrich. Sadly, Amalie left no record as to how the giant deadly snake was collected. ROB VALENTIC

people were advertised for sale by her employer among a list of 'other mammals'.

For more than 50 years, Dietrich's taipan in Hamburg was the only known specimen. Two New Guinea snakes were collected in the 1880s, but those specimens sat anonymous and unstudied in the bowels of the British Museum. It was not until 1922 that another Aussie taipan made itself known to science, when an enthusiastic ornithologist rode over it. William McLennan (1882–1935) had been employed to collect biological specimens in tropical Australia. Birds and their eggs were his main target, but he also obtained spectacular snakes if he had the opportunity to do so. In March 1922, McLennan was riding his horse through long grass near Coen in tropical Queensland when he saw a huge snake beneath him. He promptly dismounted and killed the snake by hitting it with a sapling. He recorded its size as "nine feet three inches in length, and eight inches in girth." McLennan had assumed that such a huge snake must be a harmless python, and he was shocked when he saw the snake's fangs. The wealthy grazier who employed McLennan (Henry Luke White, 1860–1927) sent the preserved specimen – plus the head of another that had been collected by an Indigenous man, Friday Wilson – to the Australian Museum.

In 1923, Australian Museum curator James Kinghorn (1891–1983) published a formal description of the giant brown snake from tropical Queensland. Although McLennan's monster was similar to the specimen described as *Pseudechis scutellatus* by Peters in 1867, Kinghorn believed that the animal deserved its own genus name as well as species name. He named the animal *Oxyuranus maclennani*, after its captor. A decade later, the confusion was resolved when an intrepid Australian anthropologist named Donald Thomson (1901–1970), with first-hand field experience of taipans in tropical Australia, realised that *Pseudechis scutellatus* and *Oxyuranus maclennani* were one and the same. With only a single specimen to look at, Kinghorn had underestimated the variation in scale-counts within the species. Ever since Thomson's work, the giant snake has been called the taipan (the term used by local indigenous people) and known by the scientific name *Oxyuranus scutellatus*.

Even that convoluted history of changing names is eclipsed by the case of the Coastal Taipan's close relative, the Inland Taipan. Based on venom toxicity, this is the world's most deadly snake. Although two specimens were obtained in 1879, and another in 1882, the species was not seen again for almost a century. Then in 1972, the species was rediscovered by John Wombey and Queensland-based herpetologists Jeanette Covacevich (1945–2015) and Charles Tanner (1911–1996) 1,500 km (1,000 miles) away from the first collecting site. And like its Coastal cousin, the Inland Taipan has been known by an ever-changing range of scientific names. The latest twist to the taipan story is more recent, with a third species (the Western Desert Taipan) found in 2007. So it's not just small harmless snakes that are being discovered nowadays – there are some monsters as well.

Part of the reason why taipan taxonomy has been riddled with errors is that collecting these fearsome animals is so perilous that few people attempt it. And of those that do, not all survive. Chapter 11 tells the story of Kevin Budden (1930–1950), a young Aussie killed by the taipan he collected for antivenom production. I vividly remember my own first encounter with a taipan, as a 22-year-old graduate student. On a field trip in Cape York in 1972, I was driving in the late evening when a huge slender brown snake crossed the road in front of me. I hit the brakes, leapt out and sprinted after the snake. I had almost caught up to it when some small part of my brain screamed out at me 'WHAT THE HELL ARE YOU DOING?' Alone, barefoot, with no flashlight, snake tongs or bag, grabbing that snake would likely have landed me in an early grave. So, for the first time in my young life, I stopped and walked away from a snake. Similar common sense by others has reduced the numbers of taipan specimens available to science.

But the taipan's lifestyle has also hindered research on the species. One of the few venomous Australian snakes to feed mostly on mammals, taipans depend upon native rats – and the numbers of those rats depend upon erratic rainfall events that provide green grass for rodent food. As a result the rats are rare most of the time, but once in a while their populations explode into super-abundance. During those brief windows of unlimited food, taipans eat prodigiously, grow rapidly, mature early, and reproduce often. Suddenly, taipans are common snakes – but within a few months the green grass is gone, the rodents have died and taipans are difficult to find for another decade or two.

The Inland Taipan (*Oxyuranus microlepidotus*) is ranked as the most deadly snake species in the world, with enough venom in one bite to kill 100 adult humans. JULES FARQUHAR

What kinds of snakes have attracted the most scientific study?

Although there are hundreds of snake species about which nobody has written even a single ecological paper, a few species have been consistently popular targets for research. We can look at the data on 'number of papers per species' to explore which snakes have been studied most often by scientists.

From the geographic patterns I talked about above, you might guess that the most intensively studied species of snake would live in either Europe or North America. And common sense suggests that non-venomous snakes would be the most popular study animals, because people avoid animals that can kill them. The best candidates would be widespread abundant species, and thus among the first snakes to be described scientifically. And you'd be correct, on all three counts. The overall winner is the European Grass Snake (*Natrix natrix*) – around 2,000 papers mention ecological characteristics of this widespread and harmless species. The silver medal goes to another non-venomous species that belongs to the same evolutionary lineage as the Grass Snake (the natricine colubrids) and is also abundant over a wide area. Found in North America not Europe, this runner-up is the Common Garter Snake (*Thamnophis sirtalis*) with 1,500 mentions. Both of those species were described by the venerable Swede, Linnaeus, in 1758. Venomous snakes then come into the medal rankings, led by the Eurasian Adder (850 papers) and the Timber Rattlesnake from North America (450 papers).

The European Grass Snake (*Natrix helvetica*) is a true 'model organism' for research in snake ecology. This species has the worst-smelling faeces of any snake I've ever handled, but that doesn't seem to have discouraged researchers. Indeed, my friend Pat Gregory claims to like the aroma. ROB VALENTIC

Those numbers reinforce the idea that over much of its history, snake-ecology research has focused on a narrow subsample of the world's snakes. But the apparently simple question of which species is the most studied is difficult to answer, because that ranking depends on which scientific name has been applied and when those names have changed. For example, the top-ranked Grass Snake (*Natrix natrix*) has recently been split into three separate species (*Natrix astreptophora, Natrix natrix,* and *Natrix helvetica*) based on genetic data. And to make the situation even murkier, two of those new 'species' contain several distinctive forms. Further work might well elevate those subspecies to full species. As a result, most papers about '*Natrix natrix*' are based on animals that modern authorities might refer to by a different name. That shifting landscape of applying labels to animals means that general patterns are significant – such as the emphasis of research on non-venomous snakes in Europe and North America – but that teasing apart finer-scale patterns is a waste of time.

How about the amounts of research on different evolutionary lineages of snakes? The graphs show that it's a dynamic picture. Studies on colubrid snakes have dominated the field in recent times, mostly based on North American species. Abundant, widely distributed and generally non-venomous (or only slightly venomous), colubrids such as garter snakes and grass snakes tick a lot of boxes for 'ideal study species'. But venomous snakes have attracted increasing scientific interest as well. Vipers have become popular species to study, and South America has become a popular place to study them. Several factors have driven this growth: for example, vipers are an important cause of snakebite and they are ideal for radio telemetry (big, heavy-bodied and unlikely to move too far). Pragmatically, it's not too risky to catch a dozen vipers and equip them with transmitters, then release and monitor them. A population-level mark-recapture study on such a species, however, would involve capturing and measuring hundreds of animals: a much more dangerous enterprise. So, radio telemetry is ideally suited to large venomous species; and the growing availability of miniature transmitters encouraged an equivalent growth of interest in viper ecology. Also, vipers are diverse and abundant in South and Central America, where scientific institutions have developed great strengths in this field of research over recent decades.

What scientific papers about snakes have had the most impact?

Although the numbers of papers can illustrate how much research has been directed towards different snakes in different places, numbers don't tell the whole story. One landmark paper is worth a thousand short notes.

We can measure a paper's impact from the number of times that it has been cited by later publications. That information is available in the same mega-repositories as we used to extract information on numbers of papers. So I went back to 'Web of Science' and downloaded the citation data as well.

Citation rates per paper have a peculiar distribution. Most papers are never cited, or they attract only a single mention. But at the other extreme, a classic paper may be cited thousands of times. So if we restrict our attention to papers with hundreds of mentions, we are looking at the crème de la crème.

In all fields of science, the most heavily cited papers are ones that suggest a new method or review a large field of study. That conclusion fits well with the results of my search. I located 40 papers about snakes that had each attracted more than 300 citations, with the gold medal (1,847 citations) going to Steve Arnold's 1983 paper 'Morphology, performance and fitness'. Based in Chicago at the time, Steve used snakes as an example to explain a new method: a way to link an animal's size and shape to its evolutionary fitness. Specifically, Steve wrote about how

Harry Greene and the author at the World Congress of Herpetology in Vancouver, Canada, in 2012. It's difficult to distinguish between similar-looking old white males at the best of times, but even harder when they switch their name tags to confuse their colleagues.

the shape of a snake's head affects its ability to swallow large prey. Most citations to that paper come from researchers working with other kinds of animals, not snakes. Nobody has gathered field data to test Steve's snake example – but the concept is clever and useful.

The silver medal (1,421 citations) goes to a larger work, entirely focused on snakes: Harry Greene's classic 1997 book *Snakes: The Evolution of Mystery in Nature*. Harry's volume is a rich and detailed review of snake biology and evolution. It's the most popular book on snakes ever written. I can testify to that popularity personally, because Harry and I are about the same age, height and general appearance (including an admirable lack of hair on top of our heads). So when Harry and I attend the same herpetology conference, students sometimes approach me thinking I'm Harry, and congratulate me on his book (or approach Harry to ask about Australian snakes). Admittedly, the tendency for Harry and me to swap name tags at social gatherings during the meetings may add to that confusion. Misidentifications have even occurred when we are side-by-side, enabling me to enjoy Harry's attempts at replying in a broad Australian accent to keep the joke going a little longer.

Returning to citation rates, the bronze medal (995 citations) is awarded to Ray Huey's landmark paper from 1991 on 'Physiological consequences of habitat selection'. Ray is a Seattle-based American biologist with a special interest in physiology. Partway through his career, to the astonishment of his colleagues, he abandoned reptiles for a decade or so to study fruit flies – but fortunately saw the error of his ways and returned to the world of scaly creatures. Like Steve's paper at number 1, Ray's paper outlines a new method – in this case, for measuring the range of temperatures available to an animal in natural environments, and their consequences for ectothermic ('cold-blooded') animals such as snakes.

Number 4 on the list (754 citations) is by Tom Fritts and Gordon Rodda, and it's a 1998 chapter that reviews the devastating impact of invasive Brown Tree Snakes on the ecosystems of a small Pacific island. Reflecting a fierce determination to keep the snakes from invading other Pacific islands, the US government has bankrolled research on Brown Tree Snakes in Guam for decades. That investment has resulted in unparalleled detail in our understanding of the system.

Citation rates fall after those first four masterpieces, as we encounter papers that provide new information about snakes rather than reviewing evidence or suggesting new methods. But again, topics are diverse and, interestingly, non-American studies begin to dominate. In paper number 5, Wales-based Jenny Daltry and her colleagues argue that the venoms of Malayan Pit Vipers have evolved to match local prey types. In number 6, Thomas Madsen and his Swedish and Australian colleagues show that introducing new males to an inbred population of Eurasian Adders eliminated inbreeding effects and reversed a decline in population size. And I wrote

Above and opposite: Because many spectacular snake species have never been studied ecologically in the field, we have no idea why some species – such as the African Bush Viper (*Atheris squamigera*) – occur in several vivid colour morphs. PHOTOGRAPHS: BILL LAMAR

number 7, which goes back to the theme of reviews – in this case, of information about sex differences in body size among snakes, and why those differences have evolved.

Looking through the list of 'top 40' papers, I would class 16 as reviews and three as 'methods' papers. Most of the rest provide original data, but the topics and species vary enormously. American garter snakes (five papers) and Eurasian Adders (four papers) were the most popular study systems, but there are also papers on snakes from places such as Guam, Australia, South Africa, Brazil, Costa Rica and France. Likewise, the topics of those 40 papers range from fundamental to applied biology.

Snake ecological research as a growth industry

The most important message from the analysis of scientific literature is the overall acceleration of ecological research on snakes. Every category has increased in absolute terms. In 2000, only a few decades into that expansion, the pattern was already so clear that my French colleague Xavier Bonnet and I wrote a paper claiming that snakes were becoming a 'model organism' in ecological research. Nobody disagreed with us.

The transition in topics studied was gradual. For example, the earliest books on reptiles focused on how to identify a snake and determine if it was venomous. They had nothing to say about the species' biology. But as information accumulated, newer books included brief ecological observations. There was guesswork involved about where each species occurs, what it eats, whether it lays eggs or produces live young, and so forth, but science is a self-correcting process. Through time, more reliable observations provided an ever-clearer picture. Snake ecology proved to be more complicated than expected, as those pioneering naturalists discovered unexpectedly high variation in ecological traits. For example, average body sizes differed not only between species, but also among populations within a single species, and even between males and females within a single population.

Snake ecology is complicated! Even within a single population, diets can differ dramatically between males and females. Female Arafura File Snakes (*Acrochordus arafurae*) are heavy bodied and large headed, and ambush large fish – whereas males are slender, small headed, and search actively for small fish. JULES FARQUHAR

The history of research in snake ecology is messy, disorganised and jumbled. There was no single revolution; no point in time or particular type of snake or specific question where we could say with confidence 'this was a turning point!' Instead, progress occurred by numerous leaps and bounds, emerging from unexpected places. Research groups sprang up, often driven by a single person, flourished, and then waned. So if we plotted the trajectory of snake ecology research, we wouldn't see a huge and ever-expanding wildfire spreading out from a single lightning strike in Henry Fitch's Kansas farmlands or Hubert Saint Giron's French forests. Instead, there were thousands of those lightning strikes, over half a century, popping up all over the world. Some of those fires flared briefly then died out; others spread and coalesced with other fires. Eventually the changes wrought by the research revolution had touched almost every kind of snake and almost every country where snakes live; but some fires started earlier than others, and some burned hotter.

Because most snake ecologists worked alone, and were fiercely independent, the field wasn't 'organised' by any professional organisation. The closest thing to an umbrella committee was the 'Snake Ecology Group', a loosely structured bunch of people who came together after Rich Seigel and Neil Ford organised the first snake-ecology symposium at a Canadian conference in 1985. That was the first time I met some of the international giants of the field, plus several younger people who would later become major figures in snake research. Momentum was increased by a symposium on snake ecology at the First World Congress of Herpetology in the UK in 1989; and then by a succession of smaller snake-ecology-focused meetings in the USA and Japan. Conversations at those conferences led to a new era of international collaboration and broadened the perspectives of emerging workers.

In summary, the period from 1980 to 2020 saw research on snake ecology burst its boundaries. A field that had arisen with a strong focus on vipers and colubrid snakes in the temperate forests and woodlands of Europe and North America became a global enterprise. New kinds of snakes in new kinds of places, studied by a more diverse array of people from a wider range of perspectives and using a wider range of methods. The 'model organisms' – species that were important at the birth of snake-ecology research – remained popular, but the range of questions asked of those systems diversified at lightning speed. I'm not sure if that phenomenal burst of activity qualifies as a 'scientific revolution', but that's what it felt like from my ringside seat.

IN THEIR OWN WORDS

Many pioneers recognised the incomplete nature of their own understanding of snake biology:

"Most savage peoples have many beliefs about snakes that most of us may regard with scorn, yet in our own ignorance we have just as strange and foolish ideas about these interesting animals." CHARLES CURRAN AND CARL KAUFFELD, 1937

"If then, our present acquaintance with their mere physical attributes is so far from complete, is it any marvel that we know next to nothing of their habits and propensities? And is it not justifiable to declare that we know next to nothing, when we are in ignorance with regard to hundred of snakes as to whether they kill their prey by the grand distinctive process of constriction or by common biting; and (with a few exceptions) cannot say which species are oviparous, and which produce living young?" ARTHUR STRADLING, 1882

And early 'snake public relations' efforts ran into the same problems as modern-day efforts. For example, how can we let the reader know what kind of snake we are referring to, when names are hopelessly ambiguous?:

"All over the world we find such titles as 'death', 'night' or 'fire adder'; 'rat snakes', 'chicken snakes'; 'grass', 'sand' and 'water snakes'; 'deaf', 'blind', 'green', 'brown' and 'black' snakes; 'ringed', 'striped', 'spotted', 'tiger', 'leopard', 'milk', 'silver', 'coral', 'harlequin' and 'carpet' snakes – some or all of these. To attempt to reduce the popular nomenclature of reptiles to anything like systematic order is to make confusion worse confounded. Go to any country and learn the common names of a snake. You will find that not only may that name be purely local and confined to a certain district, so that the creature may assume half a dozen aliases as you proceed, but that in all probability the same word is applied to half a dozen other snakes as well." ARTHUR STRADLING, 1882

My favourite author, Catherine Hopley, suggested an ingenious but incorrect answer to explain why it can be so difficult to identify snake species in the tropics. The correct answer, courtesy of modern genetics analyses, is that the tropics contain a remarkably high number of snake species. Not realising this, Catherine suggested that perhaps there were just a few species but they frequently interbred with each other to create a great diversity of forms:

"In tropical or semi-tropical regions, where closely-allied species abound, it may be suspected that hybrids not unfrequently create confusion as well as a multiplication of supposed 'species' not likely to cease. In our small London collection, hybrids have been produced at least twice within a few years; and we fear that the habit of hibernating in mixed multitudes leads to some immorality among the ophidia."
CATHERINE COOPER HOPLEY, 1882

She was wrong about why tropical snakes are difficult to identify, but it was a clever idea.

One of the most magnificent snake species (and the author's personal all-time favourite), the Red-bellied Black Snake (*Pseudechis porphyriacus*) is abundant in eastern Australia. ALANA DE LAIVE

PART 2

DEVELOPING A TOOLKIT FOR SNAKE RESEARCH

Snakes are difficult to study. At its core, research on snakes is a struggle between people who want to find things out and snakes that refuse to co-operate. So to obtain useful information, researchers had to invent ways to find snakes, catch them, measure them, determine their sex, identify their recent meals, and so forth. In this section of the book, I look at how trailblazing biologists overcame the challenges of working on a recalcitrant study animal with a peculiar body shape.

Chapter 3

First, catch your snake

To study snakes, you need to outsmart them. That's easier said than done when your adversary is built close to the ground and has a world-class ability at playing 'hide and seek'. For millions of years, snakes have been fine-tuning their invisibility. In a tropical climate where it can stay warm without leaving shelter, an ambush-foraging snake may stay well hidden in the same place for months on end, waiting for a furry meal to wander past. One radio-tracked Reticulated Python spent two months hidden underground within a Singapore sewer-pipe, staying in the same place while consuming dozens of rats – and as a result, growing substantially larger. Likewise, some captive vipers literally don't move for weeks on end; zookeeper Jim Murphy told me of a Temple Viper in his collection that stayed immobile for so long that a spider attached one end of its web to the snake's head. The web remained in place for more than six weeks.

The sad reality for wannabe snake finders is that evolution has enshrined any trick that makes a snake more difficult to see, including superb camouflage as well as the ability to remain motionless for weeks. Even experienced snake biologists fail to find most of the snakes around them. And if a snake spends its life beneath the ground, underwater or in the tree-tops, the problems are magnified a thousandfold.

So, what methods have snake researchers developed to work with serpents?

Using other people's snakes

The easiest way to get your hands on lots of snakes is to persuade other people to catch them for you. Cash can be a powerful motivation, especially in countries where the local people are impoverished. For example, Indian surgeon and biologist Edward Nicholson (1839–1920) wrote that: "The European in India can do little himself beyond keeping a sharp look-out whilst walking for exercise or after game; by far the greater part of collections are made by employing the patience and acuteness of Indians in this laborious pursuit. In stations where a reward is given by the authorities for every cobra that is killed, other snakes will often be brought in, and an arrangement with the police will bring these to anyone willing to give a

How can a researcher ever hope to understand the private life of a Green Tree Python (*Morelia viridis*) that spends its life in the trees and is almost invisible in the foliage? PIXABAY

small reward. Where public money is not devoted to this philanthropic object the best way is to make generally known amongst toddy-drawers, fishermen, grass-cutters and Indian camp-followers in general, that a reward will be given for every snake that is brought in."

Even in a wealthy country, some sections of the population can be forced into snake-finding duties without financial reward. In a classic early study in 1953, Finnish researcher Perrti Viitanen (1929–2022) surveyed the abundance of Eurasian Adders. These small snakes are difficult to see but Pertti was a schoolmaster and so was able to assemble a volunteer army. He conscripted his high-school students to form a cordon, with each student five metres (five yards) from the next as they walked slowly through adder habitat. In his paper, Perrti doesn't mention asking for parental permission beforehand.

Other motives for contributing snakes have played a role as well. For an early settler afraid of snakebite, the first problem was to know what level of danger was posed by the local snakes. To do that, the snakes had to be identified – and the easiest way to do that was to kill snakes and send them to a museum. Other people were (and are) motivated by a more personal thrill – the challenge of capturing a potentially dangerous animal. In modern research programs, the people who actually catch the snakes include a semi-anonymous army of students and 'citizen scientists' – that is, volunteers. And roles evolve over time. When I began my annual research

A proud young snake-collector in Escuinapa, Mexico, in 1904.
JOSEPH H. BATTY (1847–1906), COURTESY OF THE AMERICAN MUSEUM OF NATURAL HISTORY

trips to New Caledonia to mark and recapture sea snakes, I caught every snake. Twenty years later, my local volunteer army catches many more snakes than I do.

Unfortunately, most of the 'other people who catch snakes for you' have their own agendas. Unless you pay them or they are snake-focused zealots looking for a reason to indulge their passions or play a serpentine version of Russian roulette, they are unlikely to knock on your door and offer you healthy animals with precise information about collection sites and times. Instead, those 'donated' animals were collected for some other reason. They may have been killed to reduce the risk of snakebite to people, or to eliminate predation on pet birds or fish; or culled so that their skins or flesh can be sold; or to be preserved and lodged in a museum.

Even if those donated snakes are dead rather than alive, they can still be valuable for ecological research. You can't study the behaviour of a dead animal, but you can measure its carcass and determine its sex; and even better, you can look inside its body to record its reproductive state, and peek inside its stomach to see what it had eaten before it died.

In the early days of ecological research on snakes, many investigators (me included) caught and killed snakes, then dissected them to obtain the information we needed. One of the most gruesome titles I've seen for any scientific paper was a 1974 one by Japanese biologist Zan Hattori and his colleagues entitled 'In front of a pile of sea snake carcasses'. But it's sickening to kill the creatures you love, so scientists looked for other ways to obtain those dead bodies. Ways that didn't involve additional slaughter. Harry Greene (in the USA) and I (in Australia) independently hit on the idea of looking inside preserved snakes in museum collections to amass data on stomach contents (diets) and gonads (reproductive cycles). Harry worked his way through selected American species, while I did the same in Australia. There are limits to what you can learn from peering into the innards of a dead snake, but it gave us information about hundreds of species – and thus, an overall framework. For the first time, we could talk about general patterns in snake diets and life histories, based on sampling the snake fauna of entire continents.

But Harry and I weren't the first people to extract information by examining an animal's entrails. A much-admired profession in Ancient Rome was 'haruspicy', whereby a self-proclaimed expert would examine the entrails of a slaughtered animal to clarify the will of the gods. For example, the appearance of the liver, heart and lungs inside a slaughtered animal's carcass would tell the haruspex whether or not the gods approved plans for military action. When Harry and I began slicing open long-dead snakes in museums to obtain insights, we were following a well-trodden path.

Museums are not the only large repositories of dead snakes. At the dawn of research in snake ecology, venomous snakes were still so unpopular that people tried to exterminate them. Early researchers such as San Diego-based Lawrence Klauber (1883–1968) dissected huge samples of snakes collected in the name of eradication. Those tragically misplaced efforts at snake control have largely disappeared, although vestiges persist in the 'rattlesnake round-ups' of the USA. And researchers are still taking data from the animals collected for those round-ups, although these days it's mostly just external traits such as size and sex. Sadly, a few of the old-style round-ups persist, including cruel practices such as forcing snakes out of dens with gasoline. But in most present-day round-ups the snakes are released rather than killed, and the activity is more about public entertainment than about snake control.

Likewise, attempts to reduce predation on waterfowl by eradicating snakes were abandoned long ago. The largest modern-day snake-culling activities are those to protect commercially

The skins and meat from large snakes – such as this huge Green Anaconda (*Eunectes murinus*) from Rio Tapiche, Peru – are a valuable source of income and food for local villagers. BILL LAMAR

raised fish. The slaughter ranges from water snakes in the USA to mud snakes in South-East Asia. And opportunistic biologists examine the carcasses of those victims, just as Klauber did with rattlesnakes in the 1950s. Another common source of freshly killed snakes involves accidental bycatch from fishing activities. Indeed, the only information on the diets and reproduction of some species of sea snakes has come from dissection of individuals that drowned in fishing nets.

People also collect and kill snakes to make money – especially in Asia, where there is a long tradition of using snake skins and eating snake meat. If the snakes are too small for belts or dinners, they provide food for commercially raised crocodiles. One village I visited in Vietnam bred and raised King Cobras to make 'snake wine', with a preserved snake in every bottle. To grow the young cobras to suitable size, the farmers require abundant food – and King Cobras mostly feed on other snakes. No problem. Thousands of small mud snakes are harvested from the surrounding paddyfields to feed the young Kings.

The skin industry is much bigger than the 'snake wine' industry, with vast numbers of snakes collected from the wild every year and turned into luxury leather fashion goods. Larger species provide more valuable skins, so pythons are a popular target. A biologist at the reptile slaughterhouses of Asia has access to massive numbers of fresh carcasses. Working with Indonesian colleagues, I exploited that opportunity to examine the life-history traits of harvested species. In the process, we gathered the first ecological data on some of the most abundant snake species on the planet.

People who look inside dead snakes often discover surprises. A curious Australian herpetologist who opened up the swollen stomach of a road-killed Eastern Brown Snake in southern Australia in 1992 was the first person in more than 30 years to set eyes on a supposedly extinct lizard, a miniature species of bluetongue skink. Snakes are good at finding creatures that are inaccessible to most other forms of searching. For example, the small bluetongues rarely leave their burrows and so are invisible to herpetologists – but easy prey for snakes. Sometimes, we can use that prey-finding ability for conservation purposes, as in the case of amphibious sea snakes that capture moray eels from coralline crevices where they are inaccessible to human collectors. Because the snakes then bring the eels back to shore to digest, the sea kraits' meals provide an easy way for us to find out what kinds of eels occur in an area, and how their populations are faring.

Finding your own snakes

Some kinds of snakes continue to defy ecological researchers. In particular, burrowing snakes are still metaphorically thumbing their noses at science, but other kinds of snakes are yielding their secrets as we discover ways to find them. Sometimes that involves learning where snakes hide away and targeting those sites at times when the snakes are curled up inside. In cool climates, a quest for warmth attracts snakes to sun-heated shelter items. A sheet of metal exposed to sunlight is a snake magnet. Some researchers deploy hundreds of these thermal oases and then check beneath them regularly.

A Timber Rattlesnake (*Crotalus horridus*) that was found hiding beneath a sheet of metal. NOAH K. FIELD

But most snakes are difficult to find while they are hidden away in refuges, so the key to increased capture rates is to understand why snakes leave their shelters and become catchable. As I mentioned above, the need for warmth is a key vulnerability in cool climates. A snake that is basking in sunlight is easy to find because it has to expose itself. Experienced snake catchers walk through bushland with the sun behind them, to get a clear view of snakes in sunny spots. And the experts pick days after heavy rain, when snakes emerge to dry out. Cool climates increase that vulnerability because a snake needs to be warm for several reasons – for example, to digest prey or manufacture sperm. To accelerate the development of her embryos so that she can give birth before the first frosts of autumn, a pregnant female snake in a cool climate simply has to bask.

Sunlight has less appeal for snakes that live in hot climates, where an animal can stay warm while it is hidden. But even in those species, the males have to find the females – and as a result, the mating season brings male snakes out into the open. In most snake species, mate-searching males range widely and are vulnerable to predators while they are away from shelter. Add in the single-mindedness of sex-searching males – a focus on females, and nothing else – and you have a recipe for disaster. Most museum collections of large snake species are dominated by adult males that were caught during the breeding season. The same problem occurs for females as well if they have to migrate to sun-warmed sites for egg laying. Such migrations are risky, so those same museum collections show a spike in the numbers of pregnant females collected in early summer.

But however you look at it, snakes are difficult to find. And sadly, science hasn't made it much easier. Knowing about seasonal cycles and habitat use can tell us when and where to look, but a snake is diabolically difficult to distinguish in thick cover. The main factor affecting success is who is looking: some people are hopeless at finding snakes whereas others are freakishly good. Many research projects have succeeded because a single member of the team had an uncanny ability to recognise a stray coil amidst thick vegetation. Likewise, many projects have failed for the lack of such a person. What makes a person a good snake-spotter? To answer that question, American herpetologist Gordon Rodda tested his assistants' ability to detect hidden objects by asking them to complete the children's puzzle 'Where's Waldo'. The people who were quickest to find the correct cartoon image also were the best at finding Brown Tree Snakes at night in the forest. An ability to notice details is vital, and the best snake finders have an encyclopedic knowledge of snake behaviour. An inexperienced collector spends hours turning over every rock, hoping to find a snake in hiding, whereas an expert at the same location restricts their search to large thin flat rocks exposed to afternoon sunlight.

The mottled patterns of a Reticulated Python (*Malayopython reticulatus*) render the giant snake almost invisible in dappled light and dense vegetation. RUCHIRA SOMAWEERA

Variation among snake-hunters in their ability to find snakes transcends cultural boundaries. On the tiny island of Lifou, east of the main island of New Caledonia in the Indo-Pacific region, the Kejeny tribe eat forest-dwelling Pacific Boas. But it's damn difficult to find a small brown snake up a tall tree in a dense tropical forest. You not only need a good eye, intense concentration and a fierce determination – you also need to think like a snake. The Kejeny honour the best snake-hunters by calling them *sie i un* (pronounced 'see ay oon'). I don't qualify for that lofty title, but I have worked beside superb snake finders in many parts of the world. Those people are extraordinary.

After a hard day in the field with nothing to show for it, frustrated would-be snake catchers must often wish for some magic technological fix – a machine that can tell you where a snake is hiding. I've heard rumours of an ingenious biologist who carried a gas-powered leaf-blower in the field while searching for Gaboon Vipers among piles of dead leaves on the forest floor, but the only method I've seen in action involves electro-shocking, where direct current flows between two terminals that are held underwater. The technique is commonly used in freshwater fisheries research. The fisherperson has a backpack with the battery, and two long poles to deliver the current. A fish that encounters that pulsating current instantly exhibits uncontrolled muscular contractions that force it to swim towards one of the terminals. If the equipment is used correctly, the fish isn't harmed; it can be scooped up in a net and measured, then released. Snakes are affected the same way so on the Indonesian island of Java, hunters prod their electroshock poles into the edges of canals and fishponds. If a water snake is hiding nearby in the murky water, it begins thrashing around and can be seized.

Another twist to the tale is to use dogs. With its phenomenal sense of smell, a dog can detect a hidden snake invisible to humans. That sounds like a great idea, and sniffer dogs receive extensive media attention. Pioneering researcher Lawrence Klauber told of a hound that located 500 rattlesnakes for its owner over a two-year period. Nonetheless, researchers who test the dog's effectiveness are lukewarm. As a graduate student, I once borrowed a friend's dog and took it with me on a snake-hunt. I was hoping that the dog would show me the location of camouflaged snakes – perhaps by barking, or investigating, or even running away – but it just ambled along in the sunshine. I finally encountered a large Red-bellied Black Snake that was also enjoying the sunshine, and stood back to let the dog discover the reptile. That way, I figured, I might see distinctive behaviour that would alert me when the dog finally found a snake of his own. But even when I dragged him up beside the snake, my canine companion pretended the animal wasn't there. He just looked the other way and pretended to be entirely oblivious of the large reptile that was hissing and coiling in front of him. Clearly, watching the dog's behaviour wasn't going to lead me to snakes.

The Brown Tree Snake program on Guam explored canine detection much more carefully than I did but their results weren't much better. It takes 18 months of almost-daily training for a dog to learn snake-detecting; and many canine contenders prove unsuitable. Some are afraid of snakes; others become bored at the monotonous task. And it's not cheap. The Guam team estimated that kennel construction cost \$30,000, and annual upkeep per dog \$10,000. In the tropics a dog can only work for two hours a day before overheating, and a canine's working lifetime is only a few years. Add in the costs of a highly trained dog handler and sniffer dogs price themselves out of the snake-detection market.

We can't all be expert snake finders, nor afford talented assistants, so the final kind of opportunity to catch snakes is perhaps the most important. It has driven an enormous amount of research. That factor is the occurrence of aggregations of snakes. These groupings arise because some kind of critical habitat is scarce (and so, snakes gather there) in an area where food is abundant (and thus, snakes are common). That habitat feature might be a small island on the flyway of bird migrations, providing a resting place for tired feathered travellers and a

The Brown Tree Snake (*Boiga irregularis*) has a broad geographic distribution across Australia and the Indo-Pacific, but has been studied mostly on one small island (Guam) where its introduction after World War II caused ecological catastrophe. JULES FARQUHAR

smorgasbord for pit vipers. Or an island in the midst of a coral lagoon, where sea kraits that feed in the ocean return to land to digest their meals. Natural features that concentrate large numbers of snakes into small areas solve the first and greatest challenge for a snake researcher – to find enough study animals.

In areas with severely cold winters, a scarcity of places to avoid freezing in midwinter forces snakes to gather in communal dens. And those aggregations are magnets for snake research. The massive garter-snake dens of Canada are the most famous example, but European researchers have also focused on dens of vipers, and other scientists have studied rattlesnake dens across the USA. In 1950, American academic Angus Woodbury (1886–1964) wrote about a den in Utah that "was discovered by sheep-herders in 1937, who, with the aid of workers from a Civilian Conservation Corps camp, killed an estimated 300 rattlesnakes and blasted the entrance in an effort to seal the den opening." They defined 'conservation' differently in those days!

Heaven for a snake enthusiast; the author beside a communal overwintering den of Red-sided Garter Snakes (*Thamnophis sirtalis parietalis*) in Manitoba, Canada. Such dens overcome the problem of small sample sizes. BOB MASON

Another snake den in Utah was a goldmine for ecological research from 1940 until 1973, when a wildfire resulted in loose sand blowing in to block the entrances. In the first phase of research from 1940 to 1949, Angus Woodbury individually marked more than 1,600 snakes to follow their den fidelity, growth and general ecology. In 1966 Harold Hirth, a professor at the University of Utah, re-started work at the same den, experimentally translocating snakes to see if they could find their way home. Bill Brown and Bill Parker, PhD students in Hirth's lab, then took over in 1969. They conducted groundbreaking population-ecology work at the den, including the use of radio transmitters.

First, catch your snake

If your quarry is a non-venomous snake, the main impediments to capturing it are the snake's athleticism and its ability to disappear into a deep crevice. If you do get your hands on the beast, you've won the battle. Many non-venomous snakes submit meekly to being captured and even if such a snake retaliates, its weapons are ineffective. All it can do is inflict superficial wounds with its small sharp teeth, or urinate and defecate profusely to dampen your enthusiasm. Large muscular snakes are the ones most capable of resisting capture. Anyone catching an American water snake or an Australian Slaty-grey Snake may lose blood in the process.

If you upsize your quarry to a large python, a bite upgrades from minor discomfort to a trip to the nearest hospital for stitches. Truly large boas and pythons – up around three metres (9-ft) long – are so powerful that constriction is a risk to life and limb. Experienced handlers tackle such snakes in teams. The person holding the snake's head gets all the glory, but the person at the other end is just as important. First, the rear end is the source of a dramatic outflow of smelly faeces. A snake able to thrash its tail around while it evacuates its hindgut can spray-paint the entire group with substances too vile for description. More importantly, the tail is a leverage point. If the snake can wrap its hindbody around a branch or rock, or even around a human limb or body, muscular contractions transmit force all the way through its body and exert a crushing power that has to be experienced to be believed. Sometimes, attempts to handle large pythons single-handedly end in tragedy.

Large non-venomous snakes such as this Black-skinned Parrot Snake (*Leptophis nigromarginata*) from Ecuador can inflict a painful bite.
BILL LAMAR

One way for snake catcher to avoid a bite is to ensure that the snake's mouth is already occupied. For example, South African snake guru Don Broadley (1932–2016) wrote in 1962: "The smaller, harmless snakes may be easily caught by holding a handkerchief in front of the head; when the snake strikes the material and hooks its teeth in the latter, it can be quickly seized by the back of the neck and picked up; this method can also be used effectively even with large species, such as the python, but in such cases a sack should be used in place of the handkerchief." Also in Africa, tribesmen from the Gbaya ethnic group in Cameroon use a variation on that method. First, the hunters set fire to grassland so that Rock Python tracks are clearly visible in the resultant ash. If a snake is located inside its burrow, one man crawls down and encourages the snake to bite onto a thick section of cowhide wrapped around the man's arm or leg. Once the snake's recurved teeth catch on the fabric, the python can't let go. The thick hide prevents the snake's teeth from penetrating into the intrepid snake-hunter's flesh, so all that remains is to extract the snake from its burrow. Pythons are powerful, so it may take several villagers pulling on the arms or legs of the snake-hunter to extract him from the burrow, with python attached. The unlucky snake then becomes the main course at a village feast.

African Rock Pythons (*Python natalensis*) are large enough to provide a feast for the village; but catching one of these formidable creatures is no easy task. JOHAN MARAIS

But the real challenge in snake catching is to subdue a venomous serpent. Again, species vary in their reactions to being picked up. Sea kraits are placid, as easy to catch as a strand of spaghetti. Some vipers likewise accept disturbance without taking affront. But at the other end of the spectrum, anybody who tangles with a Bushmaster or Black Mamba needs confidence, calmness, quick reflexes and a modicum of luck. And if their heart isn't pounding by the time the snake is in the bag, they are tougher than I am.

The best advice I ever saw about catching deadly snakes is in a delightful 1962 book by South African dentist Walter Rose (1884–1964). Rose was never employed as a herpetologist, although he took up an honorary position at the South African Museum for a few years. Walter's humour pervades the book, beginning with his short biography which notes that he was "born at an early age". Under the heading 'Chapter 39. Advice to the Inexperienced on Catching and Handling Poisonous Snakes', the entire text of the chapter consists of a single word – "DON'T".

Especially if the quarry is fast-moving and deadly, experienced snake catchers decrease the

Most non-venomous snakes have small teeth that can't do much damage to a human hand. But beware larger species that eat birds! To prevent the bird from escaping, such a snake must hang on tenaciously after the strike – and so is equipped with formidable dental weapons. This image shows the business end of a Rough-scaled Python (*Morelia carinata*). RUCHIRA SOMAWEERA

risk level by choosing where and when to launch an attack on the snake. Like an astute army general who selects a battleground that favours their own troops, wily snake catchers don't leap onto a serpent as soon as they see it. One impressive example involved an elderly farmer from tropical North Queensland in the 1960s. His farm contained Coastal Taipans, massive fast-moving elapid snakes with deadly venom. Taipan bites were usually fatal in those days but on the other hand, a live taipan commanded a rich reward because its venom could be used to make the scarce antivenom. Tackling one of these agile giants single-handed in the middle of the day would have been suicidal, so the old man devised a better way.

If he encountered a taipan in his fields, the farmer followed the snake at a respectful distance as it wandered about in search of rats or mates. When the taipan eventually retired to a hollow log to spend the night, the farmer crept away and then returned at dawn. Hiding in the scrub a few metres from the log, the old man waited until the snake emerged and crawled slowly across to a patch of sunlight to bask – and then, and only then, did he run across and seize the snake, and wrestle it into a sack. Cold and slow, the snake was unable to resist – and could be captured safely.

Different types of snakes require different kinds of catching gear. For a spitting cobra, eye protection is essential. Those snakes aim for their tormenter's eyes, and even a tiny drop of venom in the eye causes excruciating pain. Most heavy-bodied vipers and pit vipers are quick to strike but slow to move, so can be manipulated into a bag or bucket with a snake-hook. In contrast, lithe elapids easily evade a hook, and must be seized either by the tail or with a pair of tongs. In the early days of Australian snake catching, the usual method was to grab the snake by the tail then pin the head down with a convenient stick. That method is simple, but it's risky. Slender-bodied snakes can hurl their bodies upwards, and catching a large Eastern Brown Snake on a hot day requires juggling and fast footwork. Most of my own PhD research in the 1970s consisted of catching elapids – initially by hand, but some terrifying near-catastrophes during the first year of fieldwork convinced me to graduate to tongs. Worldwide, nowadays most snake catchers use implements of one kind or another. Hooks, tongs or rakes were standard equipment for American and European snake catchers from the earliest days, because picking up a viper by the tail is asking for trouble. Ditto for a too-small or too-large elapid.

The grumpy African snakeman C.J.P. Ionides (1901–1968) is often credited with inventing special tongs for tree-dwelling snakes such as Green Mambas. Ionides was certainly the first to use the system of "pincers at the end of a long pole operated by a handle at the base" but in his autobiography, Ionides credits a museum curator, Norman Mitton, for constructing the first version. Later versions of Ionides's tongs included clamps that could be fastened shut, so the snake could be securely held without requiring the operator to exert pressure on the handle.

Krystal Tolley giving serious thought about how best to capture this Black Spitting Cobra (*Naja nigricincta*), because it can spit venom as well as bite; and antivenom doesn't work well against the venom of this species. KRYSTAL TOLLEY

It's difficult to grab a fast-moving snake if you're halfway up a tree, but it's even more difficult to hang onto that snake if you need both hands to clamber back down to the ground.

The next important innovation was the hoop bag – a long cloth sack with a handle, rather like an over-sized butterfly net. Devised by Charles Tanner (1911–1996), a pioneer of venom extraction in Australia, the design allowed Charles to pick up snakes by the tail and drop them straight into the bag without having to pin them down first. The hoop bag is now standard equipment for Aussies, often used with tongs to keep the catcher's bare hands away from the business end of an enraged taipan or Australian Brown Snake. Some snake catchers have developed a modified approach that dispenses with handling the snake at all. Just hold the opening of the hoop bag vertically beside your leg close to the ground, then step on the tail of the departing serpent. Hey presto, it spins around and launches a strike towards your leg, ending up with its forebody well inside the hoop-bag. Lift the bag upwards, and the task is complete.

Like snake finding, snake catching is more of an art than a science. The best snake-handlers I know are people who routinely 'milk' venomous snakes to extract venom. Indeed, many techniques that simplify the task of handling a deadly snake were invented by people who caught snakes for venom rather than research.

Safely handling a venomous snake by holding its head requires calmness and a clear understanding of the species you are dealing with. For some vipers, the main danger is to the snake – a gyrating serpent can fracture small bones in its neck. For large muscular elapids such as the King Brown Snake and Snouted Cobra, beware any coils around your arm or elsewhere – they give the snake a leverage point to pull backwards against your restraining grip, inexorably moving those fangs closer and closer to your fingers. And for a few species, such as the side-stabbing snakes of Africa, there is no safe way to hold the snake behind the head. These viper-like burrowers (also known as stiletto snakes or mole vipers) can slash backwards with their huge fangs, impaling a finger that would be out of reach of any other snake. They don't need to open their mouth to do so; even a firm grip of the head doesn't protect the handler. That unusual ability reflects the snakes' way of feeding – they penetrate deep into rodent burrows, slide their head down past the rat, then jab backwards to impale it on a fang and deliver their venom. That foraging tactic translates into catastrophe for any snake-handler who doesn't know the risks.

Snake-handling technology continues to evolve. Some people swear by high-tech gloves impervious to a snake's fangs; others construct their own snake-pinners from kitchen utensils that were designed to mash potatoes. There's no single correct way to handle a deadly snake, but there are a lot of wrong ways to do it. Experience helps. After a lifetime catching lithe fast-

Some elapid snakes, such as this Black-necked Spitting Cobra (*Naja nigricincta*), have evolved dilute venom that can be sprayed towards an attacker's eyes to cause intense pain. Goggles are essential gear for the snake catcher in areas where these species occur. PHILO BECK

moving elapids, I'm comfortable handling even the largest and most deadly species. But I'm way out of that comfort zone when I am face-to-face with a viper. Even a small one. To me, a viper is like a rusty hand grenade – I can't predict if and when it will explode without warning.

In his 1962 book about African reptiles and amphibians, the joyful Cape Town dentist and animal-lover Walter Rose quotes from an early (1937) magazine designed to prepare missionaries for the challenges of working in Africa. The story gives a flavour of just how badly people misunderstood snakes. And remarkably, the advice was about non-venomous pythons. The article says: "Remember not to run away, the python can run faster. The thing to do is to lie flat on the ground on your back with your feet together, arms to the sides and head well down. The python will then try to push its head under you, experimenting at every possible point. Keep calm, one wiggle and he will get under you, wrap his coils around you and crush you to death. After a time the python will get tired of this and probably decide to swallow you without the usual preliminaries. He will very likely begin with one of your feet. Keep calm. You must let him swallow your foot. It is quite painless and will take a long time. If you lose your head and struggle he will quickly whip his coils around you. If you keep calm, he will go on swallowing. Wait patiently until he has swallowed about up to your knee. Then carefully take out your knife and insert it into the distended side of his mouth and with a quick rip slit him up." I'm not sure if this mind-bogglingly bad advice was an attempt at humour, or a classic early example of 'fake news'.

Transporting your snake

Most snakes are captured far from home, so you need to keep the snake safe and secure while you transport it. That's not too difficult in the short term; pioneering Indian snake biologist Edward Nicholson drolly observed in 1874 that "the only inconvenience of having a nine-foot python or hamadryad [King Cobra] coiled round one is that he is apt to make a mess on one's clothes." But holding a snake in your hands for a long time is a poor tactic, especially if the animal is venomous. A millisecond's inattention enables the animal to squeeze its way out of your grip to deliver a bite; and prolonged pressure behind the head can injure it. Even if the snake is not venomous, a large python is difficult to restrain for long periods. One example of those difficulties woke me late at night on a field trip in tropical Australia. A helpful but snake-naive colleague had been returning home when he found a Carpet Python crossing the road. He captured the animal and seized it firmly behind the head. Lacking a receptacle for the 2-metre (6-ft) serpent, he simply got back into his car and maintained his grip as he drove back to town. By the time he reached my house the snake had wound several coils around the steering wheel as well as his arms. I was awoken by a frantic beeping of a car horn in my driveway, and I came out to find my friend jammed up against the steering wheel and unable to move without releasing the angry python.

The traditional snake-carrying device is a cloth bag, preferably with tape attached for tying the top. Stitching across a lower corner of the bag can produce a safe triangle for fingers to grasp the bag without exposing them to a bite from the snake within. It's amazing how large a snake can be crammed into a small bag, but a larger container makes things easier. Ionides the African innovator developed the 'reverse-bag' technique, whereby you invert the bag, put your hand into it, and grasp the snake's head through the bag. Then you turn the bag back right-side-out, with the snake's head inside, and push the rest of the body into the bag after it. You hang onto that head grimly until the mouth of the bag has been tied shut, then you let go.

Transporting a giant boa or python back to base camp is never easy. Scrambling up rocky slopes with several people attached to the same snake requires co-ordination and strength. You can solve that problem by putting the snake in a bag, but few bags large enough to hold a gigantic snake can resist the battering ram of a snout propelled by metres of muscle. My

This commercial hunter of frogs and snakes in Java, Indonesia, has devised an effective way to transport his captures. MIRZA KUSRINI

colleague Jesus Rivas developed a creative way to deal with the enormous anacondas he studied in South America. He wrestled a thick football sock over the snake's head, covering its eyes, then taped the open end of the sock to the snake's neck. Unable to see its tormentors, the snake soon calmed down.

Cloth bags are most frequently used as snake receptacles, especially pillow slips because they are cheap and easily available. Snakes generally settle down well inside a cloth bag, but there are innumerable tales of escapes through tiny holes. Experienced snake biologists

The bigger the snake, the bigger the bag. The author wrestling a large Red-bellied Black Snake (*Pseudechis porphyriacus*) into a hoop bag in southern Australia, after first seizing the snake with tongs. TERRI SHINE

insist on premium-quality bags, creating a small but profitable niche market for convicted felons in government prisons. The best bags I ever used were ones that I purchased from an Australian jail.

For sea snakes, the problem is to give the captured snakes an opportunity to breathe during the remainder of an underwater collecting trip. I use a floating O-ring of Styrofoam inside a barrel-shaped mesh bag whose sides are held apart by circular wire struts. The snakes are placed into the bag via an opening at the bottom, sealed by a plastic clip. The captured snakes can surface to breathe whenever they need to, reducing stress. I stole the idea from a wildlife documentary I watched, that showed more experienced divers using a similar device.

If you need to transport a snake over a longer distance, you can ship it via specialised companies that provide escape-proof containers, and deal with the rules and regulations required to convey a venomous animal from one place to another. But in times gone by, people simply popped their snake into the mail. Often just in a cardboard box, with the snake secured inside a cloth bag or a nylon stocking. Survival rates were high – snakes are tough – but the potential for disaster was obvious. It was commonplace for a snake to escape from its bag and spring out of its package as soon as the box was opened. One Australian Tiger Snake smuggled overseas in this way bit a postal worker in a California mail centre. When I was a graduate student, my colleagues would evacuate the tea room whenever I began to open a box labelled 'live reptile'.

Trapping snakes

Because snakes spend so much of their time hidden away, inaccessible to collectors, searching for active animals is a challenge. Is there a more efficient way? One solution is to set out traps that intercept and capture snakes as they move around. That way, investigators can lie back and check their email inbox as their traps fill up with serpents. The most common type of trap consists of a cylinder or rectangle made of mesh or wire, with inward-pointing funnels at one or both ends. Inside the trap the narrow ends of those funnels are well above ground level, so a snake that enters the trap through the wide end of a funnel finds it difficult to escape.

Most snake scientists credit the illustrious Kansas-based ecologist Henry Fitch with pioneering the use of funnel traps to catch snakes, but the idea wasn't original with him. He never claimed that it was. The real pioneer was a snake-hater. Albert M. Jackley (1880–1950) was known as 'the Saint Patrick of South Dakota' because of his zealous efforts to exterminate Prairie Rattlesnakes from that state. One magazine compared Jackley's zeal to that of Captain Ahab in his pursuit of Moby Dick.

Albert Jackley proudly surveys his day's slaughter of Prairie Rattlesnakes (*Crotalus viridis*) at a snake den in South Dakota.
SOUTH DAKOTA STATE HISTORICAL SOCIETY

Jackley's anti-snake fervour resulted from personal experience with snake-related tragedies: a schoolfriend lost a leg after being bitten, and in later life, two of his adult friends died from snakebite. Initially snake-killing was just a hobby for Jackley, but in 1937 he gave up his real-estate business to take charge of the rattlesnake-control program of the South Dakota Department of Agriculture. Jackley used many methods, including fumigating dens with poisonous gases such as chlorine and formaldehyde; but his most effective tactic was to install wire-netting traps with flap-covered entrances leading into the rocky cleft from which snakes emerged after hibernation. Any snake leaving the den crawled past the flap and into the trap and could not escape. The traps could hold dozens of snakes, and Jackley personally killed 4,500 rattlesnakes during the autumn of 1942 alone. In a 1939 article he explained his philosophy about such massacres, concluding that: "Man was created for a purpose and has his place … by the proper exercise of our God-given faculties we shall change nature so that it will administer more bountifully to our pleasures in life." (p. 11). In short, Jackley was a religious zealot.

Eradicating snakes was also the primary motive for American biologist Ralph Imler (1906–1986), but for pragmatic rather than spiritual reasons. Imler was a renowned bird biologist, conducting some of the first detailed studies on everything from Bald Eagles to crows, and occasionally venturing into sea lions. In those early days, when professional biologists were few and far between, they worked on a greater diversity of species than is true of their modern-day counterparts. In his snake study, Imler deployed traps in the early 1940s to control Bull Snakes that were eating duck eggs at a Nebraska wildlife refuge. The snake-driven reduction in the numbers of shootable adult ducks irked sportspeople, so the snakes were targeted for eradication. Importantly, Imler's traps didn't require a snake den. The traps had funnels at both ends, and they were placed beside drift fences to channel wandering snakes into the trap's entrance. Imler's design was more popular than Jackley's because it could be deployed anywhere. Henry Fitch refined Imler's prototype to make it smaller, simpler and more efficient. Instead of using a drift fence, Henry exploited natural obstacles such as logs or rock walls to channel snakes towards the trap.

Modern-day researchers frequently use funnel traps in conjunction with drift fences, to increase capture rates by directing a moving snake into the funnel entrance. Often, an array of traps around a drift fence will include pit traps as well. These are open-topped smooth-sided buckets sunk into the ground so that animals moving along the drift fence fall in and can't climb out. Pit traps work well for ground-dwelling frogs and lizards, and for snakes too small to escape. Legendary American reptile ecologist Whit Gibbons and his team at the Savannah River Lab in South Carolina deployed thousands of snake traps along kilometres of drift fences, with every unit checked daily for decades. It required prodigious effort, but the resultant capture rates were phenomenal. Whit enjoys a legendary status among American herpetologists, partly due to his prodigious research output but also to his decades-long success in finding government funds to employ some of the best young biologists in the country. A list of Whit's proteges reads like a who's who of the next generation of US herpetology. A famously genial man, the only time I ever saw Whit in a bad mood was when I stopped by his house in Georgia one day while he was watching a football game on TV. His beloved Alabama team was losing, and Whit wasn't a happy man.

Most research on snake-trapping has been done for the original purpose of traps – that is, to remove 'problem' animals. This issue spawned parallel projects in southern Japan and the Pacific island of Guam, focusing on different snakes and different problems. In the Ryukyu islands of southern Japan, a large pit viper known as the Habu (revered as 'God of the Forest' by some local tribes) poses a major risk of snakebite. In some years, more than four bites per 1,000 people have been reported. Mortality is rare, but permanent crippling is common. Although large, Habu are difficult to find in the wild: they are beautifully camouflaged in mottled brown, and spend long periods lying in ambush for their prey. The tropical climate means that the snakes never need to bask in open sites. Unsurprisingly, then, Japanese researchers have devoted enormous effort to building a better Habu trap.

A Brown Tree Snake (*Boiga irregularis*) investigates a snake-trap on the island of Guam. US DEPARTMENT OF AGRICULTURE

Digging pitfall traps into hard ground is no job for the faint-hearted. It's a lot of work, best accomplished by a group of people as in this photograph of a South African survey team. GRAHAM ALEXANDER

In Guam, on the other hand, the culprit is the slender Brown Tree Snake. It was accidentally brought from Guadalcanal (in the Solomon Islands) to Guam in American military equipment after World War II. Only mildly venomous, the snakebite risk to humans is minor – but the snake achieves high densities in its new home, exterminating native birds and mammals and causing power outages by climbing electricity poles and bridging between the wires. And such as the Habu, a Brown Tree Snake is difficult to find in the wild. The snakes are active only at night, and they spend much of their time high in trees.

Those factors motivated intensive research to build a better snake trap. Both the Habu and Brown Tree Snake projects achieved higher trapping rates if a live rodent was placed in the trap to attract snakes – but that approach raised ethical issues as well as increasing the workload of the research team. Sadly, chemical cues from rodents were nowhere near as effective as real rats. And because small snakes grow up on a diet of lizards before switching across to rat burgers, a rodent-baited trap catches only adult animals. Typical capture rates for traps are around one snake per 100 days, although some studies with the Habu have achieved much higher success. Aspects such as funnel design are critical – for example, including a flap on the inner side of the funnel slightly reduces the rate that snakes enter the traps, but massively decreases the numbers that escape after entering. A hiding place for snakes within the trap also reduces escape rates (the snake just curls up inside its new shelter) and more surprisingly, it also increases entry rates (the snake can't see inside the shelter so it enters the trap to check it out).

Snake-traps enable researchers to catch snakes 24/7, but they require frequent monitoring to ensure that captured animals don't overheat, freeze, drown, or dry out. The traps catch everything from spiders and frogs through to rodents, so collateral impacts can be severe. Traps are especially useful for fast-moving snake species where capture by hand is a daunting challenge, or where the habitat offers inaccessible refuges into which a snake can escape. But traps can also be a death warrant for captured animals in an area infested by hungry ants. And larger predators (such as ravens in Australia, and primates in Africa) can learn the location of a trapline, and systematically visit it daily (sometimes, timed to happen just before the researcher's daily checks!) to clean out any edible reptiles. Some researchers have resorted to sending off colleagues as decoys to attract the ravens' interest just before the real trap-checkers sneak away in a different direction.

During my PhD in Australia in the 1970s, I constructed Fitch-style funnel traps to overcome a problem. A small waterbody near the town of Uralla was named Racecourse Lagoon because locals had constructed a racecourse around its periphery. The race-goers drank a lot of beer, prompting the installation of large bins to collect empty cans and bottles. The bins were rarely emptied, so each was usually filled with empty beer cans to at least a metre depth.

Javan snake catchers electrofishing for water snakes and mud snakes, after draining most of the water from the pond (with the hose in the background); and carrying a captured Puff-faced Water Snake (*Homalopsis buccata*) to the bank of the canal. PHOTOGRAPHS: MIRZA KUSRINI

Australian Tiger Snakes loved those bins; the cans and bottles were heated by sunlight so a snake could warm itself up by basking on the surface of the rubbish, instantly diving down into the metal and glass matrix if disturbed. Frustrated by the sight of Tiger Snake tails slipping out of my reach, I contructed mesh snake-traps with funnel entrances and buried them in the upper layers of the rubbish. Whenever I checked the bins, I found plump Tiger Snakes inside the traps.

Traps can work in water as well as on land. Many studies on water snakes use Fitch-style traps, for example. While I was studying Arafura File Snakes in tropical Australia, radio tracking showed that these large aquatic snakes move through the shallow edges of waterbodies as they forage at night. I deployed fyke nets in those sites: that is, funnel traps with a long mesh leader extending into deeper water, to channel foraging snakes into the funnel entrance. Sure enough, the traps filled up with file snakes.

Funnel-based trap designs are not the only solution for catching snakes. The commercial harvest of giant Reticulated Pythons in Indonesia is based mostly on hand collecting by farmers, who capture pythons they encounter serendipitously during routine agricultural activities. But traps are used in other circumstances. For example, a snake track in the dust leading under a house reveals the likely presence of a python. It may not emerge from that shelter site for weeks, but it can be captured by tying a live chicken to a fish hook, connected to thick line, and throwing the unfortunate bird into the cavity beneath the house.

Sumatran snake catchers also use another kind of trap. They string nylon mesh nets along the surface of ponds, to intercept any large snake swimming across. The snake's head and forebody go through the mesh, but its thicker midbody cannot fit through – so the snake turns around and tries to exit through another part of the mesh. Before long it is hopelessly entangled.

Traps often catch species you didn't expect to see, even in areas where you have spent many hours turning cover items and searching for active animals. For example, Whit Gibbons and his team thought that Scarlet Snakes were the rarest snake species at their Savannah River study site – until they deployed all those pit traps. They caught 550 Scarlet Snakes in the first summer of trapping, far more than any other species. The species leapt in status from 'rarest' to 'most abundant'. Because different ways of catching snakes target different species, using a variety of methods is the only way to get a comprehensive picture of the snake fauna of an area.

Recording natural behaviour

Recording snake behaviour in the field is a challenge, for one simple reason. Most snakes either flee from you, or they sit still until you leave. Snakes are experts at the waiting game, and the world champions in this respect are the ambush predators. A popular foraging strategy among snakes, 'sit-and-wait foraging' has evolved independently in many species including pythons, vipers, colubrids, file snakes and elapids. In extreme cases, such a snake is about as mobile as a dining-room table. My American doppelganger Harry Greene watched one female Bushmaster, a giant pit viper from Central America, for 15 days. The snake barely moved a muscle over that entire period, sleeping by day and raising its head to survey the game trail in front of it at night. The boredom of watching an immobile snake do nothing for 15 days would have had me bashing my head against a tree, but Harry enjoyed the experience. He was overjoyed when his snake captured a large rodent on the 15th night.

Lacking Harry's superhuman patience, other researchers exploit remote cameras. Find a snake in ambush posture and set up a camera behind it so that you film anything that happens in the snake's field of view. The camera only records when something moves, so you don't have to watch endless hours of boring video. Rulon Clark and his students have used that technology to conduct groundbreaking studies on Sidewinders, small rattlesnakes of the American southwest. The camera footage shows that kangaroo-rats can discourage strikes by the snakes; and that the kangaroo-rat's athleticism usually enables it to evade a strike even if one is launched.

Other researchers have used automatically triggered cameras to record the behaviour of invasive Burmese Pythons in the Everglades of Florida. The main challenge here is a technical one: a snake in a tropical swamp is about as warm as its background, so that temperature-triggered systems designed for mammals and birds don't fire when a snake slithers past. But that problem can be overcome by manipulating background materials, or by setting the camera to take shots at regular intervals. The technology is evolving rapidly, and remote cameras have become standard equipment for field biologists.

IN THEIR OWN WORDS

Some early advice about snake catching reveals extensive experience by the writer. That's especially obvious for expatriate Englishmen who found themselves in India:

"A cobra standing at bay can be readily captured; put the end of a stick gently across his head and bear it down to the ground by a firm and gradual pressure; he will not resist; then place the stick horizontally across his neck and take him up. You must not dawdle about this; sharp is the word in dealing with snakes, and they have as much respect for firm and kind treatment as contempt for timidity and irresolution.... Some snakes allow themselves to be caught without the slightest attempt at resistance. The gentle *Tropidonotus stolatus*, *subminiatus*, and *plumbicolor* allow themselves to be taken up, and in dry weather the offer of a drink of water will at once gain their hearts. But most snakes are strongly opposed to being captured, and some show their independence by snapping viciously. *Tropidonotus quincunciatus* and *Ptyas* both fight for their freedom even at the earliest age, and, though they resign themselves philosophically to a domestic life, are always a little uncertain to handle; their bite is, however, quite harmless, and not very painful." JOSEPH FAYRER, 1872

"The collector of snakes must study their habits if he wishes to be successful in his search for specimens; and I can only give a few indications as to the likely places for them. Dry nullahs leading down to tanks are a good find for amphibious snakes such as the *Tropidonoti*; tussocks of grass in wet paddyfields often afford shelter to the ground vipers; the neighbourhood of houses is affected by *Lycodon*; the old galleries of white ants' nests are the refuge of various kinds of snakes, cobras included; the earth-snakes are to be found under large stones, and the hollows of old trees containing decaying vegetable matter are often chosen by snakes as a nest for their eggs. The squeals of a frog caught by a snake can never be forgotten if once heard, and they often enable the collector to surprise a snake at his meal. Snakes may often be captured while swimming, as they are readily detected in the water." JOSEPH FAYRER, 1872

"The collector need provide himself with no implements beyond a bag and his walking-stick, which, if placed on the neck of any snake, will permit of its being grasped without trouble. If the specimen has to be carried any distance and is too large to be stowed into a pocket, no bag being at hand, a piece of string to bind him to the stick will be found useful, as holding a large snake by the tail is inconvenient, and holding him by the neck becomes irksome, especially in the case of a venomous kind. It must be remembered that the great mobility of the maxillaries will often enable a snake to turn round on your fingers when you think he is quite secure; therefore, take care to place your finger and thumb on either side of the neck, never above and below it." EDWARD NICHOLSON, 1874

But snake-scientists in other parts of the world also had advice to impart:

"We can easily kill serpents by blows with a stick, and breaking their vertebral column; but besides that this method could only be adopted with the smaller species, it has the disadvantage that the specimens thus killed are of little utility for the cabinet. To avoid this, it is better to fix them to the earth with a staff provided with a sort of pincers on its end, by which their bodies may be seized near the head. Large species, or those that inhabit trees, we are often obliged to shoot with a gun. Aquatic snakes sometimes are caught in the fisherman's nets, and this is probably the only method to obtain them, since in swimming they never expose any part of their bodies above the water. But the greater number of innocuous serpents are easily taken with the hand, either in seizing them by the neck or by the tail. Several, however, have the power of turning round to bite, while others soil their assailant with a foetid fluid, which they can eject to a considerable distance." HERMANN SCHLEGEL, 1837

"During my journey in North America, I traversed in 1848 a region situated to the west of Arkansas, where rattlesnakes are very common. ... Having remarked that, after making themselves heard, they had little disposition to fly at persons a little way from them, I conceived the idea of taking them in the following manner. I attached a thread to the end of the ramrod of my gun, and made a slip-knot at its free extremity: I then went to the snake, which I had heard or which had been pointed out to me by the Osages with whom I travelled; I excited it; and when it raised itself up, threatening and hissing, I passed my running knot round its neck and pulled it up. The snake did not then make any movement or any effort to disengage itself, but remained straight as a stick. It was easy to kill it...." M.A. TRECUL, 1876

Speculation about the reasons for snake behaviours was rare, but intriguing:

"In 1879, while out with the Hayden Survey, I was detained about a week by high water, on the south bank of the San Juan River, near the line between New Mexico and Colorado. While out one day with my guide, we came across a very large bull snake (*Pityophis* sp.?). The reptile was suspended on some small dead oak trees about two feet from the ground. These little trees were about as thick through as the snake, and the bark was ringed and spotted much as he appeared. We went close to the snake, but he did not stir, remaining apparently stiff and rigid like the sticks upon which he lay. We viewed him for some moments, commenting on his singular position and appearance, when 'Frank' finally shot his head off. As this snake closely resembled, in size and color, the little slender oaks which abound in that region, and which are often found bent to the ground, dead, it occurred to me that he was practicing deception, either to enable him to capture a bird or other prey, or to conceal himself from his enemies." CHARLES ALDRICH, 1879

And everyone loves a good snake story:

"In walking through a canyon about two miles east of Oakland Cal., one spring morning, I met with a fine specimen of the California Milk Snake (*Lampropeltis boylii*). Having disabled it by a blow across the back, I wrapped it in paper and put it in a bag, intending, when I sat down to rest, to skin it, and to examine the contents of its much-distended stomach. About noon I opened the paper and was not a little startled to find that my Milk Snake, so strongly characterized by alternating belts of black and white, was apparently transformed into a garter snake of about the same size, with longitudinal stripes. The first impression was that I had got hold of one of the deceiving tribes of the 'old serpent' himself, but ... I ventured to look closer, and found that the garter snake must have been swallowed whole by the Milk Snake, which, on recovering from the stunning blow I gave, had disgorged its prey, and then succeeded in crawling through a hole in the bag." J.G. COOPER, 1876

Although professionals didn't adopt snake-trapping in earnest until the 1950s, amateurs were way ahead of them:

"Snake-hunting has been a pastime here with school-boys for years. In some places, particularly on the north side of open stony ridges that are studded with low scrubby vegetation, and where grass-trees, zamias and banksias abound, flat stones are laid about to serve as traps during the winter, and are examined from time to time. In this way a great many reptiles are caught." GERARD KREFFT, 1869

"In the western portions of East Africa the Black-lipped Cobra (*Naia melanoleuca*) is found, and the writer received a number of specimens which were ingeniously caught by means of a bent stick and a snare set over their holes. As the snake emerged from its retreat the spring was released, and the reptile was suspended in the air by its neck." CONSTANTIN J.P. IONIDES, 1918

Chapter 4

Obtaining data from a squirming reptile

Even for an animal with a simple body plan, there are several things that ecologists might want to measure, record or estimate. I'll begin with the obvious candidates such as species, body size, sex, prey items and reproductive state. Many methods used to estimate those characteristics arose early in the history of snake ecology, but new technology has provided additional options.

What species is that?

If all you see of a snake is a tail disappearing into a burrow, working out the species involved is little better than guesswork. But even with a serpent in hand, people untrained in the intricate details of reptilian classification may struggle to identify the species involved. With more than

Determining the correct species identification for a tiny blind snake – such as this New Mexico Blind Snake (*Rena dissecta*) – is a daunting task even for experts. NOAH K. FIELDS

four thousand snake species to choose from, the differences between one species and another may come down to trivial issues such as the number of belly scales or fragmented head scales. Only an enthusiast or a masochist tries to identify a tiny worm-like blind snake, for example … the task requires a good microscope and enormous patience.

Snakes lack the obvious distinguishing features that make it easy to tell a dachshund from a greyhound, or an ostrich from a swan. No arms, legs, beak or antlers – just a more-or-less tubular body with a tail at one end and a head at the other. Some species, of course, are immediately recognisable from their colour – such as a Red-bellied Black Snake – or their size – such as an anaconda. In practice, a snake researcher soon learns to recognise the local serpents, and often a quick glimpse suffices. But when that same researcher travels to another part of the world, the snakes are not so easily classified. After a lifetime spent working with snakes, I am still incapable of identifying most species of rattlesnakes, blind snakes or sea snakes.

Misidentifications were common in the early literature on snake biology, compounded by ambiguous descriptions of species and a lack of high-quality images. And in cases where similar-looking species were combined under a single scientific name, it can be impossible to work out what species was involved in some of the early reports. Fortunately, things have improved steadily. Accurate well-illustrated books about snake identification are now available for most parts of the world, and the internet gives access to an astounding amount of information at the click of a mouse. Online resources such as iNaturalist not only provide photographs of snakes from every part of the world, but even identify your snake for you.

How big is that snake?

One of the most important features of any organism is its body size, and common sense says that we need to measure two dimensions: length and weight. Both are tricky with snakes.

'Body length' seems like a simple idea, but exactly what do we mean? Do we include the tail as well, to give total length? That raises problems because male snakes have longer tails than females, in order to fit their reproductive organs into the tailbase. Also, the tip of the tail is the most vulnerable part of the body when a snake is fleeing from a predator, and many tails are truncated by a beak or a bite. Other snakes lose their tail tips due to parasite attack. So, tail lengths are affected by a snake's sex and by injuries, leading most researchers to measure both tail length and body length. The latter measure is termed 'snout-vent length' because it is taken from the tip of the snout to the vent (that is, the opening to the snake's digestive and reproductive systems).

But even the apparently straightforward notion of snout-vent length is difficult to assess accurately. How do you measure the length of a large squirming serpent that is unfeasibly

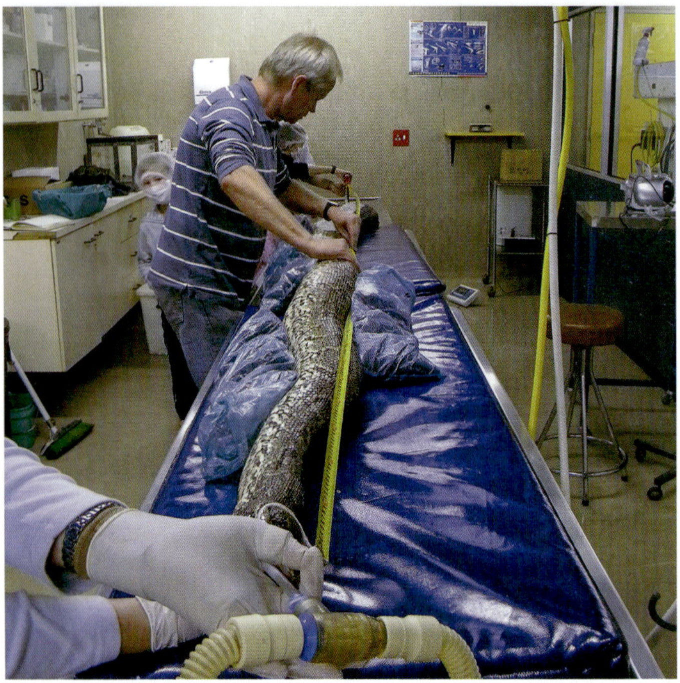

Measuring snakes in the field is a simple task with a small animal like the Red-sided Garter Snake (*Thamnophis sirtalis parietalis*) the author is handling in this image from 1998; but for an accurate estimate on a larger snake you may need to anaesthetise the animal first, as with this African Rock Python (*Python natalensis*) being measured by Graham Alexander. MARY-ANN COSTELLO

muscular, is joyfully voiding its latest meal out of both ends of its body, and that possesses a deadly venom? Snakes wriggle when held, resist being straightened out, and are incredibly flexible. Measuring the body length of a large python, for example, requires several muscular human beings. And snakes are stretchy as well – measuring the length of a snake is like measuring the length of a piece of elastic. The more you stretch it, the longer it is. When I went into the field with pioneering snake researcher Henry Fitch, I was struck by his methodical approach to measuring his study animals. Henry kept a cloth measuring tape tucked into his belt, so he could hold it alongside a snake as he held it out. And he stretched those snakes so hard I feared for their backbones.

Most people who conduct long-term mark-recapture studies on snakes insist on measuring every snake themselves, to assure consistency. But that isn't always possible. While I was working at the huge dens of garter snakes in Manitoba, we measured hundreds of snakes every day: too many for a single person to do it all. These are small docile snakes, so I didn't expect much discrepancy among the snake-measuring team. But just to check, I asked everyone on the team to measure the same test group of a dozen snakes. Surprisingly, one of the students assessed snakes as being 15 per cent shorter than everyone else. He was a kind-hearted soul, reluctant to stretch the snake out fully – and that affected his estimates of body length. I had to apply a correction factor to every measurement that he made.

There are at least three problems with stretching a snake out along a measuring tape. First, you need to standardise how firmly you stretch the animal to make it straight. Second, stretching a snake may injure it, especially for heavy-bodied snakes that thrash around. The neck is slender, with many small bones. It's easy to inflict serious damage. And third, holding a snake by the back of the neck as you stretch it out places your hand very close to the business end of an enraged animal. One small slip, and there's a fang in your finger.

If you are prepared to sacrifice precision for a reduction in risk and stress, you can encourage the animal to crawl into a transparent plastic tube so narrow that the snake is unable to turn around. Keep a hold of the tail, allow the snake to stretch out at full length inside the tube, then place the measuring tape alongside the tube to estimate body length.

Another approach, that takes longer but gives more accurate results, is to place the snake inside a 'squeeze box' with a soft foam-rubber base and a Perspex lid that fits snugly inside the main box. By pushing down on the snake with the transparent lid, the animal can be held firmly in position. No stretching, no danger to either the animal or the handler. The researcher can then use a crayon to draw on the Perspex along the middle of the snake's back, and later measure the length of that line.

Moving even further, you can anaesthetise the snake before you manipulate the unconscious animal into position and take its measurements with minimal risk to either participant. The method is well suited to projects that focus on small numbers of large venomous snakes.

OK, you might think. Measuring snakes is difficult. Why not just weigh them? Mass is tricky as well. A snake weighs more if it has swallowed a prey item; and developing offspring can weigh as much as the female who is carrying them. Researchers routinely record mass and body circumference, but there is no simple 'gold standard' number to tell you how big a snake is.

This Ornate Blacktail Rattlesnake (*Crotalus ornatus*) has consumed a huge meal, massively increasing the snake's total mass. NOAH K. FIELDS

Apart from the body and tail, the other obvious feature of a snake is its head. To measure head width, you need clear rules for deciding exactly where on that tapering head you place your calipers. For head length, you can't just measure along the midline because there's no simple way to decide where the head finishes and the neck begins. Most researchers measure jaw length instead. You might expect that head lengths would be easier (as well as safer) to measure on a preserved snake than a live one, but snake heads are flexible and often are deformed when the snake is jammed into a jar of preservative. Some researchers have given up on external measurements and rely on X-rays. In short, measuring a snake is not as easy as it looks. New technologies pose less risk to both the snake and the snake-handler, but most of us still measure and weigh snakes the old-fashioned way.

How old is that snake?

Snakes grow rapidly when they are young, but the body length of an adult snake may not change at all over many years. Knowing the age of such an animal could illuminate rates of growth or annual survival. That's critical information if a researcher wants to measure the ability of a population to withstand threats imposed by habitat loss, food shortage or invasive predators. But sadly, snake researchers have struggled to solve the mystery of an animal's age.

Early American naturalists thought the rattle of the rattlesnake might add a segment with each passing year. In 1634, colonist Thomas Morton (1579–1647) wrote "there is one creeping beast ... that has a rattle at his tayle that does discover his age; for so many years as hee hath lived, so many joints are in that rattle." Before long, though, biologists realised that the number of segments on a rattle only tells us about the number of times the snake has sloughed its skin, which may bear little relationship to age; and that in most free-living rattlers the terminal segments are lost through accident or injury. In 1951, American researchers LaMarr Heyrend (1927–2016; later to specialise in child psychiatry) and Anson Call (1937–2022; son of one of the pioneering Mormon families of Utah) regretfully concluded, based on annual captures of rattlers at a den in Utah, that "it is obvious that some snakes of the same age have different numbers of rattles."

The number of segments on the rattle of a Timber Rattlesnake (*Crotalus horridus*) may tell you how many times the snake has shed its skin during its life, but it won't tell you the animal's age. NOAH K. FIELDS

In seasonal environments where snakes are inactive during winter and feed and grow only during summer, an individual's age can be determined from growth rings in its bones. Just like the rings in a tree, wide marks indicate periods of rapid growth (summer) separated by periods of quiescence (winter). But the method requires the direct examination of bones, so it can't be applied to live animals. And even then, bone remodelling during growth can eradicate earlier rings as newer tissue is deposited.

Using annual rings to infer age, technically called 'skeletochronology', has been applied more often to lizards than to snakes. Many researchers clip toe-tips off lizards to identify individuals if they are later recaptured; each animal has a unique combination of missing toe-tips. Those toe-clips can be sectioned and examined under a microscope to count annual rings. No need to kill a lizard to work out its age. For snakes, the only studies that could easily use the method would be ones where large numbers of recently killed animals are available – such as in the commercially harvested snakes of tropical Asia, or sea snakes that drown in prawn trawler nets. But seasonal variation in climate (and thus, growth rate) is minor in many tropical climates. As a result, there may be no consistent pattern of annual rings in bones. I tried this method to age Water Monitor lizards in Sumatra, but gave up after finding no clear age signal in the bones.

Another way to estimate ages is to look at seasonal distributions of body sizes. If you collect a large sample of snakes from the same place, you can plot the body size of each animal against the time of year that it was collected. In cool-climate areas, most lizards and snakes are born or hatched over a brief period late in summer. With luck, you can see a cohort of newborn or newly hatched snakes appearing in late summer, and follow that cohort through the next year or two of their lives. Your graph of body sizes of captured animals through the months should show a scatter of points that correspond to two-year-olds and another for three-year-olds. But before long the fastest-growing two-year-olds overlap in size with the slowest-growing three-year-olds, so your estimates of age become unreliable. The method was popular in early studies of snake ecology and gave plausible estimates of age at sexual maturity; but it can only be applied to the youngest age classes.

Most recent snake studies that report on population age structure have gathered their data the hard way: by marking then recapturing individuals over long periods. If you individually mark a snake in its first year of life (when its body size reveals its age), then you know how old it is every time you recatch it. The problem is that recapture rates are low, marks can become difficult to distinguish, and few field studies are funded for more than a few years. In practice, most long-term mark-recapture studies on snakes are labours of love, with a deeply committed researcher (and sometimes, their long-suffering partners and children) maintaining the work in their spare time, decades after the funding has dried up.

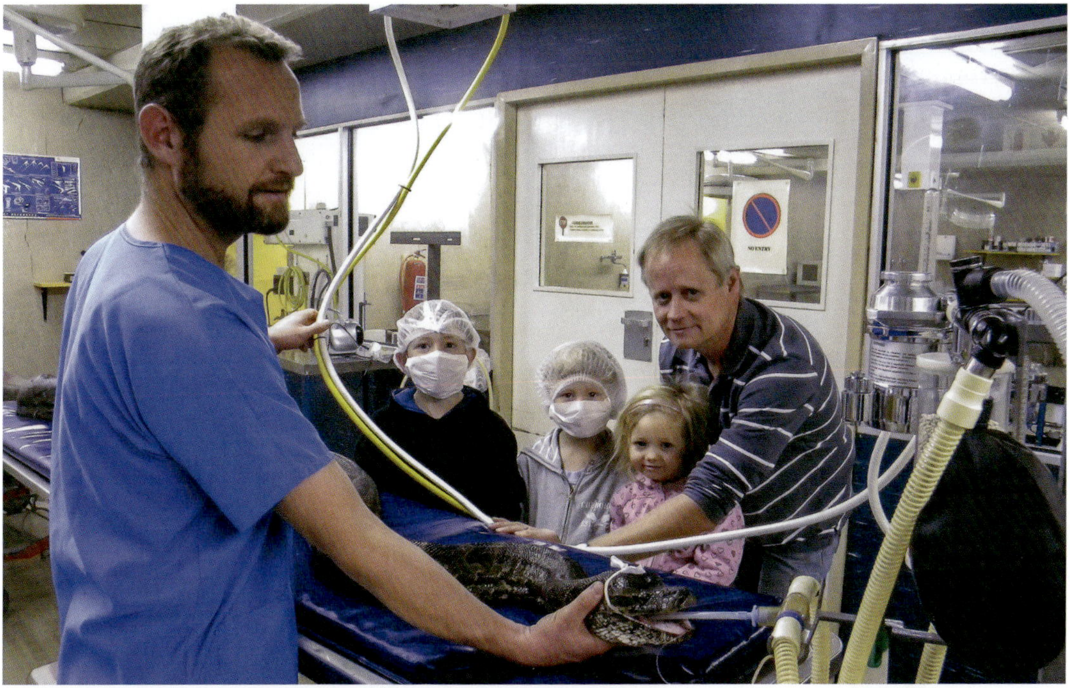

Funding for research on snake ecology is difficult to obtain, and fieldwork can enforce long absences from the family. Those twin pressures encourage researchers to involve family members as assistants. Young Amy Alexander and her siblings are important members of the research team led by their father, Graham Alexander, in tasks as diverse as supervising transmitter-implantation surgery into Rock Pythons (*Python natalensis*) and carrying a radio-implanted Puff Adder (*Bitis arietans*) to be released back into the wild. PHOTOGRAPHS: MARY-ANN COSTELLO AND GRAHAM ALEXANDER

Colour is complicated! This Coachwhip (*Masticophis flagellum*) demonstrates how a snake's colour can differ along its body, and these Australian Lowland Copperheads (*Austrelaps superbus*) show how colour can differ between two individuals from the same population. PHOTOGRAPHS: NOAH K. FIELDS AND JULES FARQUHAR

Although few species of snakes have been studied long enough to provide robust estimates of age structure, it's already clear that there is enormous variation among species. Ambush-foraging vipers in cold climates can delay sexual maturity for a decade, whereas active-hunting frog-eating keelbacks in tropical swamps can begin breeding at a few months of age. In between those extremes, males of many snake species mature at around two years of age, and females a year later. Well-cared-for captive snakes often live for 20 years, but predators, disease and accidents cut short the lives of most wild specimens.

We desperately need a better way to determine the age of a live snake. Genetic markers such as DNA methylation rates and telomere sizes provide accurate indicators of age in birds and mammals, so the Holy Grail may yet be achieved for snakes as well.

The colour of a snake

An animal's colour is one of the first things we notice about it. But there's nothing simple about the colour of a snake. The belly is usually a different colour than the upper surface of the body, and the front end can differ from the back end. The tail can be banded, as in some rattlesnakes. Individuals from nearby populations can differ in colour and many snake populations include jet-black as well as typically coloured individuals – and sometimes, a single clutch or litter can contain offspring of several different colour morphs. Some (but not all) juvenile Australian brown snakes are strongly banded, whereas adults are various shades of brown.

To make it even more complicated, an individual snake can change its colour through time. Green Tree Pythons don't achieve their bright green colours for a year or two after hatching, after a period spent as yellow or red babies. Some snakes even switch backwards and forwards between different colour patterns. In the Australian semi-desert, Inland Taipans are black in winter and yellow in summer. In the rocky escarpments of Kakadu National Park, Oenpelli Pythons are drab brown by day but transform into shimmering grey ghost-like creatures every night. Male Eurasian Adders exhibit bright black-and-white zigzag bands in springtime but adopt sombre brown hues in summer.

So although they lack the dramatic colour patches of socially displaying lizards, snakes exhibit a diverse chromatic array. Those colours must play significant ecological roles but sadly, we don't understand what's going on. Plausible explanations are available for a few of the patterns I've mentioned above, mostly relating to camouflage (best to resemble the local background), thermoregulation (darker snakes heat up quicker) or escaping from enemies (bands can make a fast-moving snake more difficult to see). But other variations remain mysterious.

To attack those puzzles, we need to score colour patterns. Snake biologists have generally put that task into the 'too hard' basket because of the subtlety as well as complexity of snake

Many species of lizards – such as this Canyon Lizard (*Sceloporus merriami*) – use bright splashes of colour to convey social information, but snakes more often rely on scent to work out who's who. NOAH K. FIELDS

coloration. Lizard biologists have been more proactive, using sophisticated machines to quantify wavelengths and reflectances of patches of bright colours. Those machines are useful because humans see a different set of wavelengths than many other species. Thus, a colour patch that reflects infrared radiation is invisible to us but may be obvious to a snake. As a result, we can measure reflectances and then use computer programs to work out what the colours of a reptile would look like to another reptile, or a bird, or a fish.

Is it a male or a female?

A snake's reproductive organs are hidden within its body. As a result, the sex of a snake is not immediately obvious. Dissection overcomes the problem but also terminates the snake's existence unless you are very careful. How can you tell if a snake is male or female without harming the animal? Snake researchers have developed several approaches.

In some snake species, distinguishing between adult males and females is straightforward. For example, a huge Timber Rattlesnake or King Cobra is bound to be a male – females don't attain those dimensions. Contrariwise, any gigantic Reticulated Python or Green Anaconda is a female. Somewhere out there in the jungles and swamps, the longest snake in the world is undoubtedly a female Reticulated Python measuring almost 10 m (30 ft), while the heaviest is a female anaconda weighing more than 100 kg (214 lb). In some species, adult females routinely weigh more than twice as much as adult males.

Although the differences are more subtle, male and female snakes can also be distinguished based on body shape. For example, female Arafura File Snakes are more heavy-bodied than are males and have larger heads. But although such sex differences are common, they are usually not obvious enough to be useful in sexing a snake. Likewise for differences between the sexes in traits such as muscular strength, relative eye size, tongue length, fang shape, venom yields and so on. Interesting, but not much help if you just want to know if the snake in your hand is male or female.

Sex differences in scale features are more useful. The longer tails of males translate into more scales under the tail, so counting those subcaudal scales may tell the males from the females. To count those tiny scales under the tail of an agitated snake, it's simplest to take a photograph and do the counts from that image. In some kinds of snakes, males possess large rough tubercles under the chin or near the vent, that provide sensory cues during courtship. Rough scales extend over most of the body in some sea snakes, helping a male to clasp his partner as he coils around her while mating.

In a few species of snakes, males and females differ in more dramatic ways. In the Madagascar Leaf-nosed Snake, males have a smooth spear-like projection from the front of the nose whereas females have a leaf-like projection. The function of that difference remains a mystery. The same theme, albeit less spectacular, is seen in Turtle-headed Sea Snakes. During the mating season, male Turtle-heads grow a unicorn-like spine on the tip of the nose. They use the spine to prod the female during courtship.

In boas and pythons, males have a small thorn-like spur on either side of the cloaca (anal opening). Those tiny spurs are the evolutionary vestiges of hindlimbs that have been lost in other kinds of snakes. Early workers ascribed several functions to those spurs. For example, American clergyman, doctor and African missionary Thomas S. Savage (1804–1880) wrote the following in 1844 about West African pythons: "The claws or hooks near the anus are sometimes protruded, it is said (and the evidence is wholly satisfactory), and inserted in the ground or under roots, thus affording a fulcrum which gives unbelievable force to the blow. These horny processes, or rudimental feet as they have been called, are also serviceable in ascending trees; they are inserted into ground and bark of the tree, constituting fixed points, which greatly facilitate the ascent." It was a plausible idea. Indeed, many burrowing blind snakes have a small spine at the tip of the tail that anchors the snake as it pushes forward into hard soil. But pythons aren't blind snakes, and Thomas got it wrong. In 1894 two amateur Trinidad-based herpetologists, newspaper editor Richard Richardson Mole (1860–1926) and entomologist Frederick W. Urich, correctly noted that the spurs are used by the male during courtship, vibrating and scratching against his partner's back and sides. Smaller spurs are present in many females also, so it's not a reliable guide to sex identification.

A male Water Python (*Liasis fuscus*) scratches a female with a cloacal spur – a tiny remnant of the hindlegs seen in the ancestors of snakes.
DAVE BARKER

In short, most of the differences between male and female snakes are subtle or temporary. For reliable sex identification, then, researchers inspect the snake's genitals.

A male snake has two copulatory organs, one on either side of its body and kept inside-out in pockets at the base of its tail. Each of these hemipenes is attached to the testis (testicle) on that side of the body. A special set of muscles can push the hemipenis out of the cloaca for use in mating, and another set of muscles pulls it back into its space in the base of the tail. Thorny spines on the everted hemipenis lock into the female's reproductive tract, keeping the male member firmly in place until copulation has concluded.

The size and shape of the hemipenis varies so much among species that it can be used to identify evolutionary relationships among different kinds of snakes. The first person to notice that diversity, and realise its value for taxonomy, was controversial American herpetologist Edward Drinker Cope (1840–1897). In 1895, he wrote that "the hemipenes ... exhibit a variety of ornamentation and armature beyond any part of the anatomy in the ophidia, and I am satisfied that they furnish more important indication of near affinity than any other part of these reptiles yet examined." Old papers on the classification of snakes include lovingly detailed illustrations of bizarre heavily spined male sex organs. A reader might suspect that snake biologists were obsessed with male copulatory organs.

Cope was a leading figure in reptile research in the 1800s, but he was a quarrelsome individual and is most famous for his lengthy and intense feud with Othniel Charles Marsh (1831–1899) about dinosaur discoveries. The two Americans initially were friends; indeed, they even named new species of dinosaurs after each other. But Cope and Marsh soon fell out. Minor disagreements escalated to full-blown conflict, with each man attempting to undermine his enemy's research projects by bribing the other's employees, and stealing or destroying their precious fossils. Even after both men were bankrupted by their rivalry, their passion remained undiminished. Not long before his death, Cope donated his skull to science so that his brain could be measured. He believed that brain size was a measure of intelligence, and that his brain would prove to be larger than his adversary's. He challenged Marsh to have his brain measured as well, but Marsh ignored the provocation.

How can you tell whether your snake is a male or a female? Researchers use two main methods – either they apply pressure to the base of the hemipenis to push it out of the snake's tailbase, or they insert a lubricated probe into that organ while it is inverted inside the tail. Female snakes have a similar orifice beside the vent, but it leads only to a small sac. As a result, a probe pushed into a female won't go as far as one pushed into a male.

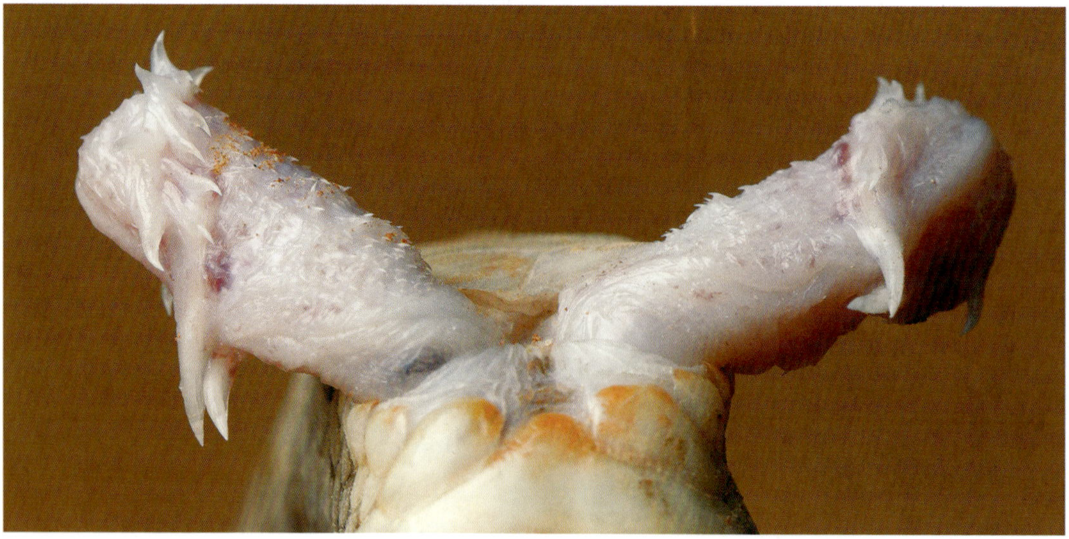

Male snakes have paired hemipenes, that can emerge from the vent by turning inside-out. Hooks at the tip of the hemipenis serve as anchors during mating. This image shows the cloacal area of a male Strap-snouted Brown Snake (*Pseudonaja aspidorhyncha*). JULES FARQUHAR

Both methods have problems. Male snakes are reluctant to extrude a hemipenis, so it takes an experienced snake-handler to pop out the organ. And with probing, it's easy to mistake a male for a female if the probe is blocked by a plug of dried gunk composed of shed skin, dried secretions or old semen. It's also easy to mistake a female for a male if the probe is inserted so firmly that it penetrates past the sac into soft tissues beneath. Even the experts can make mistakes. In his pioneering study on American Copperheads, Kansas-based Henry Fitch reported that 75 per cent of the babies were males; but it was an error. He had pushed too hard with his probe, and many of Henry's 'males' were in fact females with very sore tails. We now know that, like most other snakes that have been studied, copperheads produce equal numbers of sons and daughters in each litter.

Another complication is that female snakes have hemipenis-like structures. They are generally much smaller than the male equivalent, but in some snake species the pockets in females are large enough to be easily mistaken for hemipenes – especially if the snake is able to evert them (as some Blood Pythons can, according to my snake-breeder colleagues Dave and Tracy Barker). Those pockets have generally been interpreted as non-functional: that is, present simply because males and females of the same species share many genes. That's the usual explanation for why male mammals have nipples, for example. Contrary to that view, though, some researchers call those structures 'hemiclitores' and suggest that they have some function (as yet unknown). There's a lot we don't know about the rear end of snakes.

For snake species with large hemipenes, you don't need to see or probe the male member to establish an individual's sex. The swollen pockets in a male's tailbase lengthen his tail and make it broad at the base, so a quick glimpse is enough to tell if the snake is male (long tail, thick at the base) or a female (short tail, quickly tapering from vent to tailtip). But some snakes have tiny hemipenes, making sex identification difficult. It's impossible to work out the sex of an African sand snake without dissection, unless you're another African sand snake.

There are other drawbacks to probing and hemipene eversion as well. It's stressful for the snake – especially for a female subjected to repeated unsuccessful attempts to evert a non-existent hemipenis. And that stress translates into a higher risk of snakebite. In one tragic case, 26-year-old Wade Westbrook died in Chattanooga, Tennessee, in 2011 when he was bitten while trying to determine the sex of a captive American Copperhead. Experienced snake-

Examining the tail of a juvenile Eastern Brown Snake (*Pseudonaja textilis*) to determine the animal's sex, while the dangerous part of the animal is restrained within a clear Perspex tube. JULES FARQUHAR

handlers reduce that risk by encouraging the snake to crawl into a narrow Perspex tube. Once the snake is halfway in, you can take hold of both the tube and the rear end of the snake. The snake can't go forward and can't go backwards; all it can do is bite the walls of its tubular plastic prison while you squeeze or probe the tailbase.

As with most other methods, new technologies are coming to the rescue. Ultrasound or radiography (X-rays) can detect internal organs and reveal hemipenis spines inside the tailbase. In some species, you can even see the outline of the male sex organs when a bright light is shone through the tail. A more high-tech genetic approach is to analyse a sample of blood or shed skin for sex chromosomes. As such methods become cheaper and easier, genetic assays will become more popular. But they will never take over entirely, because some snake species don't have sex chromosomes. And in others, incubation conditions in the nest over-ride the sex chromosomes, turning a genetically female snake into a functional male. As a result, snake researchers who need to determine the sex of their study animals will be squeezing tails and counting scales for many years to come.

Eggs or baby snakes?

About three-quarters of snake species reproduce by egg laying (oviparity). The female lays her eggs and hatchlings emerge a month or two later. But the other 25 per cent use a different tactic: viviparity. Embryonic development occurs inside the mother's body, so she produces fully formed offspring not eggs. The swollen hindbodies of pregnant snakes aroused the curiosity of early collectors, and some of the earliest writers clearly were surprised to find well-developed offspring within the mother's body. For example, in 1887 the New Jersey-based naturalist H.C. Young wrote about a water snake (likely a Common Water Snake, *Nerodia sipedon*) he had shot and killed near Salem: "Upon examining the snake (which was almost as thick as my forearm) I found it contained considerable of a bunch which I supposed to be something it had swallowed; but upon cutting it open I found it contained small snakes in a bag, each one in a separate division formed as it were by a twist in the bag. I took them out, and found there were thirty-three of them of different sizes, a number of the smaller ones having a portion of an egg attached to them, which they appeared to be absorbing, the larger ones having already absorbed theirs. I was then convinced that while the land-snakes lay eggs in the earth, to be hatched by the heat of the sun, the young of the water-snake are actually hatched in the belly of the mother."

Initial over-generalisations ('vipers are live bearers; all other snakes lay eggs') soon gave way to a more nuanced view. For example, the young Charles Darwin wrote in his field diary in 1836, after killing a Tiger Snake in Australia: "The abdomen being burst in catching the animal: a small snake appeared from the disrupted egg: hence ovoviviparous: is this not strange in Coluber?"

There are two ways to find out if a species is live bearing or egg laying. Either you can dissect a pregnant female (does the oviduct contain eggs with thick shells, or embryos inside thin membranes?), or you can observe egg laying or live birth in captive animals. Even a single observation of egg laying or live birth gives a strong clue to reproductive tactics, because it's rare to find a species where egg laying occurs in some areas and live bearing in others. It's even less common to find cases where females within a single population differ in their mode of reproduction.

Sadly, dissecting a snake doesn't tell us whether or not she cares for her eggs or offspring after they have left her body. Most egg layers deposit the eggs in a nest and then abandon them, but a few remain with the clutch until hatching. The pioneering English author Catherine Hopley quoted a 1665 report of maternal care: "some affirm to have seen snakes lye upon their eggs as hens sit upon theirs." Pythons were popular captives in zoos and thus were the first species known to brood, but maternal attendance of the eggs is now known to be widespread. Unfortunately, the list of snake species that show parental brooding remains woefully incomplete.

Is that female pregnant?

It's easy to distinguish pregnant snakes by their body shape; the mother's abdomen is grossly distended. Palpation will confirm if that lump is a part-digested meal (squishy, and mostly in the midbody) or eggs (firm, and in the hindbody). The only difficulty comes with muscular tree-climbing species, where the abdomen remains streamlined and distension of the body is more subtle.

Rates of reproduction vary incredibly among animals. At one extreme, a queen African Driver Ant can produce tens of thousands of eggs every day. At the other extreme, a female elephant produces a single calf once every five or six years. Snakes don't rival ants in their fecundity, but some are impressive. Many tropical snakes produce multiple clutches of eggs within a single season, often consisting of a dozen eggs at a time. If the weather is good and prey are abundant, such a snake may produce 100 eggs within a single season.

At the other extreme, though, some kinds of snakes bear young infrequently. The first detailed report of this 'slow' life-history tactic came from German-born but American-based biologist Hermann Rahn (1912–1990), who is famed for his later research on bird eggs and for his role in the development of aerospace medicine. But in his early days, Hermann worked with snakes. Specifically, he was given 64 freshly killed Prairie Rattlesnakes from overwintering dens in Wyoming. Rahn's dissections in 1942 showed that about half of the adult female rattlers

This Grey Rat Snake (*Pantherophis spiloides*) is still tightly coiled around her newly laid eggs. BILL LAMAR

had large ovarian follicles and had mated recently – clearly, they would have given birth that year (if they hadn't been slaughtered). But the other half had tiny follicles and had not mated. Rahn concluded that in this high-elevation population, female rattlers only produce a litter every second year. That was surprising, because studies on other snake species in captivity had reported annual clutches. And dissections of the same rattlesnake species from a site in Colorado, by Laurence Klauber, had found annual cycles also.

But as studies accumulated, it became clear that biennial reproduction was common in female rattlesnakes – even in areas where other kinds of snakes produced clutches every year. In 1951, another researcher at the Utah den, Henry Glissmeyer (1880–1970), reported that: "The Striped Racer, the Blue Racer and the garter snakes have annual cycles of egg development ... In contrast ... the rattlesnakes ... appear to have a biennial cycle in which females return to the den one fall with enlarged eggs and the next year without them." Intriguingly, though, Glissmeyer's data hinted at a dynamic situation. Although the overall average over 11 years was 49 per cent of adult females reproductive, the actual percentages of pregnant females per year varied from 12 per cent to 67 per cent. At around the same time, French biologist Hubert Saint Girons and other European workers were discovering a similar pattern in European vipers: variation among years, but with less-than-annual reproduction in colder parts of the species range. We now have many more examples of that same flexibility, from many different evolutionary lineages.

The fact that female snakes are often emaciated after laying, and take a long time to rebuild their energy reserves, provides a compelling reason why they don't (or can't) produce a large clutch every year. But why not produce a small litter every year rather than a large litter every second year? In one of the first scientific papers I ever wrote, in 1979, Jim Bull and I proposed an explanation. We had noticed that pregnant snakes stop feeding and concentrate instead on

To escape from the egg, hatching snakes use a special (and temporary) 'egg tooth' on their snout to cut through the fibrous shell. Like the eggshell, that egg tooth is lost in live-bearing (viviparous) species. PIXABAY

basking to warm their developing embryos. Starving for months is a huge energy cost that is just as high if you produce a small litter as if you produce a large one. As a result, the most efficient tactic for a female snake is to delay pregnancy until she can produce a large litter, even if this means waiting a year or two to do it. That way, she offsets the high cost of pregnancy with a large not a small litter.

How many babies or eggs?

The number of eggs or developing babies held inside a female snake's body is important not only for that female (it will contribute to her evolutionary fitness) but also for the wider population. The more offspring are laid or born, the faster that a population can increase, and the better it can withstand new threats. Reflecting that dual significance, researchers have paid special attention to estimating brood sizes. Many early reports provide accurate information about the topic, albeit with a few surprising twists; for example, an anonymous author wrote in 1786 that litter sizes in snakes are variable but always consist of an even number (they don't).

One way to measure clutch and litter sizes is to keep a female snake in captivity until she produces her eggs or babies, but that requires a long time. Pregnancy can last for three months or more. For field-based projects, one option may be to capture snakes in the last few weeks of pregnancy and keep them in outdoor cages. In the lab, it is straightforward to keep females throughout pregnancy. As a result, captive snakes have yielded detailed information on issues such as the proportion of ova that have been fertilised. Infertile eggs generally aren't absorbed back into the female's body – they simply pass out at egg laying or birth, as hard yellow chunks of yolk. Another parameter that is easy to measure is water content of the egg or the egg-like package containing the offspring. Egg-laying female snakes add water to the egg before it is laid, giving it a reserve of fluid to help it survive in a dry nest. Live bearers don't need that insurance, so females reduce water reserves to fit more babies into their swollen abdomens.

Snakes are so secretive that a fieldworker is unlikely to observe egg laying or birth. Instead, we estimate brood size by palpating the female snake's abdomen. The number of bumps tells you the number of babies. It's easier with egg layers than with live bearers, because the eggshell provides a firm shape for your fingertips to recognise. Late-term embryos inside live-bearing females are squishy, making it difficult to know if you are feeling a few big embryos or a larger number of small ones. And you need to be gentle – palpation that is too firm or too frequent can damage developing embryos.

Once again, technology is providing alternatives. Ultrasound or X-rays can be used to count embryos or eggs, but those methods require expensive equipment and are difficult to bring into the field. Returning pregnant snakes to the laboratory for processing takes time and imposes more stress on the snake. It's easier and quicker, even if less accurate, to gently palpate the snake's abdomen.

What did the snake have for lunch?

Snake biologists have a huge advantage over lizard biologists when it comes time to investigate feeding habits of their study organisms. Most lizards eat dozens of small insects every day. And the tough chitinous exoskeletons of insects must be broken down before the nutritious inner body parts can be digested. As a result, lizards have strong jaws and teeth that reduce a grasshopper to mush. Hundreds of small chunks. An investigator looking inside a lizard's stomach to identify the remains of prey items needs patience, and ideally childhood experience in assembling jigsaws. Many lizards also eat plants – flowers are especially popular – increasing the challenges of prey identification.

Snakes have opted for a different approach, far more user-friendly for scientists. First, all snakes are carnivores. Well, almost. In 2016, Noman Al Moktadir and Md Kamrul Hasan found a Checkered Keelback eating boiled rice that had been discarded by university students. Second, most snakes eat vertebrates not insects. Third, they consume a small number of large

This Japanese Rat Snake (*Elaphe climacophora*) is consuming a bird far larger than the snake's own head. KIYOSHI NAKAYAMA, PIXABAY

The long slender shape of snakes makes them well-suited to swallowing long slender objects, including other snakes. Sometimes the dinner item is a snake of a different species, as in this Coachwhip (*Masticophis flagellum*) being overpowered by a Texas Indigo Snake (*Drymarchon melanurus*). NOAH K. FIELDS

Sometimes the meal consists of a snake of the predator's own species, such as this cannibalistic Cape Cobra (*Naja nivea*). BRYAN MARITZ

prey items rather than a large number of small prey items. And fourth, they swallow intact prey items rather than grinding them into fragments with their teeth. Even after a day or two inside the snake's stomach, a mouse or lizard remains identifiable. In a few cases, it's even easier to identify the snake's last meal. For example, the famous Thai biologist Stanley S. Flower wrote: "In May 1897, a python, 2,820 mm (or 9 ft, 3 in) in length, was found in the Wang Luang (King's Palace); I was told that it had swallowed a pet cat and then become too fat to get away through the hole by which it had entered. On opening the snake, I found a full-grown Siamese cat with a bell hung around its neck." Flower was an extraordinary man; indeed, the renowned writer Rudyard Kipling (author of the classic 1894 children's novel *The Jungle Book*) wrote that Flower was "one of the most interesting men I have ever met." Flower's career spanned many professions, from army officer to museum curator, conservationist and manager of the Egyptian Camel Transport Corps during World War I.

Of course, looking inside a snake's stomach isn't feasible if the snake is still alive, so fieldworkers need a different approach. It's possible to identify and even measure a prey item by carefully palpating the snake's midbody region. If you want to be 100 per cent certain, the snake may co-operate by regurgitating its meal for you. It wants to lighten the load in order to make a getaway, but it's a convenient response. Smelly, though. Anyone who has opened a cloth bag in the morning, to admire the snake they caught the night before, will be aware of the special odour and texture of half-digested rats. And the disappointing reality that a snake smeared in rodent paste looks and smells less attractive than you remembered from last night.

If voluntary regurgitation isn't happening, careful pressure from the fingers can force a prey item upwards from the stomach and out of the snake's mouth. A quick look can confirm the ID before you slide the item back down again. Palpation works well for slender smooth prey items such as eels but is dangerous if the serpent's meal features spiky appendages. Bird claws and fish spines can tear open the snake's gut lining if inexpertly pushed around, so it's best to leave them in place. In the unlikely event that anyone reading this book finds a snake that has swallowed a porcupine, I'd suggest extreme caution.

Snakes tend to select safe hiding places after they feed, so you may not find that snake until the prey item is well and truly digested. But all hope is not lost. Snakes exhibit extreme generosity to their captors by providing faecal samples, free of charge. That's not too informative if your snake has been eating frogs, but any prey item with keratinised structures – such as mammal hairs and lizard scales – may reward a bit of time spent peering at poo under a microscope. Every mammal species has slightly different hair structures, so it's possible to work out the identity of a long-gone meal by careful analysis. Likewise for reptile prey – a smooth scale may be from a skink, a rough scale may be from a dragon, thick rectangular scales are from a monitor lizard's tail, and an elongate belly-shield on the petri dish tells you that your snake is a cannibal.

Palpating prey items out of snakes and examining snake poo in detail have been standard techniques throughout the history of research on snake ecology. But the world is changing. For investigators who prefer high-tech approaches, you can scan snake poo for DNA fragments from various kinds of prey; or use stable isotope analysis to work out what kind of animal was eaten.

In particular, stable isotopes are providing new insights into feeding ecology. You can work out what an animal has been eating by examining chemical isotopes in its blood, or in tiny muscle-tissue samples, or even from a few scales. Different prey types have different isotopic ratios, transferred to the snake when it eats those prey. Andrew Durso and Stephen Mullin used isotopes to show that hognose snakes in Illinois eat lizards when young, shift to toads as adolescent snakes, then focus on turtle-eggs as adults. High-tech methods like this will soon be mainstream.

For snakes that feed on large prey items, how can you tell whether or not a snake has eaten anything since the last time you handled it? In one of the first detailed ecological studies of free-ranging Eurasian Adders, in 1971, English biologist Ian Prestt (1929–1995) wrote: "A larger spot of brown paint was put on the back of the neck. This was lost when a snake swallowed food, the enormous swelling of the neck, causing extensive separation of the scales and cracking of the paint which then fell off, thus indicating that a snake had eaten. Quick-drying enamel paint was used and was applied with a small brush while the viper was held in a gloved hand. The paint marks were, of course, lost when the skin was shed and so had to be replaced at intervals." Strangely, nobody else seems to have used Ian's ingenious method in the decades since his original paper. He never got a chance to do so himself, either, because his career took him into the prestigious role of Director General of the Royal Society for the Protection of Birds. And you probably can't learn much from dabbing paint onto feathers.

Identifying individual snakes

A mark-recapture project is a waste of time unless you can recognise an individual when you recatch it. To achieve that goal, you either rely on pre-existing differences among individuals, or apply a mark to enable later recognition. Researchers have used both options.

At first sight, one small brown snake looks very much like another. But as you spend time handling those snakes, you notice subtle variation in traits such as the position, width and shape of blotches or bands. Scales can be equally informative; in some viper populations, for example, every individual has a unique pattern of scale fragmentation on the head that doesn't change from the animal's birth until its death.

Katja Claus photographs every Eurasian Adder (*Vipera berus*) that she captures, enabling her to identify individuals when they are recaptured even many years later. TERRI SHINE

If you look carefully enough, individuals almost always differ in some respect. For example, some snakes have a mixture of scale types under the tail – a few scales stretch across the entire width of the tail whereas others are divided in half. It's quick and easy to record the scale-pattern signature of each individual, helping to confirm its ID. Knowing the animal's sex cuts the number of possible IDs in half; and knowing its capture location and body size further restrict ID possibilities on recapture. Scars from predator attacks are common, as is loss of the tail tip due to predation or parasite infection. Such injuries can enable individual recognition.

But recording pre-existing individual differences is a huge information-processing challenge. Far easier, then, to give each animal a unique mark. Early researchers tried methods such as jaw tags, freeze-branding and tattoos. Some even tried implanting radioactive tags, with the predictable result of tumours at the implantation site. But most people adopted a simple approach that had been invented in one of the first 'snake ecology' projects. In 1933, American biologists Frank Blanchard (1888–1937) and Ethel Beulah Finster (1881–1980) clipped the edges of scales beneath the tail. These small wounds left scars, enabling the authors to recognise individuals even many years later.

Modern snake ecologists still use the method, with a tweak introduced by Bill Brown and Bill Parker in 1976. The two Bills, American students working at the renowned Utah snake dens, suggested clipping belly-scales (ventrals) not tail-scales (subcaudals) – an easier method because belly-scales are bigger; and they proposed a numbering system so that each snake had a readily counted number. The first ten scales above the vent are numbered 1 to 10; the next nine are 20 to 100; and the next nine are 200 to 1,000. And so on. Thus, a snake with clips at belly scales 3, 13 and 23 above the vent is number 543. Scale clipping doesn't cause much pain; snakes generally don't even react to it. The wounds heal quickly and remain recognisable for years, especially if the cut edges of the scales are cauterised with heat. That method is now used almost universally, except for snake species which lack belly shields (such as file snakes) or in which wounds heal so rapidly that the marks disappear (like sea snakes). For such species, researchers resort to branding (with either heat or cold) or implanting tiny

The creators of the most widely adopted snake-marking protocol, Bill Parker (left) and Bill Brown (right), as graduate students during fieldwork at their Utah snake den in 1972.

microchips like those used to identify domestic pets. If a researcher can afford it, microchips provide accurate and rapid individual IDs that streamline snake processing dramatically in mark-recapture programs.

For short-term behavioural studies, researchers often paint numbers or colour-coded bands on the snake's body. In dark-coloured snakes, shaving off the upper part of a few scales to reveal the white tissue beneath can provide an obvious but temporary scar. Such marks are lost when the snake sheds its skin a few months later. In one evolutionary lineage, the rattlesnakes, paint can last for much longer because scales on one part of the body are never shed. A rattlesnake builds up its rattle by retaining specialised scales on its tail tip when it sloughs its skin, resulting in longer rattles as the snake grows older. My colleague Marty Martin, from West Virginia, exploited that situation by writing numbers on the base of the rattle so that he could recognise individuals whenever he recaptured them.

In practice, long-term mark-recapture studies rely on redundancy of information. Scale clips are quick and easy to read but they can regrow, or a scar from a predator's attack can resemble a clip. And of course, there's always human error when you clip the wrong scale. So as well as scale clipping, researchers record unusual marks, scars, colour patterns and scale counts. Most individuals are identified from their scale clip, but for ambiguous cases we drill down into the information and photographs from earlier captures to check the ID.

Two recent developments – one social and one technical – are changing the ways that researchers recognise individual snakes. The social shift involves community concern about animal welfare. Increasing opposition to interference with wild animals means that techniques that were once mainstream, such as scale clipping snakes or toe clipping lizards for identification, are now controversial. Researchers need approval from ethics committees, and some of those committees now forbid toe clipping or scale clipping on the grounds that it causes stress. Technological solutions such as microchips are preferred. Frustratingly, those views are based on human intuition rather than evidence. When my student Tracy Langkilde and I measured stress levels in lizards, we found that toe clipping was kinder than microchipping. But nobody listened.

The second driver of that revolution is our increasing ability to recognise individuals without marking them. As computers become more sophisticated, it is feasible to photograph snakes and use algorithms to quantify subtle differences among individuals. This can enable individual recognition with no need to inflict physical marks. The computing challenges are substantial, however, and the method is still in its infancy. If it was easy, farmers would already be using the approach to recognise individual horses, sheep or cattle, rather than using brands or eartags. But things are changing.

How to kill a snake humanely

How should you kill a snake? Ecologists don't enjoy killing animals, but sometimes there is no choice. The animal may be badly injured; or it may be an invasive species that cannot be released back into the wild without imperilling native fauna; or euthanising animals may be essential for a research program. The early naturalists often dripped tobacco juice from an old pipe into the snake's mouth. These days, fewer snake catchers in Western countries smoke pipes but most have refrigerators and freezers, in which case the simplest solution may be to put that reptile into a fridge to cool down; and after a few hours, transfer it to a freezer. Death is painless.

To my frustration, the use of cold for euthanasia of reptiles remains controversial. It's not for lack of evidence. Measurements show minimal activity inside the brain of a cold snake or a cold frog. Being moved to the freezer doesn't register a blip. The animal doesn't feel a thing. But cold-based euthanasia has three problems.

First, it doesn't work well for species that live in cool climates. Reptiles and amphibians adapted to function under cold conditions keep on wriggling even at low temperatures.

The second problem is a social one. Killing an animal with cold sounds cruel. As warm-blooded animals, we would experience great stress and pain if killed by freezing. Our bodies would fight the encroaching cold. But that's not the case for reptiles. They get cold every day (or night) and so it's not stressful. And they are dead before they know anything dangerous is happening.

And third, killing an animal with cold seems old-fashioned. Ethics committees include veterinary practitioners who are trained in the use of chemicals for euthanasia. High-tech solutions with powerful drugs sound more modern than putting a snake into the fridge then the freezer.

What if your aim is to kill vast numbers of snakes that are hidden in dense jungle? Researchers on the island of Guam developed a way to slaughter invasive Brown Tree Snakes by dropping poison baits (each attached to a dead mouse) from low-flying helicopters. The acetaminophen toxicant kills snakes rapidly, but apparently poses little risk to other wildlife. The method can't eradicate Brown Tree Snakes, because juvenile snakes are unaffected (they prefer lizards as prey, not mice) – but it can make a dent in snake numbers.

IN THEIR OWN WORDS

Many early authors wrote about absurdly huge snakes. For example:

"A gigantic serpent is said to have dwelt on the banks of the river Belgrada, between Utica and Carthage, and to have destroyed many soldiers who had gone to its haunts for the purpose of procuring water. Regulus was, therefore, compelled to employ against it the most effective military engines then known, as darts hurled at him glanced off the scales, when a ponderous stone, hurled by one of them, slew the reptile; and his skin, when taken to Rome, measured a hundred and twenty-three feet." *Cassell's Popular Natural History,* 1881

"The largest of our European serpents (*Coluber quadrilineatus*), inhabiting Italy and Spain, often attains the length of six feet. According to Metaxa, it was a snake of this species that is stated to have swallowed a child on the Vatican mount, in the time of Claudius. The boy was taken out of this non-venomous reptile's stomach unmutilated. A respectable writer says, in allusion to this account: "We do not think it at all incredible, and more likely to be true than otherwise. We remember seeing a very small young child deposited on the pavement of a church in Lisbon, quite naked, to wait until some charitable person should order it to be buried, that a very moderate-sized snake might have swallowed, had such a one met with it in its haunts." *Cassell's Popular Natural History,* 1881

In response to absurd claims about gigantic snakes, people who wrote more scientific reviews felt the need to point out the errors involved:

"Many travellers, and especially those of a more remote age, speak of serpents of a monstrous size, which they say they have encountered in their travels in intertropical countries, and which they state as reaching to forty feet and upwards. In whichever country these great reptiles are found, they apply to them the name of Boa Constrictor, familiar to all, although the true Boa Constrictor of systems yields much in dimensions to other species of the boa and the python. The numerous researches of modern, well-informed, travelling naturalists have belied many of the fables which have been promulgated on the nature of these ophidians. We now know that the most gigantic do not surpass twenty to twenty-five feet in total length; that their thickness is not above seven inches in diameter; and that the received notions on the great size of some species, only repose on the vague surmises of the natives." HERMANN SCHLEGEL, 1837

As time went on, writers bemoaned the difficulty of accurate estimates of body size, even for live snakes:

"It is possible that many larger snakes have been killed, but they are generally measured by the eye only, and we all know how apt one is to exaggerate the size of such quarry; there is nothing so good as a tapeline, if truth is to be ascertained; but people do not generally care to be very particular, and after relating snake stories for years they make the size of the reptile increase as their story grows old." GERARD KREFFT, 1869

"Of many possible measurements that can be taken, snout-vent length (SVL) is the most important and also one of the most difficult to obtain. The body of a live snake is highly elastic and can stretch or contract to yield measurements over a wide range of values." HENRY S. FITCH, 1987

Because it is difficult to establish the age of a snake, myths of extreme longevity abounded:

"Among the many attributes ascribed to the serpent, longevity is one which has especially fitted him to become the emblem of eternity. Renewing, say the learned in magic lore, his youth with the changes of his skin, accident alone can deprive him of life." VARINA ANNE DAVIS, 1888

Astute observers were aware of sexual dimorphism:

"Sometimes, as we have stated above, the livery of the two sexes presents considerable varieties at different periods of life. The males have often a more thick and longer tail than the females, probably because they have the organs of generation lodged in a cavity at the base of that member; the females, on the other hand, acquire a size greater than that of the male, and their trunk is then of a more considerable volume." HERMANN SCHLEGEL, 1837

And some brave pioneers tried to summarise broad ecological patterns:

"Most ophidians choose their food indiscriminately from among the three first classes of vertebrate animals. The aquatic species live more or less exclusively on fishes, according as their mode of life devotes them to the liquid element. The species of small size, especially the terrestrial and burrowing snakes, pursue insects, mollusca, worms, or other animals of the lower classes. Tree serpents prefer birds, not because this species of nutriment is better suited to their taste, but because it is more within their reach." HERMANN SCHLEGEL, 1837

The earliest records of fecundity mostly involve exceptionally large (and thus memorable) clutch or litter sizes:

"The number of young which ophidians produce at a single deposition of eggs, differs considerably in the different species. I have observed in several Calamarire not more than ten; some Colubri lay from twenty to twenty-five; I have found thirty and more in the Trigonocephalus atrox, and it is said that our Ringed Snake lays as many as forty." HERMANN SCHLEGEL, 1837

"A 'spotted spreading adder' was shot in two, near the middle; when eighty-seven young were taken from her body. ... This occurred within the last two weeks, and in the presence of nearly a dozen persons, from several of whom I have gathered the facts." J. SCHNECK, 1882

Remarkably, modern snake biologists individually mark snakes in almost the same way as Frank and Ethel did in 1933:

"The method of marking devised consists in snipping a piece from a caudal scute and recording the number of the scale thus marked." FRANK N. BLANCHARD AND ETHEL B. FINSTER, 1933

It's comforting to see that humane treatment was an issue even in the earliest scientific studies:

"Another convenient way of killing a snake without injury is by blowing into its mouth a drop or two of the oil from a dirty tobacco pipe, or administering a few drops of strong decoction of tobacco. But the systematic collector will find that carbolic acid affords the readiest mode of killing specimens for the museum. The liquid should be passed down the throat of the snake by means of a glass pipette about nine inches long. Twenty drops thus administered will destroy a large cobra in a couple of minutes. The snake is put to no apparent pain; it soon shivers, becomes insensible and dies with paralytic symptoms." EDWARD NICHOLSON, 1874

The Woma Python (*Aspidites ramsayi*) is a widespread but rarely encountered inhabitant of Australian deserts. ALANA DE LAIVE

PART 3

SNAKE RESEARCH IN THE LAB

In order to understand something, first of all we need to describe it. Without a clear grasp of what is happening, any attempt to explain something is doomed to failure.

In the case of snake ecology, ideally we would gather our information in the wild so that our insights relate to snakes in the real world. But fieldwork on snakes is challenging. In the previous chapter, I talked about methods that researchers use to record the sizes, shapes, food habits and reproductive biology of their study animals. Later in the book, I talk about how radio tracking filled in a major gap by giving us detailed stories about the day-to-day lives of free-ranging snakes.

But sadly, there are limits to what you can achieve in the field. You can't spend hours counting scale numbers on a newly caught snake if biting ants are crawling up inside your pants, or the rain is pouring down on your head, or nightfall is imminent and your camp is an hour's hike away. Far better, then, to put that snake in a bag and record the data at your leisure.

Transporting a snake to the lab also opens up opportunities that are not available in the unpredictable and ever-changing conditions of the field. Some measures can be made within hours or days of first capture, whereas others rely upon long-term captivity. If you keep your snake in a cage, you can control the conditions that it experiences. And by doing so, you can move from description to experiments.

Chapter 5

A snake in the lab is worth two in the bush

If we bring our newly captured snake back to the lab rather than releasing it, the list of things we can assess increases dramatically. Some of the new opportunities include measurements that are too time-consuming and fiddly for field-based research, whereas other options involve questions we can't ask unless we keep the snake around for a while. For example, some behaviours will only be manifested if the snake is well adjusted to living in a cage. And it's easier to expose a snake to some treatment or other, and monitor the long-term effects of that experience, if you don't have to wander around in the forest trying to relocate the animal a year later.

This chapter looks at methods of obtaining data over a brief timescale – keeping snakes captive for long enough to measure their abilities or responses, but not setting up long-term captive colonies.

The earliest experiment I could find on snake biology was a simple study by 'Lieutenant Tyler', about his 1849 observations on captive snakes from a small Caribbean island. Tyler fed one species (the slender and elegant 'Couresse', or St Lucia Racer) to another (the large and muscular 'Clibro', or Underwood's Mussurana). Intrigued by rumours that the predator swallows his prey alive, Tyler notes that: "I have satisfactorily proved that the Clibro does not kill his prey before he has swallowed it, by allowing a Clibro to swallow a Couresse, all excepting the very point of his tail, then pulling him out, after a short interval giving it to him again, pulling out the Couresse by the tip of his tail as before, and keeping him alive for months afterwards." That certainly qualifies as an experiment (Tyler manipulated something and recorded what happened as a result), although its brutality would outrage any snake-lover. Sadly, the Clibro is now extinct, and its smaller relative the Couresse ranks as among the rarest snakes in the world – a tragic example of the dismal fate of snakes on small islands.

The next example I could find of an experiment on snake ecology was one that was planned by the greatest biologist of all time – the reclusive Englishman, Charles Darwin – but does not seem to have ever been conducted. In a letter to his cousin The Reverend William Darwin Fox on 17 May 1855, Darwin wrote: "My dear Fox. … As you live on sandy soil, have you lizards at all common? If you have, should you think it too ridiculous to offer a reward for me for lizards eggs to the boys in your school; a shilling for every half-dozen, or more if rare, till you get two or three dozen and send them to me. If snake's eggs were brought in mistake it would be very well, for I want such also: and we have neither lizards or snakes about here. My object is to see whether such eggs will float on sea water, and whether they will keep alive thus floating for a month or two in my cellar. I am trying experiments on transportation of all organic beings, that I can; and lizards are found on every island and therefore I am very anxious to see whether their eggs stand sea water. …. Your most troublesome friend, C. Darwin."

Fox never managed to supply those eggs, because the only abundant lizard species in the UK (the European Common Lizard) bears live young rather than laying eggs. The great man had forgotten this bit of basic biology. But it didn't take long for him to realise his mistake and in a follow-up a week later, Charles admitted: "I had quite forgotten when I wrote to you, that the very common British lizard is ovoviviparous!" So, Darwin's experiment was doomed from the outset.

In a more successful experiment in 1888, Indian biologist Ghore Pore set out to test whether or not snakes can hear airborne sounds. To do so, he arranged for a snake-charmer and his flute to be positioned either in front of the cobra (as usual) or behind it – and thus Pore could show that these snakes were 'dancing' to the snake-charmer's movements rather than his music.

Moving forward, one of the most elegant examples I could find of an experimental study came from a short paper by Edward Green (1861–1949), an expatriate Englishman who was born in Sri Lanka and schooled in England, but then returned to Sri Lanka and spent much of his life there as Government Entomologist. In between studies on insect pests, Green contributed papers to the fledgling natural-history journal *Spolia Zeylanica*. In one of his first papers on snakes, in 1903, Green integrated indigenous knowledge with observations of a captive snake, then tested the snake's responses with experimental stimuli. The paper is so short that I can reproduce it all here: "A freshly captured specimen of *Dryophis mycterizans* supports, by its actions, its popular native name of 'Eye-piercing Snake'. When first placed in the cage it repeatedly struck at my face, though it would not take notice of my hand under any circumstances. It also struck repeatedly at the eye-pieces of a pair of binocular field-glasses. It struck at a piece of white sponge to which a small black disc had been attached (to represent an eye), but it never hit the disc, always catching hold of the sponge itself." Edward Green was a true pioneer of experimental studies of snake behaviour.

The Green Vine Snake (*Ahaetulla nasuta*) from Sri Lanka is renowned for its habit of striking at people's eyes. RUCHIRA SOMAWEERA

The innovative contributions of those pioneering naturalists were the first small steps towards measuring snake behaviour in the laboratory. In modern-day snake research, that trickle has become a tidal wave.

Serpentine Olympics: measuring a snake's performance

Some kinds of behavioural trials work even with a snake that is obsessed with escaping from you. Specifically, you can measure the animal's ability to make a getaway. As a result, the easiest 'performance' to quantify is the speed that an animal can crawl or swim or burrow. If a snake is hell-bent on escape, and you place it on a raceway of some kind, the animal will hurtle as quickly as it can along that route towards freedom. The raceway can be as simple or as sophisticated as you like, and can be set up either in the field or the laboratory. At the 'simple' end of the spectrum, we measured speeds of garter snakes in the field by marking a central location in a flat grass-covered area (using a beer can as the marker) and then spray-painting concentric circles onto the ground at various distances around the central point. A snake released beside the beer can would race away as fast as it could, in a straight line, and we could record the time taken to cross each circle.

The next step up in sophistication involves a channel to keep the snake on the straight and narrow as it sprints away from you. I've built these raceways for several studies, using three boards. One board is laid on the ground as the base, and the other two are nailed upright on either side of the bottom one. The base board must be rough, to give the snake purchase as it moves along, but the raw materials are easy to obtain. To compare speeds of sea snakes on land and in water, we used the same raceways on dry land as in the ocean shallows.

For the ultimate in sophistication you can employ a laboratory version of the raceway, with electronic movement detectors embedded on the walls at regular intervals. As the snake wriggles past those detectors, its speed is recorded on a computer. It's more precise than the field-based methods, and the lab setting makes it easier to manipulate factors such as room temperature. Even in the field, though, some snake-filled bags can be put into the fridge or the shade, whereas others sit in the sunlight or on a heated car seat.

A raceway lets us measure how a snake's size, sex and body temperature affect not only its speed, but also its anti-predator tactics. Cold snakes curl up and strike at the investigator, whereas hot snakes sprint for the open end of the raceway. There are always a few unco-operative animals that try to climb out over the side walls, or that insist on going halfway down the raceway then turning around and going back the other way. But with a little patience, an investigator can obtain repeatable measurements of each individual's athletic ability.

Speed and endurance on a horizontal raceway are only the beginning; a creative investigator can devise many other biologically meaningful challenges. How is speed affected if the racetrack is inclined at an angle rather than flat? How well can the snake climb a rough or smooth surface?

A simple raceway constructed to measure crawling speeds of reptiles in the field. JULES FARQUHAR

Speed is quick and easy to measure, which is one of the reasons why the Olympic Games have so many events based on running rather than on other biologically significant tasks such as the speed and efficiency with which you can digest a meal and pass it through your body. OK, there are other reasons as well for omitting those activities from the Olympic Games. But snake biologists can take a broader view than Olympics organising committees and measure a wide variety of performances. With a high-speed video camera, you can measure the speed and accuracy of a snake's defensive strike, and how those abilities shift with the snake's size and body temperature. You can even assay the amount of venom expended in a bite, by allowing the snake to strike a sponge that retains the fluid. The possibilities are constrained only by the researcher's creativity.

Looking for love

When it comes time for a male snake to find a female, he faces a huge challenge. Snakes are scarce in most parts of the world, so blundering around randomly to locate a mate won't work. An inconvenient lack of ears makes it impossible for a snake to find a mate by listening for calls, as frogs and birds can do. Humans in search of romance can use visual cues to find and evaluate a partner, but a snake's eyes are too close to the ground for him to see very far. Male snakes haven't totally abandoned visual searching – looking for females may pay off in a crowded snake-den or in the ocean, where no other information is available – but smell usually offers a better clue. The forked tongue of a snake – larger in males than females – provides an exquisitely sensitive scent-detection system. And fortunately for lusty male snakes, females produce skin chemicals that reveal a snake's sex, rub off against grass and rocks when the snake moves around, and persist for days or even weeks. For a snake, like a dog, the world is a complex mosaic of chemical trails.

Following a scent trail is a distinctive behaviour, easily simulated in the lab. Anyone who keeps pet snakes in a cage will notice the frantic tongue-flicking of an amorous male during courtship as he explores his mate's body; and the equally frantic tongue-flicking that such a male directs towards the base and sides of his tank after the female is removed. Such observations led to some of the earliest experimental research on snake behaviour. In the 1930s Harry John Clausen (1904–1972) and the frenetic Gladwyn Kingsley Noble (1894–1940) conducted elegant experiments in the laboratory to work out how garter snakes locate and follow the trails of other snakes, and what sense organs they use in that process. But even before that American work, European scientist Franz Baumann (1885–1961) published a groundbreaking paper in 1929 that described male European Asp Vipers tongue-flicking the scent trails laid down by females.

Snakes rely on frequent tongue-flicking to obtain chemical evidence about their surroundings. This is an American Copperhead (*Agkistrodon contortrix*). NOAH K. FIELDS

What happens after boy meets girl?

How fast you can slither or how high you can climb is important, but when it comes to evolutionary success ('fitness' in Darwinian jargon), nothing matters as much as reproduction. As a result (or perhaps due to personal obsessions), snake ecologists have devised several ways to monitor the ability of male snakes to overcome their rivals, and to achieve a coupling with a female.

Few snakes are abundant enough for an investigator to measure the effect of traits such as body size on the tactics and mating success of a male snake in the field. So to find out if size really does matter, the best approach is to set up trials with recently captured males during the mating season. If you use field enclosures close to the snake's usual domicile, a male may be so busy looking for romance that he ignores being captured and deposited in an outdoor cage. Indeed, some male snakes are so single-minded that they continue to fight and mate even if transferred to a glass cage in the laboratory.

Outdoor cages work well for mellow snakes that recover quickly after being disturbed. As a result, outdoor cages have been pivotal to revealing the sex lives of garter snakes and sea kraits. But not everyone likes to be cooped up in a cage. Some snakes take weeks to settle down, making it impossible to study their behaviour. When I put Shedao Pit Vipers in open-topped cages, the only behaviour I ever saw was snakes threatening to bite me.

Being colour-coded and labelled for individual identification doesn't distract these Red-sided Garter Snakes (*Thamnophis sirtalis parietalis*) from the important business of courtship and mating. CHRIS FRIESEN

That variation in response can occur even within species. Once when I was staying with pioneering biologist Hubert Saint Girons at his chateau in the French countryside, he proudly showed me a set of outdoor cages that he had built to study the local Asp Vipers. All of the mesh enclosures had fat and happy vipers coiled up inside, but I was surprised to see an equally fat viper coiled up on the outside of the fence. When I pointed the animal out to Hubert, he laughed. This was a male viper that had lived in the area for years, and often spent his time beside the cages. But if Hubert picked him up and put him inside the cage, the snake never settled down – constantly searching for an exit. As soon as Hubert put him back outside, the snake calmed down. He liked the habitat but insisted on liberty.

Trials with captive snakes have told us a lot about snake sexual shenanigans. For example, in species where males fight with each other, the larger male almost always wins. These wrestling matches are a test of strength, so a bigger male has an advantage. But what happens in snake species where the males don't fight, and instead form groups of writhing suitors around a female? At first sight the orgy looks like chaos, but studies of European Grass Snakes and Red-sided Garter Snakes show that the male who wins the mating is a bit bigger, a bit stronger, a bit better at pushing other tails out of the way.

Body size plays out in other aspects of reproductive rivalry as well. For example, bigger males are better courters. If we put a single male plus female garter snake in an enclosure, a large male rapidly convinces the female to mate with him, whereas a smaller male takes longer to achieve that goal. Again, it's probably about courtship vigour.

And larger size is especially important for a male if the object of his affections is a large female. Larger females have larger litters, so a male who mates with a larger female will sire more offspring. That pay-off attracts suitors to big females, making things difficult for a small male in the mating frenzy around a large female. At least in Red-sided Garter Snakes, small males realise this, and move to Plan B. That is, focus their efforts on the smaller females – the ones that are ignored by larger rivals. In mating groups around the den, small female snakes are courted by small males, and large females are courted by the bigger males.

But this isn't a hard-wired choice. Suppose you are a large male garter snake. You would rather court large females, but the only ones you find around the den today are small. Should you ignore them, hoping to find a bigger female, or should you change your tactics? Garter snakes adopt the policy that if you can't be with the one you love, then love the one you're with. On a day when only small females are active, they are courted enthusiastically by big as well as small reptilian Romeos. There's no easy way to document that flexibility with free-ranging snakes in the chaos around a den. Instead, you need experiments to control the numbers and sizes of snakes in outdoor cages.

The process of courtship, as demonstrated by these Aesculapian Snakes (*Zamenis longissimus*), is less vigorous than the combat bouts between rival males, as in these King Brown Snakes (*Pseudechis australis*). PHOTOGRAPHS: WERNER PRIEWASSER, PIXABAY; AND GARY STEPHENSON

More generally, cage trials show us that male snakes adjust their tactics to available opportunities. For example, a male garter snake who finds himself alone with a female can concentrate on courtship. But as the number of competitors increases, a male puts less effort into the energy-sapping work of convincing the female to mate. That task can be left to the other males. Instead, a sensible male in a large mating group focuses on pushing rival tails away from the female's cloaca. Video recordings of courtship in different-sized groups show that's exactly what he does.

Likewise, a small male garter snake is out of his league in the frenzy of the den, so he disperses to nearby woodlands – a place where unmated females are scarce, but competition from other males is less intense. We can document those behavioural differences by field studies comparing snakes in the den to snakes in the woodland – but to understand the rules of the game we need to run trials in cages as well, so we can eliminate confounding factors.

Delving into even more detailed questions, cage trials have shown that a male snake's shape as well as his size affect his ability to obtain a mating. In particular, the length of his tail relative to his body can affect how dexterously he can push away the tails of his rivals in a 'mating ball'. Male garter snakes and Yellow-lipped Sea Kraits with average-sized tails outperform their long-tailed and short-tailed competitors in mating-trial experiments.

Watching captive snakes forage

Because ecology and behaviour are intimately intertwined, you can't understand a snake's diet without knowing how it finds and subdues its prey. There are a few places in the world where you can watch snakes finding prey in the wild, but such places are scarce. More often, the most you can hope for is a quick glimpse of some interesting behaviour. Captive snakes are more forgiving. Accustomed to humans around them, they ignore the large primate with a lab coat and a clipboard who is standing next to their cage taking notes.

Descriptions are useful, but experiments are even better: that is, you can ask a question. For example, what characteristics of a potential meal does a snake use when deciding what to have for lunch? Is the snake's strike stimulated by the smell of the prey? Or the prey's movements? Or its appearance? Or all three? You can answer those questions easily with a docile captive snake. If it relies on scent to identify its food, smearing the scent of a favourite prey type onto an otherwise non-preferred prey will induce feeding. If it relies on movement, a dead prey item will be ignored until you jiggle it. And so forth. In practice, different snake species use different cues – but scent and movement are often key to triggering a strike.

If you keep a snake in captivity for long enough for it to settle down and begin feeding, you can also assess its performance at tasks such as swallowing (how does a snake's head size affect its ability to swallow a large prey item, and the time it requires to do so?) or the snake's ability to penetrate deep into a narrow crevice to obtain a prey item. All of these studies experimentally manipulate some aspect in order to measure how that factor affects performance.

In the 1970s, American researcher Gordon Burghardt discovered that garter snakes are ideally suited to studies of this kind. These mellow little snakes thrive in captivity and ignore the investigator if presented with a cotton swab that has been smeared with chemical cues from a frog or mouse. Ta-da, the researcher can measure a snake's level of interest in different scents by counting the number of times the serpent flicks its tongue in and out when it encounters that smell. Suddenly, snake ecologists had a 'model system' for lab-based studies on behaviour. Information and insights accumulated rapidly.

Small, non-venomous, abundant, widely distributed and mellow: Common Garter Snakes (*Thamnophis sirtalis*) are perhaps the most user-friendly snake species for behavioural research. NOAH K. FIELDS

Experiments can show how a snake finds its prey, as well as how it decides what to eat. Bandy-bandy snakes are Australian elapids, named for their boldly contrasting black-and-white rings. They are poorly known because they spend most of their lives underground. Dissections of museum specimens show that these colourful serpents feed only on burrowing reptiles (blind snakes) that are seen above ground even less often than bandy-bandies. With most of the interesting behaviour occurring beneath our feet, hidden from human eyes, the only way to discover how a bandy-bandy finds a blind snake is to take both players into the laboratory.

The answer is that blind snakes deposit scent on the ground as they move from one ant-nest to another, and bandy-bandies follow those faint trails. Although there's no way to test that idea in the field, the lab makes it easy. We can drag a blind snake along a certain path across the cage, then remove the blind snake and watch how a bandy-bandy reacts when we put her in that cage. Sure enough, a hungry bandy-bandy spends most of its time on the pathway of blind snake aroma. Trails left by snakes of other species, or lizards, or anything else, are ignored; it's the smell of a blind snake that matters. As an undergraduate student, Australian snake-enthusiast Matt Greenlees showed that bandy-bandies are very good at detecting those subtle chemical cues, and very choosy about which paths they follow. Matt did so well on that undergraduate project that I recruited him to work in my research team – where he stayed for the next 18 years.

An ambush-forager faces an even more daunting challenge: to find a site where it can lie in wait, hidden from approaching prey and predators but able to strike out if an edible meal appears. Ambushing snakes often lie hidden in dense cover, facing out towards a path used by mammals moving through the undergrowth. The ideal perch may be above the path, or beside it, or even below it if the snake hides itself in shallow water waiting for a thirsty mammal or bird to have a drink. When selecting an ambush site, scent provides the best clue. Mammals are smelly and they often mark their paths with urine, making the snake's job easier. Experiments show that snakes base their ambush-site choice on several factors, but the scent of prey is overwhelmingly important for species that eat frogs, lizards and mammals. Scent is of no use if you are waiting for a bird, though, because a bird leaves no scent trail. Instead, the snake switches to visual cues.

For example, American snake researchers Robert Cooper and Steve Mullin showed that Grey Rat Snakes locate bird nests in the same way that a human observer would do – the snakes watch adult birds to see where they are going. To show that this response was driven by visual cues rather than scent, the investigators 'flew' a model bird strung on a wire to an artificial nest-hole. As predicted, the snakes watched the model, then climbed the tree that contained the fake nest.

Danger at dinnertime

Observations and experiments on captive snakes can also address the next step in the snake's dining sequence. Is the food safe to eat? The skins of many amphibians contain poisons potent enough to kill a snake, or super-sticky adhesive that glues a snake's mouth to nearby vegetation. Ben Phillips and I noticed that after an Australian death adder strikes a toxic or super-sticky frog, the snake immediately releases the frog and waits for it to die before swallowing it. Non-toxic non-sticky frogs are engulfed immediately, but if the frog is poisonous or sticky, the snake checks it from time to time by tongue-flicking its corpse. Only after the poisons or the glue have broken down – which takes about 20 minutes – does the death adder begin ingesting its meal.

The next step, of course, is to get that prey item into your stomach. The long slender body of a snake enables it to penetrate into tiny crevices in search of prey. But that body shape also introduces a challenge: how can a snake swallow a prey item larger than its head? Laboratory-based biologists have looked in detail at how snakes accomplish that extraordinary feat. One useful tactic is to make the prey item smaller. For example, a toad under attack inflates its lungs, swelling to a size too large to be swallowed; but enlarged teeth at the rear of a hognose snake's jaw puncture the unfortunate amphibian to let the air out.

Swallowing an inflated toad is like swallowing a pumped-up balloon; the snake's best tactic is to puncture that bubble so it can ingest the deflated prey. This image shows a Common Garter Snake (*Thamnophis sirtalis*) at dinnertime. NOAH K. FIELDS

An even more important tactic is to evolve flexible joints within the skull, enabling stretching to an almost-unimaginable degree – and with technologies such as real-time X-rays, we can watch in detail at how those joints perform as a rat takes its final journey down the gullet of a snake. But for snakes that specialise on difficult-to-swallow prey, there are other tricks as well. For example, African egg-eating snakes don't have teeth (making it easier for the egg to slide down into the throat) but they have projections on the backbone that extend into the oesophagus. Powerful muscles push the egg against those spines, breaking the eggshell and crushing it so that the juicy contents flow into the snake's stomach. Then the empty eggshell is regurgitated, and the snake wanders off to find a quiet place to digest its uncooked omelette.

Some like it hot

Snakes control their body temperatures by shuttling between sunlit patches and shade, and by selecting suitable retreat sites. Once a snake has settled into captivity, it shows the same behaviours – creating an opportunity for experimental studies on snake thermal preferences. A hot snake is better at detecting predators and prey, striking accurately, fleeing quickly, digesting rapidly and so forth. But on the other hand, high temperatures increase metabolic rates and so use up more energy. Based on that trade-off, we expect snakes to adjust their preferred body temperatures depending on local conditions. For example, eating a large meal should motivate the snake to find a warm spot where digestion can proceed rapidly.

That's an easy prediction to test. You can place an underfloor heatlamp under one section of the cage and iceblocks under another. Then you can record the snake's position in the cage when it's hungry and again after it's been fed. And sure enough, a snake that has just eaten a large meal will select warmer conditions. It will selectively heat up the bulge in its stomach, shifting as the bulge moves down. In a similar way, a pregnant snake maintains high temperatures for her unborn young.

Female pythons take that trick to a whole new level, by wrapping around their eggs and generating heat through muscular contraction. In essence, the snakes cease being 'cold-blooded' (ectothermic) and switch to a 'warm-blooded' (endothermic) lifestyle to keep their babies warm. That remarkable ability has been known since 1862, when physiologist P.L. Slater convinced an English manufacturing company to construct sensitive quick-reading thermometers so that he could measure temperatures inside the coils of an egg-incubating African Rock Python in a London zoo.

Brooding pythons coil around their eggs to protect them from predators, and can shiver to generate the heat needed to keep their eggs warm. This image shows a brooding African Rock Python (*Python natalensis*) and her eggs. GRAHAM ALEXANDER

One of the other factors that affects a snake's body temperature is its colour. Under identical conditions of sunlight, air temperature and so on, a black object heats up faster than a pale one. The effect is familiar to anyone who owns a black automobile. Because species of snakes differ in so many ways (size, shape, behaviour, habitat, etc.), it's difficult to tease apart the role of colour by comparing across species. But conveniently, many species of snakes exhibit more than one colour morph. It's common to find jet-black (melanic) individuals as well as paler individuals within a single population of species such as Eurasian Adder, rattlesnakes, garter snakes, Japanese Four-lined Snakes or death adders. That provides an ideal opportunity to explore how a snake's colour affects its thermal regimes. As predicted, a dark snake (or even just the skin of a dark snake) heats faster than a pale one. And as we'd expect, the most likely places to find jet-black individuals of usually pale-coloured species are in colder climates. Species such as Inland Taipans take it even further, turning darker during cooler times of the year.

A snake's body size also affects its thermal biology. For example, Diamond Pythons are ambush predators that live in a cool climate (at least by Australian standards). Adult Diamonds grow to around 5 kg (10 lb) and consume mammals (such as possums and rats) that are active only by night. So, adult Diamonds are nocturnal. But younger Diamonds feed by day instead, lying in wait for lizards. Why the switch in foraging times and prey types? My student Danielle Ayers showed that it's all about rates of cooling. To remain alert and ready to strike instantly if a meal comes by, the snake needs to stay warm. No problem for an adult python that can form a tight coil, reducing the surface area over which it loses heat as the night drags on. But a juvenile Diamond can't play the same game. Careful measurements of captive snakes showed that small pythons can't remain warm enough for long enough to feed on small nocturnal mammals such as mice. The snake loses heat too quickly, even if it is coiled. For a small python, the only option is daytime ambush from a sun-warmed site. And so, mice are off the menu.

In summary, laboratory-based studies have given us a detailed view of how an elongate limbless animal overcomes the challenges of life. For example, how it can find a suitable mate and deal with competition from its rivals, can find and kill and swallow its food, and can control its body temperature. In most cases, the original observations that spawned the research came from the field. But to work out exactly what is going on, we needed to bring the snake into captivity where we can take our measurements with greater precision, and in a more standardised environment.

IN THEIR OWN WORDS

Scientists weren't the only people to keep pet snakes:

"A lady of somewhat eccentric habits domesticated a number of snakes as pets; and not only did they recognise her, but would come and wreathe themselves around her arms and neck, but would often creep over and entwine themselves about her visitors, to their amazement and terror. It was otherwise with one belonging to Mr Bell. He kept a snake that would come to him every morning at breakfast for a draught of milk, and would then crawl under the sleeve of his coat, enjoying the warmth; but he would fly from strangers, and hiss if they attempted to touch him."
Cassell's Popular Natural History, 1881

"These are certainly endearing animals which can be trained to dance with a stick and the pipe, and to play dead. ... My friend Mr D. Vognetz has a ringed snake which is so tame that she crawls up and down in the room like a domestic bird, often climbs up on him, crawling up the arms and into the bosom. But it does not easily approach anyone else. He puts it in his pocket, goes into the garden with it and as soon as he emits a loud whistle, similar to the tone with which at mating time they call their mates, it comes to him, crawls up on him, lets him put it in his pocket and remains there without moving until he takes it out again. Since these crawling reptiles often grow exceptionally large, this has provided opportunity for all kinds of fables." JOHANN MATTHAUS BECHSTEIN, 1797 (translated from German in Heichler and Murphy, 2004).

The frustrations of observing snakes in nature convinced early researchers that captive animals might be the only solution:

"Until steps are taken to keep Indian snakes under observation in properly constructed serpentaria in this country, our knowledge regarding their habits will remain limited as it now is." HERBERT MUSGRAVE PHIPSON, 1891

One of the first important observations derived from captive snakes was about a topic that was impossible to measure in the field: that is, the frequency of feeding:

"A feast and a fast is more the custom of snakes than frequent feeding; their prey is generally sufficiently large to afford their digestive organs exercise for several days, and during this time they take their ease lying in wait for another meal. The possibility of keeping snakes in captivity entirely depends on their temper; some snakes feed readily, others are sulky and obstinately refuse food. Amongst the latter are cobras; I do not know how they manage with them in zoological gardens, but I have never seen a cobra feed, and I think that, unless fed by force, he will starve himself to death. The chain-viper *Daboia* is very sulky; if caught when in good case it will live for six months or more without food or drink; but the cobra does not survive its voluntary starvation for more than a month or six weeks. Jugglers either feed their cobras by cramming them with milk or curds, or else let them loose when the lives of their captives are endangered; probably their experience in snake-catching enables them to re-capture their prisoners at a future time." EDWARD NICHOLSON, 1874

Chapter 6

Long-term experiments in the lab

To answer some of the most interesting questions about snake biology, short-term captivity isn't enough. The only way to explore long-term cause-and-effect relationships is to manipulate the snake's environment – such as its incubation temperature in the egg stage, or its food supply as an adult – and then see how those experiences affect the individual's life over the next few months or years. For work of this kind, you need to keep a snake in captivity for quite a while. The early researchers in snake ecology didn't have the skills or the facilities or the resources to maintain colonies of captive snakes, but such colonies played a pivotal role when snake ecology research reached its golden age late in the 20th century.

With access to long-term captives, the questions you can ask are limited only by your ability to think of new and interesting experiments. For example, you can retest an individual time and again to check whether some characteristic of that animal is consistent throughout its life. The obvious characteristics in this respect are colour patterns or scale counts, but behaviour is equally interesting. Snakes have personalities, just as cats and dogs do. That's true within a population as well as across species. Shy snakes stay under cover; active snakes move around frequently; sociable snakes cuddle up to their cage-mates. When tested years later, individuals act in the same ways as before. That behavioural variation has important ecological consequences; a bold snake can find new habitats whereas a shy snake can survive despite a high abundance of predators. We still have only the faintest glimmerings of how an individual's behaviour affects its life in the wild.

Nature versus nurture

If you obtain your snake when it is young, you can ask one of the most fundamental questions in biology. Are an animal's characteristics shaped by its genes versus by its environment? The answer isn't always obvious. For example, it's generally true that snake species that consume large prey have large jaws. Blind snakes that only eat ant eggs have tiny skulls, whereas pythons that eat antelopes have massive heads. The obvious mechanism responsible for that correlation is evolution. If small prey are abundant, even small-jawed snakes can get plenty to eat. There is no penalty to having a small mouth, so evolution maintains genes for that trait. But if all of the prey are large, a serpent with jaws too small to swallow them starves to death. Over the generations, genes for large jaws take over that snake population.

But there's another possible explanation, even though it sounds unlikely. Perhaps a snake that is given large prey – almost too big to swallow – develops larger jaws? By analogy, human athletes who mostly use the limbs of one side of their body (such as shot-putters) grow larger stronger bones on that side. French biologist Xavier Bonnet is one of the most innovative thinkers I know. A less courageous person would have seen that idea as too unlikely to be worth testing, but Xavier loves to challenge orthodoxy. So he decided to test that idea with a litter of Gaboon Vipers that had been donated to him by a local zoo. These are creatures of nightmare for people who don't like snakes; Gaboon Vipers have potent venom and the longest fangs of any snake species. But they are also stunningly beautiful, with complex hues that camouflage them against the forest floor. Xavier used them to see if a snake could grow a larger head if it ate larger prey.

A Gaboon Viper (*Bitis gabonica*) is superbly camouflaged against the forest floor. BILL LAMAR

Sure enough, when Xavier raised the deadly babies on different diets, young snakes given large prey items increased the size of their jaws and so were able to eat those super-sized lunches.

Their brothers and sisters, fed on smaller mice, developed normally sized heads. The differences were nothing like as large as the difference between blind snakes and pythons, but the pattern was clear. It was a staggering example of flexibility – and it was only possible because Xavier was able to control the snakes' access to prey of different sizes. Such a study couldn't be done in the field.

Another kind of 'nature versus nurture?' question involves geographic variation in growth rates and body sizes. In any widely distributed species, snakes from some areas are larger than from other areas. Climatic factors can explain that divergence in some cases, but not all – especially if the areas with giants versus tiddlers are close together and so, have identical climates. Is the difference in body sizes between the two populations due to 'nature' (genetic differences) or to 'nurture' (differences in food supply)?

In an early example of such a study, Swedish biologist Thomas Madsen noticed a peculiar pattern during his fieldwork on European Grass Snakes. Over most of the species' range females grow larger than males, and feed on toads that are too large for males to swallow. But on the Swedish island of Hallands Vadero, which lacks toads, female Grass Snakes only grow to the same size as males. To see if this was an evolutionary effect (adaptation) or just a direct response to the lack of large prey, Thomas raised baby snakes in the lab. When given unlimited food, females grew larger than males in island snakes as well as in mainland snakes. There was no need to suggest complicated evolutionary stories; island females were small simply because they couldn't obtain large meals.

On the other side of the world, American researcher Anne Bronikowski has been intrigued by puzzles ever since she was a small child. It was a natural progression to search for puzzles in her professional life, and she was fascinated by differences in growth rate between two nearby populations of Western Terrestrial Garter Snakes in California. So, like Thomas, she raised babies in the lab with constant food supply but under thermal conditions like those experienced at the two sites in the field. Sure enough, baby snakes grew fastest under the conditions experienced in their source population. Mountain-meadow snakes grew fastest if kept at mountain-meadow temperatures, and lakeshore snakes grew fastest if kept at lakeshore temperatures. Divergent growth rates in these snakes are the result of evolutionary adaptation, as well as direct effects of temperature and food supply.

The indelible marks of early-life experiences

Some parts of an animal's life cycle are easier to study than others. For example, we know more about the ecology of adult snakes than about the ecology of juveniles, because young snakes are rarely encountered in the field. More vulnerable to predators, they adopt a cautious approach;

and they don't have to expose themselves for reproductive functions such as maturing sperm or accelerating the development of embryos. The most mysterious life-history phase, though, is the one before birth. Developing embryos are hidden away inside their eggs or inside the uterus of their mother, and for a long time were ignored by ecologists. Recent years have overthrown that neglect. We have learned that the ecological interactions of embryos play a vital role in snake biology.

The earliest phases of an individual's life, while it is still an embryo, are very sensitive to surrounding conditions. That's why pregnant women are encouraged to stop smoking and to stop drinking alcohol. Embryonic snakes are equally at the mercy of their environment.

Great Plains Rat Snake (*Pantherophis emoryi*) hatching from its egg. By the time it emerges from its egg, a snake has already been affected by its incubation environment in ways that can influence the animal's ecology and behaviour for the rest of its life. BILL LAMAR

Biologists have long regarded embryos as organisms-in-progress – little blobs of tissue gradually taking shape as they develop, but incapable of doing anything clever until they hatch out of the egg. We were wrong. Chinese scientist Weiguo Du and colleagues recently showed that the embryos of reptiles affect their own destinies by moving around within the egg. In a natural nest, the side of an egg closest to the sunlight-warmed soil is warmer than the other side of the same egg, furthest from that heat source. Faced with that opportunity to get warm, embryos of turtle, snake and lizard species move towards the hottest part of their egg. That warmth-seeking behaviour enables the embryo to develop faster, and in some kinds of turtles an embryo can even affect whether it develops into a male or a female. It's an extraordinary ability for such a tiny creature and emphasises how a small shift in incubation conditions can influence the rest of a reptile's life.

The first impetus for studying environmental effects on embryos came from a three-page paper that was published by Madeleine Charnier (1919–2002) in a small African journal in 1966. Born in France, Madeleine was 26 years old when she moved to Africa to join her brother, divorce her husband, and take up an academic job at the University of Dakar. She conducted some of the first detailed research on African lizards, and especially on the brightly coloured dragons called rainbow lizards that were common around the university campus. Embryonic development was one of her main interests, so she incubated many clutches of eggs – and serendipitously she discovered a remarkable result: eggs that developed under cool conditions produced daughters, whereas eggs that were kept warmer hatched into sons. Very few people read the paper and it was ignored – perhaps because it was written in French, or because its author was a Frenchwoman living in Africa, or because it was published in a low-profile local journal. It may have seemed too weird to be true. But in 1971, Claude Pieau discovered the same situation in a French tortoise, using larger sample sizes and a stronger experimental design, and published his results in a major journal. People began to look seriously for temperature-dependent sex determination in reptiles. Today, Madeleine's paper on sex determination in rainbow lizards ranks as one of the most highly cited zoology papers from the 1960s.

Examples began to accumulate, smashing the long-held assumption that an individual's sex always depends upon its genes. In most mammals, an individual with two X chromosomes is a female, whereas an individual with an X and a Y is a male. But reptiles are more complicated. Some turtle species have genetic sex determination, but in many others (as well as quite a few lizards, the Tuatara, all crocodiles and many turtles) the sex of an individual depends on the conditions that it experienced as an embryo. The same is true in at least one species of snake, and probably more. And sex isn't the only characteristic that is affected by developmental conditions.

The sex of an Inland Bearded Dragon (*Pogona vitticeps*) is usually determined by its sex chromosomes; but if the nest becomes too warm then high temperatures can over-ride the genetic instructions and reverse the young lizard's sex. JULES FARQUHAR

The ecology of embryos is easy to study in egg-laying species. We can incubate newly laid eggs in the lab, with some kept cool whereas their clutch-mates are kept warmer. Or some can be kept dry while others are kept moist. Or some can be kept at constant temperature and moisture, whereas others are exposed to fluctuations. We can track the effects of such manipulations by monitoring the growth rate of embryos; and we can even eavesdrop on their heartbeat rates without having to open up the egg. After that it's simply a matter of recording when those eggs hatch, and what kinds of youngsters emerge. How big are they, what sex, how active, how fast, how smart, and so forth? The results are clear. The conditions that an embryo experiences can affect the kind of animal that it turns into.

Mother knows best – usually

The sensitivity of embryonic development to external conditions places a heavy responsibility on a nesting female. Her choice of nest site and her timing of egg laying will affect not only the rate of development of her offspring, but also their size, shape and behaviour – which in turn will affect their chances of survival. That responsiveness has favoured careful nest-site choice. The best research on this topic blends laboratory-based incubation studies with detailed fieldwork, confirming that mothers choose sites that provide ideal conditions for the embryos. Timing matters as well; for example, swamp-dwelling Keelback snakes in tropical Australia nest only during the dry season, because wet soil is harmful to offspring development.

Keelbacks have another trick to identify ideal nesting sites as well. When she is ready to lay her first clutch of eggs, a female Keelback returns to the place where she hatched – that is, where her mother laid eggs. The fact that the female has survived to breed is evidence that the nest site where she developed is a good one, so it makes sense to use it again. Keelback matriarchs on the wall of Fogg Dam in tropical Australia pass on that knowledge about a good nest site to their daughters, who in turn pass it on to their own daughters. The end result is a long line of generations all using the same site, like landed gentry continuing to occupy the estate founded by their distant ancestors. All it takes is a gene that says 'when you first hatch, pay careful attention to where you are, and return there when it's time for you to breed.'

The Keelback (*Tropidonophis mairii*) is Australia's only representative of the natricine snakes, a widespread evolutionary lineage that dominates the snake fauna in many other parts of the world. Thanks to decades of painstaking research by Greg Brown, the Keelback now ranks as among the best-known snakes ecologically. JULES FARQUHAR

Biologists have explored the development and consequences of many different characteristics, but some of the best opportunities involve differences between the left side and right side of the body of an individual. The same genes control both sides of the body, so we might expect each side of the body to be a mirror image of the other. But that's not what happens. In practice, no organism is exactly symmetrical. Paired appendages are slightly different between right and left sides. Small differences in shape of the ears and length of the fingers in human beings show that development doesn't always proceed perfectly, especially if the embryo is exposed to challenging conditions.

Scale asymmetries are common in snakes. For example, hatchling snakes often exhibit a few incomplete ventral scales: half of a ventral shield (belly scale) on just one side of the body, rather than a full shield extending all the way across. X-rays of those scales reveal abnormalities in the skeleton. Usually, each ventral shield is associated with a pair of ribs. A crawling snake uses the edges of each belly scale as an anchor across rough ground as it moves, with muscles attached to the ribs pulling the snake along. But in asymmetric snakes, that orderly correspondence between belly shields and ribs breaks down.

Why focus on this kind of asymmetry? Because it provides a simple measure of long-term effects of embryonic experiences. A highly asymmetric adult body suggests that as an embryo, that individual encountered difficult incubation conditions. That link enables us to

By basking in sunlight, a pregnant Common Garter Snake (*Thamnophis sirtalis*) can ensure that her developing babies are kept at the best possible temperatures. NOAH K. FIELDS

use asymmetry as a time machine, enabling us to infer experiences during an individual's early life from its body measurements as an adult. There are two questions that we can ask. First, what causes asymmetries? And second, do asymmetries affect how an individual functions?

The first strong evidence on the causes of scale asymmetry came from a study on live-bearing snakes. In 2002, Chicago-based biologists Steve Arnold and Chuck Peterson kept pregnant female garter snakes under a range of thermal regimes in the laboratory, then scored scale asymmetry in their offspring. As you might have guessed, a mother's temperature during pregnancy affected the frequency of asymmetric scales in her babies. The best temperature (lowest number of scale abnormalities) was around 27°C (81°F) – which was also the average temperature selected by pregnant females in the wild. Lower or higher temperatures imposed developmental stress, increasing scale asymmetry.

Garter snakes are live bearers, so embryonic temperatures are controlled by how much time the mother spends basking in sunlight while she is pregnant. Egg-laying reptiles are at even more risk of developmental disruption, because the mother can't buffer climatic impacts on embryo temperatures. All she can do is find a suitable spot for a nest, then wander off and hope for the best. Sometimes, that's not good enough. In tropical Australia, tenacious field biologist Greg Brown incubated eggs from wild-caught Slaty-grey Snakes to explore the impacts of developmental conditions on hatchlings. Quiet, introverted and possessed of almost superhuman perserverance, Greg is a modern-day reincarnation of the pioneering American snake biologist Henry Fitch. From decades of work, Greg discovered that the main problem for embryos of the Slaty-grey Snake is being too hot. High-temperature incubation resulted in more scale asymmetry.

The reverse problem applies in colder climates. Swedish biologist Kristin Lowenborg showed that to find warm incubation sites in the chilly Swedish climate, European Grass Snakes exploit a smelly option: mounds of horse-droppings that farmhands pile up beside the stables. Decomposition inside the poo-pile creates warmth. But even so, grass snake eggs often develop at cooler temperatures than do the eggs of most other snakes. Do those low temperatures disrupt development? Yes, they do. Cooler poo-piles generate snakes with asymmetric belly-scales, reducing the crawling speed and stamina of those babies.

Does scale asymmetry affect a snake's life in other ways as well? American researcher and crossword guru Bob Mason and I looked at that question in the garter snake dens of Manitoba, where we had access to vast numbers of snakes. If you are measuring hundreds of snakes a day, it's easy to find a few with scale asymmetries. I put those asymmetric snakes aside, together with symmetric animals of the same sizes, and used them in standardised mating trials in outdoor cages. Sure enough, a male snake with asymmetric ventral shields was less able to obtain a mating; and if an asymmetric male did mate, he used the hemipenis on the side of the body opposite to that extra half-rib. Likely reflecting their lower ability to obtain matings, most scale-asymmetric males didn't even try very hard. Instead, they dispersed to the feeding grounds instead of staying around the den to seek mates. In short, a male snake's sex life was affected by the temperatures that his mother had selected while she was pregnant with him, years beforehand.

Although the effects of incubation temperature have been the most popular research theme, other factors are important as well. Eggs that develop in dry nests may be in trouble because the yolk dries up, so the hatchling can't resorb it and leaves those energy reserves behind when it emerges from its shell. But embryos have tricks to deal with that situation. Even a brief period of wet conditions enables a snake egg to store water inside it, for later use during dry conditions.

Australian Tiger Snakes (*Notechis scutatus*) are closely related to the ancestors of modern coral snakes. JULES FARQUHAR

Childhood experiences fashion the adult

Developmental plasticity doesn't just occur during the embryo stage. The habitat in which a young snake spends its first few months of life can affect the snake's later behaviour, in the same way as large prey can affect a Gaboon Viper's jaw size.

My debonair French colleague Fabien Aubret investigated the role of such flexibility in the evolution of sea snakes from land snakes. Rising sea levels may have been a key stimulus to that transition. During warmer-than-usual climatic periods, melting glaciers caused sea levels to rise, transforming coastal hills into isolated islands. A snake on such an island had few feeding opportunities on its ever-shrinking island, whereas fish were abundant in tidal pools. Through time, individual snakes that exploited that new opportunity prospered, leaving more descendants than individuals that stubbornly clung to their ancestral habitat. That is, land snakes evolved into sea snakes.

It's an interesting idea, but how would it work out in practice? Fabien spent several years in Australia working with me on that question. The ideal species with which to explore the scenario was the Australian Tiger Snake, a venomous land-dweller closely related to sea snakes. Conveniently, Tiger Snakes produce large litters of small offspring – beefing up sample sizes and enabling us to compare siblings in our experiments. But the downside of using baby Tiger Snakes was that they are deadly, and I didn't like the idea of having hundreds of highly venomous baby snakes at the university. Newborn snakes are superb escape artists, and even a single escapee might cause catastrophe on a university campus. Fortunately, the Australian Reptile Park offered to house the toxic youngsters for us.

Fabien set up three types of tanks. One had mostly dry ground, one had mostly tree branches, and one was filled with water except for a few dry spots. That forced the young snakes to spend most of their time either crawling (in the dry tank) or climbing (in the tree-branch tank) or swimming (in the flooded tank). Fab put siblings into each type of tank, to control for any differences among litters. Sure enough, testing 11 months later showed that the type of cage had a strong influence on two important characteristics of the young snakes. First, practice makes perfect – snakes from dry-land tanks were the fastest crawlers, branch-tank snakes were the best climbers, and water-tank snakes were the fastest swimmers. Second, the young snakes preferred the habitat in which they had been raised. When given a choice, the water-tank snakes headed for the water whereas the land-tank snakes headed for dry land. That kind of flexibility supports the scenario I outlined above. Snakes on a shrinking island would not only have become more adept at swimming, but also would have spent more and more time in the water. Hey presto, that flexibility would assist natural selection to turn land-snakes into sea snakes.

You are what you eat

The habitat in which a snake grows up is only one of many environmental factors that affect its later life. The most obvious other factor is food supply: a snake that eats more not only grows faster and matures sooner, but it may change its approach to life. A remarkable study on captive European Common Lizards in France by Manuel Massot and Pedro Aragon reported that a single hearty meal of caterpillars given to a newborn lizard, just two days into its life, transforms the animal's subsequent existence. For example, lizards that are fed as babies stay close to home for the next two years rather than dispersing further afield.

Surprisingly, our best data on this topic for snakes come from a field study rather than laboratory work. On a tropical floodplain in Australia, some Water Pythons hatch out in years when newborn native rats are abundant, offering easy prey. In other years, the rats stop breeding before the pythons hatch, and a young snake ekes out a precarious living. Thomas Madsen and I showed that a python born into a world of abundant furry meals takes an optimistic approach in later life, allocating most of its surplus energy to growth. In contrast, a python born in a bad year is more cautious, laying down fat reserves rather than growing.

As field studies of snakes accumulated, ecologists began to realise how much rates of growth and reproduction vary from year to year, even in the same population. The snakes are fat, healthy and pregnant in some years, and emaciated and non-pregnant in others. For many wild snakes, life oscillates between feast and famine. It doesn't require a genius to identify the most likely reason for those fluctuations. More food is available in some years than in others.

That scenario plays out in different ways in different ecosystems. In temperate-zone North America, annual fluctuations in rodent abundance drive reproductive output in rattlesnakes. Ditto for vipers in the forests of France. In tropical Australia the timing of monsoonal rainfall each year affects the abundance of fishes, frogs and native rats; and as a result, determines the body condition and reproductive output of Arafura File Snakes that feed on those fishes, Keelbacks that feed on those frogs, and Water Pythons that feed on those rats.

But correlations between weather, prey abundance and snake characteristics don't actually demonstrate that a snake's food intake affects its biology. Perhaps good years for prey abundance are also 'good' in other (unmeasured) ways that affect snakes? To understand the mechanisms involved, American biologists Rich Seigel and Neil Ford conducted landmark studies with captive garter snakes, looking at how food supply affects a snake's growth and development. Before long, the list of species studied and topics examined grew rapidly.

As expected from the field data – and from common sense – more food translates into fatter, faster-growing snakes that are more likely to reproduce. But controlled lab experiments told us a lot more. For example, in *Homo sapiens* nutrients from the food eaten by a pregnant woman can be transferred to the developing foetus. Poor maternal nutrition has severe consequences for the baby. But in live-bearing snakes, few nutrients are transported across the placenta. Maternal starvation during pregnancy is bad news for the mother – she will be emaciated after giving birth and may die as a result – but the babies are unaffected. At the other extreme, high rates of feeding during pregnancy don't benefit the babies, but they result in a plump and healthy mother who is soon ready to breed again. A female's feeding rate in the year *before* she reproduces has different effects. Depending on the species, she may use extra food to increase the number of offspring that she produces, or the size of those offspring.

That lab work not only showed that variation in feeding rates can drive variation in snake biology. It also showed just how little food a snake needs to survive. Early snake keepers had already noticed the remarkable ability of snakes to withstand prolonged starvation – for example, in 1896 Englishman Arthur Stradling commented: "Of all the phenomena pertaining to a snake's life-routine, those incidental to its dietetic peculiarities are perhaps the most striking: if there be one thing more remarkable than the way it eats it is the way in which it doesn't eat." And that anorexia wasn't for lack of trying on Stradling's part; he devoted much of his life to developing better ways to keep snakes in captivity.

By switching off growth and reproduction, a starving snake scales back its metabolic rate to stay alive until the good times return. One of the tricks a snake employs between meals is to downsize any internal organ systems that aren't being used. For example, it's a waste of energy to maintain a thick lining to your stomach if you aren't likely to find another prey item for weeks or months. Far better to let your stomach lining shrink to almost nothing, and kickstart it again only after you find food. Likewise for the reproductive tract; female snakes that skip reproduction for a year or two don't waste energy maintaining a large muscular oviduct during that period of celibacy. In the wild, snakes hit the 'pause' button during the tough times, then leap back out of suspended animation as soon as the good times return. Modern biologists are using sophisticated equipment to explore the remarkable energy efficiency of snakes.

Social snakes

Looking into the eyes of snake is like gazing at an alien life form. Lidless, unblinking, and – especially for large and regal species – aloof. It's easy to imagine our fellow mammals having a social dimension to their existence, but it's difficult to imagine snakes cuddling up with each other. As large warm-blooded animals, we tend to write off small cold-blooded animals as stupid. Snakes also do things in slow motion, remaining immobile for hours; and they are shy and difficult to observe. In the opinion of many biologists, then, snakes rank as among the least social kinds of animals. But are snakes really solitary and asocial?

Frustrated by the refusal of captive snakes to feed, many early snake keepers resorted to force-feeding. In this image from the Australian Reptile Park, renowned pioneer Eric Worrell is forcing minced meat into a King Cobra (*Ophiophagus hannah*).

Ironically, social behaviour was the focus of some of the first integrated lab and field experimental work on snakes. In 1936, two researchers from the American Museum of Natural History described how DeKay's Brown Snakes – small harmless snakes generally found hiding beneath rocks – were found in aggregations in the field, year-round, as well as in captivity; and that gathering together in tight clumps benefitted the snakes by reducing their rates of evaporative water loss. But the authors went much further, conducting extensive experiments to identify the sense organs used for aggregation. They did this by blocking the nostrils or eyes of captive snakes, or surgically removing the tongue-tips, or painting snakes different colours, or adding mirrors to change visual cues and so forth. To see if chemical cues came from the snake's skin or its vent, they taped up the cloaca of some animals. To extend their insights to trail-following, they experimentally manipulated chemical cues to work out which kinds of information were used by a snake following the trail of another snake, or a trail scented with prey chemicals. That paper by Harry John Clausen and Gladwyn Kingsley Noble was so far ahead of the field that reading it today invokes a sense of awe – although some of the treatments employed in the 1930s are repugnant to modern sensibilities.

Clausen and Noble's work was largely ignored by subsequent workers. In retrospect, snake ecologists have asked too little of their organisms. We didn't look for complex social systems because we assumed that snakes were 'simple'. That was foolish. Snakes are limbless lizards, and many lizards are social beings. In the highlands west of Sydney, Black Rock Skinks live in family groups, with parents protecting their kids from homicidal neighbours. In the arid grasslands north of Adelaide, armour-plated Shingleback Skinks are monogamous throughout their decades-long lives.

But Clausen and Noble's pioneering efforts were not entirely ignored. The myth of asocial snakes was challenged by Oklahoma herpetologist Charles Carpenter (1921–2016), who placed captive snakes together and watched them interact. In the 1970s, Carpenter took aim at the prevailing view that snakes live solitary lives. Charles argued instead that snakes communicate and interact with each other. A tidal wave of subsequent research showed that he was correct, and we now have a far more nuanced view of social interactions among these legless reptiles.

For most snake species, though, we still have little behavioural information from the field. That applies even to spectacular behaviours such as male-male combat bouts, where intertwined rivals raise their forebodies off the ground and seek to topple their opponent. Most records of male-male combat are brief observations, these days accompanied by photographs because mobile-phone cameras are so common and wrestling snakes allow close approach before fleeing. Nonetheless, there are still many widespread and abundant species in which male combat is expected (based on related species, and larger body sizes in males than in females) but has never

It's common for fieldworkers to find snakes together. Usually we don't know why this happens, as in these two Eastern Racers (*Coluber constrictor*). NOAH K. FIELDS

The distinctive chin-rubbing behaviour of the amorous male reveals that these two Puff Adders (*Bitis arietans*) are sharing a romantic moment. XAVIER GLAUDUS

been reported. The same situation applies with parental care. It's difficult to find a snake nest in the wild, let alone to document nest guarding by the parents.

For most snake species in the wild, we either have NO observations of natural behaviours, or a tiny number of anecdotes. As a typical example, the only description that I could find of male-male combat in Forest Night Adders is hidden within a 'popular' magazine article written by the indefatigable Arthur Loveridge (1891–1980). Welsh-born Loveridge emigrated to Kenya at 25 years of age, to take up a position as a museum curator in Nairobi. But the World War I broke out soon afterwards, so Loveridge joined the East Africa Mounted Rifles and went to war. He managed to combine cavalry duties with snake-collecting, survived the war, and later returned to museum work at Harvard University in the USA. But Africa still called to him, so he made several more collecting trips there – and wrote a series of entertaining books about his adventures, with titles like *Many Happy Days I've Squandered* and *Tomorrow's a Holiday*. His joy in fieldwork is inspirational. One typical anecdote involves his attempt to get his hands on a collection of preserved snakes that soldiers had seen in a farm close to the frontline of battle. To look for those specimens, Loveridge hid in a truck filled with soldiers – a decoy designed to attract an attack from the enemy – to reach the rumoured treasure trove of preserved snakes. But sadly, the house had been burned down by the time that Loveridge arrived.

Loveridge's report about male-male combat in Forest Night Adders in 1940 runs as follows: "Next day our 'boy' Zachio, engaged in setting the table, was bringing something from the kitchen (a fire in the open) when he jumped, yelled 'snakes' and made a dash for the tent. Snatching up my snake-stick, I ran back along the narrow path, freshly made through a luxuriant growth of vegetation. Thirty feet from our tent I caught sight of two velvety-green night adders, which had been scared into the grass by Zachio's appearance and were now returning. The anterior third of each was raised high, and so flattened that for a second I thought they were young cobras. They were almost intertwined, their lower portions so close together that I pinned both down with my T-ended stick. At this one reptile began to savagely bite the other's neck, enabling me to seize both together with the forceps. In this way I carried them back to the lethal tin in which some hundreds of snakes were destined to pass their last moments. 'A courtship performance', thought I, but subsequently, on examining the two beautiful creatures, found both were males; so it was nothing but a fight after all – the flattened necks an attempt at intimidation!"

Prolonged associations between female pit vipers and their newborn offspring suggest maternal care, but the details remain sketchy. This image shows an American Copperhead (*Agkistrodon contortrix*) and her babies. NOAH K. FIELDS

Many behavioural observations of captive snakes are based on just a few individuals, because the work is done in zoo collections or private homes where space prohibits large numbers. Even so, some of those results are fascinating, and hint at sophisticated social systems. For example, French snake keeper Cornelius DeHaan reported that captive 'sand snakes' (subfamily Psammophiinae) rub themselves – as well as other snakes, and even their territories – with special secretions from a gland near the nose. According to Cornelius, those chemical signals are the basis for a complex social system – different from anything yet reported in other snakes.

Recent years have seen a new generation of snake researchers begin studies on snake sociality, using experimental methods to shine a light on behaviours unnoticed by earlier workers. For example, American biologist Rulon Clark obtained three litters of Timber Rattlesnakes, raised the offspring separately for more than two years, then placed groups of snakes together in open-topped cages where the snakes were free to select their own resting-sites. Males either didn't recognise their brothers and sisters, or they didn't care. But female rattlers preferred to stay close to their sisters, whom they recognised (presumably by scent) despite having spent their lives apart. Often, sisters were found in physical contact with each other. That single well-designed experiment opened our eyes to the sophisticated social capabilities of snakes. Field studies have lagged behind, but the situation is changing.

The assumption that snakes are antisocial loners has come under strong challenge from studies that look at the simple issue of what snakes are found together. In the lab, American researcher Morgan Skinner found that some individual garter snakes prefer each other's company – similar to Rulon Clark's study with rattlers. But does this happen in nature as well? Fortunately, a government department in Ontario, Canada, had funded Megan Hazell to check for effects of road construction on a population of Butler's Garter Snakes. By looking under rocks, the researchers had recorded locations of more than 3,000 individuals over 12 years. Sure enough, when Morgan and Megan analysed those data, they found a strong pattern. Groups of snakes were consistently found together, suggesting that they like each other's company. Female snakes were far more social than males, with many of the groups (of up to 46 snakes) centred around older females.

Patterns of association between individuals hint at long-term social bonds. This image shows Baird's Rat Snakes (*Pantherophis bairdi*) sharing a shelter-site. NOAH K. FIELDS

What turns a snake into a social being rather than an antisocial loner? In one intriguing study, my French collaborator Fabien Aubret showed that hatchlings from eggs of Viperine Snakes that are incubated singly in the lab produce less 'social' hatchlings than do eggs that are incubated in a group (as would occur in nature). The young snakes from isolated eggs are very active, but less likely to cuddle up to another snake.

The flip-side of sociality is aggression. Zookeepers in South Africa told me that pairs of huge Snouted Cobras would vigorously defend their territories (and thus, cages) against other members of the same species. I was sceptical, so they threw a large male into a cage containing a pair of these snakes – and within a few minutes the three snakes were engaged in a dramatic struggle, biting as well as wrestling each other. The chaos continued until the intruder was evicted. Perhaps such behaviour is rare – but I note an interesting statement about Indian Cobras by the famed expert Albert Günther (1830–1914), in his 1864 book *Reptiles of British India* (p. 340): "This snake …. will live in captivity for years. Two may be well kept together; and it appears as if they felt some attachment for each other, for when they are excited by having food brought into their cage, or by some other incident, they will frequently fight each other, raising the anterior part of the body, spreading the hood, and darting as if to bite, but always carefully avoiding to wound. When, however, a third individual or any other snake is brought into the same cage, they attack and kill it." That sounds like the behaviour I saw at the Transvaal Snake Park, in a different kind of cobra in a far-distant country and more than a century later.

Other investigators have explored interactions between species. In 2014, American researcher Michael Edgehouse and his colleagues reported that one species of garter snake actively drives another away from preferred foraging habitats inside large outdoor enclosures. I don't know of any other examples of this kind of aggression, but that may be because nobody has looked for it.

How smart are snakes?

Early writers on snakes saw the reptiles as stupid. For example, South African dentist-turned-herpetologist Walter Rose drily commented in 1962 that "the exhortation to be 'wise as serpents' does not demand any high standard, for, although snakes are somewhat higher than fish in general development, they are little if any higher in intelligence." Even zealous supporters of snakes were dismissive of their intellect. In 1895, English physican Arthur Stradling wrote that "their brain-power is so limited that the marvel is how they have ever managed to survive" and "the intelligence of the whole of ophidia is so low that no kind of training or education is possible." Nonetheless, Stradling grudgingly admitted that a few species of snakes (such as the King Cobra) might display glimmers of intelligence.

In 1899, Thai-based expatriate biologist Stanley Smyth Flower (1871–1946) described bockadams (Asian water snakes) as having "more intelligence than most snakes and appreciated being petted: when I came to the tank in which they were kept they would often of their own accord come to me and climb up my arm and remain round my neck or curled up in a pocket sometimes for hours till replaced in the tank, while they resented being touched by anyone else, which was remarkable, for other snakes I have kept as pets never objected to being picked up by anyone (who was used to handling snakes)." In 1888, Guiana-based John Joseph Quelch (b.1854) described how a 2.5-metre (8-ft) anaconda learned the best place in a room to hide while its cage was being cleaned, and that it remembered the location of that hidey-hole for at least four months.

In 1882, American naturalist H.A. Brons suggested that garter snakes hunting fish in a drying pool were "all acting in concert", implying a level of co-operative organisation unlike anything ever described for snakes. Was it just a figment of Brons's over-active imagination? Perhaps not. In 2004, Indian biologist Sandeep Sharma described how eight Checkered Keelbacks gathered around a school of small fish and tightened the circle until the fish began jumping into the air, at which time they were seized by the snakes. The manoeuvre was repeated three times, suggesting it was no accident. And in 2023, the jet-setting Sri Lankan ecologist Ruchira Somaweera and his colleagues described pack-hunting groups of Erabu Sea Kraits in deep water off Lombok Island in Indonesia. The leading snakes entered coralline crevices and flushed out fishes, providing a meal for their followers.

Snakes have small heads, and thus small brains, compared to the size of their bodies. As a result, a snake's brain is only about half the size of that of a lizard of the same body mass. Does this mean that snakes are stupid? Sadly, it is more difficult to evaluate an animal's intelligence than to measure its size or speed.

To assess learning, the investigator presents a stimulus associated with either punishment or reward to see if the animal can associate the stimulus with the consequence. One of the simplest tests involves habituation: that is, the ability of an animal to learn that some frightening stimulus is in fact harmless, so they can afford to ignore it. Snakes are capable of that kind of learning. A recently captured snake attempts to flee or retaliate when it is handled, but it soon learns that those responses are futile and unneccessary. Captive rattlesnakes stop rattling when the lid of their cage is opened. In garter snakes and Cottonmouth Moccasins, an individual's species and sex and age affect how quickly it habituates to handling. Corn Snakes, rat snakes and cottonmouths rapidly learn the location of shelter items within their cages, whereas Spotted Pythons do not. Juvenile cottonmouths can learn to associate a red card with the location of food, and Burmese Pythons can learn to push a response key to open a door and obtain a reward. So some snakes definitely *can* learn some things, but the details remain mysterious.

Some of the most popular 'pet' species remain poorly known in the wild. For example, Corn Snakes (*Pantherophis guttatus*) are one of the most frequently kept 'pet' snakes, but we know very little about their ecology in the field. BILL LAMAR

One problem with this field of research, like many others, is that positive results are more interesting than negative ones. As a result, scientists are more likely to publish a paper about successful learning trials than unsuccessful ones. If a researcher finds out that their pet serpents are dumb as doorbells, the resulting dataset may languish in laboratory notebooks and never be transformed into a published paper. It's not very interesting to describe something that didn't happen.

My own scientific forays into learning in snakes have been frustrating. For example, my team discovered that many Australian predators rapidly learn to avoid toxic Cane Toads as food. A marsupial, crocodile or frog that eats a small toad becomes nauseous and avoids toads as prey thereafter. Anybody who has eaten a sickness-inducing meal can relate to that effect. Garter snakes can learn taste aversion like this, but our attempts with Aussie serpents were a dismal failure. The snakes never realised that toxic toads were a poor dietary choice. I can see the ghost of Arthur Stradling sadly shaking his head and saying: "I told you so; snakes are stupid."

Snakes without fathers

One advantage of keeping a snake in a cage for a long time is that every once in a while, the animal does something that knocks your socks off. Something ludicrously unexpected. You can't plan for that to happen, but if you spend enough time with an animal it may reveal a secret that astonishes you. So it was with 'virgin birth', which is technically called 'parthenogenesis'.

In most species of animals, there are two sexes. Indeed, the need for both males and females is so obvious that it's difficult to imagine any other way of functioning. However, a substantial number of reptiles and amphibians (and a few birds and fishes) have found that other way.

In 1974, legendary American taxonomist Sam McDowell (1928–2014) was examining blind snakes. Sam was a tall lean man who reminded me of Abraham Lincoln. Often chewing on the stub of an unlit cigar, he was a groundbreaking figure in snake classification in the days before the genetics revolution. Sam scrutinised snakes in intricate detail, dissecting them to find arcane features – such as muscle attachments to bones – that clarified evolutionary connections between groups. One of the most puzzling groups was the blind snakes, small earthworm-like burrowers whose external characteristics varied little across species. In the 1960s, New Zealand herpetologist and wildlife tour guide Joan Robb (1921–2017) realised that the hemipenis of males could be used to identify natural groupings. She spent years dissecting these tiny serpents and drawing detailed diagrams of their genitals.

Joan's approach revolutionised blind snake classification, but Sam hit a snag when he tried to apply it to a tiny blind snake species from South-East Asia. The Brahminy Blind Snake is also called the Flowerpot Snake, because it has been spread across the world by people transporting flowerpots with enough soil for a threadlike snake to be carried along. Sam dissected 144 of these tiny snakes – no easy feat – but was unable to describe the genitals of the males because there *were* no males. Every Brahminy Blind Snake is a female. When she matures, she lays eggs that contain genetic copies of herself – clones. That trick has helped the Brahminy Blind Snake to spread widely. It takes only one pioneer snake to found a new dynasty.

Several species of lizards have abandoned the need for males, so Sam's discovery of virgin birth in blind snakes was not too surprising. But the next step was remarkable. In 1997, American zookeepers Jean Dubach, Agatha Sajewicz and Ray Pawley reported that a long-term captive Arafura File Snake gave birth to two litters of offspring over a three-year period. The remarkable aspect here was that this is an Australian species, and the female in question had been transferred to an American zoo (in Illinois) shortly after she was born. In the five or more years between birth and breeding, she had never even seen a male of her own species. The closest potential mate was thousands of kilometres away. The babies were almost identical genetically to their mother, confirming that this was a case of clonal reproduction.

Female snakes generally rely on mating to provide sperm for the production of offspring – but if a female has no access to a male she may be able to go ahead and produce offspring anyway. That insight has come from studies on long-term captives, including species that are impossible to study in the field such as these Jameson's Mambas (*Dendroaspis jamesoni*), so we can obtain captivity-sourced data from a wider variety of species. PIXABAY

Also in 1997, another American biologist, Gordie Schuett, described virgin birth in rattlesnakes and garter snakes. Before long, cases accumulated for many types of snakes. Earlier studies had recorded females producing offspring after a long period without access to males – but had attributed that situation to long-term storage of sperm inside the female's reproductive tract (that is, her oviduct). The mounting evidence from genetic analyses confirmed that female snakes of normally sexual species can switch to virgin birth if no males are available. It happens in both egg-laying and live-bearing species. These fatherless offspring are all females in 'primitive' snakes such as boas and pythons, but all males in 'advanced' rattlesnakes and garter snakes. Whether or not parthenogenesis is a viable reproductive tactic remains unclear, because it is generally associated with birth defects. Still, a few offspring may be better than nothing. The list of species capable of facultative parthenogenesis continues to grow, and now includes fishes, crocodiles and birds.

Without studies of long-term captive snakes, facultative parthenogenesis would never have been discovered.

IN THEIR OWN WORDS

Today, when captive snakes are commonplace, it is difficult to imagine the horror that people once felt for a snake – any snake. Those feelings were so intense that anyone who contemplated keeping a snake in a cage was likely to be regarded as an idiot or a psychotic:

"So general is the repugnance of mankind to the animals composing these classes, that their study has been overlooked, and they have usually been considered as beings which it was not only necessary but meritorious to destroy. A part of this vulgar prejudice is derived from education, and perhaps some of it may originate from the fact that several of them are furnished with venomous fangs, capable of causing intolerable sufferings and death. To the naturalist and physiologist, however; to those who study nature through her various modification of form and structure, they present some of the most interesting objects of contemplation. Their utility, either in diminishing various noxious animals, or in furnishing food themselves to others, has been lost sight of; and because they were cold to the touch, with a naked slimy skin without hair or feathers, they have been considered as loathsome and hideous, although their structure displays as much of the omnipotence and care of the Creator as can be seen in those which are considered to be the most gorgeous and beautiful of his animated beings." JAMES E. DEKAY, 1842

The admiration of snakes is a key motivation for many early writers, but they generally suppress their enthusiasm. When it comes time to describe colours, however, that fervour shines through:

"It is not possible to lay down fixed principles on the item of colours in ophidians. Sometimes uniform and dull, sometimes shining with a brilliancy equal to that of precious stones, their tints are infinitely varied, and very differently disposed, not only in the various races, but often also in species of the same genus… Many climbing serpents, for example, present a livery of uniform green, absolutely resembling that of the leaves; while others ... in this respect resemble small naked branches; and, lastly, in the *Dipsas*, the system of colouring simulates the old stem of a tree covered with fine and luxuriant mosses. The serpents which frequent fresh water are generally remarked for their sombre and uniform tints; the green, the yellow and the blue colours which ornament the bodies of sea-serpents confound them with the waves in the vast ocean. The inhabitants of the desert ... are scarcely distinguishable from the sand, so uniformly spread over those dismal wastes; other snakes, the burrowers, are recognisable by their beautiful shining, strongly iridescent colours, among which red is predominant on the lower parts. A multitude of other ophidians present colours which sometimes imitate the dusky brown of a boggy soil, marshy, or shaded by thick forests, sometimes the green of herbs, sometimes the diversified tints of places clothed with mosses and lichens; and some have their livery adorned with the most brilliant hues, in rivalry of the splendours of the flowers of a tropical vegetation." HERMANN SCHLEGEL, 1837

"The African viper and her young one baffle the artist's palette in their prismatic hues." CATHERINE COOPER HOPLEY, 1882

Setting up facilities for long-term maintenance of snakes in captivity was a major logistical challenge, but that didn't stop people from planning how it might be done:

"The best habitation for snakes would doubtless be a verandah fenced to a sufficient height with wire gauze ... provided with water and shrubs sufficiently to gratify the desire for coolness and shade. Such a serpentarium would enable interesting observations to be made on the habits of snakes. The floor should be strewn with sand; it would not often require renewal owing to the inoffensive nature of the uric acid excreta of snakes ... (Snake's dung was, some years ago, of value; about three shillings per lb. was the price, if I remember right; it was used as a source of uric acid for the manufacture of mitrexide, a brilliant purple dye. This was shortly before the discovery of the aniline dyes) ... Observations regarding the casting of skin and teeth, the laying, incubation and hatching of eggs, the oviparous or ovoviviparous nature of various snakes are very much needed." EDWARD NICHOLSON, 1874

Diamond Pythons (*Morelia spilota*) exploit the rich food supplies of suburban gardens in south-eastern Australia to thrive even in large cities such as Sydney. ALANA DE LAIVE

PART 4

SNAKE RESEARCH IN THE FIELD

One theme of this book is that our understanding of any topic develops sporadically. There are periods of steady but slow accumulation of information, punctuated by brief upheavals when a breakthrough identifies new questions, new insights and new perspectives.

The stimulus for that new understanding can be a new way of thinking, or a new form of analysis, or even just a new study system. But the most powerful catalyst for a rethink is a new method. Armed with that state-of-the-art tool, researchers can investigate previously inaccessible topics. In the case of snake ecology, the first revolution was the application of mark-recapture methods by pioneering researchers such as Henry Fitch in Kansas and Hajime Fukada in Kyoto. The techniques weren't especially innovative, although Henry's use of traps for research rather than snake control was new. The breakthrough was to demonstrate the rewards that can be reaped from fieldwork on snake ecology if you are prepared to put enough time and effort into it.

The next revolution was technological. The ideal way to understand the day-to-day life of a snake would be to follow it as it goes about its business. But that's a formidable challenge. Even if you manage to find and catch your snake, you probably won't see it again after you release it. Long-term mark-recapture programs overcome that problem with sheer dogged persistence, but the pioneers of snake ecology must have yearned for a magic new technology that could enable them to relocate snakes.

When that technology appeared, it transformed the field. In the 1960s and 1970s, the electronics revolution was creating new gadgets that spawned new possibilities. For snake biologists, the key innovation was radio telemetry. The earliest radio transmitters had been large, clunky and short-range – but soon, engineers were producing powerful miniature versions. The ***beep-beep-beep*** of a telemetry signal could reveal the location of a snake even when the animal was hidden within its burrow or among the dense foliage of a rainforest tree.

Chapter 7

Using radio transmitters to pry into the snake's private life

Scientists have learned a great deal by catching snakes and recording their size, sex, feeding habits and so forth. But to really understand an animal's biology, a snapshot isn't enough: you need to monitor an individual as it moves about its natural habitat. That is a huge challenge: how can you stay in touch with a creature that is usually hidden away? By solving that challenge, radio telemetry revolutionised snake research.

Attaching a transmitter to an elongate animal

Wildlife biologists used transmitters on other kinds of animals long before applying them to snakes. That transition required not only miniaturisation, but also a way to attach the unit to a snake. A transmitter can be affixed to a collar around the neck of a deer or a lion, but that won't work with a snake. A loose collar falls off; and a tight collar prevents the snake from swallowing a large meal. A transmitter attached to the outside of the body creates a bump that prevents the snake from fitting into its rocky crevice and risks entanglement. The best option is to put the unit inside the snake's body.

The easiest way to get a transmitter inside a snake is to lubricate the unit with cooking oil, open the snake's mouth, and slide the electronic gadget down into the stomach. If the telemeter is the right size, it will lodge there. Early investigators also tied heavy nylon thread around the snake's forebody to prevent regurgitation. Forcing the transmitter down a snake's throat is more difficult if the snake is venomous – an oil-lubricated transmitter is slippery and the snake's fangs are dangerously close to your fingers as you push the unit down. And, as you've guessed from the nylon-thread method, some snakes regurgitate the unit – or, if it's small enough, pass it all the way through the gut and out the other end.

Peter Harlow (left) and the author carefully force-feeding a radio transmitter to a Red-bellied Black Snake (*Pseudechis porphyriacus*). Working with venomous snakes requires intense concentration! TERRI SHINE

During fieldwork with Australian snakes, my research assistant Pete Harlow devised a method that was less stressful than force-feeding a transmitter to a snake. We persuaded free-ranging snakes to swallow the transmitter voluntarily. To do so, we put transmitters inside dead mice and dangled those mice in front of foraging snakes. As their name suggests, Red-bellied Black Snakes are jet-black above and scarlet on their sides and bellies. They are the Australian equivalent of the large cobras of Africa and Asia. I only had a few weeks for the study, so I needed to get transmitters inside the snakes without disturbing them. Surgery was out; recovery would take far too long. So instead, we fed transmitters to the snakes.

Black snakes are voracious. We killed and eviscerated white mice, inserted transmitters into their body cavities, stitched them up, and then I dangled an electronically enhanced rodent in front of the first snake I found. The snake didn't hesitate, and within a few minutes the transmitter was safely inside its stomach, where it lodged until I gently palpated it back out a week later. And the method worked just as well with every other snake we found. 'Snake-

By inserting a radio transmitter inside a freshly killed mouse, then placing the mouse near a hungry snake, we convinced free-ranging Red-bellied Black Snakes (*Pseudechis porphyriacus*) to swallow the unit. Compared to force-feeding transmitters to snakes, it was a lot less stressful both for us and for the snake. TERRI SHINE fishing' was so much fun we kept doing it even after we had used up all of our transmitters.

For long-term studies, a better option is surgery. Make an incision in the snake's side, insert the unit, and sew up the hole you made. But to do that, you need to put the snake to sleep. That requires anaesthesia. The earliest studies used cold to immobilise the reptilian patient. As its body temperature drops, a snake loses the ability to move around and sinks into unconsciousness. As a graduate student, I used a quintessential Aussie approach to snake anaesthesia, by placing chilled cans of beer around the scaly patient. Within a few minutes the snakes were immobile and unresponsive to my scalpel.

Cooling down to the point of unconsciousness sounds awful to a human being, because we function at a high internal temperature. Throw us into a snowdrift and we begin to shiver – that is, our muscles contract to generate heat. We fight the cold with every weapon at our disposal. But a snake is different. It functions over a wide range of temperatures. For many snakes, cooling down is a normal part of life. Every afternoon, the snake moves out of the sunlight and retreats to a cool safe shelter. A drop in internal temperature doesn't ring any alarm bells, nor is it painful. Organ systems just slow down. Before long the animal's metabolism is ticking over slowly, not using much energy, to leap back into action when sunlight reappears the next morning. In effect, a cold snake is in suspended animation. That slowdown is a natural part of its daily cycle.

As I discussed earlier with respect to euthanasia (killing), cold-based anaesthesia was unpopular with the ethics committees that sprang up in the 1990s to oversee university research. Forbidden to anaesthetise their animals with low temperature, snake biologists turned to drugs. For a while we used ketamine, known as 'Special K' in the party-drug scene. Once popular for anaesthesia of humans during medical procedures, ketamine fell out of favour when patients reported having nightmares under the drug's influence. We don't know if snakes also experience nightmares, but ketamine has another problem as well – it renders a patient unconscious for many hours. Ideally, you want to anaesthetise your reptilian subject for just long enough to insert the transmitter.

In time, inhaled gases replaced injectables. The simplest approach was to put the snake inside a plastic bag containing anaesthetic-soaked cotton wool, but it was difficult to get the dose right. A gas-mixing machine designed for cats and dogs was a better option, stimulating collaboration between reptile researchers and veterinary surgeons.

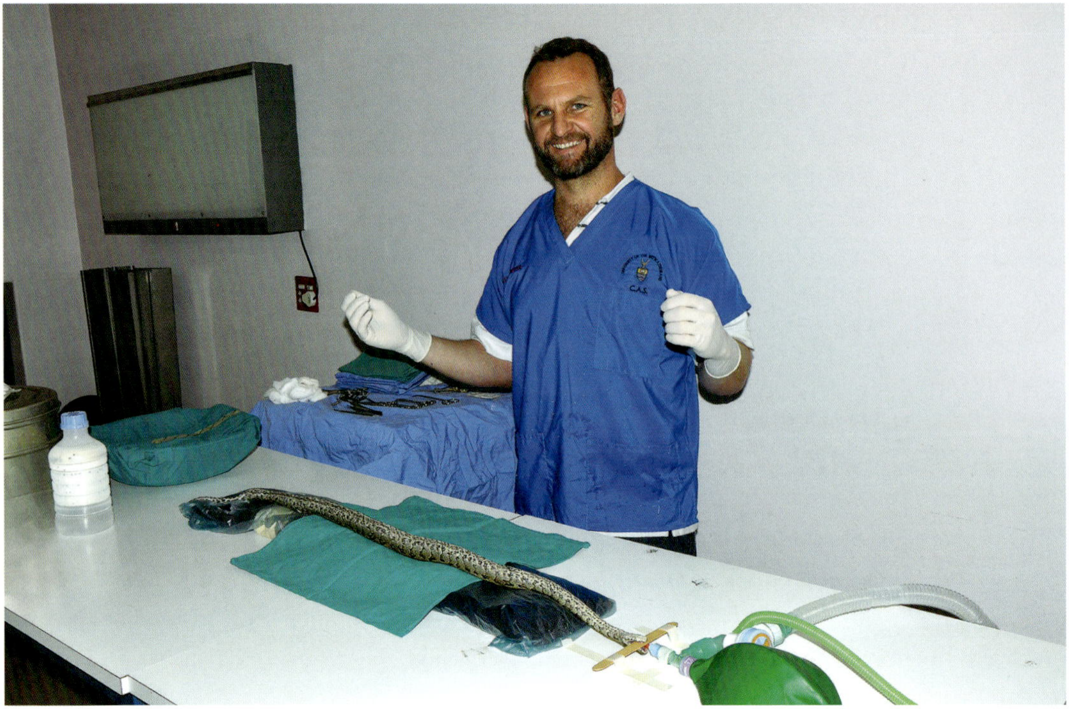

In the early days of telemetry research, scientists performed their own surgeries. Increasingly, though, that work is now performed by professional veterinary surgeons such as Leith Myer, here seen implanting a transmitter into a young African Rock Python (*Python natalensis*). GRAHAM ALEXANDER

Anaesthesia of snakes requires patience, because reptiles work on their own timeline. Most mammals and birds take several breaths a minute, but snakes can delay their next breath for much longer. That ability is partly due to the snake's low metabolic rate: it's an energy miser, so can survive on a single lungful of oxygen for far longer than we could. But also, snakes have a lot of practice in holding their breaths. For example, they often find themselves in tight underground tunnels with little airflow. Or laying in ambush for hours, when the bodily expansion due to a deep breath would reveal their position to wary prey. Or swallowing a prey item so large that it blocks their mouth for an hour or more, obstructing the airway. Snakes extrude their windpipes snorkel-like from the mouth while swallowing big meals, to obtain air – but regardless, the life of a snake often involves long periods between successive breaths. Sea snakes routinely stay underwater for 30 minutes. If a snake detects anaesthetic gas in the air, it may decide to stop breathing until the smell goes away. As a result, surgery on snakes requires patience.

The alliance between veterinary practitioners and snake researchers had many positives – notably, vets are experts at suturing thin membranes and fragile skin. But there are difficulties as well. I attended one conference talk where vets had implanted transmitters in snakes, and almost all of the snakes died within a few months after they were released. The reason for that mortality was that the vets had routinely injected a mega-dose of antibiotics after surgery. Those antibiotics help to fight post-operative infection in cats and dogs, but the slow metabolic rates of snakes meant that the toxic drugs stayed in the snake's system for months, and eventually destroyed their kidneys. Snakes are very different from mammals and need different techniques.

The same kind of misunderstanding often arises post-operatively, when vets want to keep the legless patient in a cage for a few days 'to allow it to recover before it is released'. That's sensible with domestic pets but a field-captured snake is highly stressed in a cage. My philosophy is to release the animal as soon as it wakes up. Even if you put it straight back into a putrid-smelling swamp, the reptilian patient will survive. Snakes are tough. I recall releasing one male garter snake an hour after surgically implanting a radio transmitter into the snake's abdomen. Before the snake left my hand it started courting a nearby female. But if you keep such a snake in a cage 'to help it recover', it may die from the stress of those unnatural conditions. Snakes aren't beagles.

The earliest transmitters had circular internal antennae – easy to put inside a snake but with limited range. In 1982, American researchers Howard Reinert and David Cundall developed a better method, threading a long antenna up inside the snake's body under its skin. Reception range for the signal skyrocketed, and radio tracking a mobile snake became easier. And transmitter longevity improved as well, because you could obtain the Holy Grail (small size and long reception distances) with less battery power. The life of an implanted transmitter was only a few days or weeks at the outset of research in snake telemetry, but within a decade it had stretched out to months – or even years if your study species was a chunky python or rattlesnake.

Most of the early transmitters were so large that they affected the snakes. But despite such problems, and small sample sizes, scientific papers began to appear based on radio tracking. Many early studies caught snakes over a wide area and then released them at a central location to facilitate tracking. That method failed to account for the fact that snakes are homebodies, intimately familiar with their local home ranges. Translocating an animal will stress it out. It will either hunker down or try to find its way home – just as I would if you dropped me in New York City or Beijing. As a result, most of the early data on snake movements were of limited value.

Researchers still translocate snakes to study their movements, but these days they do it on purpose. All over the world, 'problem' snakes are captured in cities and released elsewhere to mitigate wildlife-human conflicts. Those snakes range from rattlesnakes in Arizona to Tiger Snakes in eastern Australia, and giant Reticulated Pythons in Singapore. And in almost every case, the snake heads home as soon as you let it go.

The earliest transmitter studies

The rapid uptake of telemetry makes it difficult to identify 'pioneers' in snake radio-tracking, but two studies by US-based researchers on body temperatures were among the earliest papers. One was of Boa Constrictors in Mexico. In 1969, Sam McGinnis and Robert Moore tracked two juvenile snakes in an outdoor enclosure, took two adults back to California to track in the lab, and tracked one large adult Boa (2.3 m long) in the field. In the following year, David Osgood tracked 13 North American Common Water Snakes (10 of them pregnant females) in outdoor cages and in the field. In both of these studies, temperature-sensitive resistors in the electronic circuitry meant that pulse rates of the signal increased as the snake warmed up. To know a snake's temperature, the investigators recorded pulse intervals with a stopwatch.

The Boa Constrictor (which has the scientific name *Boa constrictor*, the same as its common name) was one of the first snake species studied by radio telemetry. PIXABAY

It wasn't long before the doyen of mark-recapture research on snakes, Henry Fitch, got into the act as well. Henry tracked an impressive sample of 67 individuals of eight species in Kansas. His colleague Hampton Shirer had constructed transmitters to study marmots and opossums, and Henry convinced Hampton to apply the methods to snakes. Their main aim was to compare movement patterns of tracked snakes with those of individuals that Henry had captured and recaptured in the same area. He concluded that putting a transmitter into a snake's stomach mimicked the effects of a large meal. That is, the snake stopped moving and hoped that the large lump in its stomach would be digested. Some transmitters in that study weighed 27 per cent of the snake's body mass, so it's not surprising that snakes stayed close to home. If you put a 20 kg transmitter inside my body I wouldn't move very far either.

The rapidly shrinking size of transmitters soon enabled telemetry of small snake species. Most researchers adopted a rule-of-thumb that the transmitter needed to weigh less than 5 per cent of the snake that was carrying it – but for a slender tree-climbing snake, even 5 per cent might be intolerable. Transmitter sizes decreased for three main reasons: better electronics designs on miniaturised circuits; improvements in battery technology; and the emergence of commercially produced transmitters. Home-made units were bigger and less powerful than the commercial units, prompting a surge of grant applications as snake scientists strove to purchase high-powered transmitters and reliable receivers.

The most impressive aspect of the radio-telemetry revolution was its speed. Within a decade, the radio tracking of snakes was mainstream. As an undergraduate student in Australia in 1971, I built my own transmitters and implanted them in lizards so I could watch behaviour in the field. And just a few years later, as a PhD student, I did the same with snakes. The technology spread around the world like a whirlwind. Ideally suited to snakes, telemetry added the allure of sophisticated technology to a field long dismissed as old-fashioned, and thus with a lingering inferiority complex. And so, aspiring snake ecologists who could afford to buy transmitters honed their skills at anaesthesia and surgery, and then spent long hours in the field waving a telemetry antenna in the air and listening for the beeping signal of a hidden snake.

Radio tracking is now a standard tool for wildlife biologists, and is commonly featured in the media. Those film clips often suggest that telemetry is a silver bullet for snake research. Just pop out to the study site each day, switch on the receiver, immediately locate all your snakes, then go home for lunch. But the sad reality is that radio tracking generates modest returns in terms of data per unit effort. You can waste an entire day slogging through the swamp, failing to find a telemetry signal – either because the snake has moved away, or it has gone deep underground, or because a wire inside the cable linking your receiver to your antenna broke when you fell over that log in the tall grass. And every once in a while, the telemetry signal leads you to a transmitter in a pile of snake poo .... because some snakes have the almost-magical ability to move the transmitter from their body cavity into their gut, and pass the unit out of their body with their faeces. Radio telemetry rendered field research on snakes possible, but it didn't make it easy.

Despite rapid progress in miniaturising radio transmitters, it will be a long time before we can apply the technology to tiny species such as the Chihuahuan Black-headed Snake (*Tantilla wilcoxi*). NOAH K. FIELDS

When snake telemetry makes you unpopular

If your study species is dangerous to humans, you run into other problems. They aren't unique to radio-tracking work, but telemetry magnifies them. To phrase it politely, dangerous snakes aren't well-liked. Local people who hear about a snake research project on adjoining land may develop conspiracy theories that the scientists are intentionally releasing hordes of deadly snakes, or are producing mutant cross-bred snakes that will devastate the neighbourhood. In his classic monograph on American Copperhead ecology in 1960, Henry Fitch complained that: "Absurd rumors such as one that thousands of poisonous snakes had been brought from elsewhere and released on the reservation, were seized upon by the local press for their sensational appeal, and as a result gained credence among many of the less well-informed country people." More recently, a major rattlesnake telemetry project in Virginia was shut down when the university employing the scientists buckled to public pressure.

Even worse, the danger to people may be real. Imagine that you are radio tracking a venomous snake that wanders over to a schoolyard and coils up beside the classroom door. What do you do? Keep quiet, and risk a fatal snakebite to a child? Tell the school – which will be a death warrant for the snake? Catch the snake and return it to its original site of capture – in which case it will probably just head straight back to the schoolyard? This isn't just hypothetical … it's a problem faced by any snake researcher who works close to human habitation. Snakes are attracted to the water and prey that flourish around houses, so it's a brave soul indeed who embarks on such a study. We need to know what snakes are doing in suburbia, to find ways to reduce their conflict with people – but such a study creates daunting challenges.

I've never had a radio-tracked venomous snake bite a member of the public, but one of our giant Scrub Pythons did try to eat somebody. My student Dan Natusch was radio tracking Scrubbies in tropical Australia, in a wilderness area dominated by rainforests and savannah woodland. There was only one house in the area, a small shop for passing tourists. At 2.28 am on the night of 10 March 2014, one of the owners of that shop was awoken abruptedly when a large 3.6 m (12 ft) male Scrubbie crawled in through the open window, seized her on the thigh and threw coils around her body. Lea-Ann fought off the snake and trapped it in the kitchen until Dan could come and fetch it. The day before, he had warned her that the snake had moved 100 m (330 ft) from the woodland to a location close to the house – but none of us expected an attack. Although the snake was long, Scrubbies are slender. The offending serpent weighed only 3.6 kg (8 lb), whereas Lea-Ann weighed 64 kg (140 lb). She was far too large for the snake to swallow, so it's puzzling that it tried.

Benefits of snake telemetry

Some of the first studies to use radio transmitters in snakes were focused on movements. For example, Henry Fitch wanted to compare activity patterns of radio-tracked snakes at his Kansas site to the movements he had recorded from scale-clipped snakes that he caught in his traps. Nonetheless, the potential for telemetry to reveal other aspects of snake biology was clear from the outset. David Osgood's 1970 study on body temperatures of water snakes offers an early example.

It's difficult to overstate the impact of telemetry on our knowledge about snake ecology. For example, studying habitat use seems straightforward, without any neeed for complex technology; you just record the habitat types in which you find and catch snakes during fieldwork. But that approach is fraught with error, because snakes are easier to see in some types of habitat than others. I had caught hundreds of Red-bellied Black Snakes before I first put transmitters into any of these animals. I had always found black snakes on riverbanks, so I expected them to stay close to water – but in fact most of my snakes wandered off to forested habitats where they were well hidden. Another consistent experience from radio-tracking studies is to find snakes up trees from time to time, even when your study species is supposed to be entirely terrestrial or even a burrower. The first few days of a radio-tracking project really open your eyes to the species' behaviour. Your preconceptions about the habitats they prefer and the distances they move are shattered.

Most snakes encountered during fieldwork are found while they are crossing the road – like this Eastern Hognose Snake (*Heterodon platirhinos*) – but that's because snakes are easy to see on roads, not because roads are a preferred habitat. Without radio tracking, we can't work out where snakes spend most of their time. NOAH K. FIELDS

Telemetry also overcomes other biases that affect hand-captures. For example, let's say that we want to document the body temperatures of snakes. If we catch all of our snakes while they are out and about, they will all be hot. If we catch them all while they are hidden beneath shelter items, they will all be cold. If we use radio telemetry, we can record body temperatures regardless of what the snake is doing or where it is doing it – so we can obtain an unbiased estimate of thermal regimes.

Telemetry also enables us to conduct field studies that would otherwise be impossible. If you can find a radio-carrying snake whenever you want to, you can observe the day-to-day life of that snake. It's a lot easier to sneak up on an animal if you know where it is. For example, one important question with highly venomous snakes is how they react to the approach of a person. In Australia, deadly Eastern Brown Snakes are abundant in farmland, leading to perilous encounters between snakes and people. We could try to tease apart snake responses to people by simply going out and recording snake behaviour, but it would be devilishly difficult. You don't see most of the snakes because they slip away to their burrows; and the ones you do see are almost underfoot before a lithe brown body erupts into a threat display.

Telemetry solves that problem, enabling better data and less risk to the investigator. My student Pat Whitaker and I took advantage of his radio-tracking research to work out what happens in those encounters. Pat's brown snakes often didn't move from one day to the next, so Pat could check the telemetry signal and be confident about where one of his snakes was located. The pulse rate of the transmitter's signal told him the snake's body temperature; if the rate was high the snake was hot, so it was almost certainly sitting above ground rather than hidden in a burrow.

Wendy Panaino radio locating snakes in the Kalahari desert of southern Africa. GRAHAM ALEXANDER

With the benefit of that knowledge, it was a low-risk exercise for one of us to walk towards the snake and record how close we got before the snake reacted; and how it reacted; and how that approach distance and reaction were affected by factors such as the time of day, the colour of our shirts and the speed of our approach. Only one snake ever tried to bite us, and that happened after Pat accidentally trod on its tail. So much for the myth of 'aggressive' brown snakes.

By overcoming the biases that plague observational data, telemetry has been transformative.

Real-estate choice from a snake's perspective

To understand how an organism interacts with its environment, we need to study its behaviour. Sadly for intending behaviourists, though, serpents are difficult to observe in the field. Well hidden, usually inactive, and ready to hurtle away if approached by a large vertical object with binoculars on a strap around its neck. Prior to the radio-tracking revolution, most snippets of information about snake behaviour were based on brief glimpses.

As a result, snake ecologists needed to exploit every scrap of data they could obtain. The easiest information to record was the microhabitat which a snake was using when it was first seen. Was it in leaf litter? Under a cover item? Or up a tree? But how much detail was appropriate? Counting the number of leaves on the tree where you found a snake won't tell you much. At the other extreme, describing habitat types in general terms such as 'grassland' and 'forest' fails to capture important variation within those categories. We need to find a compromise: habitat characteristics that give us useful insights but don't take all day to score.

That challenge was overcome in two landmark 1984 papers by an American biologist, Howard Reinert. He radio tracked Timber Rattlesnakes and American Copperheads in Pennsylvania. Because these heavily built ambush foragers stay put when approached, Howard could pinpoint each snake's resting place. Importantly, his sample sizes were respectable: he surgically implanted transmitters into 41 snakes and recorded their locations every two days, for a grand total of 725 locations. As far as possible, he divided that sample evenly between his two study species, and between males and females within each, and between pregnant and non-pregnant females. He was even able to compare two different colour morphs of male Timber Rattlers.

Whenever Howard found a snake, he measured 14 structural features of the habitat within a metre (1-yard) of its location. Those factors included the per cent of ground covered by rocks versus leaf litter versus logs, the numbers and heights of woody stems, and distances to the nearest rocks, logs and tall trees. He also scored sun penetration through the canopy, as the per cent of open sky compared to foliage. By comparing the habitat in spots that snakes chose to other sites within his study area, Howard could test whether snakes chose habitats at random, versus selecting specific conditions.

Howard's snakes were choosy about the places they sat, and a snake's habitat use was affected by its species. Copperheads liked young forests, whereas Timber Rattlers liked all forests. Habitat choice also was influenced by reproduction (pregnant females liked open rocky sites) and colour (melanistic male rattlers liked mature forest with fallen logs whereas pale-morph males liked young forests with leaf litter). Other snake researchers soon adopted the new approach.

Snakes are adept at exploiting seasonal food resources, and the resulting concentrations of venomous snakes can make life interesting. These photographs show Thilo Bell searching for Cape Cobras (*Naja nivea*) that gather in the communal nests of Sociable Weavers (*Philetairus socius*) in southern Africa; and a cobra peering down from inside one of the nests. PHOTOGRAPHS: THILO BELL AND BRYAN MARITZ

One of the strongest patterns revealed by radio tracking was that snakes spend different seasons in different places. The first examples involved European and North American snakes living in areas with cold winters. Shelters deep enough to escape the cold were few and far between, forcing animals to congregate in rocky outcrops on high ground. With the advent of warmer conditions in springtime, the snakes moved down into more thickly vegetated valleys – often to the edges of streams or swamps where food was more abundant.

Similar seasonal shifts play out all over the world. In temperate-zone Australia Broad-headed Snakes spend winter under sun-warmed flat rocks, but as the weather warms up in springtime the snakes move to the forest and climb into tall trees. A related species, the pugnacious Stephens' Banded Snake, remains in treetops all year except for autumn, when female rats are weaning their babies. For a few weeks, a snake that stays on the ground has access to a supermarket full of easily caught furry morsels. Seasonal shifts in habitat are common even in the tropics, where snakes can remain active year-round. On floodplains in tropical Australia, monsoonal flooding each year inundates low-lying areas and drives native rats out of their soil cracks and downstream to higher, drier levee banks – and Water Pythons are not far behind. Oenpelli Pythons hide among the branches of seasonally fruiting trees to capture the bats and birds that arrive to feed on those fruits. In the aquatic Arafura File Snakes of tropical Australia, males spend the long dry season in shallow waterbodies full of the small fish they love to eat, whereas adult females head to deeper billabongs to eat larger fish. In short, the availability of food shifts with the seasons, and snakes migrate accordingly.

My long-term research assistant, Melanie Elphick, searching for a radio signal from Red-sided Garter Snakes (*Thamnophis sirtalis parietalis*) in Manitoba. RICK SHINE

Even if a snake remains in the same habitat year-round, staying in the same place is a poor option after you have eaten most of the locally available prey. Radio tracking shows that snakes typically remain at a site for a while then shift elsewhere. After a few foodless days and nights, it's time to check out another restaurant. For example, Pat Whitaker found that as soon as an Australian brown snake had gobbled up most of the mice within a burrow system, the snake moved to another underground larder where rodents were still abundant.

Measuring snake temperatures

Food isn't the only driver of habitat selection for a snake, because it's easier for a snake to control its body temperature in some places than others. For example, recall Howard Reinert's conclusion that certain species and sexes prefer open habitats that offer basking opportunities.

To evaluate the role of temperature in snake habitat selection, we need to measure the thermal regimes that are available in each kind of habitat. Researchers initially did so with snake-like models, such as water-filled inner tubes from bicycle tyres, with temperature-measuring devices inside them. That offered a way to assess what temperatures were available to a snake, to compare to the snake's actual temperatures (as monitored with the radio-transmitter signal). In the early days, though, technical obstacles were horrendous. I spent hours burying cables that ran from snake models to large and bulky temperature recorders, with daily trips to replace batteries. But within a decade or two, we could buy temperature recorders small enough to be surgically implanted in a snake.

Now that we could measure temperatures in different habitats and in free-ranging reptiles, we needed a way to analyse those data. In 1993, American biologist Paul Hertz and two colleagues proposed a new way to do that. First, they recorded reptile body temperatures and environmental ('operative') temperatures at the same sites. Then, from lab studies, they calculated the thermal preference of each species: that is, how warm does it want to be? From those measurements, they could estimate how well the study animals maintained their preferred body temperatures despite varying environmental temperatures. Predictably, the thermal challenge was tougher in some habitats than others; and some species were determined to stay at their perfect temperature whereas others were less fussed about it.

Studies of temperature regulation became popular, especially in species of lizards that are active by day and select very precise body temperatures. A graph of body temperature versus time of day in such an animal shows an impressively constant plateau throughout the day. In contrast, the graph for a snake is ragged. Snakes are more interested in hiding than in shuttling between sunlight and shade. An ambush predator lying in wait won't give away its position by moving. It happily trades off precise body temperatures for the opportunity to capture a meal. Another inconvenience is that with such a long slender animal, it's not clear where we should measure 'body temperature'. A snake that partly emerges from its underground burrow and lies with the front half of its body in sunlight, can be ten degrees warmer in the front end than the back end.

As research widened to include new species in new places, it became clear that regulating body temperatures carefully is a priority only for some kinds of reptiles in some kinds of habitats. In a nocturnal snake or lizard, for example, basking in the sunlight isn't an option. And most reptiles occur in the tropics, where the major thermal challenge is to avoid overheating rather than to warm yourself up.

Even reptiles tucked away under shelter items can still thermoregulate. In 1989, Ray Huey and his colleagues studied garter snakes in California – or more accurately, they studied the rocks that their garter snakes were hiding under for most of the day. A hefty rock was slow to heat and cool, never reaching the snake's preferred thermal level. A super-thin rock heated and cooled too fast, so was too hot by day and too cold at night. Intermediate-sized rocks were ideal, and they were the ones preferred by snakes.

Broad-headed Snakes (*Hoplocephalus bungaroides*) thrive in cool climates of south-eastern Australia by selecting sunlight-exposed rocky shelters that remain warm into the night. JULES FARQUHAR

More generally, radio telemetry showed that a snake could control its body temperature without having to bask in the sunlight like an extroverted lizard. In Australia, Eastern Brown Snakes move around inside their soil burrows to track shifting temperatures in the sun-warmed soil. Broad-headed Snakes beneath sun-exposed rocks push up against the lower surfaces of the heated rocks to warm up in the morning, then cool down at midday by a subtle shift that brings them into contact with the cooler rock beneath. Hidden within hollow tree branches, Stephens' Banded Snakes move to places where the sunlight hits those branches, warming up the snakes inside. On small islands in New Caledonia, sea kraits snuggle up to warm-blooded seabirds inside their burrows. Many snakes thermoregulate while hidden away inside inaccessible shelters. But with a transmitter beeping away inside the animal, we can work out what's going on even when the snake is invisible to human eyes.

IN THEIR OWN WORDS

The biggest frustration with radio telemetry of snakes is to accept the snake's relaxed timetable. Most human beings aren't patient enough to wait for hours until a snake does something. That inactivity was noticed long before telemetry, mostly from observing captive snakes:

"A good number [of snakes] pass a great part of their existence in a state of languor, or listlessness resembling sleep, and that do not disturb themselves, unless when some animal approaches them, which they seize when they are inclined, relapsing afterwards into a profound lethargy, which renders them sometimes for a considerable period incapable of hunting for food." HERMANN SCHLEGEL, 1837

Before telemetry was developed, the only snakes whose movements could be monitored from one day to the next were those that left physical tracks. Sidewinders are small rattlesnakes that leave very distinctive tracks in the desert sand, enabling early researchers to measure movements and home ranges over short periods:

"Apparently the Sidewinder does not inhabit a certain permanent refuge, but rambles at night over the desert and settles down for rest at any convenient place, spending each day at a different point, chosen at random. It may be however, that the individual returns during the following night or nights to the point from which it started, thus maintaining a territory covered in several nights, but this does not seem very likely." WALTER MOSAUER, 1933

One of my favourite papers about reptile thermoregulation is by James Heath, who pointed out that stable body temperatures of snakes and lizards in the field don't necessarily mean that the animals are actively choosing that temperature. We'd expect thermal stability just from physical principles, when rates of heating equal rates of cooling. To demonstrate that fact (and frustrate the hell out of over-zealous thermoregulation researchers), Heath measured temperatures inside water-filled beer cans:

"In order to determine whether the distribution of temperatures of inanimate objects would be distinguishable from those obtained from reptiles under similar conditions, I substituted water-filled metal cans for reptiles. Thirteen cylindrical metal containers (beer cans) ... were filled with tap water ... Eleven were placed so as to receive direct sunlight throughout a full day. Two were kept in full shade."
JAMES EDWARD HEATH, 1964

Chapter 8

Testing hypotheses in the field

Careful observation is the foundation of knowledge – and as a result, almost all field-based studies on snake ecology (including radio-tracking studies as well as mark-recapture research) are descriptive. Our data reveal what's happening in the field, and as the information accumulates we begin to see patterns. In turn, those patterns suggest explanations. Working with live snakes is enormously enjoyable, but my favourite part of doing snake science is that glorious moment when a new idea pops into my head, and I can see a way to find out whether or not it is true.

Where do new ideas come from?

You have found a snake, and caught it, and measured it, thereby transforming your encounter with that serpent into numbers on a spreadsheet. And you've done it enough times, in a sufficiently organised way, that you have a dataset suitable for revealing new facets of snake ecology. Even better, your work has revealed an interesting pattern. Congratulations. But your job is only half done. Now, you need to work out the reason for that pattern.

The best research doesn't just provide new information; it also proposes new ways of thinking. It opens our eyes to connections between topics. It shows us a new dimension to what our study animals are doing, or how best we can illuminate their biology. In short, landmark studies convey new ideas. Where do those ideas come from?

The history of research is festooned with examples of creative people who saw things that were hidden to mere mortals. Galileo, Einstein, Darwin .... famed not just for their scientific results, but for their new perspectives. Nobody doubts the impact of those conceptual revolutions, but understanding the birth of ideas is elusive because we don't know how our brains work.

For example, one common path towards the birth of a new idea involves misunderstanding someone else's suggestion. You read or hear something, but you misremember the details. You may use that idea for years before finally going back to check the original source and discovering that the concept driving your work is actually your own brainchild, not one borrowed from a colleague.

Common sense says that if we have a bold new idea, we will be able to recall how that idea arose. But we can't. Most people who have groundbreaking revelations report that the breakthrough suddenly appeared to them, fully formed. It usually cropped up when they were doing something else. New ideas are produced in our unconscious brain. Mysterious cognitive machinery works away in the background, eventually generating a new idea and sending it into a part of the brain where we can 'see' it.

The implication is clear but frightening. Much of the time, we don't know what we are thinking about. Processing is going on behind the scenes. By analogy, many of us spend hours looking at computer screens – but all we see is the interface, not the networks through which electrons fly around to produce patterns on the screen. The process of generating new ideas in a human brain is equally mysterious.

That doesn't mean that producing ideas is random, of course. Some people do it more often than others. Nobel Prize-winners brave enough to explore reasons behind their success preach some unlikely virtues – such as ignorance (if you are deeply knowledgeable about conventional ideas, you won't look outside them), arrogance (if you accept that somebody else knows the topic better than you do, you'll stop trying), laziness (new ideas won't arrive while you are labouring away at 'normal science') and so forth. Many of those personality traits are directly opposite to those we celebrate in run-of-the-mill scientists. Perhaps that's why so many of the new ideas come from the brains of so few people.

Research also tells us that the best new ideas don't come from geniuses who attack a question by concentrating on it for hours. Individuals with stratospherically high IQs are no more likely to give birth to a new idea than are individuals with not-much-more-than-average IQs. And pondering a problem at length rarely generates a truly new insight. Instead, there's something important about letting ideas jump back and forward between the conscious and unconscious brain, and then allowing the mind to range widely.

How about the birth of new ideas in snake ecology research? Even if the process is mysterious, do certain situations foster new ideas? When I ask my colleagues for first-hand accounts of how they invented novel insights, they just shrug. So I have to rely on my own experience here; a shaky platform because sample sizes are low and memory is fallible. But I can tell at least one story about the origin of a new idea.

Part of the answer lies in 'fortune favouring the prepared mind'. If a researcher has already thought long and hard about a topic, a new idea is likely to pop into their brain. That's what happened to Thomas Madsen and me in August 1991, when we were living in a small demountable house in tropical Australia conducting research on pythons. During the day when the biting flies were buzzing and the pythons were hiding, we analysed some old data sets from

In my experience, the field provides one of the most fertile breeding grounds for new ideas. It's a bit less comfortable than the lab, and less controlled – but informal conversations can suggest new hypotheses. Some of the new ideas come from discussions around the campsite, and others arise while measuring recently captured animals prior to releasing them. TERRI SHINE

A recently mated female Eurasian Adder (*Vipera berus*), blissfully unaware of the complex and sophisticated sperm-selection mechanisms at play inside her uterus. TERRI SHINE

Thomas's PhD studies on Eurasian Adders in Sweden. One day we turned to a puzzle: why did most female Eurasian Adders mate with several males each season, even though a single mating gave a female snake more than enough sperm to fertilise her litter? We ran statistical analyses to compare a female's mating history to her body size, her age, her litter size and so forth, hoping to find some evolutionary benefit to multiple mating. But nothing came out.

The next day was picnic day at the field station, where we joined the farm hands for a barbecue and games. I was too busy playing cricket to think about snakes. But that night as I lay in bed, too sunburned to sleep, I had a flash of inspiration. Perhaps female adders with multiple partners could somehow choose to use sperm from distantly related males rather than close relatives? That way, they could spare their offspring the costs of inbreeding. To test that idea, we just need to compare a female's mating history with the proportion of her offspring that are healthy rather than dead or deformed. When I told Thomas about the idea at breakfast, he laughed. He'd had exactly the same thought while washing up the dishes after dinner, and he had already found his field notebooks and located the information on stillbirths. It took him until 3 am, but it was worth it. The pattern was exactly as we had predicted. The more males a female mated with, the healthier her babies.

The idea challenged conventional thinking about sex roles in animals, by showing that females as well as males could benefit from 'promiscuity'. The fact that Thomas and I had the same brainwave at the same time suggests that all it took was a day off, playing cricket, to light the same spark in two overheated brains.

A person's background and training also affect the way their brain works, and thus the kinds of new ideas they invent. In recent years, a combination of changing experiences (driven by cultural shifts as well as emerging digital platforms) and a more diverse cohort of researchers (see Chapter 13) is generating exciting new ideas about snake ecology.

Testing ideas with experiments

By itself, an idea is entertaining but unsatisfying. For that brand new hypothesis to be really useful – to help us understand why snakes act they way they do – we need to go back out into the real world and gather data to see if our new insight holds up.

Many grand and wonderful ideas are impossible to test. For example, scientists have speculated that competition between species can affect the composition of a local snake fauna. If species A competes too much with species B, they can't both live in the same area. It's plausible, but how could you test it? The only robust evidence would come from experimentally reducing (or increasing) the numbers of one of those species, and see what happens to numbers of the other one. That would be an enormously ambitious project. And as a result, the idea of competition between species has stayed in the 'too hard' basket – still talked about, and possibly true, but as yet untested.

The most useful ideas are those that can be tested either by assembling more information (to look for patterns predicted by the new idea) or by manipulating what's going on – that is, by conducting experiments.

Experiments are the gold standard. Progress in a research field accelerates when we move from describing what's going on, to testing ideas about why those things are happening. In short, hypothesis testing. The natural world is mind-blowingly complex, but we can make sense of it one step at a time by developing plausible explanations and then using experiments to find out which explanation is correct.

Bob Mason in a den of Red-sided Garter Snakes (*Thamnophis sirtalis parietalis*) in Manitoba, Canada, recording the responses of free-ranging male snakes to various scents. Vast numbers of super-tolerant snakes make this an ideal place for field experimental research. CHRIS FRIESEN

To conduct experiments, we need to isolate cause and effect. For example, as I discussed in a previous chapter about lab-based research, we can tweak one aspect of a snake's life – say, the amount of food that it eats, or the temperatures it experiences as an embryo – and record what happens to that animal as a result. The approach is powerful because we can directly compare individuals that have had identical experiences except for that one factor. We don't have to rely upon correlations. If a change in Factor X causes a shift in Trait Y, we have nailed down cause and effect.

The easiest way to conduct experiments is to take the animal out of its messy, complicated natural environment and pop it into a cage where we can control thermal regimes, water and food supply, cues from predators and other snakes, and so forth. In that simplified world, we can manipulate the factor of interest and record what happens. But there's a downside to that approach as well. In simplifying the snake's environment, we may lose components that really matter. A pampered pet snake behaves differently than its wild cousin who has spent its life escaping from predators and searching for food.

Is there a way to get the best of both worlds – the power of experiments plus the reality of the field? Yes, there is. You can conduct your experiments on free-ranging snakes. It isn't easy because a newly captured snake is unlikely to be thinking about anything except escape or retaliation. To conduct experiments in the field, you need to gather your data without frightening the snake. Difficult, but not impossible. And it's damn good fun.

Cowards, bluffers and warriors

What's the easiest kind of behavioural experiment to conduct on snakes in the field? That is, what response could you measure to something that you do? No prizes for guessing 'the snake's reaction to you'. The experimental stimulus is simple – it's you, walking towards the animal. And the response is easy to record, because the snake has a limited range of options. Does the animal rely on camouflage, remaining immobile? Or does it flee? Or rattle its tail, hiss and strike?

To identify factors that affect a snake's behaviour, we need to think like a snake. My friends Jesus Rivas and Gordon Burghardt summed it up beautifully when they wrote in one of their scientific papers that 'we have to wear the snake's shoes'. Gordon is a pioneer of behavioural research on snakes, and Jesus is a larger-than-life field ecologist and star of wildlife documentaries. Famously, he spearheaded field research on the mighty anaconda. He also spent a few years as the presenter for TV documentaries about snakes, where his first name created difficulties when interviewing deeply religious snake-handlers from a small cult in the southern USA. They couldn't bring themselves to introduce their Venezuelan-born visitor as 'Jesus'.

This Sri Lankan Trinket Snake (*Coelognathus helena*) has decided that attack is the best means of defence – but given a chance, it would happily switch to rapid retreat. RUCHIRA SOMAWEERA

'Thinking like a snake' is easy to say, but hard to do. It's difficult enough to understand the perspective of a human being from a different culture or gender, or a different age. It's far more challenging for intuition to cross the species boundary. Although many pet owners claim to share the innermost thoughts of their canine or feline companions, research shows that most people misinterpret the behaviours and body postures of their pets.

Thinking like a snake … what would that feel like? Emerging from your cool overnight shelter to bask in the sunlight, barely conscious of what is around you …. then feeling your brain and body coming to life as heat seeps into your body, shunting that sun-warmed blood to organs that need extra heat … then extruding your tongue-tips to obtain chemical information about the silent world around you. It's a very different scenario than bounding out of bed to grab a cup of coffee and go to work.

But I agree with Jesus and Gordon. The best way to understand snakes is to put yourself in the snake's place. Its response to your approach is a good place to begin.

First, what are the snake's options when a gigantic primate walks up to it? It can really only do one of three things. The first is to remain immobile, to evade detection. The second option is escape: it can slither away. Or lastly, it could stand its ground and try to intimidate the intruder by inflating its neck, hissing, striking, or rattling its tail in dry grass. Cobras raise their forebodies and erect their hoods, a terrifying apparition if it suddenly materialises in front of you. Rattlesnakes vibrate their tail tips, warning that the snake will not tolerate closer approach.

There are other options as well, but their function is puzzling. Some small snakes make popping sounds by pushing air out of the cloaca, but these subtle snake farts don't seem terribly frightening. Likewise with brief squeaks from non-venomous species such as the Ornate Snail-eater from South America, or the tiny Claw-snouted Blind Snake from Australia. And the bandy-bandy, that lifts loops of its body off the ground when approached. Or death feigning, when a European Dice Snake or an American hognose snake lies on its back with its mouth open and its tongue protruded. I'll leave these bizarre displays as problems to be solved by future research, and stay with the three general responses: hide, run or retaliate.

Death feigning has evolved in several distantly related types of snakes, but I'm still puzzled as to why it works. In this photograph, an Eastern Hognose Snake (*Heterodon platirhinos*) is trying to convince a potential predator (the photographer) that it is well and truly dead.
NOAH K. FIELDS

Some of the most effective 'don't tread on me' displays involve visual signals. American Cottonmouth Moccasins (*Agkistrodon piscivorus*) take the name 'cottonmouth' from the brightly white interior of the mouth – a dramatic signal that is best respected. NOAH K. FIELDS

Thinking like a snake, which response should you adopt? You might doubt that a 'simple' snake could make such a decision, especially when it's so cold that its brain is barely functioning. But you'd be wrong. Today's snakes are the descendants of individuals that have avoided predators for millions of years. Generation after generation, the only individuals to survive were the ones that opted for the most effective responses. Any behaviour that helped them to survive was encoded in their genes and passed on to their descendants. Even if they lack complex intellects, we can expect snakes to react effectively to any looming threat.

So, back to our question. For example, what factors should encourage a snake to rely on camouflage rather than escape or active defence? Body temperature is important. A cold snake is a slow snake, so escape is out of the question. Either rely on crypsis or launch into a spectacular threat display. The equation is the same for snakes that are slow for other reasons – such as being heavily pregnant or having just consumed a large meal. Or for a snake that can't see clearly because it is about to slough its old skin.

So a hot snake heads off at full speed away from you, but a cold (or pregnant, or recently fed) snake lies immobile. And if that cold snake realises it's been discovered, it may launch into a spectacular (though poorly co-ordinated) threat display. Even inoffensive species such as Red-sided Garter Snakes take a deep breath to expand their bodies, making themselves look larger and more formidable. That bodily expansion reveals the bright red skin between their scales, which is hidden except when the snake is trying to scare away an intruder.

A snake's size matters as well, because a smaller snake is more vulnerable to predators, and is slower and less capable of intimidation. Another factor that should (and does) affect snake responses is the local environment. Fleeing is a poor option for a snake in a large open field, that cannot reach cover without a long period of dangerous exposure. But if the same snake is close to a burrow or a bush, escape is feasible.

By seeing the problem from a snake's perspective, then, we can generate predictions. A snake's response to our approach should be affected by several factors, some relating to the snake and some to the local environment. To test those predictions, we just need to approach free-ranging snakes in a standardised fashion and record what they do.

Studies of this kind support the idea that snakes choose their anti-predator responses based on the factors I've listed above. However, precise patterns differ among species. For example, juvenile Shedao Pit Vipers are more likely to strike out than are adults; and colder snakes and those in trees rely on crypsis whereas warmer snakes on the ground flee or display. Australian Tiger Snakes from predator-free island populations ignore humans whereas snakes from mainland habitats are more skittish. Sea kraits flee at night and when in the water – where rapid escape is feasible – but not by day and when on land. Female Keelbacks that are carrying eggs (and thus are slow) flee an approaching human from greater distances than do non-pregnant females. In contrast, mate-searching male Keelbacks are too focused on reproduction to notice the approach of a water buffalo, let alone a person.

To make the predator-prey encounter more realistic, some researchers use models of real predators. That way, we don't have to assume that an approaching human stimulates the same response as an approaching mongoose or fox. At the garter snake dens in Manitoba, for example, we used a plastic crow on the end of a stick to frighten free-ranging snakes. It was fun, but I doubt that a cold snake had any clear idea of what was coming towards it. Prodding with a human finger produced the same responses as prodding with our plastic crow. We would have obtained the same results if we had used a fluffy pink unicorn.

Contrary to popular belief, one response that is almost never seen is aggression. By and

Earthwatch volunteer Keith Vanning testing the responses of a Red-sided Garter Snake (*Thamnophis sirtalis parietalis*) to an approaching 'predator' – in this case a plastic crow. BOB MASON

large, snakes don't 'attack' people. In 1958, American herpetologist Clifford Pope (1899–1974) wrote that "snakes are first cowards, then bluffers, and last of all warriors." That is, a snake's rule is 'run away if you can; if not, look frightening; and only launch a strike as a last resort'. A warm snake generally flees when approached. In a tropical climate where snakes are always warm, most bites to humans occur when a snake thinks that it is under attack. For example, sea snakes rarely sink their fangs into swimmers or skin-divers. Instead, most bites occur after the snake is caught in a fisherman's net.

But in nature, there are very few rules that aren't occasionally broken. American zookeeper and raconteur Jim Murphy wrote in 2015: "An adult male racer was the only snake in my career to have aggressively attacked me without provocation. I encountered this male courting a female in the wild during high school and this suitor likely wanted privacy. I retreated and the snake continued to pursue me, wildly striking." Some attacks on people by snakes are attempts at predation by over-optimistic constrictors that, despite their large size, would be unable to swallow an adult human being. Our radio-tracked Australian Scrub Python that tried to swallow Lea-Ann falls into that category, as do the Brown Tree Snakes in Guam that crawl in through open windows at night and chew on newborn human babies. Some of the other 'attacks' involve snakes that have no other way to retaliate because they are caught in a fishing net, or because a human is blocking their only escape route.

Fishing for snakes

Scoring a snake's anti-predator reponses, as I've described above, is the easiest kind of 'natural behaviour' to record; all the scientist does is record what happens when a snake detects an approaching person. Ideally, though, we would also like to understand a snake's interactions with prey. To study that topic in the wild, we need to present a stimulus to an undisturbed snake. 'Undisturbed' is the key word here. Adept at detecting intruders, snakes are unlikely to wait around long enough for that intruder to begin asking questions. Creeping up to a free-ranging snake and presenting it with a fake prey item sounds impossible.

But the same challenge lies at the heart of recreational fishing. Many kinds of fishing involve presenting a free-ranging predator with an artificial stimulus (a bait, or lure, or fly) that conceals a hook, and deceiving the fish into believing that the stimulus is real. If that approach works with fish, why not with snakes? Just delete the hook and change the stimulus. Attach a fake prey item to thin nylon line and dangle it from the end of a fishing rod in front of a passing serpent.

Fishing for snakes has never been popular with researchers, with a few exceptions. I'm one of those people. I've used the method frequently. Ever since childhood I've enjoyed fishing

To examine how well male Red-sided Garter Snakes (*Thamnophis sirtalis parietalis*) were able to follow females of their own species, I attached a dead (predator-killed) female snake to a fishing line (plus makeshift rod) and dragged her along the ground. The males were easily fooled. JONATHAN WEBB

with artificial lures or flies, and dangling a lure in front of a snake gives me the same thrill as depositing an artificial fly in front of a trout. As a result, I've seized every opportunity to sneak up to free-ranging serpents with a fishing rod in my hand and a gleam in my eye. I suspect that I've dangled more objects in front of free-ranging snakes than has any other human being in history. Sadly, the *Guinness Book of World Records* doesn't include that category.

Beyond the fun factor, snake-fishing enables an experimental approach – controlling the stimulus while working in a natural environment. Knowing a species' diet from looking inside the stomachs of dissected specimens is useful but it doesn't tell us the whole story. Does a snake have an empty stomach because it wasn't hungry or because it hadn't found prey? What sensory systems does a snake use to locate its next meal? And how does a snake decide what prey items to consume and which to ignore? The trusty fishing rod provides a way to answer those questions.

Is the snake anorexic?

Almost every field study reports that most snakes have no food in their stomach at the time of capture. That result reflects low feeding rates, coupled with a tendency for recently fed snakes to hide away. But there are other factors as well. If reproduction is incompatible with feeding, for example, a snake has to choose one or the other. A male viper can either search for receptive females or lie in ambush for prey. It can't do both. Likewise, a swollen body due to enlarging offspring may make it impossible for a pregnant female to enter a narrow burrow where her prey are hiding, or even to fit prey into her stomach.

The garter snakes of Manitoba illustrate this trade-off between feeding and mating. It's easy to tell if a garter snake has fed recently – the remains of that meal emerge from the rear end of the animal, to be smeared all over your fingers. That happened often when we picked up garter snakes away from the big communal dens, but it never happened when we were handling snakes at the dens themselves. Why aren't the snakes feeding while they are at the dens? There are only two possible answers: either the snakes refuse to eat (focusing instead on sex), or else there aren't any edible items at the den.

Testing between those explanations was easy. Bob Mason and I dug up earthworms from a compost pile, tied them to line attached to a fishing rod, and dangled the worms over a den full of snakes. Every snake we tested grabbed the worm like a graduate student finding an unclaimed donut in the university cafeteria. So garter snakes at the dens will eat if prey is available. It's just that worms are scarce at a den with thousands of hungry snakes. We don't need complicated explanations about snakes prioritising sex over food; but it took an experiment to establish that fact.

Food trumps sex, even for a male Red-sided Garter Snake (*Thamnophis sirtalis parietalis*) that is enthusiastically courting a female in the Manitoba dens.

How does a snake detect its prey?

The first step in obtaining a meal is to figure out if the object in front of you is edible. How do you decide? Vision and smell are the most obvious cues, but there are other possibilities as well. For example, how about body temperature of the prey? And in a water snake, there's another option: water vibrations.

At the height of the midsummer monsoons in tropical Australia, Macleay's Water Snakes gather in vast numbers at the flooded edges of waterbodies. Native fish sleep at night close to the water's edge. Those sleeping sites are usually in dense vegetation, providing protection from predators, but rapid flooding extends the water's edge onto open ground. The sleeping fish are exposed and vulnerable – and the snakes know it. Medium sized and heavy bodied, the snakes cruise along the water's edge to grab unwary fish. A great chance, I thought, to break out my fishing rod.

With colleagues Greg Brown and Melanie Elphick, I crept quietly along the water's edge at night, with a dead fish or a hook-free plastic lure dangling from the rod tip. To see if snakes key in on prey based on water vibrations as well as visual cues, Greg held a transparent plastic shield between a snake and the lure as I jiggled it. Sure enough, snakes attacked if the shield was removed but ignored the jiggling fish if the shield blocked vibrations. And further evidence of the role of vibrations came from watching snakes chasing fish. Fish responded to approaching snakes by flipping up out of the water, landing a few centimeters away and then dashing off. The splash of a fish hitting the water near its head drove the snake into a frenzy, slashing around with its mouth open and clamping down if its teeth encountered anything fishy.

So, was vibration the key? To find out, I drove into town and purchased a child's water pistol. That night, I aimed the pistol near the first foraging snake that I encountered – and to my delight, the resulting splash drove the snake into hysteria. And in between swatting mosquitoes and dodging crocodiles, we found many other snakes to test – and every time, the splash was effective. A snake's best chance of grabbing a fish comes as it flips back into the water – and so, disturbance to the water arouses a hungry snake into frenetic activity. For a Macleay's Water Snake, water vibration is the most reliable cue to catching a fish.

Not all prey items create vibrations, though. For Turtle-headed Sea Snakes on coral reefs of the Indo-Pacific, every meal consists of tiny fish eggs. The snakes tongue-flick as they search for fish nests, suggesting that scent is the most important cue. To test that idea, I set out small bundles of cotton cloth among the coral. Some bundles contained fish eggs, and others were empty. The two types of bundles looked identical, but one emitted egg smells – and sure enough, foraging sea snakes were far more interested in those offerings than in nearby 'control' bundles. Snakes are specialists at detecting faint chemical traces, and scent drives the foraging biology of many species. Not all of them though. Hadas Tsairi and Amos Bouskila used semi-natural enclosures in the Judean desert to show that Saw-scaled Vipers select ambush sites based on the cover of bushes not the scent of prey items.

For snakes that eat endothermic ('warm-blooded') prey, temperature provides another cue about a prey item's location. Pit vipers derive their common name from forward-facing facial pits that can detect tiny thermal differences. The pits have attracted sophisticated laboratory study and at least one field trial. Shedao is a small island in north-eastern China, famed for its abundance of pit vipers. The snakes feed on small birds that use the island as a stopover as they migrate between Siberia and South-East Asia. With an average of one pit viper per square metre, almost every tree is draped with snakes lying in ambush for an unwary feathered meal. And like many island species, the pit vipers of Shedao are unafraid of humans so I could approach closely without disturbing them. To test the role of prey temperature, my 'lure' was a feather-covered nylon stocking enclosing a balloon full of either hot or cold water. I dangled my lure in front of ambushing pit vipers, mimicking the movements of a small bird. Often, a strike was so fast that it was difficult for me to be sure that the snake had moved at all. But

Greater Sea Snakes (*Hydrophis major*) search for Coral Catfish (*Plotosus lineatus*) on a falling tide, as water with catfish scent flows out from cavities in the coral and tells the snake where to find a meal. CLAIRE GOIRAN

scoring was easy because the snakes' fangs puncturing the balloon generated a spectacular 'pop' and water gushed from two small holes. Snakes were more likely to launch a strike at the hot model than the cold one, demonstrating that a hungry pit viper prefers a warm meal.

Other researchers have conducted field experiments on snake foraging also, but without fishing rods. The Brown Tree Snake team on the Pacific island of Guam designed traps to remove these devastating invaders. Part of that work involved testing the cues that attract snakes to traps, including visual versus olfactory cues (a live bird versus bird-scent). The same approach has been applied in Florida to improve trapping success for invasive Burmese Pythons in the Everglades. Although the work has a practical aim – pest control – these studies qualify as field-based experiments on the foraging responses of snakes.

Another form of prey-searching behaviour has also been a classic topic for research. It addresses the issue of how a snake can find an already-envenomated prey item – for example, when a rattlesnake strikes a rodent but then immediately releases it, waits for the prey to die, then tracks it down to eat. Some snakes hang on grimly after they have seized their intended meal, but that's risky if your dinner has fast reflexes and sharp claws or teeth. So ambush-foraging snakes such as vipers often strike then release. They mostly rely on the scent trail of the bitten prey – or even the scent trail of the snake's own venom – to locate it, and such a snake can distinguish the rat it struck from an otherwise similar rat that doesn't have venom coursing through the body. If no scent trail is available, the snake can use airborne cues to find its food. In short, the predatory strike initiates a complex and stereotyped set of behaviours that help a snake to relocate its meal.

Happiness is a warm meal

After consuming a large meal, a captive snake moves to a warm place in its cage because digestion works faster at higher temperatures. We might expect to see the same pattern in the wild. Sure enough, if you offer a free-ranging snake a large prey item, the snake stops moving around after its meal and instead, finds a safe place where it can bask in the sunlight (or under a sun-warmed cover item) until its prey has been digested.

Most studies on this topic have placed a recently killed prey item close to a radio-tracked snake, so the snake encounters the free meal and swallows it. But Greg Brown took the procedure a step further by training free-ranging snakes to accept food from his hands. During his PhD in Canada, Greg began by placing dead fish near Common Water Snakes; but to offer fish to specific snakes Greg attached the fish to an extendable car radio antenna with an alligator clip so he could hold it next to the snake of his choice. Before long the snakes learned to associate Greg with an unlimited smorgasbord. Instead of fleeing, they climbed into his canoe. No time for the radio antenna; he had to offer fish by hand. More than once an overly zealous snake grabbed Greg's fingers rather than the fish. Training those wild snakes gave Greg a great experimental study, proving that a meal doesn't change a water snake's basking behaviour. But his study had disturbing consequences for other researchers who were studying birds in the lake. Students returned from the field white-faced, with tales of ferocious snakes storming into their canoes.

Turning mice into snakes

Showing that a snake's reproductive output depends upon its food supply is more difficult in the field than in lab trials. Nonetheless, several brave souls have done it. As a PhD student, Emily Taylor placed dead rodents near some of her radio-tracked Diamondback Rattlesnakes in the Arizona desert, one to four times a week. Nearby snakes monitored at the same time were not pampered in the same way. Snakes with access to the extra food grew faster and they were more likely to reproduce in the following year. With those strong experimental studies

Northern Water Snakes (*Nerodia sipedon*) feed on fishes, and usually catch their own. NOAH K. FIELDS
For an experimental study, Canadian researcher Greg Brown trained these snakes to accept food from his hands; but sometimes the snakes' enthusiasm made them mistake Greg's finger for a fish. GREG BROWN

behind her, Emily soon obtained a professorship position, but she retains her sense of humour; her social media name is 'snakeymama'. In a follow-up study a decade later, Emily and her own students repeated the experiment but offering additional water not food. Again, the effects on rattlesnake reproduction were spectacular. Those studies provide direct evidence about the factors that drive snake reproduction in the wild.

Standing back to take an overall look at field-based experimental studies on snake ecology, it's clear that the opportunities are exciting. For example, I could only find a single study that looked at the consequences of experimentally manipulating some aspect of the snake's appearance on its foraging success. Terry Farrell, Peter May and Paul Andreadis painted the tails of Pygmy Rattlesnakes different colours (black or yellow), to test the idea that tail colour affects the success of caudal-luring behaviour. It didn't work – a snake's new tail colour didn't affect its rate of feeding or growing – but it was a hell of a good idea.

There's no place like home

Most animals have distinct home ranges, rather than wandering long distances. Cross-country travel is hazardous, and there are advantages to knowing the local layout – where to find food and shelter, where to bask safely, and so forth. Snakes are homebodies as a result, and mark-recapture studies generally reveal that an individual remains within a small area throughout its life. What happens, then, if you capture a snake and release it somewhere else?

That question has real-world significance, because snakes that venture close to houses are often captured and removed to reduce danger to the householder. Mitigating this human-wildlife conflict is a huge enterprise worldwide, with thousands of snake catchers removing unwecome serpents from the living rooms of distressed homeowners. Sadly, such translocations are often futile. The displaced animal wanders around trying to find its way home, at high risk from predators and highway traffic. And if the snake makes it all the way home, any benefit from its removal is eliminated.

Homing has been documented in snake species from sea kraits through to rattlesnakes, and appears to be widespread. In some studies, investigators have radio-tracked snakes that were translocated at the same time as others that were not. Emily Taylor and her team found that not only did translocated rattlesnakes move about more, but parts of the brain associated with direction-finding expanded.

How can we ask a snake what kind of habitat it prefers? A radio-tracking study can show that those preferences differ among species, and even between adults and juveniles, or between males and females, or change with season. But we need experiments to tease apart the reasons behind those patterns.

For example, radio tracking shows that snakes spend a lot of time in places where they obtain food. But is it the food that attracts them, or some other characteristic of the site? A place with shelter might also contain food, and it might be the shelter that attracts snakes. To test the idea that snakes key in on food directly, we need an experiment. In 1990 American biologist David Duvall and his colleagues performed one of the first field experiments in snake ecology. In Wyoming, Prairie Rattlesnakes move long distances every spring from their overwinter dens to their summer feeding ranges. Do they stop when they encounter prey-rich areas?

Some of the first experiments on habitat selection by free-ranging snakes were conducted on Prairie Rattlesnakes (*Crotalus viridis*).
NOAH K. FIELDS

To test that hypothesis, the researchers radio tracked migrating snakes in springtime. When the snakes ceased moving each day, the scientists deployed cues from Deer Mice (a common prey item) in snakeproof cages. Some cages contained live Deer Mice; others had chemical cues from Deer Mice; and yet others were controls (no scent or live mice). Sure enough, snakes that encountered mice stopped migrating and assumed ambush positions. Male snakes were easier to fool than females; they stopped for mouse scent alone, and two male rattlers stayed beside the mouse cages for the entire 21-day study. It was a convincing demonstration that Prairie Rattlers are looking for food as they leave their dens in springtime.

That pioneering study was followed by many others. In one of the most ambitious studies, the Florida-based 'Pig Team' sprayed frog scent within their study area and showed that Pygmy Rattlers chose to lie in ambush in the frog-smelling areas rather than in nearby places sprayed only with water.

Other straightforward experiments involve cases where snakes regularly use more than one type of habitat. For example, the garter snakes of Manitoba usually stay at ground level, but occasionally hundreds of snakes climb into small trees beside the dens. We noticed that tree climbing occurred after rain showers that cooled the ground, suggesting that snakes climb to stay warm. We tested the idea with lab trials but also with a simple field experiment. When we lightly sprinkled snakes with water, they went straight up into a tree. Habitat use in snakes must often be driven by these kinds of dynamic thermal mosaics.

In the case of the broader question 'why do snakes use habitat X rather than habitat Y?', the gold-medal standard approach would be to modify the available habitat to create two options and see how the snakes respond. That's simple in theory but difficult in practice, because it takes a lot of work to modify habitats. One successful study of this type was by my student David Pike, on Broad-headed Snakes that live in rock outcrops among eucalypt forests in eastern Australia. Historical photographs show that the forest is becoming denser, with fewer opportunities for snakes to find a sun-warmed rock for shelter. To test if forest overgrowth was a problem, David cut down some shade trees. Hey presto, the rocks were exposed to sun again, and the snakes' favourite prey items – Velvet Geckos – moved back in. The snakes weren't far behind.

Because many snakes are mobile and long lived, it's difficult to know if a change in habitat that affects snake abundance does so via dispersal (snakes move into or out of the new habitat) or an actual increase or decrease in snake numbers overall. Nonetheless, it's an important question. Most habitat-manipulation experiments haven't continued for long enough to detect strong effects, but at least two pioneering projects have achieved that aim. In a French forest, Xavier Bonnet and his colleagues removed trees to allow sunlight penetration, stimulating the growth of thick shrubs that favoured rodents and the snakes that fed upon them. In African savannah habitats, US-based researcher Douglas McCauley and colleagues exploited an ambitious experiment that had removed large herbivores such as elephants from some plots but not others. By regularly checking under cover boards, the scientists found that Olive Hissing Snakes as well as their rodent prey were more common in the absence of large herbivores.

How to arouse an amorous male snake

Snakes spend more time looking for food than they do looking for mates, so it's easier to conduct experiments on feeding than on reproduction. But there are places where male snakes are so intensely focused on finding mates that they ignore human intruders. The huge garter snake dens of central Manitoba provide the perfect system.

That opportunity has transformed our understanding of communication systems in snakes. Over decades at the big dens, Bob Mason single-mindedly explored the chemical basis of sex recognition in Red-sided Garter Snakes. After his discovery that skin chemicals enable a male garter snake to distinguish the sex of another serpent, Bob and I used that information to run experiments in the field. For example, we rubbed cotton swabs over female snakes, then laid those cotton swabs on the ground beside the den. Any male who encountered a female's swab launched into courtship overdrive, but a male-scented swab was ignored. Even a single tongue flick can tell a male about a female's species, body size, body condition, and even her sex life – in particular, whether or not she has recently mated.

Is scent the only information that a male garter snake uses to locate a female? Nope. There are other clues as well, and males use all of them. For example, emerging females are instantly courted by dozens of males. As a result, the easiest way for us to find female snakes was to look for a writhing pile of bodies. To test the idea that male snakes key in on frantic movement,

Courting Red-sided Garter Snakes (*Thamnophis sirtalis parietalis*) at a Manitoba den. CHRIS FRIESEN

I thrashed a rope around – and lovestruck male snakes hurtled over to it. Any pile of writhing snakes is likely to have a female inside it, so it pays a male to look for movement.

What other cues might alert a male garter snake to a romantic opportunity? Males use every shred of information available. For example, most females in the den have recently emerged from hibernation and thus are mud covered and cool, whereas the males courting them are clean (from moving through wet grass) and warm (via basking). Does a lustful male garter snake look for muddy cool snakes? Yes he does. When I smeared mud on a male snake, it increased his sex appeal. Likewise, cooling a snake down in the fridge made him a magnet for the other males. Over millions of years, natural selection has fine tuned the ability of males to find females. Today's snakes are masters at that art.

Those mate-finding skills extend to the faint scent trails that are laid down on the ground as a female slithers along. We dragged female snakes through the grass, then recorded the response of males that encountered her trail. The males immediately took off along the trail we had laid, fervently tongue flicking the ground in search of the elusive female who had passed that way. Male trails were ignored.

If you can turn on a male garter snake's libido with chemicals, maybe you can turn it off as well. Watching courting groups at the den, I was impressed by the abrupt end to the writhing turmoil around a female. As soon as she begins mating with one of the males, the others give up and head off to look for action elsewhere. How do they know that it's futile to continue? Perhaps they can smell the successful male's sperm? To test that idea, we put pairs of snakes inside empty plastic margarine containers and used a small aquarium pump to push air past the stimulus snakes and towards males courting a female. If the stimulus snakes were mating, the targeted males gave up and went elsewhere. If the stimulus snakes weren't mating, the target males kept courting. It was the first evidence that snakes use airborne scents when making decisions about sex.

We also devised experiments to explore female behaviour. For example, female garter snakes don't just mate with the first male who comes long. It takes prolonged vigorous courtship to convince a female to mate. Why does she resist? Is this because she just doesn't want to mate, or is there a hidden evolutionary advantage? For example, a female who resists for as long as she can may end up mating with the most vigorous male – and he probably has the best genes, giving her offspring the best chance in life.

How do you ask a female snake whether her resistance to courtship is real, or just a clever tactic to pick the best mate? When I first visited the dens I saw many female garter snakes apparently trying to leave, but failing because they were swamped by frantically courting males. Is that because the female benefits from attracting many suitors so she can pick the best one? Or more simply, is it too difficult to climb a steep rocky slope out of the den with twenty wriggling males on top of you? To test the idea that females are doing their best to escape, we smeared some newly emerged females with a chemical that discourages male courtship. Others were smeared with a 'control' chemical that had no such effect. When we did this, the females that were given a free pass to avoid male harassment zipped out of the dens as soon as they could whereas the others took much longer to disperse. The females weren't actively attracting males in order to get the best mates; they were just trying to get away.

It's the mating season, and this male Turtle-headed Sea Snake (*Emydocephalus annulatus*) is frantically courting a diver's flipper – even though it's difficult to understand how he could mistake it for a female snake. ALINE GUEMAS

Emboldened by success with sex-crazed garter snakes in Manitoba, I applied the same methods to amorous male Turtle-headed Sea Snakes in the shallow waters of Indo-Pacific coral reefs. I attached ropes of different colours and textures to fishing line, and then dragged my models through the water. During the snakes' mating season, any male sea snake that saw the rope swam over to it and began courting. The males didn't care about the rope's colour or texture, but tongue flicking a rope pre-soaked in female chemicals (pheromones) drove the males to new heights of sexual enthusiasm. Those trials showed that mate-searching male sea snakes rely on their eyes to find a female, with their sensitive tongue tips only coming into the picture after they are up close and personal. Clearly, a male snake's tactics are affected by the evolutionary transition to life in the oceans. Unlike their land-dwelling ancestors, male sea snakes can't follow chemical trails to find romance. First, the sex-identifying pheromones are water-insoluble. And second, female sea snakes don't rub against the coral as they swim around. As a result, male sea snakes rely on visual cues to find females, and then check them out by tongue flicking when they are close enough. Male sea snakes have bigger eyes than females, to help deal with the challenge of murky water – but even so, their eyesight is poor. So mate-searching males approach anything they see moving around – even human divers. That behaviour leads to lurid tales of 'attacks', when all that is happening is a sad case of mistaken identity.

But there's still a lot we don't understand about sexuality in snakes. The biggest puzzle is that males are the choosy sex, not females. Many studies show that male snakes select their courtship targets based on traits such as body size and condition – but nobody has ever demonstrated the same choosiness in female snakes. Maybe it's just too difficult to resist.

IN THEIR OWN WORDS

Some people hate to speculate:

"The great curse of science, the grasping at finite inferences on insufficient data, has been exemplified in none of its branches to a more disastrous extent than in ophiology. When we reflect on the variable character of serpents and nearly everything connected to them, it would seem as though especial care should be taken in guarding against convictions based on anything but the most abundant evidence, where questions concerning them are involved; yet scientific men have promulgated their hypotheses as proven facts on the strength of isolated cases, and great travellers who have been famous for their erudition in other departments of natural history have given the weight of their names to vulgar rumours which have been reported to them of things ophidian. Better, far better, to fall back upon the veriest superstition and folklore than to find ourselves on ground which is beset with pitfalls of error like these beneath its seeming solidity." Arthur Stradling, 1882

But others enjoy nothing more than a good flight of fancy:

"False facts are highly injurious to the progress of science for they often endure long; but false views do little harm for everyone takes a salutary pleasure in proving their falseness; and when this is done, one path to error is closed and the road to truth is often at the same time opened." CHARLES DARWIN, 1871

"I love fools' experiments. I am always making them." CHARLES DARWIN, 1896

"Any one who has studied the history of science knows that almost every great step therein has been made ... by the invention of hypotheses, which, though verifiable, often had very little foundation to start with; and, not unfrequently, in spite of a long career of usefulness, turned out to be wholly erroneous in the long run." THOMAS HENRY HUXLEY, 1887

Field experiments on courtship and mate-finding behaviour rely on the enthusiasm of male snakes. That ardour was noticed early in the history of reptile research:

"Though cold-blooded, their passions are strong." CHARLES DARWIN, 1871

"It is remarkable to notice the tenacity and intent with which the males persist in following up the females during the time of sexual desire." GEORGE EUGENE BEYER, 1898

Snake experts struggle when commenting on stories of 'aggressive' snakes, because although the experts have never been attacked themselves, it's impossible to categorically deny the possibility that every once in a while, a snake goes ballistic. For example, the African pioneer Ionides caught hundreds of Black Mambas, and regarded them as inoffensive unless harassed; but nonetheless feels compelled to say:

"Of alleged entirely unprovoked attacks by Black Mambas I have little reliable evidence. There is the account by my friend Charles Pitman in his book *The Snakes of Uganda*, in which he gives the case in Southern Rhodesia many years ago of a rogue Black Mamba that started by chasing sheep and goats and ended up killing eleven people, most of whom died within half an hour." CONSTANTIN IONIDES, 1965

Chapter 9

Studying snakes without studying snakes

Some of the most important interactions in nature involve the eternal conflict between predators versus prey. In that conflict, a snake can play the role of either killer or victim. Because most snakes are small and harmless, they are popular menu items for animals ranging from centipedes to snake eagles. And on the other side of the coin, snakes are superb predators that can overpower and consume animals far larger than themselves.

To understand the interactions between eater and eaten, you need to study both of the parties involved; and even a snake-obsessed investigator can find themselves working mostly on the animals that are eaten by snakes, or that eat snakes, rather than on the snakes themselves.

Masters of camouflage

There are no vegetarian serpents. To survive, a snake has to find, capture and kill its prey; and those prey will do their best to avoid being found, captured and killed. This evolutionary battle, playing out over millions of years, has produced spectacular results. For example, it has fine-tuned traits that render ambush-foraging snakes almost invisible and has developed sensitive snake-detection systems in prey.

A snake hidden in foliage is difficult to detect even by a species with outstanding eyesight, such as *Homo sapiens*. The challenge is formidable. Ambush-foraging snakes remain immobile for days on end, and their intricate colour patterns are beautifully matched to local backgrounds. The risk posed by predatory snakes has fashioned prey species to be experts at detecting snakes. For example, lizards can recognise even a faint whiff of snake odour and avoid sites with those tell-tale warning signals. Given the choice, a heat-loving Australian velvet gecko prefers a cold crevice *without* snake smell to a warm one *with* snake smell. It pays to be paranoid.

If a lizard, tadpole or salamander detects the scent of snakes, the potential prey changes its behaviour. It may flee, or stop moving, or remain under cover. If a foraging rodent encounters snake scent in a food patch, it goes elsewhere. If a snake lies in wait in a tree laden with ripe fruit, even the hungriest birds stay away. The shed skin of a snake inside a bird's nest discourages egg predation by squirrels. In short, snakes are scary.

Above: Ambush predators are beautifully camouflaged against the background, to escape detection by both predators and prey. Although fully exposed, this American Copperhead (*Agkistrodon contortrix*) could easily escape detection. NOAH K. FIELDS
Below: This Puff Adder (*Bitis arietans*) is almost invisible among dead leaves. XAVIER GLAUDUS

The scent of a snake can even change the way that an embryo develops. Lab studies have shown that tadpoles of the endangered Mallorcan Midwife Toad grow longer tails with deeper tail muscles, and develop more rapidly, if they detect the presence of predatory viperine snakes. Those changes likely protect the tadpoles. Even more intriguing, though, are cases where the developing embryo is tucked away inside the mother's uterus, and it's the mother not the baby that detects snake scent. In a laboratory experiment, my student Sharon Downes and I exposed pregnant lizards to the scent of snakes. Remarkably, the babies produced by mothers who smelled that frightening aroma were unusually fast running, had longer-than-usual tails, and tongue flicked at frenetic rates if they encountered snake scent. Those characteristics would help a young lizard to detect a snake and flee from it, so it looks like an adaptive response. But how could it work? We don't know any pathway by which a mother could transmit that warning to her unborn offspring. Intriguingly, though, other research has shown that stressed pregnant lizards add hormones to their eggs that affect embryonic development.

How have such anti-predator defences affected snake evolution? Increasing paranoia in prey favours increasing counter-adaptations in snakes. For example, the snake may need to blend into its background so well as to be undetectable. In snake species with a wide geographic range, local races match local backgrounds. In species that shift habitats with age, colour can shift as well. For example, Green Tree Pythons take their common name from the colour of adults, whereas juveniles are bright red or yellow. The young snakes live on the forest edge, where their colours hide them from prey and from predatory birds; whereas adults live in the forest canopy where green provides the best camouflage.

In snake species that occur across diverse habitats, local populations often evolve colouration to match local backgrounds – such as in this Horned Viper (*Cerastes cerastes*) from pale-sand deserts of the Middle East. PIXABAY

Camouflage can be so effective that it's humbling for a snake researcher who follows the signal from a radio-tracked snake and then tries to find the animal visually. You know it's there – the radio receiver is beeping loudly – but sometimes you need to stare at a patch of ground for minutes before you finally see the snake. Even more embarrassing, the animal can be fully exposed – but blends so beautifully into the background that it is well-nigh invisible.

Camouflage sounds like a simple issue at first sight, but not all eyes are created equal. For example, birds detect different wavelengths of light than do snakes or mammalian predators. As a result, specific types of camouflage work best against specific enemies. If we understand the physics of vision, we can work out how obvious a particular snake coloration is to a predatory bird versus to another snake.

Visual resemblance to the background may not be enough, though, if the creatures you are hiding from rely more on their noses than their eyes. Carefully controlled trials by Graham Alexander and his students on the Puff Adder, a large heavyset ambush predator in southern Africa, show that these snakes are virtually odour-free. Even acute sniffers such as dogs, Meerkats, cobras and elephants can't distinguish between 'control' cloths and those containing the scent of Puff Adders. Invisibility to a prey item's nose as well as its eyes is a powerful weapon in the Puff Adder's artillery. These lethargic vipers even retain fully digested remains of prey within the rectum for weeks – even months – before taking a toilet break. That prolonged constipation may further reduce smells that would be detectable by predators.

Long periods of immobility are important also. Movement not only makes a snake visible; it also smears scent around. Lab experiments show that Australian velvet geckos are more reluctant to enter a crevice with widely distributed snake scent than a similar crevice where the scent is restricted to a central area. It pays an ambushing snake to stay still.

Luring prey to their doom

Although most ambush-foraging snakes try to be invisible, some species keep most of their body hidden but flaunt one small part of it – the tail or the tongue – to attract prey items.

Tongue luring to attract prey has been recorded in only a handful of snake species, but may be widespread. A foraging snake flicks its tongue tips in and out of the mouth frequently to search for chemical cues, and a hungry prey item could easily mistake the flickering object for an edible insect. Tongue luring has been reported mostly in aquatic snakes, but Puff Adders may also use their flickering tongues to attract amphibians on land. Puff Adders also lure with their tails, making this the only species with a lure at each end of the body.

The possibility of tongue luring was mentioned in the 1880s, early in the history of snake research. Catherine Cooper Hopley noted the behaviour in 1882, and one of her contemporaries

Although Puff Adders (*Bitis arietans*) are well camouflaged both visually and chemically, they are not invisible. Predators that locate and consume them include the Cape Cobra (*Naja nivea*) and the Ratel or Honey Badger (*Mellivora capensis*), as shown by the gruesome remains of a pregnant female Puff Adder. PHOTOGRAPHS: BRYAN MARITZ AND GRAHAM ALEXANDER

described it in detail a few years later. Arthur Stradling (1851–1902) was friendly with Hopley – indeed, he once offered her a live rattlesnake, but she politely declined. In one of his many papers about captive snakes, Stradling described how he put a live hen in a cage with an anaconda and saw the hen making "a determined dab at the snake's tongue, sometimes two or three dabs in quick succession, every time the quivering black line caught her eye. My own idea is that she mistakes the tongue for a wriggling worm". Stradling also described "how a Scarlet Tanager in Costa Rica had been attracted out of a tree down close to a snake by its quivering tongue, the only moving thing about it … one of the chief uses of the mysterious little organ is to attract insectivorous animals."

Tail luring is much better understood. It occurs in snakes of several different lineages, often accompanied by modified colours or shapes of the tail tip. The snake lies hidden with only its tail visible and twitches the tip in a way that makes it look like a small insect. An unwary frog (or lizard, bird or shrew) that approaches that seductive twitching is in desperate trouble.

The undisputed Gold Medal for 'most spectacular tail lure' goes to the Spider-tailed Horned Viper of Iran and Iraq. As the snake's name suggests, the tail ends in a chunky section bordered

As its name suggests, the Spider-tailed Viper (*Pseudocerastes urarachnoides*) has a tail tip that looks like a spider – and when waved about, it attracts hungry birds. MATTHIEU BERRONEAU

by long drooping scales, with a stunning resemblance to a spider. Birds seem to be the main victims of this elaborate ruse. But although nobody doubts the prey-attracting power of such a lure, scientists disagree about luring in other species of snakes. For example, can a rattlesnake's rattle play this function, as well as making a warning sound?

Have the colour and movement of a snake's tail tip been fine-tuned by natural selection to make an effective lure? To assess that possibility you can take the system into the lab and ask two questions. First, do snakes initiate luring only in the presence of a potential meal? And second, do factors such as the lure's size, colour and movement affect its success in attracting prey? In 2002, American biologist Randall Reiserer was the first to examine those topics with large sample sizes and a clear framework. He examined luring behaviour of four species of vipers in the lab and found that luring was initiated by different prey types in each snake species. Importantly, Randall also pioneered the use of model prey items (painted rods) so that he could alter the size, shape, colour and movement of the artificial lure. That way, he could conduct experiments on how lure characteristics affect the response of potential prey.

My student Mattias Hagman took that work a step further in studies of the Northern Death Adder, an ambush-foraging Australian elapid snake. As you might guess from his name, Mattias is Swedish – but his lifelong passion for reptiles and amphibians led him to Australia to do his doctoral research in my lab. I was surprised when my new graduate student proved to be a tattoo-covered drummer from a Swedish rockband, but Mattias settled rapidly into a very different world. One of his most interesting studies involved death adders, perhaps the most unusual of Australian snakes. Like all of the other dangerously venomous Aussies, death adders are elapids – and worldwide, almost all elapids are slender and they actively search for prey. But death adders ambush their prey, like vipers in other parts of the world; and thus have evolved viper-like body shapes, and behaviours. That similarity extends to tail luring. Mattias found that (just like vipers) death adders are selective about when they wiggle their tails. Lizards attract more interest than frogs and are more likely to approach the lure. Mattias also attached a severed death adder tail to a machine that waved the tail tip, to see how prey responded. Small lures were more attractive than larger ones, perhaps explaining why juvenile death adders lure more often than adults.

In follow-up work with death adders, we found that caudal luring can also backfire. Our study site was overrun by toxic Cane Toads, and about half of our radio-tracked death adders died when they ate the poisonous toads. Sadly, one of the reasons for that death toll was tail luring. Cane Toads stimulate intense luring by death adders, and the toxic amphibians enthusiastically approach that enticing tail. A strategy that had worked well for death adders for millions of years was transformed overnight into an ecological trap. Like a doomed hero in

In snake species that lure prey with their tail tips, the lure is often brightly coloured – especially in young individuals, such as this American Copperhead (*Agkistrodon contortrix*). NOAH K. FIELDS

a Shakespearean drama, death adders bring their fate upon themselves.

We still have a lot to learn about luring by snakes. Many ambush-foraging snakes could benefit from attracting prey items, and caudal luring and tongue luring may not be the only options. For example, the pelagic Yellow-bellied Sea Snake has a unique lifestyle. All other sea snakes are closely tied to coral-reef habitats, where they mostly rely on active searching to catch their prey. But the Yellow-bellied Sea Snake drifts about in the open ocean, floating on the surface most of the time. It eats tiny fish – and uses a fiendishly clever method to do so. The floating snake looks like a stick, and fish gather beneath such an object because it offers protection from attack by birds. But after fish have accumulated under its body, the Yellow-bellied Sea Snake swims backwards – bringing its mouth close to those edible hitchhikers. A sideways snap, and the snake has dinner. It may be the only snake that uses its entire body as a lure.

The Yellow-bellied Sea Snake (*Hydrophis platurus*) drifts at the ocean surface, attracting edible fish by mimicking a floating stick. This photograph shows fish gathering beneath a distinctive all-yellow individual of this widespread species, in the Golfo Duce of Costa Rica.
SUSAN BESSESSEN

Fish are also the target for the Taiwan Eastern Water Snake, a highly aquatic species that sometimes spends hours with its tail and hindbody anchored to the bottom of a deep clear-water pond, and with the forebody raised vertically. Jean-Jay Mao noticed that in this position, a patch of bright white scales under the snake's neck reflects the sunlight – looking a lot like a shiny fishing lure. Jean-Jay never saw the snakes catch fish, but he speculates that maybe – just maybe – that colourful patch and unusual posture have evolved as a reflective lure. More generally, flecks of colour on a well-camouflaged snake (such as a juvenile Green Tree Python) might look like a swarm of edible insects, luring insect-eaters to their doom. At the risk of offending my American colleagues, I also think that a tightly coiled rattlesnake looks a lot like a cowpat. Perhaps in the days when huge herds of Bison roamed the plains, resembling a faecal pile rendered you inconspicuous – or even, attracted small animals that feed on dung-eating insects?

Luring a prey item through visual cues isn't the only prey-luring option. Smells might attract prey closer as well. Ambush-foraging Veiled Chameleons exude chemicals that attract flies, providing easy meals for the lizard. It's only a short leap from there to a scent-based system that attracts bigger prey. So far as I know, nobody has ever looked to see whether snakes that lie in wait produce perfumes that lure their prey closer. But I suspect that an ambush predator that has to wait for weeks between meals will use every prey-attracting trick that it can.

The Veiled Chameleon (*Chamaeleo calyptratus*) attracts insect food by producing a chemical that entices flies. NOAH K. FIELDS

Don't tread on me!

Although most snakes are well camouflaged against their surroundings, a few species opt for the opposite tactic: a colour pattern that stands out from the background. Several types of venomous snakes exhibit boldly contrasting black and yellow bands, advertising their deadliness. Some of those colours are hidden until a snake mounts its defence display, revealing brightly coloured skin between its scales or flashing an iridescent belly to startle a predator. That flexible strategy enables the snake to remain hidden during its day-to-day life, only revealing bright colours when its life is in danger.

But some snakes take the idea of 'bright colours' much further. They flaunt hues so intense that even a myopic predator could detect them from far away. The most famous examples of that tactic are coral snakes, highly venomous American elapids that are boldly ringed. Depending on the species involved, the rings may be black and yellow or black and red, or combinations of those colours. Instead of hiding from predators, these snakes draw attention to themselves.

Some snakes, such as this Eastern Coral Snake (*Micrurus fulvius*), have abandoned the idea of camouflage entirely, opting instead for bright colours to advertise their toxic venom. MATTHIEU BERRONEAU

An association between bright colours and toxic defences is widespread among animals ranging from wasps to poison-arrow frogs, so it's not surprising that snakes use the tactic as well. A predator that attacks a deadly snake is in mortal danger, and the snake that is attacked is likely to be injured also. Far better for both participants, to avoid that confrontation. Natural selection should favour predators that recognise and avoid toxic serpents; and deadly snakes that make that task easier for the predator by exhibiting unambiguous eye-catching colours.

Mimicry

If the only snakes to bear warning signals were toxic, that would be the end of the story. But strangely, almost-identical brightly banded patterns are also seen in a few non-venomous snakes. Why advertise your presence if you are edible? The answer to that question involved contributions by three of the 19th century's greatest biologists.

In 1848, two young British naturalists sailed from Liverpool to Brazil to embark on a massive collecting spree. Henry Walter Bates (1825–1892) and Alfred Russel Wallace (1823–1913)

were amateur naturalists who planned to collect insects and birds for sale to English museums and private collectors. The vast expanse of rainforests along the Amazon River provided a treasure trove of exotic animals for enthusiasts back in England. After a year together near Belem, the two friends went their separate ways. Bates spent nearly eleven years in the Amazon, obtaining the first specimens of many bizarre species. On his return to England in 1859 he wrote a best-selling travel book about his adventures.

An astute observer, Bates noticed that one type of colourful butterfly was never attacked by birds. He guessed, correctly, that these gaudy smelly butterflies were poisonous. Strangely, though, another type of butterfly in the same area, belonging to a harmless group, looked just like the poisonous ones. As Bates travelled up the Amazon he recorded that the colour patterns of the poisonous butterflies changed – and the colour patterns of the harmless ones changed as well, maintaining the resemblance.

The similarities were too striking to be coincidental, and Bates hit upon an explanation. The non-toxic species benefitted from imitating the toxic models because predators mistook the harmless butterflies for poisonous ones and so did not try to eat them. The process he described was later named in his honour, as 'Batesian mimicry'. Published in 1861, just two years after Charles Darwin's landmark book *On the Origin of Species*, Bates's idea was a beautiful illustration of the power of natural selection.

Darwin was delighted to have the example. In 1862, the great Charles sent a gushing letter of praise to Bates. "Dear Bates," he wrote, "I have just finished, after several reads, your paper. In my opinion it is one of the most remarkable and admirable papers I ever read in my life." Darwin then reveals his usual modesty – "I rejoice that I passed over the whole subject in the *Origin*, for I should have made a precious mess of it. You have most clearly stated and solved a wonderful problem" – as well as his antagonism to critics of natural selection – "Your paper is too good to be largely appreciated by the mob of naturalists without souls, but rely on it, that it will have lasting value, and I cordially congratulate you on your first great work." Darwin was desperately short of good examples of natural selection, and mimicry was ideal.

Meanwhile, Bates's companion Alfred Russel Wallace had travelled further afield to collect specimens – to the Malay Archipelago. Working in that remote area, Wallace made seminal contributions to biogeography and famously, he also came up with a startling new idea: the concept of natural selection. In 1858 he sent a manuscript outlining his ideas to none other than Charles Darwin – the man who had had the same idea several years earlier but had never published it for fear of controversy. Wallace generously acknowledged Darwin's prior claim to the theory, even writing a book about natural selection that was titled *Darwinism*. In my opinion, the two men deserve equal credit.

A harmless American species, the Arizona Mountain Kingsnake (*Lampropeltis pyromelana*), looks very much like a venomous coral snake.
NOAH K. FIELDS

Like Bates, Wallace also wrote a best-selling account of his tropical adventures (dedicated to Darwin). And also like his fieldwork companion, Wallace noticed the resemblance between co-occurring poisonous and non-poisonous butterflies. But he couldn't explain it, and wrote to Darwin to ask if he could think of an interpretation. In the end, it was Bates who delighted the great man by solving the puzzle with the idea of mimicry.

But then Wallace comes back into the picture. He realised that resemblances between poisonous and non-poisonous species were not just restricted to butterflies. In 1867 he wrote an extensive review of mimicry with an entire chapter devoted to snakes. As Wallace wrote, "We can hardly have more wonderful and more conclusive cases of … protective mimicry than are afforded by these various species of American snakes." Ironically, then, the most compelling case of Batesian mimicry among vertebrates occurs in the coral snakes of South America, but neither Bates nor Darwin had recognised that fact. Bates had spent more than a decade in the Amazon and must have encountered many coral snakes and mimics; in his travel-adventure book *The Naturalist on the River Amazons* (1863) he talks of "the coral-snake, which is a most beautiful object when seen coiled up on black soil in the woods." Darwin had spent a few months in Brazil also, and in *The Voyage of the Beagle* he mentions a coral snake collected on the Rio Macaè north of Rio de Janeiro. But it was Wallace who saw the relevance of Bates's mimicry hypothesis to coral snakes, and to the brightly coloured harmless snakes that resemble them so perfectly.

The discovery of mimicry in snakes was only a small part of Wallace's contributions to science. He had broad-ranging interests and wrote prolifically about topics such as whether or not there was life on Mars; the unjust social and economic system of Britain; and the environmental impacts of human activity. Later in life, his passionate belief in spirituality led him to conclude that the higher mental faculties of humans could not have arisen through natural selection. He was an anti-vaxer in the early 1880s, opposing mandatory smallpox vaccination because he doubted its effectiveness. Misfortune dogged him, for example when his entire collection of specimens from years of work was lost at sea when a cargo boat sank; and ill-advised investments in railways and mines kept him poor.

The idea of mimicry spread like wildfire, championed by Darwin's supporters. In an 1890 paper in one of the first Australian natural-history journals, the Reverend George Dutton wrote a review of mimicry in animals. He was clearly an enlightened clergyman: "Among vertebrates, too, we can find examples of mimicry. In a genus of snakes (*Elaps*) a very prominent peculiar colouring is seen. The snake always bears about with him a very legibly written notice to all whom it may concern, that he is poisonous to eat as well as in biting. Very like this is a harmless edible snake, *Pliocercus equalis*, which from its resemblance to the poisonous species enjoys immunity. … Defenceless creatures, by their resemblance to ones protected in a special way, are themselves protected. It is important not to be taken for what they are – eatable, defenceless creatures." But at the end, Reverend Dutton couldn't resist from expressing his abhorrence of such ungentlemanly behaviour: "Of the morality of such hypocrisy I shall not here speak."

Testing the mimicry hypothesis

In the 150 years since Bates and Wallace proposed mimicry as a powerful force for the evolution of colour patterns in snakes, many authors have joined the fray. Indeed, coral-snake mimicry ranks as one of the most popular but still-controversial ideas in snake research. Detailed resemblances between venomous models and non-venomous mimics have been identified. Those analyses include comparing times of evolutionary origin of presumed models versus mimics, as well as careful investigation of the degrees of similarity.

The main alternative explanation for those remarkable resemblances is that some unknown feature of the local environment favours a particular kind of colour pattern. As a result, that pattern has evolved independently in venomous and non-venomous snakes. For example, a banded pattern can make a snake more difficult to see as it moves through leaf litter in the twilight. That idea also predicts a correspondence in geographic variation between venomous and non-venomous species, although it's difficult to explain why some of the resemblances are so incredibly precise.

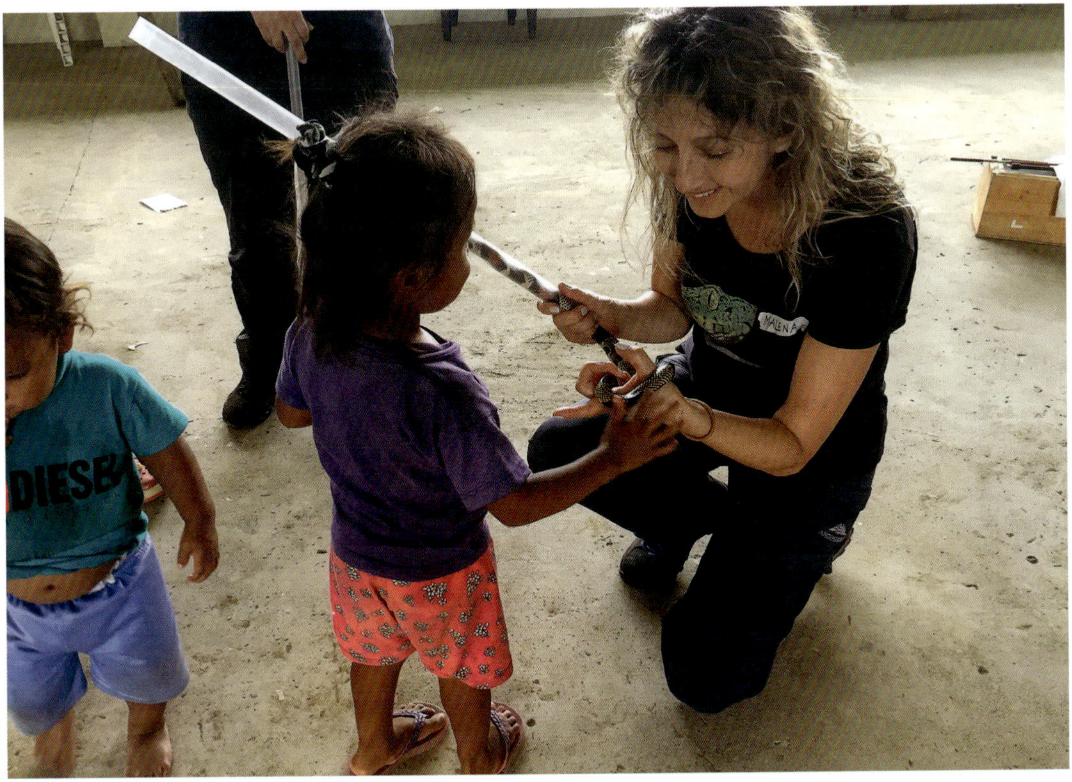

For an Amazon Kichwa child, learning the difference between deadly coral snakes and their harmless mimics is a matter of life and death. In this photograph, researcher María Barragán-Paladines is teaching a child in San Isla Community how to distinguish between this Ecuadorian Milk Snake (*Lampropeltis micropholis*) and the co-occurring deadly coral snakes.

Critics of the mimicry hypothesis point to the Scarlet Kingsnake, a black-and-red banded burrower that is common across a large swathe of North America where coral snakes are sadly lacking. How can the kingsnake be mimicking a non-existent toxic model? But coral snakes were once widespread in much of the kingsnake's range, so the non-venomous snake may benefit from those colours if predators retain their ancestral aversion to brightly banded reptiles. Well, maybe. And how can mimics evolve if the model (the toxic species) is much less common than the harmless mimics? Theory suggests that mimicry wouldn't function very well in that situation. Perhaps there is something about a brightly banded body that discourages predators, regardless of mimicry?

To escape from this kind of ambiguity, we need experiments. For example, does a harmless snake's resemblance to a dangerous species affect its vulnerability to predators? That's a difficult challenge because predation is rarely observed. By definition, a successful predation event only occurs once in the life of the prey item. The key development came from a US-based biology professor, Susan Smith, in 1975. She had the idea of using painted wooden dowels to test the responses of predatory birds to various colour patterns. As predicted by the mimicry hypothesis, tropical birds avoided red and yellow (coral snake-coloured) models but pecked at other chromatic options.

Susan's work was with captive-raised birds, suggesting that their aversion is innate rather than learned by an unpleasant outcome from previous encounters. That's a useful result, but it would also be good to take the experiment into the field. In 1981 two Swedish biologists, Goran Nilsson and Claes Andren, used hard-plastic models to look at predation rates on melanic (black) versus typically coloured Eurasian Adders, with a slice of sausage beneath each model. If the model was displaced or the sausage disappeared, it was scored as a predation event. Another Swede, Thomas Madsen, took the method one step further. He constructed his models of soft plasticine so that any attack would leave beak or tooth impressions. To test the idea that yellow spots on the neck of a juvenile European Grass Snake frighten away predatory birds, Thomas set out plasticine models with and without neck-spots. As he predicted, birds rarely pecked the neck-spot models.

The next great leap forward came in 1993, when an American graduate student, Ed Brodie, applied the plasticine method to coral-snake mimicry. He deployed models of snakes in the Atlantic lowland forests of Costa Rica. Some of the models were coloured like coral snakes, whereas others were brown. To check that attack rates were not influenced by detectability against the forest floor, he placed some models on sheets of white paper to make them obvious. When Ed retrieved his plasticine models, many of them had beak marks or tooth marks from predatory birds and mammals. And as the mimicry hypothesis predicted, brightly banded models were attacked less often.

Soon, deploying plasticine models became part of the snake-ecology research toolkit. Some people used simple versions that only an optimist would call 'snake-like', whereas others opted for ultra-realistic clay tubes wrapped in photographically printed fabric bearing an exact likeness of the snakes in question. On a personal level, my only attempt to deploy plasticine models ended in failure. I wanted to test the idea that in Manitoba, predatory crows are more likely

Snakes are frequently killed and eaten by birds including hawks – such as this Square-tailed Kite (*Lophoictinia isura*) carrying a Macleay's Water Snake (*Pseudoferania polylepis*) in tropical Australia – and herons – such as this Great Blue Heron (*Ardea herodias*) swallowing a North American Banded Water Snake (*Nerodia fasciata*). That predation imposes strong evolutionary pressures on snake colour patterns, to evade detection or to advertise toxicity. PHOTOGRAPHS: PIXABAY

to attack a solitary garter snake than a group of courting snakes. So I placed some plasticine models separately, and others in small groups. Unfortunately, by the time I checked my models, most of them had melted in the Manitoba sunshine. All I found were small pools of plasticine.

Other scientists have had more success. Dozens of studies have repeated Ed Brodie's methods, in areas with and without coral snakes. Some of the results are difficult to interpret, with banded models being attacked more rather than less often, but predators generally avoid banded models. As a result, most researchers think that mimicry explains the evolution of 'coral-snake' colour patterns in non-venomous snakes. But it's not a universal consensus. Science thrives on disagreement; the purpose of erecting a general explanation is to encourage other people to try to shoot it down. For every advocate of the mimicry hypothesis, there is a vociferous detractor. In 2024, independent British researcher Henri Mouy suggested that many of the snakes that exhibit coral-snake colours are preyed upon by other snakes – and that peculiar features of snake vision (they focus on objects by moving the lens back and forth) make red colours and bands difficult to see. If so, those bright patterns might have evolved to deceive predators rather than to resemble other snakes.

The major weakness in evidence for coral-snake mimicry comes from the artificiality of plasticine or clay models. Are beak marks evidence of predatory attacks, or are they due to curious birds checking out strange stationary objects? If the model doesn't deceive the bird, those responses may be about curiosity or scavenging rather than predation. Adding to that uncertainty, there are reports of predators avoiding banded models but attacking live coral snakes.

To overcome that objection, ideally our models would resemble moving rather than stationary snakes, and we would watch the interaction directly. That's difficult with land snakes, but my French colleague Claire Goiran and I overcame that problem by exploring snake colour patterns in a very different system: sea snakes on coral reefs.

Most sea snakes are highly venomous and many of them are banded in colour. Although none are as brightly hued as coral snakes, that banding might warn predators such as fishes and seabirds. Similarly banded patterns in eels and octopuses have been attributed to Batesian mimicry of deadly snakes. To test the idea that predatory fishes avoid banded snakes, we used snake-shaped fishing lures that swim through the water in a realistic fashion when pulled by a line. After painting the lures in various colours, Claire and I had great fun snorkelling through shallow-water reef areas with one of us dragging the lure behind us while the other watched for fish responses. To my delight, solid-coloured lures were attacked by large predatory fish whereas banded lures were almost never seized. And because the lures were moving, and we were watching, we are certain that the encounters were about predation not scavenging.

Many highly toxic sea snakes, such as this Slender-necked Sea Snake (*Hydrophis coggeri*), are banded in bright colours – a pattern that may deter predatory fishes from attacking them. CLAIRE GOIRAN

Deadly sea snakes and coral snakes aren't the only potential models out there for a non-venomous snake. Toxic invertebrates such as centipedes, millipedes and flatworms might be dangerous or noxious enough to repel predators, conferring protection on small burrowing snakes with similar colour patterns.

The most widespread toxic models, though, are other snakes. Over much of the world, large heavyset vipers are abundant and offer plausible models for other kinds of snakes (and for each other; venomous species may benefit from a common resemblance). Looking for similarities in colour between vipers and other snakes is a tricky business, because that colour pattern may have evolved for camouflage rather than mimicry. But the evidence suggests that mimicry of vipers is common. Using computer-based artificial intelligence methods ('deep learning'), French biologist Thomas de Solan and his colleagues analysed the resemblance between venomous vipers and non-venomous snakes across western Europe. Non-venomous species that occurred in the same places as vipers were more similar in appearance to the venomous snakes than expected by chance, with around 8 per cent of non-venomous species identified as likely mimics of vipers. In an experimental study, Wolfgang Wuster and his colleagues from Bangor University in Wales deployed 813 plasticine models in European fields to show that the dorsal zigzag pattern of Eurasian Adders is avoided by predators.

The topic of mimicry between harmless and venomous snakes is of personal interest to me, because it landed me in hospital. On a field trip in Oklahoma, I seized a small snake that was swimming across a creek. I was 99 per cent sure that it was a Banded Water Snake – but I was wrong. It was a juvenile Cottonmouth Moccasin, that repaid my interference by biting me on the finger before I could release it.

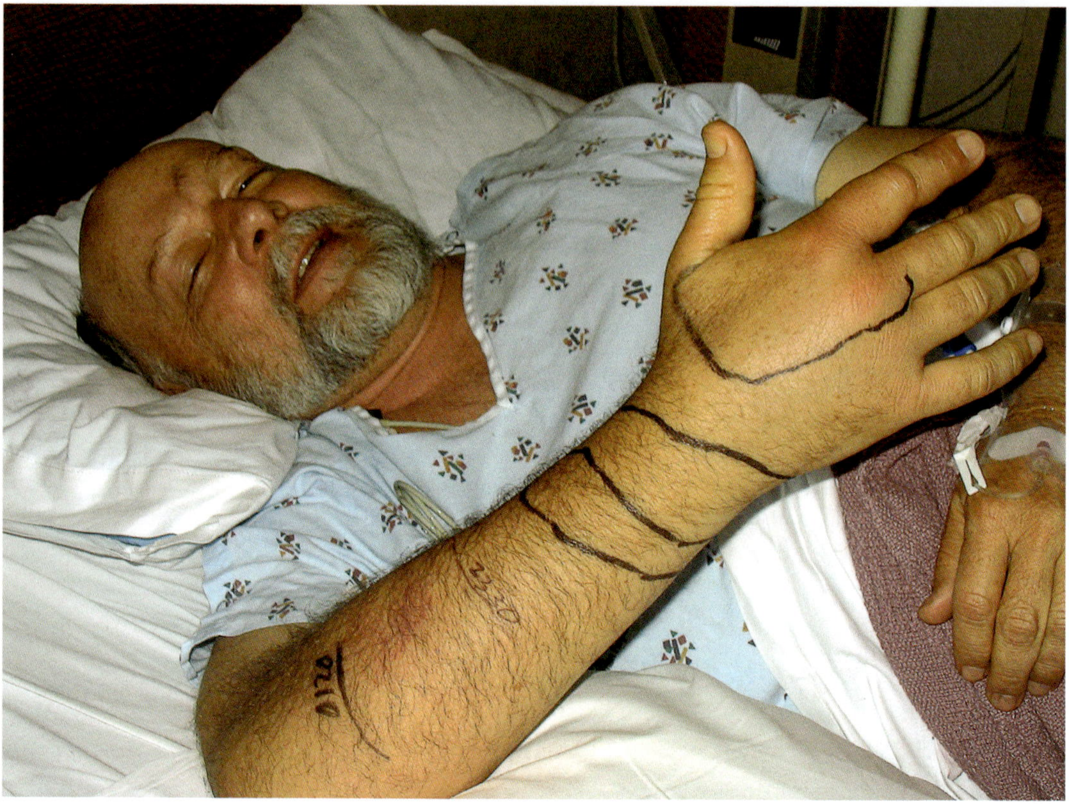

The consequences of failing to distinguish between a toxic snake and a harmless mimic species. The author in an Oklahoma hospital after mistaking a Cottonmouth Moccasin (*Agkistrodon piscivorus*) for a Banded Water Snake (*Nerodia fasciata*). The lines on the arm show the extent of swelling at different times after the bite. JONATHAN WEBB

I spent three days in hospital after that bite, and I was mercilessly teased by my US colleagues about my foolishness. To their experienced American eyes, a Cottonmouth looks nothing like a water snake. While searching through old scientific papers for this book, however, I encountered the following note by G. Brown Goode in 1873: "A friend recently brought me from Florida a fine specimen of Banded Water Snake (*Tropidonotus fasciatus*) which had been given to him … as one of the dreaded moccasins (*Ankistrodon piscivorus*). The resemblance was so perfect that I did not detect the error until I examined the head. I have since examined the specimens of this species in the Smithsonian collection and find that in many individuals the coloration imitates that of the moccasin to perfection. It would seem that the species are not distinguished by the Florida people. Is this not a fair case of protective mimicry?" I wish that I'd read that note before I encountered the snake in Oklahoma.

Sometimes, the difficulty of distinguishing between harmless and venomous snakes leads to tragedy. Chapter 15 tells the story of Joe Slowinski (1962–2001), an expert snake researcher from the USA, who made the fatal mistake of carelessly handling a deadly krait in the belief that it was a harmless mimic species.

Mimicry can extend beyond physical appearance. Some non-venomous snakes also imitate the sounds produced by venomous species. In North America, harmless snakes twitch their tailtips in dry leaf-litter to make a sound like the rattle on the tails of their venomous neighbours. In Europe, harmless Viperine Snakes (as their name suggests) resemble co-occurring vipers in body shape and colour, and especially in having a large triangular head. Like vipers but unlike related harmless snakes, Viperine Snakes produce a loud, long, low-frequency hiss that sounds like that of a true viper.

Displaying a King Cobra (*Ophiophagus hannah*) to the public at the Australian Reptile Park.

In the Middle East, Saw-scaled Vipers take their name from the rough edges of their body scales. An agitated viper forms loops with its body and rubs those scales against each other to produce a hissing sound. Non-venomous snake species that occur in the same area do the same thing. Lastly, one of the most truly bowel-loosening sounds in the natural world has to be growling by the King Cobra. Lower-pitched than a typical snake hiss, it is produced by resonating chambers within the giant snake's airways. A large harmless snake species that overlaps with the King Cobra in distribution, the Oriental Rat Snake, has evolved the same trick. In 1899, legendary snake expert Stanley Smyth Flower wrote of the rat snake: "When angry it utters repeatedly a curious threatening sound, audible some yards off, best described as 'roaring', something like the deep growling of a big dog. It also rears its head up like a cobra and dilates its neck." As far as I know, nobody has ever tested responses of predators to those growls, but I reckon it would work on me. A four-metre (12-ft) snake, forebody raised from the ground, staring at me and emitting a loud low-pitched growl … I'd think twice before attacking such a beast.

Sadly, mimicking deadly snakes may backfire in a world dominated by humans. Although other snake predators are deterred by the viper's zigzag coloration, people who kill snakes out of fear or ignorance may be likely to kill a viper mimic even if it is non-venomous. Those cases of mistaken identity may be a powerful threat to Smooth Snakes in the northern part of their European range. The effect of a snake's colour pattern (and size, and shape) on responses of redneck snake-killers would be interesting to clarify, but most people have no idea about the identity of snakes they encounter. And frankly, most snakes remain unseen. My student Christa Beckmann placed rubber snakes on a road in tropical Australia at night, to see if motorists would avoid snakes or try to run them over. In fact, neither of those things happened. Most drivers didn't see the brightly coloured model snakes on the road.

IN THEIR OWN WORDS

The effective camouflage of snakes was evident to the earliest naturalists:

"On a footpath, a grass plot, or in a museum case, a Carpet Snake is so striking an object, by reason of its bulk, its sweeping curves and mottled pattern, that a casual observer would regard it as a conspicuous animal, which would everywhere obtrude itself on his attention. Yet, in the recesses of its native forest, that casual observer, and even a sharp-eyed naturalist, might brush against it, or walk over it without noticing it. An experienced collector once related to me how startled he was when searching in the bush, by the sudden apparition, as it seemed, of a huge Carpet Snake a yard away. Not till then had he realised how the mottled marking of the reptile perfectly imitated the litter of grey and brown dead leaves, and how the curves of the body answered to a fallen limb." EDGAR WAITE, 1898

Likewise, the close resemblance between harmless and venomous species was frequently commented upon:

"*Xenodon macrophthalmus* ... may be at once distinguished by its large eye and by its dilatable neck, the scales of which show an arrangement very similar to that of a cobra, for which it is frequently taken. All the specimens I have seen show unmistakable signs that their captors considered it best to kill them from a distance, and to inflict a death wound as near to the head as possible." ALBERT CARL LUDWIG GÜNTHER, 1864

"A curious fact has been lately brought to my notice by a friend of mine, Mr H.M. Oakley, in connection with the *Dasypeltis scabra*, Linn., or Egg-eating Snake – the '*Eijer eter*' of the Dutch colonists – which, if not already well known, may prove of interest to some of your readers. The specimen obtained by Mr Oakley was caught at Hout Bay some twenty miles from Cape Town, and is about three feet in length, and its size, markings, and colour bear sufficient resemblance to those of the Berg Adder (*Clothos atropos*, Linn.) to be easily mistaken for that snake. It also has keeled scales, generally characteristic, at the Cape, of venomous species. Its head has, however, the long lacertine shape distinctive, here, of harmless snakes, but, when aroused and alarmed or irritated, it flattens it out until it assumes the usual viperine shape of the 'club' in a playing card. It then coils as for a spring, erects its head with every appearance of anger, produces a hissing noise with its scales, not unlike the hiss of a Puff Adder or cobra, and darts forward as if to strike its fangs into its foe, and in every way exactly simulates the motions of an irritated Berg Adder. This snake has, however, neither fangs nor teeth (which, indeed, would not be required for egg-swallowing), and is not poisonous, a fact which was placed beyond doubt by Mr Oakley repeatedly placing his finger in the reptile's mouth. This seems a clear instance of mimicry of another species for defensive purposes, but I am not aware of another instance among ophidians." W.H. TOOKE, 1886

Spending most of its life down soil cracks in inhospitable semi-desert regions of Australia, the spectacular Collett's Snake (*Pseudechis colletti*) remains a creature of mystery. ALANA DE LAIVE

PART 5

HEROES AND MARTYRS OF THE REVOLUTION

Research on snakes is an interaction between animals and scientists, and we can't understand that process without exploring both sides of the equation. Looking at snakes is the easier enquiry to pursue and is the focus of most of this book.

The human dimension is more difficult to tease apart.

What kinds of people are attracted to animals (such as snakes) that arouse fear and disgust in most other people? And what kinds of questions attract them, and how do they try to answer those questions?

As you might expect, some of the early snake-enthusiasts had remarkable lives – and sometimes, sudden deaths. For snake biologists both past and present, the risk of fatal snakebite is never far away.

As with so many other aspects of human society, research into snake ecology has been changing through time, and the pace of that change has accelerated. Over the last few decades, it feels to me as if research on snakes has shed its old skin and is emerging as a new kind of organism. The international community of snake researchers is changing at lightning speed. Using methods that would have been unimaginable even a few years ago, a new generation of researchers is transforming our view of the much-maligned serpent.

Chapter 10

The pioneers: a ragtag assemblage of zealots

What kinds of people love snakes? I should know. I have spent decades conducting research on snakes of many different kinds, in many different places, with a diverse array of fellow snake maniacs.

If you don't share our obsession, then studying snakes seems like a foolish career choice. But the people who have taken that path are living the dream.

Snakes are profoundly unlike 'normal' animals such as dogs, cats and parrots, so you might expect that the people drawn to these legless living tubes are weird themselves. But in most ways, 'snake people' are the same as the rest of the human race – tall/short, fat/thin, smart/stupid, extrovert/introvert, shy/bold, gay/straight, male/female/other, and so on. There is more variety among the attendees of a reptile-biology conference than among the crowds at most concerts, or art galleries, or football games.

The only characteristic that unites the serpent fraternity is a passion for snakes. Typically, an intense passion. Most 'snake people' are obsessed from childhood. Elderly snake biologists wear T-shirts emblazoned with rattlesnake images, and younger scientists have tattoos of snakes writhing along their arms and legs.

For a 'normal' person who sees snakes as just another kind of animal, or as a creature to be avoided, it is difficult to imagine the intensity of a true believer's attachment. I know many people whose trajectories in life – choice of jobs, places to live, partners and so on – have been driven by their obsession with snakes. When the long-suffering partner of a snake zealot finally delivers an ultimatum – 'it's either me or the snakes' – the reptile enthusiast almost always opts for the reptiles.

To fully appreciate the passion of a true snake devotee, we need to look at the early days of 'snake research'. Before the rise of professional science, an enthusiast had to find ways to spend time with snakes while being paid to do something else. Zealous individuals looked for jobs as clergymen, soldiers or physicians – professions that gave access to tropical countries abounding in reptiles.

To a snake-lover, a Ball Python (*Python regius*) is a subject of immense fascination. PIXABAY

One of the most enthusiastic disciples of the serpent world was Arthur Stradling (1851–1902), an English physician with no formal zoological training but a lifelong obsession with snakes. Arthur's passion was evident early in his life, encouraged by his father who once bribed the keeper of a travelling menagerie to drape a python around the neck of his son. Later in life, Arthur recounted that story with gratitude.

After he completed his medical degree, Arthur was employed as a surgeon aboard ships owned by the Royal Mail Steam Packet Company, criss-crossing the oceans of the world delivering mail and packages. His medical duties paid his salary, but Arthur's motivation was the opportunity to visit tropical Asia and Central and South America. He filled his cabin at sea with a diverse assortment of reptiles, ranging from crocodiles to sea snakes, with the aim "not only of studying them and matters connected with them from a scientific point of view, but of living in close and constant companionship with them."

In more than a decade of wandering the oceans with his reptile pets, Stradling had numerous adventures and misadventures. Smallpox and malaria almost took his life, but his most perilous voyage was on a steamer from Rangoon to Shanghai. The steamer was commanded by pirates,

Arthur Stradling and his son preparing to feed a captive Boa Constrictor.

who used the cover of night to raid small villages along the coast. Stradling writes of "... shrieks, flames, the report of firearms and the clash of steel" as his shipmates plundered Chinese villages. After four months on the pirate ship, Stradling devised a cunning plan to escape. He shared his supply of medicinal morphine with the crew, waited until they were all drugged, then stole a dinghy and rowed to land. Fearing reprisal, he hid in a tomb before setting out barefoot to walk 300 km (200 miles) to the nearest village, hiding in tombs and ditches along the way. That nightmare trip took 22 days.

Back in Europe, Stradling decided to focus on captive snakes. He published prolifically in outlets ranging from respectable scientific journals through to popular magazines aimed at young readers. He was an unabashed advocate for snakes, enthusiastically portraying these misunderstood animals in a positive light. Aided by his fellow snake-lover Catherine Cooper Hopley, Stradling bombarded the English public with a barrage of entertaining stories that framed snakes in a positive way. Stradling frequently lampooned scientists whose only experience was with preserved animals, stressing instead the importance of looking at live specimens – ideally, in the field. And his voice was among the first to call for snake conservation.

Scattered amongst Stradling's novel observations and insights, however, were some dreadful mistakes. For example, he claimed to have heard a snake scream "like a child"; and he foolishly transported British snakes to faraway places such as South America and Asia and released them to see if they could survive. But we all make mistakes, and Stradling eventually recognised and admitted his folly.

All pioneers attract criticism, and Stradling's high public profile stimulated frequent abuse. For example, his attempts to immunise himself with injections of snake venom were derided as irresponsible. Stradling also offended animal-welfare advocates by feeding live mice to captive snakes, motivating fictitious reports of Stradling's death (by snakebite) in newspapers and even in scientific journals.

Sadly, Arthur Stradling died just a few years later, of a cocaine overdose. An accident had left Stradling with severe back pain, which he tried to allay with narcotics. His life descended into a spiral of substance abuse. Unable to work, his personal life fell apart as well: his marriage collapsed, and he became homeless. In 1902, his body was found beside his bed, surrounded by bottles of cocaine and morphine. It was a tragic end to one of the pioneering free spirits of snake research.

The snake tribes: 1. Snake exhibitors

It's tempting to think of 'snake people' as a single tribe, united by their obsession. But a closer look reveals several different ways that a person can interact with snakes.

The tribes with the longest history are the showmen (and less often, showwomen): people who exhibit snakes to the public. The earliest versions of that profession include the snake charmers of India, with their choreographed displays of cobras 'dancing' to the tune of a flute that the snake can't hear. It's not far from there to sideshow performers in the circus, thrilling crowds by handling deadly serpents. Forsaking nomadic existence, other devotees display snakes in cages and open-air pits, often with snake handling included as entertainment. Those set-ups range from small-scale roadside snake shows and snake-fondling religious sects through to large reptile houses at major zoos. Despite the enormous range in background and expertise of the people involved, they all exhibit snakes to the public.

The growth of television generated a profitable offshoot of that exhibitor tribe: people handling snakes on a TV screen. Again, that TV tribe was diverse. At one extreme a sober presenter informs and educates; at the other, a larrikin over-emphasises the snake's danger and torments an animal into retaliating on camera.

Grace Olive Wiley (1883–1948) was a high-profile American advocate for snakes and other reptiles, who courted controversy by handling deadly snakes with her bare hands. She scorned gloves or tongs when dealing with cobras, mambas, rattlesnakes and Gaboon Vipers. Her bold approach to snake taming attracted considerable publicity, especially in Chicago where she was employed for two years (1933–1935) as curator of the Brookfield Zoo's reptile collection. Newspaper reporters loved her, partly because it was unusual for a woman to hold a curatorial role in those times.

Her bosses at the zoo were less enthusiastic. Appalled by her cavalier approach, they ordered her to desist. She refused, and compounded the problem by overseeing security so lax that 19 snakes escaped their cages during her tenure at the zoo. Wiley was unrepentant, telling

Snake charmers ply their trade across much of Asia, usually focusing on the spectacular but relatively easy-to-handle cobra. PIXABAY

reporters that "I do not feel I was guilty of carelessness. I just forgot, simply forgot, to close the door to the cobra's cage after I cleaned it." She was dismissed from the job in September 1935. Despite the publicity she attracted for the zoo, her risk taking had financial implications. Because of her, the zoo's insurance policy cost them more than Wiley's annual salary.

Grace Wiley free handling a large King Cobra (*Ophiophagus hannah*), in a way likely to induce hysteria in any modern workplace safety committee.

When she left Brookfield Zoo, Wiley took her snakes with her and set up a private roadside exhibit in Cypress, California. She also trained and handled snakes for the movie industry. Wiley continued to court the press, and her death at the age of 65 was due to a cobra bite while she was posing for a journalist. Frightened by the photographer's flash, the snake bit Wiley when she tried to restrain it. Tragically, her only vial of cobra antivenom was broken in the confusion after the bite, and the local hospital did not have antisera for exotic species. Grace Wiley died less than two hours after being bitten.

Although snake exhibitors and TV presenters frequently claim that their activities contribute to research, that claim is patent nonsense. So why pretend? One reason is increasing public opposition towards keeping animals in cages. 'Wildlife should be left in the wild', runs the mantra of the Animal Liberation Front and similar groups. Facing that antagonism, zoos worldwide now profess to be actively involved in conservation. In some cases, that's just window dressing, designed for public relations. The actual investment into research is trivial. But in an increasing number of other cases, wildlife parks and zoos are playing a constructive role by recording useful information and collaborating with researchers. Especially for species that are now so rare as to be impossible to study in the wild, captive colonies may provide the only opportunities to document critical ecological and behavioural traits.

The snake tribes: 2. Snake keepers

The next snake tribe also comprises people who keep snakes in cages, but not to exhibit to the public. These are the pet keepers. The idea of snakes around the house is not new; farmers have kept rodent-eating snakes in barns for centuries. But the tsunami of interest in snakes as domestic pets is a new development. High prices for strangely coloured pythons spawned a vigorous industry. Some professional snake breeders are expert not only in husbandry, but also in the genetics underlying colour patterns. It's a multi-million-dollar industry, with 'snake expos' attracting thousands of buyers every year.

Snake breeding is a sophisticated pursuit, and the best breeders have exceptional expertise. Indeed, many important discoveries in snake reproduction have come from attempts to generate striking colour patterns that increase a snake's commercial value. The first photo shows a typical colour pattern for wild Blood Pythons (*Python brongersmai*), whereas the other three shots illustrate colour patterns produced by selective breeding: a 'batik-matrix' morph, a red-orange albino, and a 'magpie' morph. All of these stunning colour patterns were created by fabled Texas python breeders Dave and Tracy Barker.

A pet snake doesn't take up much room, and it doesn't need to be fed and exercised daily like a dog. In many ways, snakes are ideal pets for people with not much room and not much spare time. There were few snake keepers in Australia during my schoolboy years, but these days pampered pythons are abundant even in high-density housing areas. As a result, the pet-keeping fraternity vastly outnumbers the professional research community – and thus, in recent years many new and surprising observations have been based on snakes in homes rather than laboratories. And if somebody notices something unusual, especially if they take a picture of the event, the internet enables that observation to be spread around far more widely than would have been possible a few decades ago. A person without scientific training may struggle to publish a full-length paper in a professional journal – that process requires anonymous external review, and journal editors are formidable gatekeepers – but many respectable publications now invite short notes from pet keepers. Modern journals such as *Herpetological Review* have sections devoted to anecdotal observations – these days, supported by photographs. I often find those short accounts more interesting than the longer papers in the rest of the journal, because most 'normal science' follows well-trodden paths. Truly new discoveries are rare. But every once in a while, somebody sees a snake doing something totally unexpected – and writes a short note about it.

If you admire snakes enough to keep one in your home, you are more likely to notice other kinds of snakes as you move around in the course of your daily activities. And so, the role of pet keeper blends seamlessly into a broader activity: observing snakes in the wild. These people usually don't actually capture the snakes they see, let alone measure them or insert radio transmitters – but they pay careful attention to an animal's behaviour. And quite often, they take photographs of what they see. The end result is a quantum leap in information about the ecology of snakes in the field, about poorly understood aspects such as feeding habits, male-male combat and social interactions. Time after time, my own understanding of Australian snakes has been enriched by gems of information from pet keepers. There's no denying the fact that some snake keepers are motivated by machismo and contribute to a negative public perception of snakes as pets – but most of the snake keepers I meet are motivated by a genuine interest in their captive animals. Those snake-friendly citizens are an invisible army that continually generates fascinating and unexpected discoveries about the serpent world.

The snake tribes: 3. Snake killers

A fascination with snakes motivates most pet keepers, showmen and so forth, with little role for financial rewards. At heart, most people in the 'pet-snake' industry and the snake-exhibitor world are more interested in Corn Snakes or copperheads than in cash and coinage. But commercial motives lie at the core of the next tribe: people who collect and kill snakes for profit. Strange as it may seem to Western eyes, snakes are commercial commodities for meat, leather and medicinal products in many parts of Asia, South America and Africa. It's a strictly utilitarian view of snakes, with no role for emotional attachments between reptiles and reptile collectors. Snakes are a resource. Millions of them are taken from the wild every year, in what generally seems to be a sustainable industry.

Feeding time at a commercial python-raising farm in Vietnam. These Burmese Pythons (*Python bivittatus*) are happily consuming rats on a concrete floor. DAN NATUSCH

The professional snake killers might seem utterly unlike the pet keepers, but there's a rapidly growing intersection between those approaches. Across many parts of Asia, snakes are being collected from the wild and kept in captivity until they are large enough to be slaughtered for their skins, meat amd medicinal products. Large non-venomous species such as pythons are the main 'livestock' for these snake farms. Typically, the captive snakes have access to sunlight-exposed areas for basking, plus indoor areas for shelter. To increase growth rates to the maximum possible, the snakes are fed or force-fed everything from rats to sausages. A snake farm looks peculiar to Western eyes, but the system is very efficient because snakes convert food into flesh much more efficiently than can a chicken, pig or cow. No need to waste energy maintaining a high body temperature! And if food becomes scarce or too expensive for a few weeks or months, you can just stop feeding your snakes until the situation improves. That flexibility is impossible with warm-blooded livestock.

The snake tribes: 4. Snake catchers

For tribe number 4, the snake catchers, the central focus is the danger that snakes pose to people – or more often, the exaggerated fear that people have about snakes. Homeowners panic when they discover a scaly coil under the pile of dirty clothes on the laundry floor, or when they see a snake disappear into a pile of building materials in the backyard. Because some snake species are attracted to suburbia, such encounters are common worldwide. Afraid that the interloper is deadly, many people call for professional help to capture the serpent and remove it. Snake-removalists can earn a good living, but it's a deeply frustrating one. Time after time, the expert arrives at a house to be met with vague stories about a snake that has vanished; or even worse, that is writhing on the floor after being injured by the homeowner.

For a schoolgirl living in suburban Sydney, Australia, a glimpse of a free-ranging Red-bellied Black Snake (*Pseudechis porphyriacus*) in local bushland can be a real thrill. MATT GREENLEES

Not all snake catchers are professionals. The word soons spreads when a house in your neighbourhood is purchased or rented by someone with expertise in snake handling. Perhaps that person is a pet keeper; less often, a scientist. Regardless, a phone call to the local snake expert is often the first reaction when somebody finds a serpent in the front yard. Over the years, I've collected a lot of frightened snakes from my neighbours' yards. But in recent times, those calls have become less common as 'wildlife rescue' organisations have proliferated. Most of those groups initially focused on mammals and birds that had been injured on roads or attacked by domestic cats and dogs – but increasingly, more of the 'rescues' concern snakes that are not injured in any way, but instead are simply unwelcome in suburbia. So an army of 'wildlife rescue' volunteers have dutifully taken snake-handling courses, and are the first responders to many snake call-outs.

A small but interesting subset of snake catchers assists police when they visit homes where snakes are being kept illegally. For example, some drug dealers use snakes as guardians, hiding the stash inside a cage with venomous snakes. Taking the idea still further, in 1993 law enforcement officers in Florida intercepted a shipment of 223 live Boa Constrictors containing packages of cocaine. The unfortunate reptiles had condoms full of cocaine stuffed up their rectums, which were then sewn shut. A suspicious customs inspector once delayed my departure from Canada to the USA when I arrived at the airport with a dozen Common Water Snakes. All of the snakes were heavily pregnant, with swollen hindbodies. It took an hour for me to convince the authorities that I hadn't stuffed the snakes full of contraband.

The snake tribes: 5. Snake scientists

The final snake tribe is my own clan: the scientists. You only choose that career path if you are hopelessly entranced by serpents. There are degrees of obsession, and a world of difference between liking snakes enough to keep one in a glass tank in your living room versus devoting your professional life to them. To opt for the latter course, you need two things. First, a passion that is truly all-encompassing. And second, the ability to ignore well-meaning feedback from friends who think that you've made a stupid decision. At best, self-indulgent. At worst, idiotic. The only kindred spirits who understand your passion are your fellow snake enthusiasts.

In one sense, the naysayers are correct. A career spent delving into the sex lives of snakes is unlikely to involve luxury yachts and private jets. More probably, it will lead to a perennial struggle to fund your research. But for the truly besotted, it is not a choice. It's a compulsion. It doesn't make sense, but it doesn't have to. For a true serpent zealot, fascination with snakes lurks in some deep-seated part of the brain. It's impossible to eradicate.

Why do some scientists focus their research on snakes instead of other organisms? I'd wager a lot of money on the simplest of all possible answers: it is driven by curiosity. That is, the stubborn belief that no other career offers as much excitement and fulfilment as a scientific odyssey into the world of snakes.

Among the scientists who study snakes, it's not an easy task to define sub-groups. Where do you fit parasitologists, for example? They have specialised methods and publish their own journals, but few snake biologists work on parasites. Among the mainstream disciplines, the most obvious divide is a four-way split between taxonomists, venom specialists, functional biologists and ecologists.

The scientific sub-tribes: 1. Taxonomists

Taxonomists focus on the classification and geographic distribution of species. Much of the earliest research on snakes was taxonomic, as science began to grapple with the diversity of snakes and how to distinguish one species from another. In the early days, it was difficult for taxonomists to keep up with each other's publications – partly because they couldn't read papers written in other languages, and partly because of long delays in obtaining such papers from other countries. To many people, there is something glorious about being the first to put a name on a 'new' species – a kind of immortality – and some brave souls described new species (often, named for their friends or supporters) based on very flimsy evidence. Inevitably, many of those taxa proved to be variants of already described species; and most descriptions were so woefully inadequate that it's impossible to work out what kind of animal the taxonomist had in front of them as they wrote their paper.

The 'cowboy taxonomists' aroused the ire of more serious professionals, who had to clean up the mess of ambiguous names created by enthusiastic but slapdash descriptions. For example, one of the most prolific describers of new species in Australia was Charles De Vis (1829–1915), a clergyman who became Director of the Queensland Museum. His descriptions appeared at a phenomenal rate, but were ambiguous, brief and obscure – and frequently, wrong. Only two of the 17 snake species described by De Vis are recognised as valid today; and even more damningly, De Vis sometimes formally described a species then later redescribed it with a different name. An eminent British scientist, George Albert Boulenger (1858–1937), was so fed up with De Vis's output that he wrote in 1885 that "through his incompetence and want of care, he will do much harm ... one can only wonder at his daring to write on subjects of which he is so manifestly ignorant."

Charles De Vis, a snake taxonomist whose enthusiasm often overcame his attention to detail.

Describing new species and working out their links to other species continues, as DNA sequence data clarifies hitherto-confusing evolutionary relationships. Nonetheless, many issues remain controversial. Indeed, taxonomy attracts people who enjoy a good argument.

I can't talk about the people who used words to describe snakes without mentioning the unappreciated illustrators whose pictures often were far more useful than the dry text within a paper. A picture tells a thousand words, and any description of a snake species is unclear without images of the beast. Modern scientific papers and books rely on photographs, but hand-drawn illustrations were the only depictions available in earlier days.

Some of the best drawings were in books from the 19th century. An accurate list of the snake species from a given area enabled people to identify a snake they had seen; and illustrations made that job a thousand times easier. Some of the illustrators were incredibly talented.

For example, Harriet Scott (1832–1910) and Helena 'Nellie' Scott (1830–1907) were sisters born in colonial Sydney. Neither was formally trained in science, because women were excluded from universities and learned societies; indeed, professional opportunities for women were non-existent at the time. Later in life Harriet wrote to a friend that she had a "great desire to distinguish myself in some way or other and if I were only a man I might do it, but as I am a woman I can't ... clearly I ought to have been Harry Scott instead of Hattie Scott." But with scientific careers out of reach, the Scott sisters used their artistic skills and knowledge of nature to become influential scientific illustrators. They created superb artwork for the first book on Australian snakes, written by Gerard Krefft in 1869. Unlike their contemporaries, the Scott sisters placed many of their subjects on realistic backgrounds and in lifelike poses. To this day, images drawn by the Scott sisters remain some of the most evocative depictions of Australian snakes.

An illustration of the Diamond Python (*Morelia spilota*) by Harriet and Helena Scott, from Gerard Krefft's landmark 1869 book on Australian snakes.

The scientific sub-tribes: 2. Understanding venom

Knowing about the distribution of snake species is only the first step towards mitigating snakebite risk. You also need to understand venoms and to develop antidotes to those venoms. That endeavour has attracted a vast amount of attention. Up until the early 20th century, antidotes were effective only by encouraging the patient to be optimistic. For example, in 1849 Lieutenant Tyler recommended "intoxication and sleep induced by administering rum punch with plenty of lime juice in it." Early showmen often spruiked home-made remedies as well, which were as effective as the rum punch but less tasty.

One surprising aspect of the early scientific literature on this topic is the willingness of pioneering biologists to force snakes to bite them. For example, George Beyer (1861–1926), a German zoologist based in Louisiana, routinely allowed newborn snakes to bite him to find out how venomous they were. In 1898 he recounted that a young Cottonmouth's bite felt like a bee-sting whereas a baby rattler's bite generated "lightning-like pain" up to the shoulder, vertigo, laboured breathing, swelling and fever for 36 hours. I don't know whether to be impressed at George's dedication to science, or to be appalled at his cavalier attitude.

Showman August Eichorn (1857–1944) 'accepting the bite' from a deadly Australian Eastern Brown Snake (*Pseudonaja textilis*). Eichorn was bitten more than 500 times in such exhibitions, but eventually died not from snakebite, but due to infection from a barbed-wire scratch. PHOTOGRAPH COURTESY OF JOHN CANN

Snakebite treatment was revolutionised in 1895 by Albert Calmette (1863–1933), a French physician who developed an antivenom against the cobra. Nonetheless, uptake was slow. The first American antivenoms were not produced until 1927, as a result of US-Brazilian collaboration. Nowadays, antivenoms are so effective that snakebite kills very few people in places such as Europe, North America and Australia. Sadly, tropical countries still have more than 100,000 fatalities per year. The tropical snakebite catastrophe is driven by climatic, social and economic factors. People walk barefoot at night, in poorly illuminated areas, and rely on traditional remedies if bitten. And the problem is compounded by agricultural practices that support abundant rodents, attracting snakes to areas around human habitation. Cobras, kraits and vipers abound in the ricefields of southern Asia.

Although most research on snake venom is about danger to humans, there are interesting questions to ask about the evolutionary processes that have generated such potent toxins. Different kinds of snakes have different venoms. For example, most elapids kill by paralysing nerve transmission, whereas many vipers destroy cells and disrupt blood-clotting mechanisms.

Why is snake venom so incredibly powerful? For some species, it seems like massive overkill. For example, Coastal Taipans are long – to almost 3 metres (9-ft) – lithe brown cobra-like speedsters of Australia. They feed mostly on relatively small mammals, such as rats – but a single bite from a taipan can contain enough venom to kill 100 adult humans. Why does a rat-eater need such an arsenal? The likely answer is that eating rats is risky business. David Fleay, a pioneering Australian naturalist and zookeeper, lost his favourite pet snake – a 2.2-metre-long (7-foot-long) Coastal Taipan named Alexandra – when a Black Rat found its way into her enclosure. Alexandra struck the rat but before she could release it, the rodent spun around and bit into the snake's neck. The rat was dead only seconds later, but so was the giant snake. Incredibly toxic venom may be the best evolutionary option for taipans in that scenario.

Milking venom from a Russell's Viper (*Daboia russelii*), a species responsible for many fatal snakebites in India. ALEXANDRA LYSENKO, PIXABAY

All vertebrate animals produce chemicals that help to digest food, such as fluids in the lining of the mouth. As a result, injecting such fluids (even human saliva) breaks down tissues – and it's easy to imagine how ancestral snakes with more-than-usually potent saliva benefitted from poisoning prey items held in the mouth. A dead mouse is easier to swallow than a live mouse, as well as being less likely to injure the snake that is holding it. From there, it's a small step to evolving more potent venoms, places to store those poisons (venom glands), and delivery systems (hollow fangs) that inject the toxins deep into the prey's body.

To study venoms, you first need to obtain a sample of the deadly liquid. That can be done in the field, as you catch your snakes, but it's a risky business because the situation is uncontrolled, the researcher's fingers are close to the snake's fangs, and hospital is a long way away. Additionally, venom begins to break down as soon as it leaves the venom glands, so those precious samples must be refrigerated immediately. As a result, most research is done with venom from captive animals. And in a laboratory setting, researchers can use sophisticated equipment to explore how different venom components disrupt cell function.

The field of venom research is too diverse to cover here; it deserves a book of its own. Much of that research focuses on the effects of venom within the human body, but from a snake-ecologist's perspective the more interesting question is how venom functions in nature – that is, how venom affects prey items rather than people. For example, does venom evolve to kill specific types of prey? Yes it does. For example, several types of venomous snakes have invaded the oceans to become sea snakes – and they all eat fish. Their venoms have evolved to be simple and similar, and good at killing fishes. Likewise, wide-ranging snake species that eat different kinds of prey in different places show geographic variation in venom components; and those components shift with body size in snake species that switch their diets as they grow larger.

The earliest studies to look at the biological function of venoms simply injected different prey types with venom from different snakes and looked for some kind of relationship. For example, if venom evolves to kill prey, we might expect that a snake species that eats frogs should have venom that kills frogs quickly. But things aren't quite that simple, so the results were confusing. For starters, does it really matter to the snake if a bitten frog dies rapidly? A few extra minutes won't matter much, if you retain a firm grip on your intended meal after biting it. The situation is different with mammal eaters, because fast-acting venom may prevent the rat from retaliating and injuring its attacker. But even with mammal-eating snakes, we don't necessarily expect the snake to have a venom that is instantly fatal to the rat – because the prey will evolve resistance to that venom as well. It's an arms race, with snakes evolving new molecular tricks to kill prey faster while prey simultaneously evolve new molecular tricks to nullify those weapons.

New technologies are transforming venom research, offering less ambiguous evidence about tactics and counter-tactics. For example, these days a researcher can look at the genome of prey to search for genetic modifications that make prey resistant to specific toxins. That's a lot more informative than just injecting a lizard with venom to see what happens.

The scientific sub-tribes: 3. Functional biologists

The next sub-tribe is the functional biologists, who compare anatomical and physiological traits among species to tease apart the evolutionary processes that adapt a species to its environment. For example, how do a snake's head shape and body shape and muscularity affect its performance at swimming, burrowing and climbing? How does a snake's ability to tolerate high salt levels affect its colonisation of marine habitats? Why don't sea snakes get 'the bends' after a deep dive? How can a snake with a small head swallow a prodigiously large meal?

Those questions are examples of a relatively new field. The pioneering 'functional morphologist' Carl Gans (1923–2009) combined a training in mechanical engineering with a

A Corn Snake (*Pantherophis guttatus*) constricting a Cotton Rat (*Sigmodon hispidus*). NOAH K. FIELDS

love of animals to frame new perspectives on animal feeding and locomotion. Carl was Jewish; born in Germany, he escaped Nazi persecution when his family fled to the USA when Carl was 16 years old. Carl's father insisted that he would financially support him through college only if he studied mechanical engineering, so that set the course of Carl's early career. But biology was his first and greatest love, and he soon changed professions to become an expert in that field as well. Carl viewed snakes as machines for crawling, or burrowing, or climbing, or eating large prey items. He used physics to measure the forces involved in those processes, and thus explore how the bodies of snakes have evolved to perform specific functions. He spawned an entire new field, 'biomechanics', incorporating sophisticated techniques from physics and physiology to monitor activity in muscles and nerves, measure pressure inside lungs, and film reptiles as they moved through experimental set-ups. Carl used complex methods but he enjoyed asking simple questions and never lost his awe of nature; one of his best-known papers is entitled 'All animals are interesting!'

One classic focus of research has been to understand how snakes subdue and swallow their prey. For example, nobody doubts that the powerful muscles of a python overcome resistance by its prey; but for a detailed understanding of that process we can take the system into the lab. For example, researchers can look at how much pressure a captive python or Corn Snake exerts as it squeezes a fake prey item (a water-filled balloon wrapped in mouse fur) that contains a pressure sensor. When the snake wraps around its artificial meal we can measure the strength of constriction.

Using a similar approach, studies in which anaesthetised rodents are constricted can clarify how a python's squeeze terminates its prey's life. For a long time, researchers assumed that constrictors kill by crushing their food, or by stopping it from breathing. But measurements of blood pressure show that constriction works by shutting down blood flow. The heart stops, as does blood flow to vital organs, long before the rodent suffocates. And constricting snakes are patient; they detect the prey's heartbeat, and don't relax their coils until the heart has stopped.

With a little ingenuity, it's possible to directly measure many aspects of an animal's performance. For example, strength is likely to be important not only for how well a snake can constrict its prey, but also for how well it can climb, and battle its rivals. Dissections and X-rays show that male snakes are more muscular than females, and that muscle mass declines in female pythons as they brood their eggs. But we don't have to rely on those indirect measures; we can evaluate strength directly. For example, we can clip a spring-balance onto a snake's tail, hold the head firmly, then let the snake contract its body as it attempts to escape. The force that it pulls can be measured from the spring-balance.

Some of the most interesting 'snake-performance' studies ask how features of the environment

Two Scarlet Kingsnakes (*Lampropeltis elapsoides*) appear to defy gravity as one descends a tree, and the other crawls along a barbed-wire fence. Functional biologists try to understand how snakes are capable of such feats. NOAH K. FIELDS

affect a snake's ability to exploit the available resources. For example, to reach a nest full of tasty fledgling birds, a snake may need to climb a tall tree. Some trees are easier to climb than others, and birds know this – and thus, often nest in tall smooth-barked trees. Are these more difficult for a snake to climb? To check out that possibility, we can measure how effectively snakes climb different kinds of trees. Release the snake low down on the tree, pointing upwards, and record what happens next. Some birds, such as Red-cockaded Woodpeckers, add to the snake's frustration by removing loose bark and digging pits that cause a copious flow of resin on the trunk below the nest. Any snake attempting to access the nest has to cross a smooth and sticky barrier. Nobody has ever conducted an experiment to see if that barrier discourages snakes – but I bet it does.

Like speed and endurance, climbing ability can be affected by a snake's size and its sex. For example, by far the best cliff-climbing sea kraits are males of the New Caledonian species. More slender than females of their own species, but more muscular than the co-occurring Blue-lipped Sea Kraits, male New Caledonian Sea Kraits can clamber up steep ridges. The other sea kraits stay close to water, but male New Caledonian Sea Kraits are mountaineers.

The scientific sub-tribes: 4. Ecologists

And lastly, my own sub-tribe: the ecologists. That category includes behaviourists as well, because most studies of behaviour focus on the animal's environment as well as the creature itself. This motley crew of scientists is united by an interest in 'the evolutionary play within the ecological theatre'. Like the functional biologists, we seek to understand how snakes function in their natural habitats, and how the characteristics of these animals have been shaped by evolution. But the traits we study are ecological dimensions such as rates of growth, body sizes at sexual maturity, differences in adult body size between males and females, and dietary habits. We also look at habitat use, movements, reproductive tactics (such as the size and number of offspring), and whether those offspring are produced as eggs or as fully formed babies.

As with any human activity, the tribes and sub-tribes I've identified are not exclusive categories. Many scientists began as pet keepers, and many venom experts have a passion for the natural history of their study organisms.

In the days before English emerged as the pre-eminent language of international research, the strongest divisions within science were geographical. For example, the groundbreaking studies of Hubert Saint Girons were published in French, and the extensive work of Chinese biologists on the pit vipers of Shedao appeared only in Chinese. Based on traditional designs used to capture rodents and eels, Japanese biologists developed funnel traps to catch deadly pit vipers – and published their results in Japanese. Research evolved independently in different parts of the world, with little cross-fertilisation, until the floodgates of globalisation were thrown open late in the 20th century.

Most authors of early notes about snakes weren't full-time herpetologists; they were naturalists who just wanted to share an interesting observation. Many were army officers, reflecting the role of warfare in colonial expansion. A high proportion of the young Europeans who travelled to tropical countries did so in the armed services, administering far-flung regions of various empires. Observations about snakes were gathered in the course of less enjoyable activities such as warfare.

Europe sent preachers as well as soldiers to the outposts of the Empire. Many well-educated clergymen were interested in natural history, because studying the natural world might reveal the grand plan of the Creator. Indeed, Charles Darwin had planned to spend his life as a rural clergyman. Snakes posed a special problem for religious fundamentalists, however, because of critical attitudes towards serpents in the Bible. How could a parson reconcile elegant animals with negative stereotypes?

After a long and mostly factual 1875 account of 'The pine snake of New Jersey', the Reverend Samuel Lockwood (1819–1894) finishes his paper with what sounds suspiciously like a sermon: "In our thinking a serpent ranks as a paradox among animals. ... Such weakness, and such strength; such gentleness, and such vindictiveness; so much of beauty, and yet so repulsive; fascination and terror: – what need of wonder that whether snake or python, the serpent should figure in the myths of all the ages, and the literature of the whole world! Yes, in the best, and the worst thinkings of men."

Another enlightened snake-loving Christian was Oliver P. Hay (1846–1930), an American professor and museum curator who abandoned his studies for the ministry but maintained his fondness for God's creatures. In 1887, he wrote: "A closer acquaintance with snakes dispels many of our old prejudices against them ...; and presents them to us as possessors of many singular habits relating to preservation of themselves and their young, and sometimes of considerable conjugal and parental affection; and by inference, enjoying as much of the favor of Heaven as most animals."

True believers at the North Carolina Zion Tabernacle in 1949, handling Timber Rattlesnakes (*Crotalus horridus*) as part of their religious devotions. RALEIGH NEWS AND OBSERVER

Snakes have always had a few enthusiastic disciples battling to reconcile the Biblical condemnation of serpents with the beauty of living snakes.

For many decades, the only published information about snake ecology comprised isolated observations. Snake research didn't make the transition from anecdotal 'natural history' to more sophisticated 'ecology' until partway through the 20th century, when a few people began to study snakes for long enough to detect general patterns. That group of professional researchers was small but influential. The revolution introduced new methods – notably, long-term studies based in the field. But just as important, the advent of professional research heralded new ways of thinking – notably, about populations rather than individuals.

The father of snake ecology research

The most influential pioneer in snake ecology was a modest American named Henry Sheldon Fitch. Henry was born on Christmas Day in 1909 and he died just before reaching his 100th birthday in 2009. Over a long career, Henry showed how much could be learnt by marking, releasing and recatching snakes at the same site over a long period.

Henry was short, lightly built and quietly spoken; a man you would walk past in the street without a second look. But his placid demeanor hid superhuman obstinacy. Born in New York, Henry moved to Oregon as a one-year-old and grew up on a farm. He developed a special fondness for snakes, and once remarked that "the real bonus was in seeing horrified adults scatter." Henry worked in government agencies after completing his university studies, and he was drafted into the army in 1941. After a stint as an army pharmacist in Europe near the end of the war, Henry undertook university studies with support from the GI Bill of Rights, which financed returned veterans. In 1948, Henry landed his first and only academic job, as an ecologist at the University of Kansas. He was put in charge of the university's natural history reservation, an area of 239 hectares (one square mile) not far from the town of Lawrence. Before Henry arrived, the reservation was a working farm. Much of the forest had been cleared to provide pastures, but dense stands of trees persisted in swampy lowlands and rocky hills. Henry wasn't keen on farming so he sold the cows and initiated research on the wildlife of the reservation. Especially on the snakes.

Realising that he couldn't catch enough snakes by hand, Henry constructed traps: wire-mesh cylinders with a funnel at one end. An animal that crawled in couldn't find its way out again. Like most innovators, Henry kept things simple. He deployed hundreds of traps in strategic locations across the reservation. And every day he went out and checked the traps, extracted the captured snakes, measured them, recorded food items and reproductive condition, and gave each individual a unique mark before releasing it at the site of capture.

Pioneering snake ecologist Henry Fitch prepares to demonstrate his method of toe clipping a rodent.

As well as his wire-mesh traps, Henry laid out hundreds of coverboards that provided attractive shelter for smaller snake species. By regularly looking beneath those coverboards, Henry greatly increased his capture rates for such species. But durable coverboards are expensive, and Henry was famously frugal – so he purchased most of his coverboards from the Kansas state surplus depot. One year they had cheap metal signs that had been used to warn of landmines in a military base. Henry thought nothing of using these as long as they were placed sign down. Unfortunately, some people who ventured on to the reservation to look for snakes flipped these metal signs over and saw the warning about landmines. This led to the rumour that you couldn't go on the natural history reservation, not because of the snakes, but because of landmines on the site.

If Henry had marked and released and recaptured snakes for a year or two, he wouldn't have learned much. Most of the marked snakes would never have been seen again. But Henry's genius lay in his persistence: he kept going for 50 years, accumulating more than 32,000 capture records. Slowly but surely, recaptures of marked animals revealed how fast they had grown, where they had moved, what habitats they used in different seasons, and so forth.

Henry documented the day-to-day lives of snakes in incredible detail. For example, naturalists in Kansas already knew that the best places to find snakes are in rocky hills in spring and around low-lying meadows in summer. But the reasons for that pattern were unclear. Perhaps snakes hibernate among the rocks and then migrate down to the meadows to feed? Or perhaps, snakes emerge from hibernation earlier in the hills than in the valleys? Because Henry kept track of individual animals, he knew they moved from the hills to the valleys. He never saw most of his snakes again after their original capture – they were eaten by hawks, or died of old age, or moved out of the reservation – but many others turned up regularly. Some were not seen for decades, but then were found again in the same trap where Henry first captured them. Remarkably, he learned, even a tiny snake could live for more than 20 years. And so, Henry wrote a series of landmark scientific papers that described life-history characteristics of all of the snake species that lived on the reservation. Those excruciatingly detailed papers are jammed with extensive quotations from Henry's field notes, documenting example after

Henry Fitch studied every species of snake on his Kansas reservation, but he is most famous for his detailed research on the American Copperhead (*Agkistrodon contortrix*). NOAH K. FIELDS

example of his encounters with individual animals over decades. It isn't exactly light reading, but the accumulation of case histories builds up into a clear overall picture. With 50 years of dedication, Henry shone a bright light into the secret lives of snakes.

Henry's great contribution, though, was not just innovation in methods or persistence in data gathering. Some of his contemporaries also conducted valuable research, but they never published it. They died with filing cabinets full of data. Henry had a different view: he was determined to communicate his discoveries to other researchers. Satisfying your own curiosity is a feeble justification for all that hard work and, importantly, for the suffering you've inflicted on your study animals. Publishing the results of your work is an integral part of the study, not an afterthought. Committed to that philosophy, Henry used his hard-won results to publish landmark papers that addressed ecological questions never before explored in any species of snake. Those papers inspired an entire new generation of snake ecologists.

What happened to Henry's mark-recapture study in the long term? If you keep such a study going for long enough, it is certain to end in tragedy. Times change, habitats deteriorate, and even an abundant species declines and disappears when environmental conditions become unsuitable. Henry's decision to remove grazing livestock from the reservation in Kansas was a godsend in the beginning – the early stages of forest regeneration were perfect for snakes, so their numbers increased. But long term, as thicker forest shaded the ground, the sun-loving snakes died or moved away. By the end of Henry's long career, snakes were difficult to find on the reservation. Capture-mark-recapture studies are not for the faint-hearted.

Early in my career, in 1986, I made a trip (OK, a pilgrimage) to the natural history reservation near Lawrence, Kansas, to meet the man who had influenced my professional life so greatly. I had read all of Henry Fitch's papers, and I wanted to understand the man behind those seminal studies. At 72 years of age, Henry still checked his snake traps every day, at a pace that my 36-year-old legs could barely match. And although twice my age, he soundly defeated me at ping-pong (table tennis). Henry was a quiet and self-effacing man, happier in the forest than in a conference room. He was well liked by his academic colleagues in Kansas, but his work seemed old-fashioned even in the 1970s. Natural history was yesterday's approach, while 'modern' ecologists were building mathematical models and molecular biologists were revealing the building blocks of life.

Henry was so low on the academic totem pole at the University of Kansas that he wasn't even given an office. But by the mid–1970s the digital revolution enabled university administrators to measure and compare the research achievements of their staff. For example, citation rate (how often a scientist's papers are mentioned in publications by other academics) is a reliable index of scientific reputation. To everyone's astonishment, the most highly cited academic at the University of Kansas was that old guy from the reservation. So they gave Henry an office, but he didn't use it much. He preferred checking his snake traps.

What was it like for me, as a mid-career researcher, to spend time with Henry Fitch? In the end, it was warmer and more personal than I expected. Henry was down to earth, pragmatic in the extreme. Most true pioneers are unusual people, isolated from mainstream society. Only a zealot could spend his life catching and releasing snakes, hoping to re-catch them one day. Fortunately, Henry lived to the ripe old age of 99 – long enough to see his contributions appreciated. The only standing ovation I ever saw at an international scientific meeting came when Henry, in his late 80s, walked into the lecture theatre to give a talk. I was in the front row, and I saw the pleasure and surprise on his honest farmer's face when the audience rose as one to applaud him. Henry felt fortunate to have spent his professional life doing things that he enjoyed, with animals that he loved, to address questions that fascinated him. By comparison, fame and fortune were to be enjoyed but not taken too seriously.

Henry Fitch and the author in 1986, photographed at the natural history reservation near Lawrence, Kansas. VIRGINIA FITCH

I've met many eminent biologists over the years. Most were unpretentious, like Henry. By the time I visited him Henry had retired and was enjoying a quiet life, wandering around the reservation checking snake traps in the morning and watching his favourite TV show (*Wild Kingdom*) every afternoon. Colleagues at Kansas told me of Henry's competitive nature during social basketball games, but I only saw that side of his personality during our ping-pong tournament. He was straightforward, unaffected, and immersed in the natural history of the local wildlife. Prosaic to a fault, Henry talked about facts not theories – just as his papers did.

Pioneers from across the globe

Of course, Henry Fitch wasn't the only pioneering snake ecologist in the USA. It's a large country, with many universities. Indeed, people who pre-dated Fitch's work could legitimately qualify as the real pioneers. Frank Blanchard (1888–1937) and Frjeda Cobb Blanchard (1889–1977), for example, worked together on the ecology of harmless snakes in Michigan. A formidable scientist in her own right, Australian-born Frjeda was the first person to demonstrate how the traits of adult reptiles were inherited by their offspring.

Further north, Canada is too chilly for most snake species – but the few that do occur there can be found in astonishing abundance. The massive dens of garter snakes north of Winnipeg, Manitoba, were a magnet for scientists. It's easy to conduct research if you can collect a thousand snakes in a day! The first ecological study at the big dens was a PhD project by an expatriate Englishman, Pat Gregory.

On the other side of the Atlantic Ocean, French biologist Hubert Saint Girons (1926–2000) was a pioneer in his own right. This proud and imperious Frenchman had a lifelong love affair with vipers. Snakes were abundant in the French countryside, including around Saint Girons's delightful chateau near Nantes in the Loire region. He combined studies in the laboratory with observations on vipers in outdoor enclosures beside his chateau. Although many of his published papers were on physiological topics or relied upon anatomical investigations, Hubert was a naturalist at heart. His papers broke new ground not only in documenting reproductive cycles in French snakes, but also in providing information about reproduction in tropical serpents. During trips to Cambodia and New Caledonia, Hubert documented many new aspects of snake biology.

Professor Hubert Saint Girons, formidable French pioneer of snake-biology research. KRAIG ADLER

In September 1988, I stayed with Professor Saint Girons and his wife Marie in their chateau. He told me with pride that the chateau had been owned by his family for three generations. We were organising a symposium to be held the following year at a major conference in the UK; but in between discussions we took long rambling walks through forests and pastureland. We even managed to catch a few vipers for his enclosures. My field notes from that day say "Hubert's eyesight is not the best, and it is surprising that he can still catch vipers so effectively. But he is like Henry Fitch – enthusiastic and stubborn." Hubert was small in stature but an intellectual giant; a man who steadfastly embraced the ideals and manners of an earlier generation.

He was perfectly groomed and neatly and formally dressed even during fieldwork. Hubert was fond of wine and cigars in the evening, and he was well known for his strong opinions about science and his opposition to modern customs and to all languages other than French.

As a young researcher, I was in awe of the great man. He had been one of the examiners of my own PhD thesis, a fact which gives me great pride. I never had the temerity to call Hubert by his first name, but we had many long conversations about snakes. I was shocked by his offhand dismissal of entire nationalities ("The young American researchers – they are just chimpanzees!") but we agreed on many things. I remember sitting with him in the shade of a tree beside his beautiful chateau and saying that I try to study snakes in ways that don't harm them. He replied: "Yes. That's why you are staying with me in the chateau, not staying in a hotel in town." Hubert's work spawned a French tradition of excellence and innovation in snake research, paving the way for later groups – most notably, that of Xavier Bonnet in Chizé – to create new and exciting Gallic perspectives on the ecology of snakes.

Although Saint Girons's sustained output of snake-ecology research sets him apart from other European workers of his generation, he was by no means the only contributor. Other viper enthusiasts produced excellent studies on the biology of these irascible little serpents. Highlights include a 1944 monograph on male reproductive cycles by a Dane, Helge Volsoe (1908–1968), who is also notable for compiling the first comprehensive review on the biology of sea snakes. Other adder enthusiasts who conducted landmark field-projects were Guy Naulleau in 1964 in France, Pertti Viitanen in 1967 in Finland, and Ian Presst in 1971 in the UK. These detailed studies clarified fundamental issues about snake movements and seasonal cycles. As a result of their labours, the Eurasian Adder has a special place in the history of research on snake ecology. Abundant even in severely cold climates, it was the ideal choice for anyone in northern Europe who wanted to study local snakes in the field.

Despite the abundance of snakes in Central and South America, ecological studies on Neotropical snakes were scarce until recently. As for other regions with major snakebite problems (Asia and Africa), early researchers focused on taxonomy, distributions and venom rather than esoteric issues such as home ranges and reproductive biology. As a result, South America was home to important research on venoms and antivenoms rather than ecological studies. But as snake-ecology research increased worldwide in the 1980s, major ecological programs were initiated by Brazilians such as Marcio Martins at the University of São Paulo and Selma Maria de Almeida Santos at the Instituto Butantan, and Argentinian boa-researcher Margareta Chiraviglio. Large and charismatic pit vipers have been the subject of much of that research, reflecting their abundance as well as their importance for snakebite.

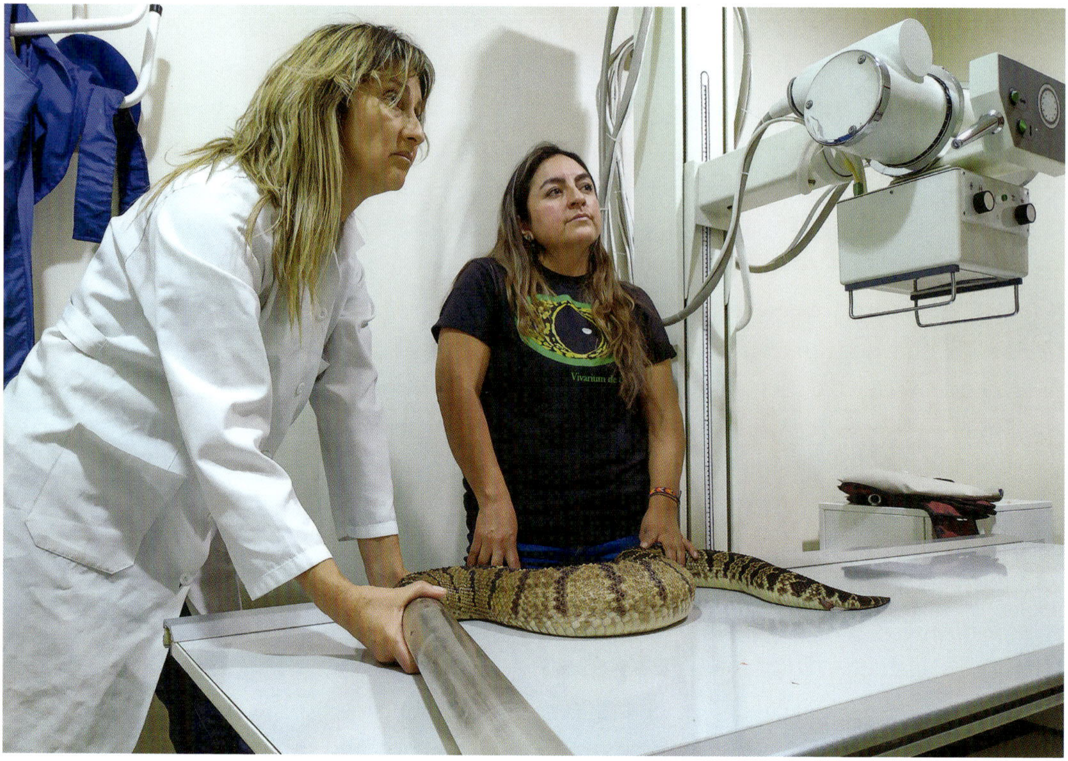

Increasing access to technology is facilitating research on charismatic snake species worldwide. In this photograph, María Barragán-Paladines is X-raying a Bushmaster (*Lachesis muta*), to check the location of its surgically implanted transmitter.

Snake ecology research in Asia

Although North America and Europe were the early powerhouses of scientific research, projects in other parts of the world were impressive also. For example, Henry Fitch wasn't the only pioneering snake ecologist to spend years marking, releasing and recatching snakes. On the Japanese island of Honshu, Hajime Fukada (1913–2002) conducted intensive studies around paddyfields. Hajime trained as an entomologist, although snake keeping was always his hobby. Like Henry, Hajime then went to war – but it was an horrendous experience for him, and he spent several years in deep shock after the defeat of Japan. English-language articles on snake ecology rekindled his interests, though, so he took a faculty position at Kyoto University. His methods were even simpler than those of Henry Fitch. Fukada peddled his bicycle from the campus to the Tambabashi paddyfields, a 15-minute ride, and caught snakes by hand. They were brought back to his laboratory for measuring, weighing and marking prior to release. Over a period of 16 years, he caught 4,769 snakes of five species. That repetitive work enabled him to accumulate the same kinds of detailed information on behaviour, movements, habitat use, growth rates, survival and reproductive biology as his American counterpart.

The snake-man of Kyoto – Hajime Fukada. KRAIG ADLER

But like Henry Fitch's experience in Kansas, Hajime's study was eventually terminated by changes in habitat. In Japan, it was due to urban expansion rather than forest overgrowth. The city of Kyoto grew, the paddyfields disappeared, an industrial estate was built, and the snakes were gone. Hajime's autobiography speaks evocatively of his passion for snakes, the chaos wrought by war, and the pain of growing old and infirm and losing personal contact with his beloved study animals.

Today, research on the ecology of snakes thrives in many countries and is conducted by people who were born there. But the early days were different. The pioneer figures for snake ecology in most tropical countries were expatriate Europeans or North Americans rather than locally trained scientists. That situation reflects the international diaspora of trained researchers, combined with economic and cultural obstacles that prevented local people from taking up a career in science. The first person to publish extensive ecological information on the diverse snake fauna of India and Sri Lanka was the physician Frank Wall (1868–1950), born in Sri Lanka but educated in England. In the Indo-Malayan Archipelago, the Austrian-born physician Felix Kopstein (1893–1939) described the biology of this rich fauna. The equivalent pioneer in China was Clifford Pope (1899–1974), an American herpetologist. Working with the American Museum of Natural History, Pope spoke fluent Chinese and made eight expeditions to Asia. His 1935 book on Chinese reptiles is full of ecological information and insights. Pope also wrote 'popular' books about snakes for the general public.

A contemporary of Pope's, Rudolf Mell (1878–1970) was an amateur German zoologist with a huge handlebar moustache and an equally over-sized passion for snakes. He sailed to China in 1908 to set up a school near Guanzhou, on the southern coast. In between teaching commitments Mell travelled widely, collecting animals and publishing books about them. Mell was a theorist and as well as obtaining information, he looked for general trends in his data. For example, he noted that mammal-eating snake species tend to have small scales whereas

The intrepid Rudolf Mell, a German-born zoologist with an unquenchable passion for Chinese snakes. KRAIG ADLER

reptile eaters have larger scales. Mell suggested that this is because smaller scales confer greater elasticity, with the skin between scales stretching more easily than a scale itself. Thus, mammal-eating snakes need small scales so the snake's body can distend when the predator consumes a chunky meal. In contrast, most reptile prey items are long and thin, and so don't require as much elasticity to swallow. Many years later I tested 'Mell's Law' with a large dataset, and sure enough, it works.

As time passed, local scholars took more prominent positions in the Chinese research effort. One extraordinary program focused on 'Snake Island' (Shedao) was rigorous and wide-ranging; but because the results were published in Chinese journals, the Shedao program remained invisible to Western science for several decades. Today, things are different. The barriers between Chinese and Western science have fallen, and Chinese research is growing at a phenomenal pace.

An African adventurer

The most colourful pioneer of snake biology in southern Africa was the elfin Constantin J.P. Ionides (1901–1968), known as 'Bobby' or 'Iodine' to his friends. Born in England, Ionides rebelled against the strict educational system of the UK and dreamed of becoming a professional hunter in Africa. He joined the army as an 18-year-old and travelled to East Africa in his mid–20s, rarely leaving that continent thereafter. After a stint in the army, Ionides turned to a life of poaching, then more respectable jobs as a hunting guide and as a game warden. He survived attacks by rogue elephants and man-eating lions but was eventually forced into retirement by ill health. At 42 years of age, severe thrombosis in both legs made it difficult for him to walk.

What could Ionides do, after abandoning his high-octane career as a game ranger? His solution was typically offbeat. Ionides turned to a new profession: collecting deadly snakes. Zoos and scientific laboratories needed live snakes for exhibits and antivenin production, and Ionides had tapped into a lucrative opportunity.

Loathing Western society, he lived in a small cottage on the Makonde Plateau in the Newala

District of Tanzania, near the Mozambique border. Adamant that foregoing European company was a small price to pay for spending time with snakes, one of Ionides's favourite sayings was "you can't have jam on it." Given his hatred for new-fangled gadgets such as fridges, newspapers, radios and ballpoint pens, his cottage was spartan in the extreme. Snakes are difficult to find in most of Africa, so Ionides relied on an extensive network of local informers. Any villager who saw a snake in the fields could send a message to the house of 'Bwana Nyoka'. Unable to walk long distances because of his thrombosis, Ionides employed two muscular young men to transport him in a specially constructed one-wheeled cart. He would then clamber out and collect the snake – but only if it had not been restrained in any way by the people who found it. For example, if the snake had been trapped under a basket, Ionides would refuse to touch it and instead, would deliver an expletive-ridden tirade. Villagers learned to simply watch snakes, not harass them. Having captured the animal and paid the informant, Ionides would then clamber back into his cart to be wheeled home.

Because Ionides saw snakes as fascinating animals, not just as meal tickets, he took notes on every snake that he captured. That included records of its size, sex, habitat, height above the ground if in a tree, and so forth. Over decades, he filled up many notebooks with those data. He also kept a running tally of his lifetime collection of snakes – including 6,663 Green Mambas, 2,159 Gaboon Vipers, 386 Cape Cobras, and so on. Most of those snakes came from within a 20-km radius of his home. His capture rates on the Makonde Plateau were extraordinary: for example, 47 Green Mambas in one two-week period. He writes that one day he caught 18 Green Mambas and one Boomslang within a three-and-a-half-hour period, and only stopped because his hands became tired. He also made trips to other parts of Africa to collect Water Cobras and Rhinoceros Vipers. Even as his leg problems worsened, he kept travelling. His final safari was to Kenya in July 1968, where he collected 27 Black Mambas. But a month into the trip, his legs failed him completely. He was evacuated to Nairobi, where surgeons amputated both legs. Complications set in, and Ionides died in September 1968.

I read a biography of Constantin Ionides when I was a student, and was immediately fascinated by this foul-mouthed antisocial misfit whose love for snakes transcended his desire for comfort or human interactions. I never met Ionides – he died 26 years before my first trip to Africa – but I often thought of those extensive notes he had kept. What a goldmine of information about a world that no longer existed! Every biography of this remarkable man mentioned the notebooks. Surely such a unique resource would have been donated to a scientific institution for safe keeping? So when I travelled overseas I searched for Ionides's field notebooks in the British Museum of Natural History and in major museums in Africa. I asked colleagues about the notebooks but failed to find even a meagre hint. Eventually I gave up the

Constantin Ionides smoking one of his favourite 'Crown Bird' cigarettes. STEVE SPAWLS

quest, accepting that the notebooks were gone forever. And then in 2018, the 50th anniversary of Ionides's death, an Englishman who had known Ionides wrote a commemorative article about him for a scientific journal. Steve Spawls told some wonderful anecdotes but the jaw-dropping moment for me was that Steve's article included a photograph of a page from one of Ionides's 'missing' notebooks.

I immediately contacted Steve, who told me that the books had been passed on to him by another legend of African herpetology, Jonathan Leakey (1940–2021). And yes, Steve would help me to fulfil my decades-long dream of analysing Ionides's meticulously recorded data. Sadly, Ionides had cut out the pages about the two species he captured most often, the Green Mamba and the Puff Adder. He sent those pages to his colleague Charles Pitman for a scientific paper that Pitman was writing. But that still left detailed information on the captures of 484 snakes of five species.

I have written more than a thousand scientific papers, but the Ionides work gave me more pleasure than almost any other. I felt that Ionides was looking over my shoulder as I analysed his hard-won data, ready to swear at me if I misunderstood anything. As I had hoped, several interesting stories emerged from the statistical analyses. For example, large Black Mambas and Rhinoceros Vipers lived on the ground, whereas juveniles of both species were often found in trees. It was a window in time to an era that has long gone. The trees where Ionides caught mambas in the 1950s and 1960s have long since been cut down. The forests no longer exist. But half a century after the death of this extraordinary man, the information he painstakingly recorded has at last seen the light of day, and gives us a glimpse into a bygone world.

Snake-ecology research Down Under

The tropical forests of the Indo-Australian Archipelago also contain a diverse array of snakes. Some of the first information about their behaviour and ecology came from a pioneering Dutchwoman, Nelly de Rooij (1883–1964), in two lengthy books that she published in 1915 and 1917. Ironically, Nelly never visited Asia herself. Her information was based on specimens in the Museum of Zoology in Amsterdam, where de Rooij was a curator. Because the Netherlands controlled much of the area between Sumatra and New Guinea (the 'Dutch East Indies'), Dutch museums received hundreds of preserved reptiles collected by explorers and

European colonists. De Rooij battled gender-based discrimination throughout her professional career, making her encyclopaedic review of Indo-Australian reptiles even more impressive.

Scientific herpetology was slow to evolve among professional scientists in Australia, my own home country, although the Indigenous people who have lived there for 60,000 years have a detailed understanding of the land and its wildlife. Australia is the only continent where venomous snakes outnumber their non-venomous counterparts, and some Aussie species have highly toxic venoms. As a result, snakebite and venoms were the foci of early research. And the ever-present danger of a fatal bite galvanised interest from the general public, spawning a long-running tradition of exhibitors at snake shows. Intrepid men and women handled deadly snakes in front of audiences and sold their home-made remedies against snakebite.

Some of those enthusiasts transitioned to professional reptile keeping in zoos but maintained their flair and appetite for public education. One of the best known was David Fleay (1907–1993), who was among the first to recognise the increasing public interest in native wildlife, and to write engagingly about his experiences as a zookeeper. Highlights of his professional life included being the first person to successfully breed the Platypus in captivity; and being the last (perhaps only) person to have been bitten on the buttocks by the now-extinct Thylacine (or 'Tasmanian Tiger'). The last known Thylacine was kept in a Tasmanian zoo and in 1933, Fleay was photographing it when it walked around behind him and took a chomp. Fleay was inordinately proud of the resulting scar. Interested in snakes as well as other wildlife, Fleay often included first-hand observations of snake natural history (including, the first records of male-male combat) in dozens of magazine articles about Australian serpents.

Another notable pioneer in public outreach was Eric Worrell (1924–1987). He created Australia's first reptile zoo, the Australian Reptile Park near Sydney, that became a magnet for snake-obsessed young Australians. But Worrell also organised information about Australian reptiles, writing numerous scientific papers and books as well as magazine articles. His contributions were resented by the scientific elite, who saw Worrell as an amateur transgressing the boundary between hobby and science.

Snake-focused Australian scientists were scarce in the early days of European colonisation, but one character stands out: Johann (Gerard) Krefft (1830–1881). German-born Krefft arrived in Australia in 1852, lured by the gold rush but soon working as a scientific illustrator for expeditions in Victoria. His drawings of Indigenous communities as well as landscapes and wildlife provide some of the best depictions of Australia in the 1850s. In 1860 Krefft was appointed as a curator of the fledgling Australian Museum in Sydney, and in 1864 was promoted to Director. In 1869 he wrote a book *The Snakes of Australia* but had to publish it himself because no commercial publisher would take it on. Superbly illustrated by sisters

Gerard Krefft, the rambunctious museum curator who offended his bosses but who also wrote a fine book on Australian snakes. STATE LIBRARY OF NEW SOUTH WALES

Helena and Harriet Scott, it was truly a landmark work. Importantly, Krefft not only described each species, but also discussed its ecology and looming conservation issues such as the widespread destruction of critical habitats.

But Gerard Krefft was a thorny character, and often fell out with his colleagues – notably with a fellow German, William Blandowski (1822–1878), during a joint expedition along the Murray River. A few years later a bitter conflict erupted between Krefft and the trustees who ran the Australian Museum. The pugnacious Krefft was accused of drunkenness and allowing the sale of obscene postcards, and was dismissed. When he refused to leave, the trustees hired two prize fighters to break down Krefft's office door, carry him out on his chair and dump him in the middle of a nearby street. Krefft took the trustees to court, won his case, and was awarded the princely sum of a thousand pounds by the Parliament of New South Wales.

As a proud Aussie herpetologist, I admire the legacy of Gerard Krefft. He was a grumpy fellow but he did excellent science, wrote about snakes for the general public, drew attention to conservation issues, embraced the then-heretical ideas of Charles Darwin, and stood up for himself in the face of bureaucratic attack. Supporting the renegade Darwin against the scientific establishment in a conservative colony wasn't easy; in one letter to Darwin, Krefft complained: "A true believer in the theory of development, I am hounded down in this paradise of bushrangers, rogues, cheats and vagabonds." Old ideas die hard. Looking through old letters in the State Library of New South Wales, I was struck by Darwin's unusually warm and candid sentiments in a letter to Krefft: "I have long respected your able and indefagitable labour in the cause of natural sciences." That's a fine epitaph for any biologist.

IN THEIR OWN WORDS

Most early herpetologists were too busy describing snakes to talk about other snake-obsessed researchers, but occasionally one will pause to reflect on their colleagues:

"Those who care for the study of amphibia and reptiles – the herpetologists, to give them their scientific title – have never been numerous; but most of them have been serious students. One reason for the fact that this branch of natural history is not very popular, is a prejudice against creatures some of which are clammy and cold to the touch, and some of which may be poisonous. People who delight in keeping newts or frogs, tortoises, or snakes, are, as a rule, considered eccentric." HANS GADOW, 1901

For a snake-lover, the almost-universal hatred of snakes, and the consequent difficulty of obtaining intact specimens for study, were a constant frustration:

"When people abroad see a live snake they rush upon it and batter it to death with sticks and stones, as though every inch of it possessed a separate and fifty feline power of life calling for special destruction; then they pick up what is left of it, and, after an uncertain interval of time, very often in the broiling midday heat of the tropics, put it into a bottle of cachasse, canha, aguadiente, or some other coarse spirit which disintegrates its actual structure, label it with the wrong name, and send it home. Such, in the case of many species, have been the only materials that naturalists have had to work upon." ARTHUR STRADLING, 1882

Chapter 11

Fallen fighters: casualties of the revolution

On 3 August 2022, as I was writing this book, my friend William H. 'Marty' Martin walked out to the shed behind his house in West Virginia to record some information from a captive Timber Rattlesnake. A veteran snake handler, undisputed expert on the species, Marty would have been confident and unflustered. But something went wrong and the snake struck him on the hand. Marty made it back to his house but he collapsed in the kitchen. He was transported by ambulance to the emergency room where he was resuscitated, intubated and given antivenom. Due to earlier bites, Marty had an acute allergic reaction to the snake's venom. He was airlifted to another hospital for more intensive care but he went into total organ failure. Marty was dead within a few hours of being bitten.

Marty Martin was one of a kind. Born in Virginia in 1941, he spent his teenage years searching for snakes in West Virginia. Lacking the financial resources to attend college, Marty joined the US Army, fought as a paratrooper in the Vietnam War, then returned to the USA to obtain the scientific qualifications he needed for a career in rattlesnake conservation.

By the time I met Marty in 1980 he already had an extraordinarily detailed knowledge of the hills of West Virginia and of the rattlesnakes that call them home. The only address I had for Marty was a trailer park – a huge collection of caravans – deep in the backwoods. When I stopped at the trailer-park office for directions, I learned that almost everyone living in the park had the surname 'Martin', and several people went by the name 'Marty Martin' – a true backwoods West Virginia situation. But fortunately there was only one 'Rattlesnake Marty'.

Slightly built but tough as teak, Marty was difficult to keep up with as he took me out into the woods to find his beloved snakes. I learned a lot from those walks – not just about rattlesnakes, but about how someone with limited financial support for research could find cost-effective ways to make a project work. Because he learned about snakes on his own, rather than from other researchers, Marty developed his own methods. For example, why spend money on expensive microchips for individual ID when you can just write a number in permanent-marker pen at the base of the snake's rattles?

Marty Martin in the backwoods of Virginia with a Timber Rattlesnake (*Crotalus horridus*), the species that dominated his life and eventually ended it. LANCE BENEDICT

Likewise, Marty ignored conventional wisdom about snake handling. I had been picking Australian snakes up by the tail for decades but had been told by my American colleagues that it would be suicidal to pick up a rattlesnake by the tail. The snake was so muscular that it could simply swing around and launch a well-aimed strike at your midriff or groin. That sounded plausible to me, so I was astonished when Marty casually seized a giant snake by the tail and held it up in the air as he recorded data. My enduring mental image of Marty is of him with the cap of a permanent-marker pen between his teeth, holding a gigantic Timber Rattler by the tail, and scribbling an ID mark on the rattles.

Marty spent most of his long career out in the Appalachian woods rather than in an office. He tramped countless miles through rough tracks, up steep mountains and across unstable talus slopes to find rattlers in their overwintering dens. He monitored twenty dens year after year, searching for snakes as they returned from their feeding ranges to the den at the end of

Marty Martin was short in stature but long on courage. This picture captures the moment when Marty returned to his field vehicle to find that a Black Bear (*Ursus americanus*) had broken into it. A few seconds later Marty charged the bear with only his snake hook as a weapon, sending the marauding mammal scurrying away. LANCE BENEDICT

summer, then again in springtime as they lay around the den entrance basking. He was an ambassador for rattlesnake conservation, funding his work through short-term contracts rather than a permanent academic position. His love affair with Timber Rattlers was eventually fatal, but I doubt that he would have wanted a different end to his life.

Why, where and when do snakes bite people?

Snakebite is an occupational hazard for any researcher who works with venomous snakes, but fatalities such as the one that befell Marty are rare. If you spend enough time working with deadly snakes, a serious bite is well-nigh inevitable. Some snake people gleefully recount their life list of 'Snake Species That Have Bitten Me', but most professional researchers are more circumspect. I agree with Rom Whitaker that "getting bitten by a venomous snake is dumb, clumsy and nothing to be proud of." But at worst, a bite is likely to mean a week in hospital, and lingering after-effects on the body part that was bitten. Modern antivenoms are highly effective.

Despite the low probability of catastrophe, nonetheless, the risk is always there. In this chapter, I'll review cases where snake researchers died during fieldwork, or when working with snakes in the laboratory. I won't dwell at length on zookeepers, because most of them weren't conducting research when they were bitten. But it's worth noting that professional zookeepers are rarely killed by the animals they care for, reflecting effective protocols and training.

Most examples of fatal snakebites to zookeepers occurred before effective antivenoms were available (such as 41-year-old Edward Rabe, bitten by a rattlesnake in Los Angeles in 1905; 41-year-old C.J. French, bitten by an Australian Tiger Snake in 1927; 52-year-old Douglas Marsh, bitten by a Fer-de-Lance in Panama in 1939; and 36-year-old Bertie Peers, bitten by a Cape Cobra in South Africa also in 1939). But several deaths were more recent, showing that snakebite can be fatal even when modern medical facilities are easily accessible. In South Africa, the Transvaal Snake Park saw two fatalities: Wanda Halligan-Jolly was only 22 years old when killed by a Puff Adder in 1971, and Paul Olsen was 25 when he lost his life to a bite from a Snouted Cobra in 1997. A Puff Adder also took the life of 37-year-old zoo director Jerry de Barry in Salt Lake City, Utah in 1964. At a Florida nature park, 22-year-old Curtis Davison

Restraining venomous snakes inside clear Perspex tubes can reduce the chance of accidental bites, as demonstrated here by Graham Alexander's photograph of a large Puff Adder (*Bitis arietans*).

died in 1989 from a bite inflicted by a large Eastern Diamondback Rattler. And in 2021, a 45-year-old keeper was found dead beside the King Cobra exhibit in an Indian zoo.

Fatal bites to 'snake people' were common in earlier times, when treatments were less effective and medical facilities were few and far between. And overall, most deaths from snakebite have been to people handling snakes for reasons other than research – usually to capture and kill them, or to keep them in cages, or to exhibit them during religious ceremonies or to the paying public.

Although the first antivenoms were produced in the late 19th century, they didn't come into common use until the 1950s. Prior to that time, fatal snakebites were common for the 'snake exhibitors' of circuses and fairs. Remarkably, most of those bites were deliberate. To spruik the benefits of their home-made remedies, handlers induced snakes to bite them as the climax of a carnival sideshow. Many of these exhibitors had had several bites already, so had developed some level of immunity. The resulting lack of symptoms helped persuade onlookers to invest in the snakebite 'cure'. But prior exposure to venom or antivenom can also have the reverse effect, inducing a fatal anaphylactic shock. Time after time, the showmen's confidence proved to be sorely misplaced.

John Cann's book *Historical Snakeys* lists 16 pioneering showmen and showwomen in Australia who died from snakebite. Most of them met their fate via the venom of Australian Tiger Snakes, but a couple were killed on international tours. 'Professor' Fred Fox (1870–1914) died in India after allowing a krait to bite him on the wrist, and Tom Wanless (1895–1921) made the mistake of inducing a Green Mamba to bite him on the arm during a show in Africa. His last words were "The Green Mamba wins."

Snake shows have disappeared from circuses and state fairs, but reptiles have become popular as pets in the home. That cultural switch has changed the venue for snakebite, but not the outcome. Most pet snakes are small and harmless, but a few snake keepers want the deadliest animals available. Inevitably, bites occur. A Google search throws up dozens of stories of snake owners crushed to death by pythons, or fatally envenomated by Puff Adders, Black Mambas and King Cobras. Most of the victims are males in their 20s or 30s. It's usually the snake keeper who is bitten, but sometimes it's a visitor to the house who runs out of luck. Or the snake-owner's child who encounters an escaped pet in the hallway.

The context of bites by captive snakes tells us a great deal about the reasons for those bites. For example, a survey of 106 bites to Australian snake handlers from 2004 to 2011 reported that the average age of people bitten was 40 years, but with a range from 16 to 81 years. Of those 106 bites, 104 (98 per cent) were to men rather than women, usually to the hands or arms. Two worrying cases involved the children of snake handlers, including a two-year-old

Most 'pet' snakes around the world are small harmless species, but a few people desire the biggest and most toxic serpents such as this Eastern Green Mamba (*Dendroaspis angusticeps*). THILO BECK

boy bitten by a highly venomous Collett's Snake. Fortunately, all of the people who were bitten survived – in some cases, to be bitten again. Three patients were each bitten on three occasions.

Alcohol contributes to many snakebites, and some people are slow to learn that lesson. A physician in Australia told me about one gentleman who kept pet snakes and was generally careful with them. But on Christmas evenings on three successive years, the lonely snake keeper drank a great deal of beer, staggered off to his cages, and grabbed an armful of Tiger Snakes with his bare hands. Next stop, the local hospital. It's an unusual way to celebrate Christmas.

Even professional snake handlers sometimes succumb to snakebite after alcohol liberates some weird inner machismo. In 1852, for example, a man named Edward Horatio Gurling died of a cobra bite. The snake was a captive animal at the zoo in London, described in a newspaper report as being "about five feet long, with a flat broad head and a yellow mark at the back of its neck." Gurling was a snake keeper at the zoo and met his end after an inebriated party with a friend that included "a quarter of gin at a public house in Shoe Lane, another afterwards, and again another at eight o'clock." A commentator at the time (in *The Daily News*, London,

23 October 1852) noted that "the gin-laden blood circulated through the brain; and reason, prudence, and the plainest sense of imminent hazard, were alike overpowered." Gurling seized the cobra from its cage, put it inside his waistcoat and then held the snake aloft by the midbody after it crawled its way out of the other side of his coat. Unsurprisingly, the snake responded by striking him in the face, seizing firm hold of Gurling's nose at least five times. He died an hour later. The jury that investigated his death concluded that "the deceased has lost his life by the bite of a serpent, known as the cobra di capello, when in a state of intoxication, and in consequence of his own rashness and indiscretion."

Drunken fatalities are so common that they rarely receive much attention in the media – unless the person involved did something truly and staggeringly foolish. One such incident in January 2009 received wide international publicity, including a 'Darwin Award'. I didn't know the victim, but the snake involved was one of my favourite species, the King Brown. And it happened in the Northern Territory of tropical Australia, where I have studied this species for decades. King Browns are Australia's equivalent to the large cobras of Africa. These huge and deadly snakes are tolerant of people but defend themselves vigorously if they come under attack. And that's exactly what happened to a local man named Gordon Lyons, who encountered a two-and-a-half metre (7.5-ft) King Brown at night on the road, where Gordon was driving with a friend.

Despite being drunk at the time, Gordon remembered that the huge fish tank behind the bar at the local hotel was empty, because the fish had died. A massive King Brown might make an interesting exhibit, so Gordon decided to catch the snake. His first mistake was to grab the snake with his left hand because, as he told a newspaper reporter, "I was holding a beer in my right one." Unsurprisingly, the snake bit him as Gordon stuffed it into a plastic bag. For reasons he could not recollect, Gordon then put his hand into the bag, enabling the snake to bite him another eight times. Gordon soon began vomiting and suffering diarrhoea, inducing his companion to assist by "trying to keep me awake by whacking me in the head and pouring beer on me." Compounding the litany of errors, his mate then drove Gordon to a hotel rather than a hospital. By the time Gordon received medical help, it was too late to save the arm that was bitten. Gordon survived for a few years but was wheelchair-bound and eventually died of complications from the bite. The outcome was a sad demonstration of the potential for catastrophe when an inebriated human being meets a deadly snake.

Although alcohol increases the risks enormously, some people are capable of astounding stupidity even when they are stone-cold sober. The most consistent contributor to fatal snakebites among snake handlers is machismo. Wrestling a deadly snake is viewed as a test of manhood. That attitude is less common among professional snake handlers than among pet

The size and power of an adult King Brown Snake (*Pseudechis australis*) make it a daunting animal to handle. And if things go wrong, these giant snakes can inflict a deadly bite. AUSTRALIAN REPTILE PARK

keepers, and rarer still among snake scientists. A few snake researchers never outgrow their adolescent bravado, but most of us don't view snake catching as a competitive sport. You can enjoy the adrenalin rush of catching a venomous snake without intensifying the experience by taking foolhardy risks.

Snakebite in front of an audience

People who handle deadly snakes to entertain the public tread a perilous tightrope. If the snake handling looks safe, it's not exciting. Thus, professional performers try to convince onlookers that their activities are desperately dangerous. Some snakes make this easy by ferociously bluffing but rarely biting. The paragon in this respect is the cobra – or at least, some types of cobra. It takes only mild harassment to persuade a cobra to raise its forebody and spread its hood, but it takes a lot more to stimulate a strike – and when the strike comes, it tends to be slow and short range. So across much of Asia, snake charmers are in less peril than they appear to be. There's a larger safety margin with cobras than with other venomous snakes.

Some snake exhibitors are experts at pretending that they are in mortal peril. The best example of trickery I ever witnessed involved a legendary Australian snake man who ran a small roadside zoo in the Northern Territory. Graeme Gow (1941–2005) wrote books about snakes, but he was more of a showman than a scientist. A small but powerful man, Graeme oozed testosterone and seemed to swell in size whenever an audience appeared to watch him handle a deadly snake. One day I brought a young woman along to meet Graeme and see his animals. A visiting American, Deborah had been volunteering as a research assistant for our work on pythons at a nearby site, and she had implored me to introduce her to the renowned snake man.

Clearly flattered by her attention, Graeme dragged a huge Australian Tiger Snake out of its cage by the tail and draped the snake across a nearby table. Then he turned away from the snake to look at the young woman, still holding the snake by the tail but with its head and body now behind him. The cardinal rule of snake handling is 'never take your eyes off the animal's head' – and Graeme was flagrantly breaching that rule. Deborah was horrified. So was I, until I realised that Graeme was staring into a large mirror on the wall behind Deb rather than focusing on the woman in front of it. And sure enough, as the snake swung around to bite him, Graeme instantly pulled his hand out of harm's way.

When I mentioned that story to other friends who exhibit deadly snakes, they mentioned an even more frightening version of Graeme's trick. While holding the snake (without looking at it), focus on the eyes of somebody in the front row of the audience. If the snake launches a strike, the startled expression on that audience-member's face gives the snake handler enough time to react before the fangs strike home. Maybe, but it sounds like Russian roulette to me.

Cobra-trainers and exhibitors depend upon the snakes' reliance on bluff rather than attack, but it pays to keep a close eye on the reptiles nonetheless. This photograph shows a man with two Monocled Cobras (*Naja kaouthia*). MICHAEL BERLOTTI/PIXABAY

And I should add that Graeme was bitten by venomous snakes more often than anybody else I've ever known. He boasted to the media about surviving 146 bites. That isn't a convincing endorsement of his approach to snake handling.

Contrary to intuition, snakebite isn't a major risk factor for professional researchers. Competent snake handling reduces the risk of a bite, and effective first aid reduces the severity of symptoms. In Australia, for example, where elapids reign and vipers don't occur, a firm pressure bandage applied along a limb can slow the venom's spread for many hours. That simple method was a serendipitous discovery in the 1970s by venom researcher Struan Sutherland (1936–2002). He was looking for a way to slow the diffusion of venom away from the bite site.

That involved injecting a macaque monkey on the limb with Tiger Snake venom, applying a ligature or splint, and then measuring venom levels in the bloodstream. Very few monkeys died because they were given antivenom as soon as the toxin began to spread. Struan told me that on the afternoon of 27 April 1978 he decided to test an inflatable splint but it had a puncture and wouldn't hold air. Struan grabbed a nearby crepe pressure bandage and applied it instead – and was astonished to find that venom levels were virtually undetectable in the monkey's blood even a few hours later. The simple bandage had worked better than the sophisticated methods Struan was exploring, and it was much easier to use in the field. Before long, most Aussie snake catchers were carrying a pressure bandage in their pocket. But of course, first aid just keeps you alive long enough to get to the hospital. The only real remedy is antivenom. Experienced researchers ensure that appropriate antivenom is available at the local hospital – and they know how to reach that hospital in a hurry.

That doesn't make fieldwork risk free, but it means that the greatest dangers come from infectious diseases, car accidents, falls, drowning and the like. Every fieldworker has stories of near misses, such as Henry Fitch's ordeal when he fell down a slope into a chilly creek on the Kansas natural history reservation, and spent the night there because the search dogs brought in to find him were hopelessly confused. Henry's scent was everywhere on the reservation, making the dogs' job impossible.

Death in the field and laboratory

Novelist Richard Conniff maintains a fascinating website entitled 'The Wall of the Dead: A Memorial to Fallen Naturalists', that lists the names of scientists who have died in the field.

https://strangebehaviors.wordpress.com/2011/01/14/the-wall-of-the-dead/

To explore the risk of fatal snakebite compared to other threats, I trolled through Richard's website to look for reptile biologists. Not all were snake specialists, but most reptile researchers study every living thing with scales, regardless of whether or not it also has legs. So I've included them as well. But I've left out researchers who were clearly focusing on other kinds of animals, and ran into snakes by accident. For example, 67-year-old fisheries biologist William Price was bitten above the ankle by a rattlesnake while fording a Californian stream. He stopped breathing within minutes of being bitten. Likewise, 41-year-old Boini Krishnaiah of the Indian Space Research Organisation likely wasn't thinking about snakes in 2022 when he went for an evening walk in Karnataka, India, and encountered the snake that ended his life. And how would you classify the death of biologist Malcolm Soule, who committed suicide in 1951 by injecting himself with snake venom after he was dismissed from his University of Michigan job for misuse of funds?

Many of the best places to find snakes are rugged landscapes, where accidents can happen at any time. This image shows fieldwork in Oklahoma's LeFlore County. NOAH K. FIELDS

The most common causes of deaths of reptile biologists in the field include diseases and conditions such as malaria (that killed crocodile specialists Jack Cox, 1952–2010, and John Thorbjarnason, 1957–2010), dysentery (Guiseppe Raddi, 1770–1829) and heat stroke (Peter Rawlinson, 1943–1991; Daniel Hamilton, 1990–2011). Septicaemia accounted for lizard-specialist Walter Mosauer (1905–1937) on a trip to Mexico. And some reptile researchers were killed by medical issues arising from fieldwork, but not manifesting until years later. Pioneering sea-snake researcher Jeffrey Graham (1941–2011) was 70 years old when he died, but the melanoma that killed him was probably stimulated by long hours of sun exposure during fieldwork decades before.

More prosaically, heart attacks brought on by the stress of fieldwork terminated the existence of Jan Rafinski (1943–2003) in Poland and prolific author Joe Collins (1938–2012) in Florida. Also in Florida, Scott Maness (1948–1981) was burned to death in a wildfire when the wind shifted the fire back towards him and his colleague as they tried to create a firebreak.

Many reptiles live on steep cliffs or high in treetops, so that a single false step can send researchers plummeting to earth far below. The body of Hungarian herpetologist Peter Torok (1989–2016) was found at the base of such a cliff in Russia. Eighteen-year-old Worth Weller (1913–1931) was collecting specimens of a newly discovered salamander species (later named in his honour) when he fell off a cliff in North Carolina. In the Pacific nation of New Caledonia, promising young Australian biologist Peter Rankin (1956–1979) fell to his death from a rainforest tree while attempting to collect Giant Geckos at night. Eminent Indian snake biologist Bupathy Subramanian (1961–2014) conducted groundbreaking studies on Indian Pythons. Tragically, he died when an apparently innocuous fall down a hill ended with him being impaled through the eye by a bamboo spike.

Water has accounted for reptile biologists as well, with drowning victims in Wyoming (lizard expert Ken Miyata, 1951–1983), Brazil (Gabriel Sugliano, 1962–2011) and Fiji (John Gibbons, 1946–1986). In India, Ambika Tripathy was studying sea turtles on Great Nicobar Island when the great tsunami of December 2004 struck.

Fieldwork often entails long-distance travel on poorly maintained roads, elevating the humble car accident to number one on the list of dangers. Researchers who died in car accidents include James Anderson (1930–1976), T. Preston Webber III (1947–1975), Benoit Mys (1960–1989) and Adao Cardoso (1951–1997).

Sadly, another major cause of fatalities during fieldwork involves members of our own species. A biologist searching for reptiles – especially at night – can be shot by locals who mistake the researcher for a criminal intruder (Ben Samphire, 1978–2009) or a wild animal (William Heinrich, 1881–1938). Several colleagues have told me of bullets zipping around them in similar circumstances; my friend Jim Berry was snorkelling for turtles in a Florida spring when fired upon by an inebriated local who had mistaken Jim for a manatee. Alcohol was also central to one of my own experiences in tropical Australia, where a drunken banana farmer routinely fired his rifle (fortunately, poorly aimed) at me when I drove past his house at night while searching for pythons. I soon learned to switch off my headlights when passing his house.

Sometimes, the people who kill biologists do so on purpose rather than accidentally. Sea-turtle conservationist Jairo Mora Sandoval (1987–2013) was only 26 years old when he was kidnapped, beaten and then killed by turtle-egg poachers while he was patrolling a beach in Costa Rica. His death aroused widespread anger internationally, leading to increased funding for sea-turtle conservation in Costa Rica. A wildlife refuge is named after him, and the 'Jairo Mora Sandoval Bravery Award' is bestowed every two years by the Society for Conservation Biology. More than a century earlier, Perry Simons (1869–1901) was murdered by his guide when crossing the Andes on a collecting expedition. Heinrich Macklot (1799–1832) was a pioneering Dutch naturalist in Java, who had the honour of a magnificent python species being named after him. Enraged when insurgents burned down his house, Macklot organised a revenge attack and was speared to death at the age of 33.

But when the general public think about the dangers of fieldwork for biologists, the first thing that comes to mind is attack by wild animals. Fortunately, fatal attacks on naturalists are rare. The only two I could find involved elephants killing Swedish naturalist Johan Wahlberg (1810–1856) and, more recently, American lizard researcher Margarita Metallinou (1986–2015). Australian media presenter Steve Irwin (1962–2006) was famously killed by a stingray barb to the chest while filming one of his shows. And I'm sorely tempted to add the name of Jean-Christophe Vivier, a veterinary practitioner who conducted surgeries to implant transmitters in sea snakes for us during our work in New Caledonia. Jean-Christophe was killed by a shark while windsurfing near Noumea in 2021. Windsurfing is not exactly fieldwork, but Jean-Christophe may have been keeping an eye out for snakes for us at the time.

When snake researchers die from snakebite

That brings us back to where this chapter began – researchers who have been killed by snakes. There's a tragic irony to loving snakes and being killed by them. Fatal snakebites to research biologists likely were common in the early days but either went unrecorded or were noted only with sketchy detail. For example, herpetologist and paleontologist Jacob Boll (1828–1880) died during fieldwork in Texas. Accounts differ, with some attributing his death to septicaemia but others implicating snakebite.

In recent cases, where we have more detailed information, I am struck by the diversity in

Large pythons such as this Rock Python (*Python natalensis*) from southern Africa can easily exert enough force to kill any adult human being. Indeed, a snake this size is a handful even for two highly experienced researchers such as Kelly Zamudio and Graham Alexander.
HARRY GREENE

the snakes responsible, the kinds of people who succumbed, and the situations in which those bites occurred.

The only scientific fatality from a non-venomous snake involves a young Swede, Eric Arttmasson (1980–2003), who was killed by his pet Scrub Python in Australia. Eric had moved from his homeland to work on snakes at an Australian facility, including research with me on Tiger Snakes. But it was his pet snake, a large Scrubbie, that ended his life one evening. Nobody knows exactly what happened.

I would have expected most deaths due to snakebite to fall upon young researchers, inexperienced in handling deadly snakes. For example, self-taught Italian-Kenyan herpetologist Emanuelle Gallman (1966–1983) was only 17 years old when he was killed by a Puff Adder while trying to 'milk' the snake for its venom. Jimmy Murray was 19 years old in 1931 when an Australian Tiger Snake bit him while he was collecting snakes for venom extraction and research. Obtaining venom for the creation of antivenom was also the primary motivation for 20-year-old Kevin Budden (1930–1950), an Australian snake-enthusiast who travelled to the tropics determined to collect a live Coastal Taipan for that purpose. Taipans are large, fast-moving and retaliate fiercely when harassed. Kevin had a stroke of good fortune by finding one of these elusive snakes while it was swallowing a rat (and thus, was unable to bite because its mouth was full of rodent). But his luck ran out soon afterwards, as he was trying to get the snake into a bag. It slipped free and bit him on the thumb. As soon as he was bitten, Budden realised that he was unlikely to survive – but he continued his efforts and finally bagged the snake. Before he slipped into a coma, he gave instructions that the snake was to be shipped alive to people who could collect its venom for antivenom production. His snake was among the first taipans to ever be captured alive, and it provided several venom samples.

But snakebite fatalities have not been restricted to inexperienced youngsters. American physician and reptile biologist, Frederick Shannon (1921–1965) was 44 years old when bitten by a Mojave Rattlesnake that he was trying to capture. Hans Schurrenberger (1925–1964), a part-time reptile collector, was 39 years old when he was killed by the bite of a juvenile McClelland's Coral Snake in Nepal. Frederick Lock was an experienced game ranger in Tanganyika, author of an identification key to snakes of that country. Late at night and just before Christmas, Locke was playing with a captive twig snake after returning from a party with friends. Believing the snake to be only mildly venomous, Lock provoked the snake until it finally obliged by biting him on the thumb. He ignored the bite but symptoms soon set in and he died on Christmas Eve 1953.

More recently, 38-year-old American biologist Joe Slowinski (1962–2001) died after being bitten by a juvenile Suzhen's Krait in a remote mountainous district of Myanmar (Burma).

Many fatal snakebites have occurred while people are 'milking' snakes to obtain venom. It's a job best left to experts, as in this photograph of a King Brown Snake (*Pseudechis australis*) being milked at the Australian Reptile Park.

Karl Patterson Schmidt, the renowned reptile researcher, who was killed by a bite from a supposedly 'harmless' snake, the Boomslang (*Dispholidus typus*). LIM L. KEMP

Joe was a leading researcher on snake taxonomy, renowned for ambitious expeditions to remote areas. A snake enthusiast all of his short life, Joe had already survived numerous bites from other snakes, beginning with a rattlesnake when he was 15 years old. He added an American Copperhead bite to his list during his student days at the University of Kansas, and a cobra bite in Myanmar.

The krait that took Joe's life was also captured in Myanmar. The animal had been captured the day before by an assistant who misidentified the snake as a harmless species – a mimic of the deadly krait. The snake had bitten another member of the research expedition on the previous day, with no effect. Joe may have believed that the lack of effect from the previous bite, combined with the identification by his assistant, was proof enough. He reached into the bag without looking and was immediately bitten. As soon as he saw the snake attached to his finger, Joe realised his mistake – but it was too late. He rapidly developed paralysis and deteriorating motor skills. Monsoonal rains prevented medical evacuation by helicopter, and the problems were compounded by international hysteria following terrorist attacks in the USA on the same day, when commercial airliners were flown into the Twin Towers buildings in New York City. Joe slowly sank into unconsciousness over a three-day period while his colleagues frantically applied first aid. Joe's body was cremated in a Buddhist ceremony in the village of Myitkyina.

Eminent snakebitten scientists

You might expect eminent older herpetologists to be safe from snakebite, because of their long experience and reduced participation in fieldwork. But many elderly reptile researchers continue to interact with captive snakes on a daily basis; enthusiasm for snakes is a lifelong affliction. And a bite to an older person is more likely to be fatal than one to a younger person.

The two most renowned cases of senior snake-researchers dying from snakebite have remarkable similarities. Both men were renowned reptile biologists, handling captive snakes

The eminent German researcher Robert Mertens was killed by a bite from his pet Southern Twig Snake (*Thelotornis capensis*), shown here in threat display by Johan Marais. SENCKENBERG MUSEUM

from an evolutionary lineage (the Colubridae) that contains mostly harmless species. Indeed, the usual common name for colubrids is 'harmless snakes'. But that proved to be wildly inaccurate for 67-year-old American biologist Karl Patterson Schmidt (1890–1957) and 81-year-old German expert Robert Mertens (1894–1975). The snakes that killed Schmidt and Mertens were tree-dwelling African species, the Boomslang ('tree-snake') and twig snake. Both have fangs in the rear of the mouth, not the front as in the better-known vipers and elapids.

Schmidt was a truly eminent biologist, having named more than 200 species of reptiles; coral snakes were his special focus. Because Boomslangs were not regarded as dangerous, Schmidt was careless as he handled a live juvenile specimen in his Chicago laboratory on 27 September 1957. The snake had been sent to him for identification. Schmidt wrote: "I took it from Dr Robert Inger without thinking of any precaution, and it promptly bit me on the fleshy lateral aspect of the first joint of the left thumb. The mouth was widely opened and the bite was made with the rear fangs only, only the right fang entering to its full length of about 3 mm." Schmidt ignored the bite, continuing to work that day but making notes on his developing symptoms. He caught the train home but developed nausea and fever with profuse bleeding in his lungs, kidneys, heart and brain. Schmidt refused medical intervention because it would disrupt the symptoms he was documenting. He continued to believe that the bite was non-fatal, but he stopped breathing and died the next day.

Like Schmidt, Mertens was a major figure in scientific herpetology. During a long career he served as Director of the Senckenberg Museum in Frankfurt and described 64 new species of reptiles. Fifteen years after retiring from his museum job, he maintained a strong interest in snakes. He was hand-feeding his pet twig snake when it bit him. The species was not believed to be dangerously venomous, despite the death of Frederick Lock 22 years earlier. As a result, nobody had bothered to develop an antivenom. Mertens lingered for an agonising 18 days before dying, keeping notes of his condition as he deteriorated. In one of his last writings, the 81-year-old noted that his manner of dying was "the only appropriate demise for a herpetologist."

Immunising yourself against snakebite

I mentioned above that frequent snakebites can create an allergy to venom or to antivenom. Indeed, I began this chapter by talking about Marty Martin, who met his end via the fangs of one of his beloved Timber Rattlesnakes. Marty was vastly experienced but previous bites had made him allergic to the venom of pit vipers, contributing to his death. Joe Slowinski also was allergic to cobra antivenom.

A snake researcher or showman who develops allergies to snakes is faced with a terrible decision. Forsaking direct contact with snakes is the sensible option, but addiction to snake handling is a powerful drug. In the 1870s, English physician and self-avowed 'ophidiomaniac' Arthur Stradling began a series of self-injections of venom that left him with arms badly scarred from wrist to shoulder. He finally abandoned the practice when he married in 1884. It's unclear whether Arthur's self-mutilation improved his resistance to snakebite, although he claims to have survived 350 bites during his career.

Injecting yourself with venom to develop immunity is technically known as mithridatism, after a legendary hypochondriac. Mithridates VI, the King of Pontus at around the time of Christ, was afraid that his enemies would try to poison him – as they had done to his father. So Mithridates began self-administering a cocktail of poisons.

If you decide to inject yourself with snake venom, though, you need to be selective. Venoms from elapid snakes – such as cobras, mambas and coral snakes – tend to be mostly neurotoxic. If the venom doesn't kill you, there are generally no long-lasting effects except a temporary loss of the sense of smell and taste. But the venoms of vipers and rattlesnakes destroy tissue, so the damage is long-lasting. That's what happened to Arthur Stradling.

The only case I can find of a group of people agreeing to be injected with viper venom was in the Amami Islands of Japan, where Yoshio Sawai and his team immunised thousands of farmers with small doses of venom from the Habu, a pit viper that inflicts many fatal bites. To reduce the effects of those injections, the venom was detoxified with formalin before it was injected. Despite initial enthusiasm, though, the project was soon abandoned.

The best-known modern-day advocate of mithridatism was Bill Haast (1910–2011), founder and director of the Miami Serpentarium. Over a long period he injected himself with diluted venom from elapids (a cobra and a coral snake), and claimed that he was immune to snakebite

Bill Haast was an American showman with a long history of working with deadly snakes such as this King Cobra (*Ophiophagus hannah*). To reduce the risks, Haast injected himself with venom to build up an immunity. GETTY/AVALON IMAGES

as a result. Haast survived more than 170 venomous snakebites and lived to the ripe old age of 100. He was still self-injecting venom at the age of 97. Even more remarkably, Bill's blood was used as antivenom for more than 20 snakebite victims. In one renowned case, Bill was flown by fighter jet from Florida to Peru to provide a transfusion of snake-resistant blood to a boy who had been bitten by a coral snake. The boy survived.

Another colourful character to try self-immunisation was Charles Tanner (1911–1996), an expatriate Englishman who moved to Australia when he was 42 years old. While working as an animal-house technician at a research facility, Charles received occasional bites from deadly snakes. Worryingly, the antivenom that saved his life began to induce severe allergic reactions. Antivenom is produced by injecting horses with increasing doses of venom, stimulating the horse's immune system to create antibodies. Because antibodies circulate in the blood, the

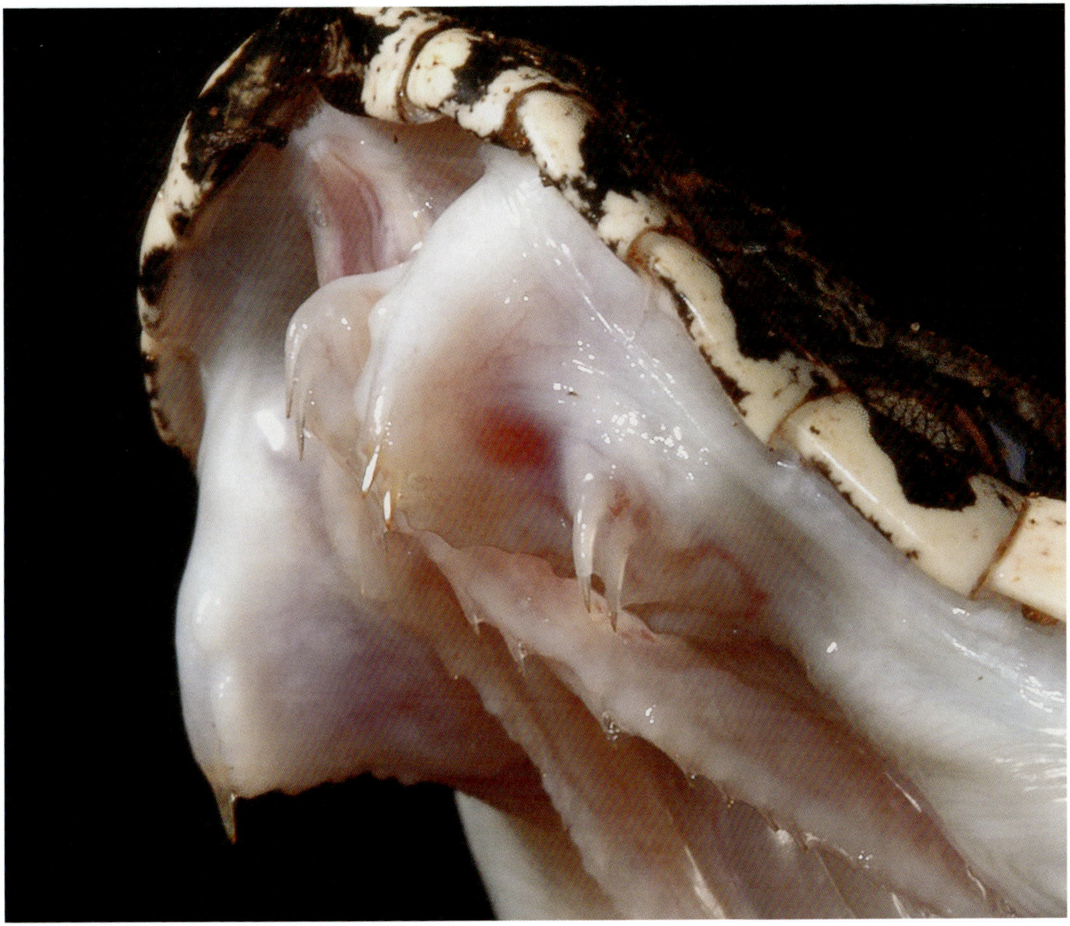

Venomous snakes often have spare fangs to replace any that are lost when they are used to strike prey. This Floodplain Death Adder (*Acanthophis hawkei*) has two fangs on one side of its mouth. JULES FARQUHAR

antivenom can be prepared by taking that blood and removing impurities, leaving mostly the antibodies ... but of course, there is still horse serum. And Charles became more and more allergic to that serum.

Unwilling to forsake a life with snakes, Charles convinced a venom specialist to inject him with increasing amounts of venom over a period of a few years, so that he could develop his own immunity to snakebite rather than relying on the immunity of horses. It worked, at least for a while.

I never met Charles Tanner in person, but we corresponded often and sometimes exchanged live snakes (sent by post, as was the custom in those days). By that time Charles had moved to far north Queensland, to live in an isolated house near Cooktown. He kept dozens of large venomous snakes, growing them to enormous sizes by force-feeding them with mincemeat made from road-killed wallabies. He milked his snakes for venom, which he then sold to the producers of antivenom.

By that time Charles had given up attempting to maintain his own immunity and was again reliant on conventional antivenom. My favourite story about this larger-than-life snake keeper centres on a bite he received from one of his captive King Brown Snakes. A veteran of such accidents, Charles wasn't too concerned. He drove into the nearest town for antivenom; the local doctor knew him well and kept antivenom for all of the species that Charles maintained in captivity.

But the usual doctor was away on holiday and the replacement medico was arrogant. Charles explained the situation, including the identity of the snake, and pointed out where the antivenom was kept. But the doctor didn't believe his disheveled patient and consulted his books instead. They advised giving Coastal Taipan antivenom if the bite was by a large brown-coloured snake of unknown species. Charles explained once again that the offending serpent was not a taipan; it was King Brown antivenom that he needed. Taipan antivenom would be useless.

The doctor refused to budge and Charles could feel the first symptoms of snakebite. So he took matters into his own hands. He punched the doctor hard enough to knock him into a corner of the office, then located the correct antivenom, filled a syringe with it, and injected himself. When the doctor recovered, he threatened to have Charles arrested for assault. But Charles pointed out that a court case might embarrass a physician who insisted on a treatment that would have killed his patient. The doctor saw the light. Charles survived the bite, and many others, and lived to the age of 86.

IN THEIR OWN WORDS

There was a real camaraderie among the early snake enthusiasts, nicely captured in this small illustration of David Fleay's generosity. In 1950, after 21-year-old Kevin (not Keith, as per the newspaper article below) Budden was fatally bitten by a Coastal Taipan he had just captured, he ensured that the animal was sent alive to a Melbourne laboratory. Budden knew he was dying but wanted the snake's venom to be used to make an antivenom, to save future victims of taipan bite. Zookeeper and prolific newspaper journalist David Fleay was given the unenviable task of opening the box containing that snake and 'milking' it to obtain a venom sample.

Fleay wrote: "...And what a beauty it was! Six feet five inches long, in the finest possible condition, its orange-red eyes glittering, the white upper lip emphasising the mouth, and only a few scales missing from the middle of the back – a superficial blemish probably sustained at the time of capture. And just as I feared, the heat of the room had put it in a most active and dangerous state. Its copper-brown body looped menacingly and it struck repeatedly to right and left." DAVID FLEAY, 1950

The venom that Fleay obtained was indeed used to make the first taipan antivenom and saved the life of a child who was bitten in the same year. The citizens of Melbourne tried to repay Fleay for undertaking that risky task of handling a taipan that had already killed one snake-catcher, but Fleay redirected the payment:

"This week a cheque for £71 8/6 was posted to Sydney to the parents of Keith Budden who was killed by the taipan snake recently 'milked' by naturalist David Fleay at the National Museum. The money was given by Melbourne people who organised a fund in recognition of Fleay's heroic act in the cause of science, but Fleay handed the money on to Budden's parents. Fleay, who kept a token amount of £5, which he will devote to natural history work, said the 'real bravery was Budden's.' The tributes paid to himself 'were too much compensation for just a little nervous strain'." *The Advertiser* NEWSPAPER, 21 AUGUST 1950

Shine's Whipsnake (*Demansia shinei*) is an elegant speedster from Australian deserts. ALANA DE LAIVE

PART 6

THE CHANGING FACE OF SNAKE ECOLOGY RESEARCH

The history of research in any scientific field is dynamic, with many twists and turns along the way. As a research field blossoms, the initial concentration of effort on a small number of topics or places, much of it by just a few people, is overwhelmed by the avalanche of new ideas, methods and practitioners. How have those changes happened for research on the ecology of snakes?

Chapter 12

New methods, new challenges

The first substantial chunks of published information about the private lives of snakes appeared in the 1800s, as small gems hidden among a diverse literature. The focus of most discussions about snakes was their danger, and how to reduce that danger. Hair-raising tales of life-threatening encounters with giant snakes were popular, as were stories about snakebite remedies. But every once in a while, those old journals include a short note describing some first-hand observation about snake biology. Some early contributions were based on dissecting a pregnant serpent to discover whether that species lays eggs or produces live young; others reported how a captive animal defended itself from humans or consumed its prey. Just snippets. There were no long-term studies.

New sources of information

The internet is making enormous datasets available, and a generation of researchers with formidable digital skills is replacing the pioneers of snake ecology. In some cases, the new technology provides jaw-dropping sample sizes. For example, a recent paper by US-based biologist Andrew Durso and his colleagues notes: "We scoured eleven online and two offline sources of snake photos in an attempt to collect as many photos of as many snake species as possible ... We collected a total of 725,565 photos – between one and 48,696 photos of 3,098 of the world's 3,879 snake species." Just a few years ago, before the online revolution, a researcher would have been content with assembling a sample size of 0.1 per cent of that number.

Other huge data repositories have emerged as well. For example, I can now check every known collection locality for every Australian snake species in the online Atlas of Living Australia. If I want to know how many snake species have been described worldwide, I can click on The Reptile Database. It's constantly updated, with new species added every week.

Websites such as iNaturalist and FrogID enable the public to upload observations. As a result, new information – often accompanied by photographs – is pouring in at a rate that would be unimaginable to Henry Fitch and his contemporaries. Increasingly, snake scientists interrogate those databases to understand distributions, seasonal occurrences, dietary habits, and so forth.

Not all newly described snake species are small and brown. Despite its dramatic appearance, the Desert Whipsnake (*Demansia cyanochasma*) from central Australia was described for the first time in 2023. BRIAN BUSH

Moving away from online 'science' resources, other platforms have photographs of snakes scattered among images of boyfriends, girlfriends, pet cats and talking parrots. Trawling through Instagram or Facebook or TikTok can yield phenomenal numbers of records. In a recent paper on African snakes, Robin and Bryan Maritz (who call themselves 'the reptile power couple') analysed more than 1,900 observations of predator-prey interactions (mostly, of snakes eating prey) from a Facebook group in southern Africa. Compared to any conventional database, the Facebook group was spectacularly productive. But even that massive sample size palls in comparison to other recent efforts. Above, I mentioned Andrew Durso's sample of 725,565 photographs. A world record, surely? No. In 2016, Uri Roll and his colleagues analysed 55.5 million views of Wikipedia pages to explore how social and cultural factors influence people's interest in particular types of reptiles.

Photographing wildlife has become very popular, spawning an enormous amount of information about snakes – and even about spectacular species such as this African Rock Python (*Python natalensis*). This giant female has the undivided attention of two eminent snake researchers, Graham Alexander and Harry Greene. KELLY ZAMUDIO

Even when that online info isn't about snakes, it can be useful. For example, meteorologists create massive datasets from weather stations and satellites. By combining those online climate databases with mathematical models, computer-savvy researchers can predict the range of body temperatures available to a reptile of any size and shape, anywhere on Earth, at any time of day and in any season. Many reptiles use environmental mosaics to regulate their own temperatures, so even a small shift in thermal opportunities can be catastrophic. Warmer weather might be a benefit in cooler climates and at some times of year, but hotter isn't always better. For example, a warm winter makes hibernation more expensive, by increasing the metabolic rates of inactive snakes. And for a snake that is active by day in a hot climate, hotter weather means less time to forage in the open before being dangerously overheated. A scientist can work that out from their office, without having to wander off into the wilds with a thermometer.

The future of radio telemetry

The toolkit for radio tracking continues to expand. Bulky short-range transmitters have been replaced by tiny powerful long-lived units that can be monitored automatically. The transmitters can be controlled remotely, switched off to save battery life if needed; and can convey information unimaginable to the pioneering researchers. For example, it's commonplace to incorporate a mortality sensor. If the snake doesn't move for a few hours, the signal changes to let you know that it's time to go out and look for a carcass not a live animal. Humidity sensors on a transmitter tell you if a snake is on land or in the water; and pressure sensors tell you how deep it dives. Doubtless we will soon see transmitters that encode variables such as activity, sleep habits, stress levels, heartrate, blood oxygen levels, ECGs, body composition and blood pressure, as are commonplace in 'smart watches' already. Accelerometers in the transmitter circuits accurately measure movement speeds.

More generally, the ways that we detect radio-tracking signals are evolving rapidly. Drone-based telemetry receivers eliminate the need to trudge through alligator-infested swamps. Miniaturised transmitters enable studies on smaller and smaller snakes. Some 'transmitters' don't even require a power source, so we can dispense with the battery and rely upon a small diode that bounces a signal back from a powerful emitter carried by the researcher. The harmonic diode system was developed to find skiers buried under the snow by an avalanche. It can only detect a diode from a few metres away, but a tiny snake isn't going to move very far.

Marine researchers use fixed listening stations to pick up acoustic beeps from transmitters implanted in sharks, dolphins, dugongs and fishes. Such receivers can even alert beachgoers to the presence of large sharks, sending a message to your smartphone to suggest that it's a bad time to go surfing. In sea-snake research in New Caledonia, we've piggybacked onto those receiver constellations to obtain thousands of records as our radio-implanted sea snakes swim past. Plans are underway to provide the same kind of receiver coverage on land as well – or even better, to detect transmitter signals from space. Satellite-based systems would be ideal for mobile species such as the sea snakes that drift for hundreds of kilometres on the ocean currents.

Gaining an evolutionary perspective

But the best example of an information avalanche via new technology doesn't centre on fieldwork. Instead, it's about what we can learn from a small tissue sample extracted from a snake – or even, from that animal's shed skin. The pace of change in genetic analyses is astonishing. Only a few years ago researchers were analysing small fragments of DNA, sequencing only a few genes. Nowadays, we can sequence the entire genome.

What's that mumbo-jumbo got to do with ecological research? Well, plenty. To understand

Olive Sea Snakes (*Aipysurus laevis*) roam huge distances in search of food. Females stay near coral reefs year-round, but males travel widely outside the winter mating season. XAVIER BONNET

why a characteristic has evolved, you need to work out how it affects an individual's ability to survive and reproduce. But an individual of what species? If the species you are studying is the only one to show that trait, it's simple. The characteristic must have evolved within your species – so your question is, 'why did that characteristic improve survival or reproduction within my study species?' But if several closely related species all share the same trait, they probably all inherited it from some ancestor. In that case, your question becomes 'why did that characteristic evolve within the ancestral species?' If that's the case (and it usually is), you need to look at the wider lineage to understand why your trait evolved. Evolutionary trees reveal how ecological characteristics have changed through time. As a result, we need to unravel relationships among snake species if we want to ask broadscale questions about snake ecology.

That's easier said than done. Snakes are a nightmare to classify. There are not many things that you can measure about a snake, because its shape is so simple; and most of the things that you can measure (such as the relative size of the head or length of the tail) turn out to have evolved lots of times in different groups of snakes. Frequent 'convergent evolution' means that resemblance in some characteristic may tell you exactly nothing about whether or not two species of snakes are closely related. For example, venom has evolved several times within snakes and has been lost just as often. As a result, modern-day venomous species are not each other's close relatives. Older schemes of classification, that used venom as an indicator of relatedness among species, fell to bits as soon as that assumption was disproved.

Until a few decades ago, it was a simple task to classify snakes as venomous (elapids and vipers, and a few back-fanged colubrids such as Boomslangs) or harmless (all other snakes). But that simple dichotomy has collapsed. There is no better example than the Tiger Keelback of Japan, locally known as the Yamakagashi. Up to a metre long, this solidly built swamp-dweller is dark green in colour with dramatic orange bands that give the snake its 'tiger' name.

Based on its evolutionary classification, we'd expect the Yamakagashi to be harmless. A perfect pet snake for your children. It belongs to a group known as the natricine colubrids (often given their own family status, as the Natricidae) – a lineage that includes well-known harmless species such as European grass snakes, North American garter snakes and Australian Keelbacks. Thousands of people are bitten each year by such species, causing nothing more than a few pinpricks in the skin. But don't get bitten by a Yamakagashi. Its venom is similar to that of a pit viper, causing horrific tissue damage that can be fatal if untreated.

And the Yamakagashi has other chemical weapons in its arsenal as well; chemicals that it obtains from its prey and accumulates in special glands behind the head. If a Yamakagashi consumes a poisonous toad, it doesn't break down the toad's powerful defensive chemicals through digestion. Instead, it transmits those chemicals through the snake's bloodstream to glands on the back of its neck. A Yamakagashi that is threatened by a predator arches its neck towards the predator, inviting a bite – or even spraying fluid from the glands.

Japanese biologist (and avid *Star Trek* enthusiast) Akira Mori and his collaborators have investigated this remarkable dual-defence system. Intriguingly, female Yamakagashi seek out toads for food before they lay their eggs, so they can add toad poison to the yolk. That way, the baby snakes hatch out with their weapons already primed. And snakes know whether or not they have toad poisons in their neck glands, so they don't rely on neck arching if the glands are poison-free.

The end result is a species using chemical defences in a much more sophisticated way than we could have imagined a few years ago. Although belonging to a group of 'harmless' snakes, the Yamakagashi delivers virulent toxins through fangs; but also fills specialised neck glands with toxins from the toads that it eats. The same 'prey toxin recycling' trick is seen not only in the Yamakagashi's Asian relatives, but in a distantly related South American species the Velvet Swamp Snake, so it must have evolved at least twice.

Although it is closely related to harmless species such as grass snakes and garter snakes, the Japanese Yamakagashi (*Rhabdophis tigrinus*) possesses deadly venom as well as potent toxins stored in special glands in its neck. MASAYA FUKUDA

Some of the problems in identifying relationships among snake species were overcome through painstaking investigations of anatomy and scale counts, but the real breakthrough came from genetics. Sequencing an animal's genes became quicker and cheaper. Before long, you didn't even have to do the sequencing yourself; you could send tissue to a biotech company and within a couple of weeks the gene-sequence data would appear in your electronic Inbox. Analysing those data raised new challenges, but fortuitously, desktop computers were spreading through the world of professional science – computers powerful enough to run those programs and crunch those numbers.

The methods used to build evolutionary trees are complicated and ever expanding. It's a vigorous field of research, with hot-blooded debates between proponents of different approaches. Some of the disagreements stem from different definitions of 'species'. At first sight that seems foolish – surely, we can all agree that a species is a group of organisms that can interbreed with each other but not with other species? Well, maybe. Some organisms never breed with anybody else – such as the Brahminy Blind Snake, the world's most widely distributed reptile. All of these tiny worm-like burrowers are female, and they give birth to daughters that are clones of mum. If they never interbreed with each other, is every individual Brahminy Blind Snake a separate species? And at the other end of the spectrum, many species happily interbreed in captivity. Nobody doubts that lions and tigers are different species in nature, but they hybridise in captivity. So do many kinds of snakes.

Other debates reflect the sad reality that differences in methods of analysis can change the form of an evolutionary tree. A major decision, for example, is the choice of an 'outgroup' – a species that is not included in the group of interest, but is used to root the base of that tree. The choice of outgroup can alter conclusions about relationships, and about how characteristics have changed through evolutionary time. Danish sea-snake biologist Arne Rasmussen once spent a few months in my hometown of Sydney, measuring museum specimens and running analyses to identify relationships. Arne had a great time socially, but the analyses were frustrating. In the acknowledgements section of a paper he wrote after that project, Arne lamented that "it's easier to find a new girlfriend than to find a proper outgroup."

The ultimate expression of serpentine 'girl power': all Brahminy Blind Snakes (*Indotyphlops braminus*) are females. TOM PARKIN

Nonetheless, genetic research has revolutionised our understanding of snake evolution. For example, many widely distributed 'species' turned out to be hotchpotch combinations of several different kinds of snakes. And in a few cases, those different kinds of snakes are only distantly related to each other – as in the case of the Beaked Sea Snake. This distinctive-looking animal causes hundreds of fatal snakebites in tropical Asia, but it wasn't until 2013 that Kanisha Ukuwela and colleagues reported, from genetic data, that this 'species' consists of two distantly related types of snakes. No wonder the antivenom wasn't working well. And the reverse problem occurs also. That is, some sea snakes that look very different from each other are genetically similar, and more closely related to each other than anyone had guessed.

Once you have a reliable evolutionary tree, how can you use it to test ideas about snake ecology? The best way is to map your ecological data onto that tree, so you can see how things have changed through evolutionary history. So, for example, you might discover that the species at the base of your tree – the first group of species to arise within that group – share some characteristic such as egg-laying reproduction. You can surmise, then, that the ancestors of the group were egg layers. But out on the farthest branches of the tree, some of the more recently evolved species give birth to fully formed offspring instead of laying eggs. That tells you that live bearing evolved from egg laying rather than the other way around. Without the evolutionary tree, you wouldn't have been able to work out which one of those tactics gave rise to the other – a classic case of 'which came first – the chicken or the egg?' In this case, it was the egg. So the tree tells you to ask 'why did live bearing evolve from egg laying?' rather than 'why did egg laying evolve from live bearing?'

But the tree does more than just identify the direction of evolutionary transitions. In the example above, it can pinpoint the number of times that the transition from egg laying to live bearing took place. And because each of those transitions is a separate event, a lineage that contains several independent transitions from egg laying to live bearing lets you ask questions such as 'what kinds of habitats favour the transition from egg laying to live bearing?' If there is only one shift between those modes of reproduction, however, you can't really ask that question because there's no way to identify a reason for any single transition.

Studies on snakes were among the first to embed ecological information onto evolutionary trees. I can claim a minor role for my 1985 review of the evolution of viviparity, but the real pioneer was US biologist Harry Greene. By superimposing his ecological data on evolutionary relationships among snakes, Harry developed powerful new ways of analysing patterns in nature. And, bless his heart, he used snakes as his examples.

To exploit that approach, we needed accurate evolutionary trees. And suddenly, we had them. Almost overnight, new methods to sequence DNA meant that a tiny tissue sample could

Although live bearing has evolved more than 100 times within lizards and snakes, most species still reproduce by egg laying. This photograph by John Weigel shows a female Rough-scaled Python (*Morelia carinata*) partway through laying her clutch of eggs.

yield a vast amount of data. Many classic disagreements were resolved rapidly. Older scientists who had spent decades arguing about snake ancestry saw all of their careful work eclipsed by a gene-based analysis from some wet-behind-the-ears graduate student. Cheap quick genomics methods revolutionised research on evolutionary relationships. We now know not only how our study organism fits within a broader family tree, but also how long ago the different species – and even, populations within a single species – split apart from each other.

Using genes to illuminate ecology

The second impact of the new genetic tomfoolery was to enable in-depth analyses of specific aspects of snake biology. For example, advances in 'venomics' helped venom researchers to identify the building blocks of complex chemical weapons in unprecedented detail. Likewise, patterns of gene expression in a pregnant snake's uterus can tell us what genes are switched on, and what genes are switched off, during the evolutionary transition from egg laying to live bearing. Or as a land-dwelling lineage of snakes adapts to exploit the ocean.

Although the Rough Green Snake (*Opheodrys aestivus*) is an egg layer, females of this species sometimes retain eggs in their oviducts for almost all of embryonic development. That ability could reveal what genes need to be switched on to allow prolonged pregnancy.
NOAH K. FIELDS

In some cases, it's actually quicker to use a high-tech approach (gene-expression data) than the old-fashioned whole-organism trials (measure responses of live organisms). For the genetic methods, all you need is a tissue sample. No need to mess around with catching dangerous snakes, settling them into captivity, and testing their behaviour. For example, Australian biologist Kate Sanders and her team decided to look into a fascinating early report by two other Australia-based researchers – Ken Zimmerman and Hal Heatwole. In 1990, Ken and Hal had reported that sea snakes can see with their tails. While Ken was diving, he often encountered Olive Sea Snakes curled up in underwater crevices with only their tails poking out. Nothing unusual there. But Ken noticed that shining his flashlight on those tails caused the snakes to move into the crevice out of harm's way.

Can sea snakes really detect light with their tails? And if so, which sea snake species have this ability and which don't; and also, what parts of the body are light-sensitive? Until a few years ago that question could only be answered by ambitious experiments with live snakes. Led by Jenna Crowe-Riddell, Kate's team hit upon a high-tech solution. They looked for 'opsin' genes – the ones related to vision – in the skin of sea snakes. And sure enough, the team rapidly discovered which species can detect light with their tails, and which parts of their body can do so.

Likewise, some of those new methods can answer ecological as well as behavioural questions with a single survey rather than requiring decades of study. For example, mark-recapture studies have been the gold standard for exploring how snakes move around, but patterns of genetic relatedness can illuminate the same issues. Dispersal away from the site of birth (or hatching) differs between males and females in many types of animals. In most mammals, the females stay close to home whereas the males range more widely. In most birds, it's the reverse pattern: stay-at-home males, wandering females. The benefit may lie in a reduction in inbreeding – if one sex disperses further than the other, most matings will be between distantly related individuals.

Snakes also show different dispersal patterns between the sexes. Males tend to be the sex with wanderlust, but the reverse occurs as well. And sometimes, even within the same species, we see both patterns. In sea kraits, for example, males leave home in some populations and females leave home in others. Detecting that pattern with fieldwork would have taken a herculean effort, so my student Amanda Lane used a simpler but more high-tech approach. She collected tissue samples from more than 400 male and female sea kraits from six islands across the Great Lagoon of New Caledonia, with information on their capture locations. Then, she looked at the genetic similarity between snakes that were caught on the same island as adults, compared to snakes that were caught on different islands. If most males disperse from their place of birth, then the adult males within an island will not be closely related to each other. They will have been hatched far from the island where you caught them. In contrast, if females are home-bodies then the adult females on an island will be close relatives, sharing many genes in common. Even tiny rates of dispersal among populations can be detected by such analyses – whereas occasional immigrants and emigrants likely would never be captured in a field study.

We can also use genetic analyses to get at the most important characteristic of all from an evolutionary perspective: that is, reproductive success. Natural selection is based on characteristics becoming more frequent if they enable an organism to leave more offspring. As a result, measuring differences in reproductive success among individuals within a population is a key aspect of evolutionary ecology. In the good old days, fieldworkers measured reproductive success by scoring the numbers of matings that a male obtained, and the number of offspring produced by each female. But in the brave new world of modern biology, genetically based paternity analyses are now routinely applied to wildlife species. Such tests require lab facilities, but it's a lot easier than trying to record a female snake's sex life throughout a month-long mating season. And genetic testing of parentage is more relevant to Darwinian fitness than is behavioural observation. For example, a male who obtained several matings might not sire any offspring because his partners used other males' sperm to fertilise their eggs. Natural selection doesn't reward copulations per se; the only currency that matters is the number of offspring that carry your genes. Using genetic analyses, my Swiss-based collaborator Sylvain Dubey showed

The Great Lagoon of New Caledonia contains sea kraits of two species – *Laticauda saintgironsi* (left) and *Laticauda laticaudata* (right) – but they use different feeding habitats and disperse in different ways. Thus, it's unusual to find the two species together like this. XAVIER BONNET

that most of the baby Slaty-grey Snakes in our study area in tropical Australia were sired by the biggest males in the population.

The list of 'ecological' issues accessible to genetic analysis continues to grow. For difficult-to-find species, a sample of water or soil can be screened for 'eDNA' (environmental DNA) – that is, genetic material left behind by an animal as it has moved through that area. Analysis of those samples can reveal the presence of a species even if the organism itself is simply too difficult to find.

In species where an individual's sex is difficult to determine from its appearance, we can use genetics. The assortment of genes within a population can reveal historical reductions and expansions in population size. Genetics can identify individuals that have dispersed from elsewhere to join your study population and can tell you from whence those adventurous souls originated. Specific kinds of changes can reveal genes (and thus traits) upon which natural selection has acted most strongly. Genetic characteristics can reveal the age of individuals. Comparisons between mothers and fathers can disclose inbreeding, and if it affects the viability of offspring.

Pregnant female American Copperheads (*Agkistrodon contortrix*) gather in safe places where they can maintain high temperatures for their developing offspring. All of the baby copperheads in an area may be born in the same place as a result of that creche behaviour, affecting genetic structuring of the species across the landscape. NOAH K. FIELDS

Genetics will never replace field ecology, but it's a powerful ally. As a non-geneticist, I console myself with the thought that somebody still needs to catch those animals, even if it's just to take a tissue sample; and more importantly, somebody has to identify the questions worth asking and interpret the answers that are obtained. To do those things, you need to understand the system. You can't do that unless you spend time in the field with the animals.

In short, the methods by which snake scientists gather information are expanding faster than a cobra's neck flattens when a mongoose comes into view.

Emerging challenges to snake research

Although our understanding of snake biology is being turbo-charged by new technologies, new threats loom. Cultural upheaval and environmental change have spawned problems as well as benefits for research.

You can't study snakes if there are no snakes left to study, and the most obvious threat to research is that snake populations are in widespread decline. Across the world, wilderness is being converted into agricultural land, housing and other 'development'. A growing human population demands more space. In the New Jersey Pine Barrens, the sunny clearings where Pine Snakes have nested for millenia are being destroyed by proliferating retirement villages.

In the Australian bushland, offtake of water for agriculture is draining the once-mighty rivers that supported amphibians and the snakes that feed upon them. On the outskirts of Kyoto in Japan, urban sprawl has eradicated the paddyfields and canals where Hajime Fukada once collected his snakes.

Physical destruction of habitats is the most obvious reason for snake declines, but it is only one of several problems. Global overviews rank habitat destruction as the number one threat to wildlife, but that destruction can be subtle. It's easy to be appalled when forest trees are felled, but a peaceful pasture scene with sheep grazing on introduced grasses may embody more loss of biodiversity. And any attempt to return a landscape to its 'natural state' is doomed to failure unless we can specify what that state is. Many 'natural' ecological processes are catastrophic for snakes. Forest regrowth eliminated the sun-exposed clearings on Henry Fitch's long-term Kansas study site, dooming his snake populations. In coastal eastern Australia, similar forest regrowth decimated abundance of the sunlight-dependent Broad-headed Snake. So when we talk of habitat destruction, it's not just about chemical pollutants and chainsaws.

Invasive species rank as the second-most-important threat. All around our planet, people are transporting species to places where they don't belong. The 1800s saw 'acclimatisation societies' set up to help homesick colonists bring Brown Trout from England to New Zealand streams, European Rabbits and Red Foxes to Australian bushland, and deer and goats worldwide. Many of those invaders have had devastating impacts on snakes. On small islands, the arrival of a new predator such as the mongoose can rapidly exterminate local reptiles. Even on a large land mass, a highly toxic species that is mistaken for an edible item can fatally poison reptile predators – such as in the case of the Cane Toad across tropical Australia. The spread of Fire Ants has been catastrophic for small burrowing snakes. Diseases can be even worse, and almost impossible to control.

Climate change is emerging as another powerful threat, partly by destroying habitats and partly by spreading invasive species. Worldwide, coral-reef ecosystems are collapsing due to coral bleaching induced by overheated water. Without those reefs to sustain them, sea snakes cannot survive. On land, wildfires are becoming hotter and more frequent, fuelled by heatwaves and invasive grasses. As glaciers melt, rising sea levels are drowning coastal habitats.

Unable to resist the challenges of environmental deterioration, some snake species will become extinct. Species on small islands will be the first to go. And even on continents, invasive predators, parasites and diseases may prove fatal to many more. It's easy to be pessimistic, but history tells us that things can change. Less than a century ago, the idea that snakes are worth conserving was heresy. Today, it's mainstream. That change in opinion enabled a seismic shift in conservation. Snakes are survivors. Even as the climate changes and habitats degrade,

Habitat destruction is a massive threat to snake populations. NOAH K. FIELDS

some species will seize the new opportunities and thrive. We will lose some fascinating species, but there will still be snakes in the suburbs.

Futile 'wildlife protection' laws

Some 'solutions' to biodiversity loss are just making the problem worse. In response to public concern, governments have created new laws to protect wildlife. And although that shift is well intentioned, it threatens snake research.

The crux of the problem is that those new laws make it more difficult to obtain research permits. For example, suppose I want to conduct a mark-recapture study on a small abundant snake species near my home in the suburbs. First I need an approval from my institution's ethics committee, to check that the scientific value of the work justifies the suffering of my study animals. OK, that makes sense. And I need a wildlife research permit from the government, to ensure that my project won't threaten any endangered species. OK, that makes sense as well.

But the sad reality is that once you set up a system of paperwork, bureaucracy can transform the process into a quagmire. In many parts of the world, applications for ethics approvals and wildlife research permits disappear into a black hole – in some cases, never to emerge. Commonly, the delays make it impossible for a new student to conduct a study on snakes. So much for encouraging new people with new ideas! Those students end up with desktop studies rather than projects on live animals.

Tragically, current conservation laws don't address the reasons why wildlife populations are in trouble. Today's laws grew out of rules to prevent overhunting of animals such as deer and ducks that are killed and eaten in vast numbers. That approach assumes that excessive harvesting is the biggest threat to wildlife populations.

But with a few exceptions (such as some of the Asian turtles collected as food), that isn't true for reptiles. If someone wants to catch a snake to keep as a pet, or to collect a few snakes for a scientific study, the long-term impacts on wild populations are likely to be zero. For any abundant snake species, more individuals are run over by vehicles every day than would be collected by scientists over the course of a year. That prolonged evaluation process by the bureaucrats doesn't address any real threat to snake populations – and it certainly doesn't help those populations to deal with habitat destruction, or invasive species, or climate change. Instead, the bureaucracy prevents scientists from gathering the information needed to understand how snake populations function. Without that information, we cannot work out how to address the real threats. Laws designed to protect wildlife are discouraging the search for solutions to biodiversity decline.

The same bureaucratic obstacles bedevil pet keepers. Powerful political lobbies based on

When distracted by social interactions, snakes often fail to notice oncoming vehicles. That's what happened to these Lowland Copperheads (*Austrelaps superbus*) in Australia. JULES FARQUHAR

'animal welfare' or 'animal liberation' oppose keeping animals in cages. One consequence of the resultant restrictions is that most reptiles maintained by pet keepers belong to a tiny number of species. The most popular pets are species such as pythons and Corn Snakes that don't occur naturally in the places they are being kept. As a result, the biology and behaviour of local snake species remains a mystery.

A disconnect between people and snakes

These days, fewer young people interact with live reptiles. For most children growing up in Western countries, a snake is a creature on a TV screen. Rates of youth participation in hiking, camping and fishing are dropping every year. The wilderness is becoming a strange and distant place. For most youngsters, the only 'real animals' – ones they can watch and touch and care for – are dogs, cats and budgies.

What are the consequences of that disconnect between people and wild animals? The portents are worrying. Surveys show that spending time in the wilderness – even the suburban-fringe wilderness – changes attitudes towards biodiversity conservation. If you don't have first-hand experience with something, you won't see it as important. And if the public doesn't care about the future of snakes, neither will politicians.

That isolation from nature also demolishes the main route by which people become researchers. Ask almost any snake scientist, and they'll tell you that their career grew from early hands-on experiences with live animals. Digital representations of animals are nowhere near as exciting. If I hadn't been able to roam bushland valleys in search of reptiles during my childhood, I would never have become a snake researcher. Where will we find the successors to Henry Fitch, Hubert Saint Girons and Catherine Cooper Hopley if the next generation of children never see a snake in the wild?

But all is not lost. Despite the allure of digital entertainment, I still encounter young people whose obsession with serpents is as intense as my own. Parents bring them into the university to meet me, perhaps hoping that a dose of reality might push young Jason or Emily away from their serpent obsession towards a more productive career. But it never works. The children leave my office just as excited about snakes as they were when they entered. Hopefully, even more excited.

IN THEIR OWN WORDS

Before Charles Darwin's ideas about evolution took hold, biologists assumed that all species were separately created by some divine presence. And thus, they wondered why the Creator had bothered to construct such creatures. The earliest speculations dismissed reptiles as unimportant. Famously, the Swedish biologist Linnaeus, father of scientific nomenclature, wrote:

"These foul and loathsome animals are abhorrent because of their cold body, pale colour, cartilaginous skeleton, filthy skin, fierce aspect, calculating eye, offensive voice, squalid habitation, and terrible venom; and so their Creator has not exerted his powers to make many of them." LINNAEUS, 1735

But as time went by, scientists looked for more positive arguments:

"Of what use are snakes? is an oft-asked question. Such a question implies the dictum that all things were specially 'created' for the use of man, and without going into the ethics of the question, it may be stated, as an axiom, that if a snake can live, move, and replenish the earth with its species, it will do so without in any way considering its utility; and snakes are by no means the only creatures who live for themselves alone. However, to speak in a more practical way, snakes do play a part in the economy of nature: they unwittingly assist in keeping in check many other forms which if permitted to increase beyond certain bounds, might become a plague, as for example, mice, frogs, lizards, etc.; had we more blind snakes we might have less white ants. On the other hand, snakes serve as food for many animals and birds, which may be more conveniently treated as enemies." EDGAR WAITE, 1898

And even in the earliest writings, some enlightened authors plead for a tolerant attitude towards these poorly understood creatures:

"The viper is by many taken for an image of malice and cruelty; but in reality she is guilty of no such thing." MOYSE CHARAS, 1673

Concerns about the conservation of snakes were raised even by some of the early writers. For example, the first book on Australian snakes had this to say about the Broad-headed Snake, now highly endangered:

"During the summer months they are very scarce … but it is not difficult to collect a good many during the cold season; they are, however, not so numerous as they were six or eight years ago, their haunts having been invaded by the builder and the gardener." GERARD KREFFT, 1869

And of course, some writers describe wanton snake killing. Henry Fitch, the revered pioneering researcher, is typically sparse with his prose. His disdain is implied rather than expressed vehemently:

"Copperheads were purposely hunted and killed, at Trading Post, Kansas, in 1958 and 1959 … the motivation seemed to be not so much the local extermination of the snakes as the competitive sport of killing them in large numbers … The method of hunting consisted of driving at night over a certain stretch of road where the snakes were abundant. Those caught in the glare of the headlights usually 'froze' to immobility and could be clubbed without serious risk to the hunters." HENRY FITCH, 1960

But sadly, most mentions of snakes in early popular writings enthiastically endorse mindless carnage. As an example, take this account of a rattlesnake hunt in Virginia, where a group of locals try to eradicate the snakes at their overwintering den:

"One of the first spring days, when the creatures creep out to sun themselves for only a few hours, retiring again at night, was the time chosen for the onslaught. The snakes were known to come forth from Rattlesnake Den on to a certain ledge of rock near their cavern; and a council of war was held as to the best approach and mode of attack. Ten years previously a similar war had been waged, when the reptiles had been almost exterminated; but of late so many accidents had occurred among the inhabitants through the fast-increasing serpents, that the farmers agreed to climb to the den and once more reduce their numbers. The boy Catlin was privileged to be of the party, and he was told to creep cautiously to an overhanging rock, whence he could see the reptiles sunning themselves on their ledge below. The rest of the party stood in readiness, club in hand. At a signal young Catlin fired a fowling-piece into their midst. There was a knot of them 'like a huge mat wound and twisted and interlocked together, with all their heads like scores of hydras standing up from the mass.' Into this horrible cluster he 'let fly', when the party, rushing with their clubs, broke the spine of hundreds by a single blow to each, while hundreds more were saving themselves by a quick return to their den.

While counting the five or six hundred slain, and holding another council of war on the battlefield, a rattle was heard of one which in the death-struggle had escaped over a ledge instead of into its cave. With a forked stick a man approached that misguided reptile and held down its head, while another brave expert seized it by the neck so close to its head that it could not turn and bite him. It was a very large snake, and young Catlin, inspired by the sudden thought, exclaimed, 'Tie a powder-horn to its tail and fasten a slow fuse to it, and let it go back into its den.'

'George, you are the best hunter in the Valley of Ocquago!' cried the man who held the snake; and forthwith the plan was agreed upon. The largest powder-horn in the party was filled to the brim from the other horns, and tied to the snake's tail by a string of several feet long; and to the horn was fixed a slow fuse of about a yard in length, made of wetted, twisted tow, in which gunpowder was rolled. This accomplished while the reptile was still firmly held, it was then set free close to the mouth of its den, the whole party speedily escaping to a safe distance.

Listening, they heard the horn rattling over the rocky floor as the snake was carrying it home into the midst of its comrades, when, after the silence of a minute or so, an explosion like a clap of thunder shook the ground on which they stood, and blue streams issued forth between the crevices around the den, and a thick volume from its mouth.

Rattlesnake Den was thus cleared of its inhabitants for many long years." JAIM CLAYTON, 1694

Chapter 13

New combatants join the revolution

Powerful new methods are changing the way that snake researchers operate, but fundamental changes also are happening along social dimensions. The latest generation of people who study snakes are more diverse in gender, age and race – and they also have a startlingly new perspective on what they are trying to achieve.

Until a few decades ago, scientists saw their job as straightforward. It was to find things out and then tell their colleagues about those conclusions. Full stop. The outputs of research were papers in scientific journals. Such papers are still the fundamental units of knowledge, and – as we saw earlier – the numbers of papers about snakes are accelerating faster than a paranoid whipsnake's getaway at midday on a hot sand dune.

But modern researchers have realised that writing papers for scientific journals is no longer enough. Gone are the days when scientists saw themselves as a group of scholars, talking mostly to each other. Educating the public about scientific results had long been viewed as 'somebody else's problem': a job for journalists, perhaps. During the first part of my own career, that was true even for fields like conservation biology. Researchers saw their role as finding solutions to ecological problems, writing papers about their results, then leaving it to other people – 'managers' – to read those papers and implement the new methods. But the world has changed. I don't know any conservation biologists who still see their role that way. The reason for that seismic shift is a tragic realisation that evidence isn't enough. In the chaotic world of modern media, the voice of science has been weakened to a whisper. To address ecological crises, scientists need to communicate with the public.

That translation of research results into on-ground actions is a formidable challenge. For example, scientists even have to explain why an evidence-based approach works better than an emotion-based approach. Unless we can convince the public that evidence matters, they will disbelieve what we discover.

So, the new generation of snake researchers has had to learn communication skills that were irrelevant to their predecessors. Scientific papers still matter, and those papers are now easily accessible. Instead of having to wander among the shelves of a university library, you

A film crew with Ru Somaweera, making a documentary about snakes. RUCHIRA SOMAWEERA

can access digitised papers with the click of a mouse. In theory, almost anyone can read those scientific papers. But in practice, most people obtain their information from websites and social media. And so, a younger generation of scientists is exploiting outlets such as films, TV shows, online blogs, websites and radio interviews. The revolution in communication pathways has transformed professional science.

But the revolution is not just in the media outlets involved; it's also in how the story is told. Yesterday's dry catalogue of facts and statistics will fail to engage a general audience. They want narratives, preferably with eye-catching images and personal perspectives. Scientists can no longer hide behind the anonymity of a white lab coat. For their work to resonate with the public, a researcher needs to present themself as a living, breathing human being who is passionate about their study organisms. And we don't have to pretend that research is just an objective search for truth. By talking about our misadventures as well as adventures, we can break down stereotypes of scientists as cold-blooded nerds. My fellow snake enthusiasts are some of the most joyful and interesting people I have ever met. As long as they don't hide behind the label of 'expert', they make fantastic media spokespeople.

If you get the balance between entertainment and education right, publicity can magnify the impact of a research project a thousandfold. The communicator's agenda is not only to explain the latest research; the publicity also addresses deeper issues by portraying reptiles as interesting rather than horrible. People need to see value in wild snakes before they sign on to conserving them. We have a great advantage here, because the public is fascinated by snakes even if they don't like them. A good story about snakes will go viral. Long after the audience forgets the details of the research, they are affected by the lingering power of the pro-serpent propaganda.

A media-savvy generation of snake scientists has taken up that challenge. Some of them – such as Jesus Rivas and Ruchira Somaweera – are polished media performers, hosting popular science documentaries on television. Canadian biologist Kate Jackson has written engagingly of her groundbreaking research on snakes in the remote African Congo, and how she overcame challenges that would have obliterated most research programs. All around the world, local biologists are regular speakers on local radio stations. With a little effort, those interviews can transform a cliché-riddled media beat-up about the danger from hordes of deadly snakes into an engrossing exploration of why snakes and people sometimes come into contact. In the process, such communicators achieve more for snake conservation than a hundred other scientists too timid to leave the ivory towers of academia.

Even if they aren't willing to throw themseleves headlong into the bruising spotlight of a media frenzy, there are other ways for a researcher to disseminate their results. One is via a media release, accompanied by photographs of animals and scientific activities. The online world is hungry for images. Likewise, a humorous title and a chatty style can work wonders. A catchy story accompanied by high-impact photographs will go ballistic. Add a compelling video and the sky is the limit.

The last two decades have seen a generational shift in the passion and ability of snake scientists to tell their stories to a broad audience. That shift is transforming the entire field. The most effective communicators now attract praise rather than disdain from their scientific peers, from promotions committees, and from funding agencies.

The communication revolution

Most scientific papers on snake ecology have been written by white males from 'Western' countries. That's not surprising. White males dominated the early history of scientific research in just about every sphere of enquiry. Indeed, they dominated society. They were pre-eminent in politics, public life and industry. If anyone ever invents a time machine, the first people clamouring to use it will be old white males, keen to re-experience a world in which they ruled.

As I mentioned in the foreword to this book, however, the first 'popular' treatise about snakes was not written by a man. In 1882, a remarkable Englishwoman named Catherine Cooper Hopley (1817–1911) set out to break down negative stereotypes about these grossly maligned creatures. *Snakes: Curiosities and Wonders of Serpent Life* drew upon scientific knowledge as well as Hopley's first-hand observations of live snakes – not only in a zoo in London, but also from encounters with free-ranging snakes in the southern states of the USA.

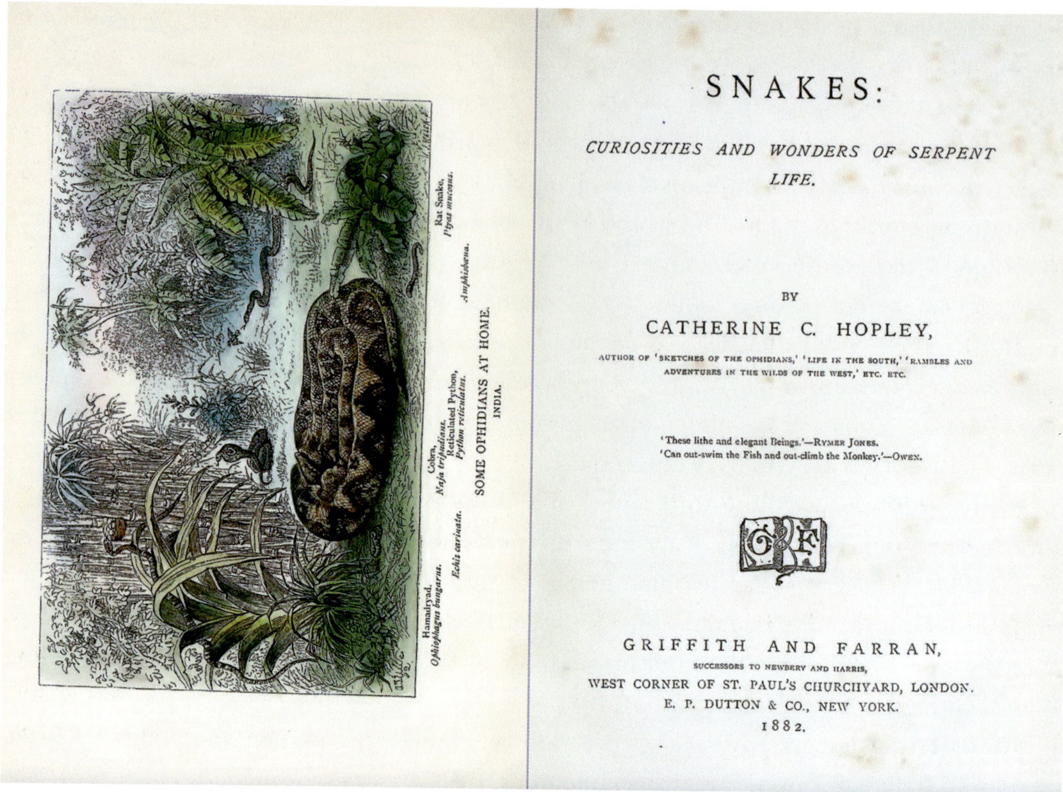

SNAKES:

CURIOSITIES AND WONDERS OF SERPENT LIFE.

BY

CATHERINE C. HOPLEY,

AUTHOR OF 'SKETCHES OF THE OPHIDIANS,' 'LIFE IN THE SOUTH,' 'RAMBLES AND ADVENTURES IN THE WILDS OF THE WEST,' ETC. ETC.

'These lithe and elegant Beings.'—RYMER JONES.
'Can out-swim the Fish and out-climb the Monkey.'—OWEN.

GRIFFITH AND FARRAN,
SUCCESSORS TO NEWBERY AND HARRIS,
WEST CORNER OF ST. PAUL'S CHURCHYARD, LONDON.
E. P. DUTTON & CO., NEW YORK.
1882.

The title page of Catherine Cooper Hopley's groundbreaking volume on snakes.

Although astonished that it "was written by a lady", reviewers of her book applauded its rigour and coverage. For the first time, English-language readers had access to reliable information about topics that had previously been the subject of myth. Hopley was a passionate advocate for snakes. The title page of her book includes two quotes that extol the abilities of serpents, one from Rymer Jones ("These lithe and elegant beings") and one from Sir Richard Owen ("can out-swim the fish and out-climb the monkey"). In a society where snakes were shunned, Catherine Hopley took on the daunting job of serpent public relations.

Hopley interacted with some of the leading scientists of the day, overcoming social barriers created by a patriarchal society and her lack of scientific training. Indeed, she dedicates the book to Sir Richard Owen, "who has graciously encouraged the studies out of which it came; and whose cordial sympathy and regard, with frankest recognition of his deep devotion to his art, gave one of its few pleasures to the short life of a dear brother of mine." I was astonished at that dedication, because most accounts of Sir Richard Owen (1804–1892) focus on his arrogance, jealousy and egotism. Owen is most famous for his role as Charles Darwin's nemesis; polite to Darwin's face but writing scathing criticisms of Darwin and his works in anonymous publications that praised Owen's own research. As the power of natural selection to explain biological diversity became clear, Owen switched approaches and tried to claim credit for the idea himself. It says volumes for Hopley's social skills that she could maintain a cordial relationship with a man described by his own biographers as dastardly, devious, sadistic, deceitful and odious. Interestingly, despite Owen's aversion to Darwinism, Hopley interprets many features of snakes in evolutionary terms. She must have been treading a narrow tightrope.

Hopley's style is far removed from the dry and dusty academic tomes of the day; she set out to entertain as well as educate, and she did a superb job at both tasks. As a pioneer in many ways, Hopley clearly saw the need to dispel myths about her favourite animals. One of her chief motivations was to educate the general populace – that is, to translate insights from scientific jargon into a form accessible to non-scientists. Fast-forward to the present day, and that need to make information widely available has become even more urgent.

Women move into snake research

Across many professions, the last several decades have witnessed a breakdown of historical barriers based on gender, race, religion and lifestyle. Some societies retain strong patriarchies, but many others do not. Once relegated to supporting roles, women now have prominent roles in scientific research.

One stimulus for that change is that gender-balanced research teams tend to outperform single-sex teams. Statistical analyses reveal that mixed-sex teams often produce more novel and high-impact scientific ideas. The reasons for that benefit remain unclear, but seem to involve the way that people interact within a team.

Pioneering tropical ecologist Dan Janzen once told me that his single golden rule for setting up field teams in Costa Rica was to include both sexes. Over several decades, Dan employed teams of local people to search the tropical dry forest for caterpillars. Under tough climatic conditions in hazardous terrain, mixed-gender teams worked together more efficiently than single-gender teams, with less conflict within each group.

But the increasing role of women in snake research isn't just about teamwork. Many women are achieving breakthroughs in their own right. Katelyn Rock and Emily Taylor from the California State Polytechnic University (plus several colleagues) recently scored genders of the authors of 62,000 scientific papers on reptiles and amphibians. And sure enough, the pattern is that women were under-represented for decades, but times have changed. We still haven't hit parity, but the proportion of female authors rose from 10 per cent to 35 per cent during the first two decades of the 21st century. It's a good start.

Numbers of papers alone only tell part of the story, because the apparently low participation of women in early snake-ecology research hides vital contributions. Even when women were not authors, they did much of the work. In 1961, biologist Clifford Pope began the acknowledgements section of his classic book *The Giant Snakes* as follows: "This is a joint endeavour, even though my wife, Sarah H. Pope, refuses to have her name on the title page. She has checked all the facts, criticized the style, written the bibliographies, typed the manuscript, and helped in small ways too numerous to mention."

Sarah Pope was not the only unsung heroine. When I visited pioneering snake ecologist Henry Fitch at his Kansas study site in 1986, I learned that his extraordinary scientific legacy was a team effort. His wife played a critical role. Petite, polite, prim and proper, dressed conservatively in the way of rural America, Virginia was 11 years younger than Henry. Like many women of her generation she had no outside-the-home profession of her own, but instead assisted her husband's career. When Henry embarked on a major review of reptile reproduction, it was Virginia who extracted information from published papers and wrote the summaries on filing cards. Hundreds of them. She showed them to me with pride. When Henry told Virginia about the snakes we had seen during our days together in the field, her observations were trenchant and well informed. She joined him on fieldwork, recording data as he measured snakes, and helped him review proofs for his scientific articles – even on their wedding night. I suspect that some of Henry's most exciting insights arose during conversations in their small Kansas farmhouse, even though Virginia wasn't an author on those papers because of cultural norms. But times were changing. Henry and Virginia's daughter Alice authored a paper in one of the top ecological journals while she was still in high school.

Although rarely given much credit, women have been catching snakes for a long time. These 'Lady Snake Hunters' pose with a day's catch of Bull Snakes (*Pituophis catenifer*) on an unknown date. TEXAS STATE LIBRARY AND ARCHIVES COMMISSION

Another example involves the greatest biologist of all time, Charles Darwin. Sickly and unable to handle social pressures, Charles would have crumbled without his wife Emma (1808–1896). He relied on Emma for almost every aspect of his existence. One of the most emotionally exhilarating experiences of my own professional life came when I visited Down House, in the county of Kent in southern England. That delightful cottage, home to Charles and Emma, has been restored as a museum. Scientists from all over the world make pilgrimages to see the place where an infirm Englishman discovered the fundamental processes that sculpt living beings. But for me, the most powerful moment came not in the house itself, but in a tiny churchyard in the town of Downe, a kilometre (half a mile) away. I was filling in time until Down House was open for visitors. I had seen Charles's grave in Westminster Abbey, but it was just a small plaque in a crowded hall – nothing evocative. I thought I might find some interesting old gravestones in the churchyard, so I wandered around reading inscriptions. And unexpectedly, one of those graves bore the name of Emma Darwin. I literally fell to my knees. It was Emma who enabled Charles Darwin to change our understanding of the world. Although they belonged to different generations and lived different lives in different parts of the world, Emma Darwin and Virginia Fitch had much in common.

Things have changed, but there is still a long way to go. Female biologists continue to face impediments to a career in research. Spouses who enable their partners to achieve scientific breakthroughs continue to be ignored. The careers of most male biologists (me included) have been grounded on the support of unsung heroines. So, the contribution of women to snake research has always been greater than is captured by authorship of scientific papers.

Gender and research

Is there anything distinctive about a female-run research program? Does the gender of an investigator influence the questions that are asked, the methods that are used, or the results that are obtained? The answer is probably 'yes', but nobody has tried to tease apart those effects. Some impacts of gender may be surprising; for example, medical researchers studying pain responses in mice reported that the scent of male investigators reduced a mouse's pain (and thus affected its behaviour) whereas the scent of female investigators did not. As a result, identical experimental protocols generated different results depending on whether the work was done by a man or a woman. I doubt that snakes are quite so sensitive to human scents, but we simply don't yet know.

Overall, the diversity among people and projects is too great for meaningful comparisons between 'male science' and 'female science'. The direction of a research project can be driven by apparently trivial aspects of the study species, study area, investigator background, and so forth. And even when a researcher stays with a single system throughout their professional lives, the approaches they use and the topics they study evolve through time.

As an example, consider Joanna Burger's landmark studies on Pine Snakes. Joanna was a pioneer of snake-ecology research; her career has spanned about the same period as mine.

Joanna Burger poses with a Pine Snake (*Pituophis melanoleucus*) at her long-term study site in the New Jersey Pine Barrens. JOANNA BURGER

The snakes that she studies are spectacular – up to 1.8 metres (6 ft) long, with bold black and white bands. The New Jersey Pine Barrens, less than 140 kilometres (85 miles) from New York City, are sandy habitats close to the northern limit of the Pine Snake's distribution. Working with ecologist Robert Zappalorti for decades, Joanna first conducted surveys for snakes and their habitats. She soon zeroed in on a critical resource: burrows used by the snakes for nesting and hibernation. She showed that snakes frequently reuse the same burrows year after year, and that the burrows are only found in sun-exposed clearings with sandy soil. Why do females lay their eggs in these open clearings? Because in this cool climate, a nest site is too cold unless it is bathed in sunlight every day. Joanna's laboratory incubation experiments showed that cool conditions produce inferior hatchlings – late to hatch, slow to emerge, less athletic, and less able to detect scent cues from predators. Incubation temperature even changes the relative numbers of male versus female hatchlings, because male embryos are less able to survive in a cold nest.

And bit by bit, Joanna began to understand the factors that threaten persistence of these spectacular reptiles. The open sun-exposed clearings so attractive to nesting sites are also popular highways for all-terrain vehicles, whose tyres tear apart the fragile sandy soil. Other threats include illegal snake collectors, and ever-encroaching construction for retirement homes. It's impossible to shoehorn Joanna's contributions into any simple category. She worked out how this system operates, why it is in trouble, and what we need to do to keep it healthy. In the process, she brought in new ideas from behavioural biology, and collaborators with relevant expertise. And she made many discoveries in fundamental as well as applied science: for example, about how incubation conditions influence the hatchlings that emerge from a nest.

Joanna's career also reveals another driver of research directions: cross-fertilisation of ideas and methods from one type of study animal to another. Joanna is an avid bird biologist as well as a snake biologist. And so, it was a small step for her to take the behavioural tests that ornithologists apply to young birds and try them out on baby snakes. Some 'new ideas' leap out of nowhere; but often, the novelty comes from taking an idea from one field of study and applying it elsewhere.

Shifting gender roles worldwide

One intriguing pattern involves the kinds of organisms that are studied by women versus men. American biologist Dawn Wilson found a clear pattern when she analysed the history of herpetological research in the USA. The first challenges to male domination of the field (as measured by authorship of published papers) came from studies on amphibians rather than reptiles. Women worked on frogs or salamanders, not on lizards or turtles. Even after female-driven reptile research became mainstream, snakes were left out of that new wave. The initial reptile work by women was mostly on lizards. Snakes came later. There are exceptions, of course, like Joanna Burger – but most pioneering female researchers worked with amphibians rather than snakes. The same pattern occurred among Indian researchers. Why was that? Dawn speculates that young female students may have been guided by their mentors towards 'less threatening' animals such as frogs. Another part of the answer may lie in a few amphibian-based researchers who actively encouraged female participation – people like Dave and Marvalee Wake in California, and Jay Savage in Florida.

Melissa Bruton checking a radio-implanted Woma Python (*Aspidites ramsayi*) prior to its release back into the wild. MELISSA BRUTON

The chest-beating macho appeal of venomous snakes can create an alpha-male atmosphere that is unwelcoming to students who don't fit that stereotype. But those barriers have broken down as well. In recent years, some of the most demanding fieldwork on snakes has been done by people like Julie Savidge on the island of Guam, Kate Jackson in Congo, Krystal Tolley in South Africa and Melissa Bruton in the Australian deserts. Rocking about in small boats on rough seas, Kate Sanders is transforming our understanding of sea snakes. Katja Claus has been capturing, measuring and releasing Eurasian Adders in the heathlands of Belgium for decades, accumulating a treasure trove of ecological information. The list of outstanding female researchers grows every year.

In global analyses of gender bias in herpetological research, the gap has narrowed faster in South American countries such as Argentina and Brazil compared to most other places. An important contributor to that change was Bertha Lutz (1894–1976), a Brazilian frog biologist and co-founder of Brazil's first woman's rights movement. Nonetheless, men continue to dominate the editorial boards of scientific journals in those countries, and tend to co-author papers with other men rather than with women. One review reported that research groups led by women had 60 per cent female co-authors, whereas those led by men had only 20 per cent. And similarly, most organisers of symposia at major conferences in Argentina are male; and on average, women tend to have shorter professional careers than do men.

Although the dominance of old white males in snake research is declining, the process has been slow. One impetus for change came at a herpetological conference in Rochester, New York, in 2018. A man with outstanding research credentials but a history of sexist behaviour was awarded a prestigious 'lifetime achievement award' by a scientific society. Mutterings of discontent began as soon as the award was announced, but those mutterings grew to a crescendo when the awardee's conference presentation contained images of young women in swimsuits. Social media exploded in outrage, and the scientific society withdrew the award. The fury of young researchers was palpable. It was a wake-up call. The upheaval made many older scientists regret our own long-term tolerance of sexism. That chaos shone a bright light on the costs to science as well as to individuals if senior figures are allowed to bully or harass younger researchers.

Several scientific societies have taken active steps to outlaw discrimination. Even before that conference in Rochester, the Australian Society of Herpetologists had approved a code of conduct for meetings to "provide an inclusive, welcoming and safe environment for all delegates", to outlaw "language or imagery that is sexually explicit and/or denigrates others on the basis of gender, sexual orientation, race, religion or physical appearance". In 2020, the American Society of Ichthyologists and Herpetologists changed the name of its journal from

Copeia because the scientist for whom the journal had been named – Edward Drinker Cope – had espoused racist views. Herpetological societies now have diversity, equity and inclusivity committees that decide how inappropriate behaviour should be punished.

Getting the locals involved

Gender of authorship has not been the only axis of change. For example, the geographical diversity of scientific papers in snake ecology is increasing (see Chapter 2). Although some authors of those papers are from Western countries – the initial strongholds of research – more and more local scientists are taking leadership roles. Asian and African snakes are being studied by Asian and African scientists – a far cry from the situation just a few decades ago.

Historians of science talk of ideas arising in some central area then being exported to far-flung places, like a US fast-food franchise going international. That's what snake ecology looked like in the early years – scientists from North America and Europe travelling to exotic destinations, living there, and conducting the first research programs on the local snake species. And that 'centre to periphery' model is still happening. Researchers from Western countries still travel to parts of the world where snakes are abundant, diverse, and unstudied. I'm one of those people.

But these days, local collaboration is central to those projects. I see a clear transition in my own research on the commercial harvest of snakes in Indonesia. I was the senior author on my 1990s papers, with an Indonesian biologist (Boeadi) as a co-author. But within a decade Boeadi was the lead author and I was relegated to second place. These days, I am well down the authorship list of papers on that system, with the research mostly done by Indonesians. It's been a natural evolution, with capacity building more important than any specific research results. Especially for conservation and management issues, local leadership is vital.

Another exciting development has been the inclusion of First Nations perspectives into research programs. In many parts of the world, indigenous people have a deep knowledge of local ecosystems. In early research projects, those people were animal collectors or assistants rather than scientific collaborators. That approach values local knowledge, but it's a long way from real partnership. For genuine collaboration, you need relationships. Romulus Whitaker's conservation work in south India offers an inspiring example of how to incorporate human beings and snakes into the same picture. Rom was born in the USA but grew up in India, and he developed a passionate attachment to his adopted country as well as to its unique snake fauna. He wanted to conserve reptiles, but also to support indigenous groups. The Irula is a tribe from southern India with a long history of snake catching, based on tracking the animals to their dens. But by the time that Rom met the Irula in the 1970s, catching snakes and killing

Good field biologists prioritise warm and respectful relationships with local people. In this photograph Bill Lamar is in Colombia, posing with a Karapana family and a large Rusty Whipsnake (*Chironius scurrula*).

them for their skins and meat was unsustainable. Every year, more than six million snakes were being killed. Snake populations were declining, and in 1975 the Indian government banned the commercial trade.

Overnight, the Irula snake catchers lost their livelihood. Rom devised an alternative plan – catch snakes to obtain venom. Each snake is milked of its venom once a week for three weeks before being released back into the wild. The venom is used to make antivenoms against snakebite. The new plan is working. The Irula have employment, antivenom is available, and snake populations are healthy. The Irula are such effective snake hunters that the Florida Fish and Wildlife Conservation Commission flew two of them to the Everglades to look for invasive Burmese Pythons. Unsurprisingly, the expert Indians caught more pythons than anybody else.

Breaking down barriers

The diversity of people on research teams is exploding in other dimensions as well. The traditional model of scientific research emphasised a restricted range of ages – generally young adults (students) through to middle age (academics). But that situation is changing. The role of volunteers became more prominent as governments slashed their expenditure on research and the internet facilitated communication between scientists and the general public. Citizen-science initiatives range from school groups surveying their local pond to sprightly grandmothers photographing deadly sea snakes. Setting up a website to explain the project to the public, and invite wider participation, is now central to any major research program. Nowadays, a research expedition may well include children and grandparents. Retirees flock to research projects in remote areas that offer first-hand encounters with wildlife.

Over the years, Joanna Burger's project on the ecology of Pine Snakes (*Pituophis melanoleucus*) has evolved from data collection by a small team of professional scientists into a major citizen-science initiative that involves dozens of non-scientists.

During my own research, I've been especially impressed by the contributions of older women to snake projects. My first encounter with 'grandmother meets snake' came via the organisation Earthwatch, which organises teams of volunteers to accompany scientists. For several years, groups of two to six such people helped Bob Mason study garter snakes at the mighty Manitoba dens. Although most of the volunteers had no formal scientific training, they were quick and enthusiastic learners. Most of all I was inspired by a septuagenarian named Ruth Nesbitt, from Vancouver, who joined us year after year. Ruth had been travelling around the world ever since she retired, but she found time to assist Bob and his team as the snakes emerged from hibernation in the cool Canadian springtime. Cheerful, skilful and helpful, Ruth integrated smoothly with students 50 years younger than herself. She contributed to the team's social cohesion as well as its research output.

Earthwatch volunteer Ruth Nesbitt was a valuable member of Bob Mason's research team at the Manitoba snake dens for several years. In this image, she is transferring Red-sided Garter Snakes (*Thamnophis sirtalis parietalis*) from one arena to another.
BOB MASON

My second interaction with grandmothers involves retired women who live in the city of Noumea in the Indo-Pacific island nation of New Caledonia. My collaborator Claire Goiran and I are studying sea snakes in the small bays beside the city, and one of our projects involves photographing sea snakes. With a good photo, we can identify individual snakes from their colour patterns. A grandmother who was swimming in the bay saw Claire photographing a snake and offered to do the same for any snakes she saw. Before long we had a formidable team of citizen scientists at work, transforming their daily swim sessions into snake-finding jaunts. Those women aren't young, but I've never met a tougher, fitter, more joyful and more dedicated snake-reseach team. The self-titled 'Fantastic Grandmothers' have recorded hundreds of giant sea snakes in our study area – vastly more than I ever expected to see. And the grandmother team has attracted a lot of interest from the media, breaking down stereotypes about gender and age as well as snakes.

Across the world, citizen scientists are sweeping away the myth that fieldwork is suitable only for middle-aged people with scientific qualifications. Other obstacles will be more difficult to overcome, but it's happening. For example, physical disabilities render fieldwork arduous but not impossible. One of the grandmothers in Noumea needs crutches to walk to the water's edge, but she swims like a fish. The pioneering African snakeman C.J.P. Ionides caught thousands of deadly snakes despite being barely able to walk. University of Nevada snake ecologist Julie Ray has been legally blind for most of her life, but that hasn't stopped her from building a successful career in research.

One of the most exciting ecological studies on snakes in North America is a long-term project on Pygmy Rattlesnakes by two professors from Stetson University in Florida. When I joined Peter May and his colleague Terry Farrell at their Pygmy Rattler site, I discovered that Peter was restricted to a wheelchair – but he still worked his way through the swampy study site, and he has played a major role in the research for many years. His attitude was nicely summed up by a bumper sticker on his car, reading 'He who dies with the most snakes wins'.

Just a few years ago, photographing snakes in the wild required expensive and cumbersome equipment. The dramatic increase in image quality from mobile-phone cameras has changed that situation, encouraging more people to document the lives of wildlife around them. This man is photographing a Speckled Kingsnake (*Lampropeltis holbrooki*). NOAH K. FIELDS

Increasing cultural diversity among snake scientists has raised awareness about other issues as well. Words are important, and some archaic terms were unintentionally discriminatory. For example, scientists writing about female-mimicking male garter snakes abandoned the term 'she-males' when we became aware of potential offence to transgender people. Likewise, 'sneaky mating strategy' could be misinterpreted as endorsing traditional sex roles; and descriptors such as 'pygmy' and 'dwarf' for small species run the risk of offence as well. Like everyone else in modern society, snake ecologists tread a tightrope between political correctness and effective communication.

Looking back at the history of research in snake ecology, the field has never been dominated by super-fit muscular white males, except on TV screens. Pioneering characters such as Henry Fitch, Hubert Saint Girons and Hajime Fukada were tough as teak, but they were never macho. Many of the obstacles that prevented women and minority groups from accessing careers in snake research were created by broader society rather than by prejudice within the ranks of scientists. Some of the older researchers were misogynistic alpha-males who resented anybody who wasn't like them (that is, male, white, heterosexual, university-educated and English-speaking). But the generation that restricted research opportunities in this way has passed on, and modern snake researchers embrace diversity. We still haven't achieved equal opportunity; historical discrimination takes generations to obliterate. But we are on an upward trajectory, towards a world which welcomes people from all backgrounds.

Taking a broader view of the history of research in snake ecology, we are seeing a return to the early days. Before the advent of professional science, advances in knowledge about snakes came from small contributions by many different kinds of people – often, from people with no special training or expertise in reptile biology. They saw something, they found it interesting, and they wrote a short note to let the world know about it. As those modest offerings accumulated, they shone a bright light onto the secret lives of snakes.

Then came the pioneering snake scientists, salaried professionals who were few in number but could focus all of their energies onto the subject at hand. Almost all of those people were white males. They integrated the scattered morsels of information, gathered extensive new data, and transformed snake-ecology research into a coherent body of knowledge. The successors of those pioneers – people like me and my colleagues and students – continued that work, and the field blossomed.

But the field evolved as well, and one of the principal shifts has been increasing diversity – not just in terms of gender and ethnicity, but also the inclusion of non-professionals. Citizen science is booming, driven by reduced government investment into research as well as by digital technologies that make it possible for almost anyone to disseminate a new observation or a new image worldwide. Before the emergence of mobile phones with cameras, an untrained person who saw a snake engaging in some interesting behaviour might have told a few friends about it, but that observation would forever remain as vague hearsay. Identifying the species in question would be nigh-impossible, for example. But a phone-based camera can provide images clear enough to satisfy even the most pedantic expert. Over recent decades, more and more notes are authored by amateur snake enthusiasts rather than professional scientists.

There's nothing magical about contributing to knowledge of snake ecology. All you need is an enquiring mind and access to snakes. Don't assume that 'this must already be known'; the chances are that it isn't. Observe what your captive snakes are doing, take photographs or video of the behaviour, and record details such as times, places and body sizes. Or if your passion is the field, stop by the side of the road to record that run-over snake, note its GPS location on your phone, and donate the specimen (if it isn't too smashed) to your local museum. Upload your photographs to iNaturalist, a web-based system that is rapidly becoming a key resource for ecological research.

Respectful coexistence with snakes is a new idea in Western societies, but it is important and it is achievable. With knowledge and tolerance, we can enrich our suburban lives by close encounters with animals that were once feared and despised. This image shows a Common Water Snake (*Nerodia sipedon*) beside a bike path. NOAH K. FIELDS

We are entering a new golden age of research into snake ecology. One in which powerful new methods can illuminate topics long inaccessible to study. In which snakes are widely recognised as valuable and interesting components of natural ecosystems. In which we can begin to base snake conservation and management on real data rather than guesswork. In which a person's race, age, gender and background do not prevent them from contributing new knowledge. The wheel has come full circle, with insights coming from a broader array of people and based on a greater range of species and places than was the case only a few decades ago. And with a more diverse array of scientists studying a more diverse array of snakes, the revolution in research on snake ecology is growing bigger and better.

An extraordinary transformation of knowledge about snake ecology has occurred during my professional career, and I count myself fortunate to have contributed to some of those revelations. As a snake-obsessed child, I could never have dreamed that I could ever be so lucky. We have learned that snakes are more flexible, complex and fascinating than we ever guessed.

In earlier days, the word 'snake' evoked fear based on fables about potent venom and aggressiveness. Today more and more people view snakes as creatures of interest, and even of beauty – this juvenile Green Tree Python (*Morelia viridis*) shows why. BILL LAMAR

Some of the new insights arose in the lab and others in the field. Some were the discoveries of professional scientists whereas others came from passionate amateurs. Some were from my own team but most were from people I've never met. Some were about snake species I know well but others were about species I'd never heard of before. Some of the information was gathered in places I know well but most came from places I have never visited. Some of the new information consisted of tiny fragments, but other discoveries came from marathon longterm projects. That enormous diversity in people, places, species and approaches has coalesced into a flood of ideas

A magnificent blue specimen of the Indonesian Pit Viper (*Trimeresurus insularis*) from Komodo Island. PIXABAY

and methods as well as observations and patterns. At long last, we are beginning to understand how snakes live their lives.

I salute the tenacious human beings whose efforts have lifted the veil of secrecy shrouding snakes, the most mysterious of beasts. Looking into the history of my own research field, I am entranced by the passion of pioneering researchers like Catherine Cooper Hopley and Constantin Ionides. Modern-day snake ecologists are indeed slithering on the shoulders of giants.

IN THEIR OWN WORDS

In Victorian-era England, a pioneering woman herpetologist needed tenacity to move beyond pet keeping, because the way forward was strewn with obstacles. The author of the first major modern book on snake biology described her experiences thus:

"After some research I learnt enough of snake nature to feel safe in proceeding with my book of Adventures, and in presenting it to a publisher. 'As a gift-book no one would look at it, and as an educational work there would be no demand for it,' was its encouraging reception. This was about ten years ago; and so far from inducing me to relinquish the subject, I began to aspire to become a means of assisting to overcome these prejudices." CATHERINE COOPER HOPLEY, 1892

Nonetheless, some of the most enthusiastic snake keepers were women:

"An equally wonderful but far more attractive sight was Mrs Mann, a graceful and charming little lady in black velvet, with Cleo coiling around her in Laocoön-like curves. The rich colouring of the beautifully marked reptile entwining the slender form of the woman, the picturesque and caressing actions of Cleo, and the responsive repose of Mrs Mann as the snake was now round her waist, now undulating around and over her head and neck, was altogether a sight never to be forgotten." CATHERINE COOPER HOPLEY, 1892

Bibliography

Most of these references relate to scientific papers, but don't be discouraged from checking them out even if you are not scientifically trained. If you go into the internet site 'Google Scholar' and type in a topic or the title of a paper, you'll find thousands of PDFs that you can download without charge – and you'll have no trouble understanding most of those papers. If references are cited in more than one chapter, I have only listed them the first time they appear.

The Black-headed Python (*Aspidites melanocephalus*) is an abundant and conspicuous element of biodiversity across the Australian tropics.
ALANA DE LAIVE

Foreword

Hopley, C.C. 1882. *Snakes: curiosities and wonders of serpent life.* Griffith and Farran, London.

Chapter 1. Emerging from the Dark Ages

Bell, T. 1849. *A history of British reptiles.* J. Van Voorst, London.

Cooke, M.C. 1893. *Our reptiles and batrachians: a plain and easy account of the lizards, snakes, newts, toads, frogs and tortoises indigenous to Great Britain.* WH Allen & Co., Limited, London.

Cope, E.D. 1876. A snake-eating snake. *American Naturalist* 10: 179.

Darwin, C. 1859. *On the Origin of Species*. Charles Murray, London.

Darwin, C. 1872. *The expression of the emotions in man and animals*. Penguin Books, New York.

Dickinson, E. 1960. A narrow fellow in the grass. In *The complete poems of Emily Dickinson* (T.H. Johnson, editor). Little Press, Boston.

Hay, O.P. 1887. The massasauga and its habits. *American Naturalist* 21: 211–218.

Isbell, L.A. 2009. *The fruit, the tree, and the serpent: why we see so well*. Harvard University Press, Cambridge.

Kinghorn, J.R. 1929. *The snakes of Australia*. Angus and Robertson, Sydney.

Montgomery, H.H. 1891. Some account of the mutton birds, or Sooty Petrels (*Nectris brevicaudus*), as seen in their homes among the Furneaux Islands, Bass Straits, Tasmania, from notes taken during a visit to the locality in March, 1891. *Papers and Proceedings of the Royal Society of Tasmania* 1891: 1–10.

Owen, C. 1742. *An essay towards a natural history of serpents*. Printed for the Author, London.

Posadas, M. 2018. Tiresias and his trouble with ambiguity in gender. *The Undecidable Unconscious: A Journal of Deconstruction and Psychoanalysis* 5: 93–106.

Quelch, J.J. 1888. The Boa Constrictors of British Guiana. *Annals and Magazine of Natural History* 7: 296–308.

Rose, W. 1962. *The reptiles and amphibians of South Africa*. Maskew Miller, Cape Town.

Saint Girons, H. 1964. Notes sur l'ecologie et la structure des populations des laticaudinae (Serpents, Hydrophidae) en Nouvelle Caledonie. *Revue d'Ecologie, Terre et Vie* 2: 185–214.

Schlegel, H. 1837. *Essai sur la physionomie des serpents. I. Partie générale. II. Partie descriptive. M.H. Schonekat*, Amsterdam.

Seigel, R.A. 1993. Summary: future research on snakes, or how to combat 'lizard envy'. In *Snakes, ecology and behavior* (R.A. Seigel and J.T. Collins, editors), pp. 395–402. McGraw-Hill, New York.

Sergueenkova, V.V. 2009. *Natural history in Herodotus' Histories*. PhD thesis, Harvard University.

Stradling, A. 1896. The tribe accurst. *The Picture Magazine* 7: 176–177.

Surface, H.A. 1906. *Serpents of Pennsylvania*. Pennsylvania State Department of Agriculture, Harrisburg.

Vidal, G.W. 1890. A list of the venomous snakes of North Kanara; with remarks as to the imperfections of existing records of the distribution of snakes, and facts and statistics showing the influence of *Echis carinata* on the death-rate of the Bombay presidency. *Journal of the Bombay Natural History Society* 5: 64–71.

Waite, E.R. 1929. *The reptiles and amphibians of South Australia.* Government Printer, Adelaide.

Williams, G.C. 1966. *Adaptation and natural selection*. Princeton University Press, Princeton.

Wucherer, O. 1863. On the ophidians of the province of Bahia, Brazil. *Proceedings of the Zoological Society of London* 1863: 55–56.

Chapter 2. The complex path of an untidy revolution

Alves-Nunes, J.M., Fellone, A., Almeida-Santos, S.M., de Medeiros, C.R., Sazima, I. and Vuolo Marques, O.A. 2024. Study of defensive behavior of a venomous snake as a new approach to understand snakebite. *Scientific Reports* 14: 10230.

Arnold, S.J. 1983. Morphology, performance and fitness. *American Zoologist* 23: 347–361.

Covacevich, J. 1987. Two taipans! In *Toxic plants and animals – a guide for Australia* (J. Covacevich, P. Davie and J. Pearn, editors), pp. 480–485. Queensland Museum, Brisbane.

Curran, C.H. and Kauffeld, C. 1937. *Snakes and their ways*. Harper and Brothers, New York.

Daltry, J.C., Wüster, W. and Thorpe, R.S. 1996. Diet and snake venom evolution. *Nature* 379: 537–540.

Doughty, P., Maryan, B., Donnellan, S.C. and Hutchinson, M.N. 2007. A new species of taipan (Elapidae: *Oxyuranus*) from central Australia. *Zootaxa* 1422: 45–58.

Fritts, T.H. and Rodda, G.H. 1998. The role of introduced species in the degradation of island ecosystems: a case history of Guam. *Annual Review of Ecology and Systematics* 29: 113–140.

Giesen, W. 1993. Mass feeding by Dog-faced Water Snakes (*Cerberus rhynchops*) in Sumatran mudflats. *Malayan Nature Journal* 46: 265–266.

Greene, H.W. 1997. *Snakes: the evolution of mystery in nature*. University of California Press, Berkeley.

Hillis, D.M. 2010. In the field with Henry Fitch. *Reptiles and Amphibians* 17: 13–14.

Huey, R.B. 1991. Physiological consequences of habitat selection. *American Naturalist* 137: S91–S115.

Kinghorn, J.R. 1923. New snake discovered on a bird expedition. *The Emu* 23: 146.

Kinghorn, J.R. 1923. A new genus of elapine snakes from North Australia. *Records of the Australian Museum* 14: 42–45.

Klauber, L.M. 1972. *Rattlesnakes*. University of California Press, Berkeley.

Kusrini, M.D., Manurung, R., Habiburrahman Faz, F., Dwiputro, A., Tajalli, A., Nur Prasetyo, H., Bayu Saputra, P., Kennedi, U.F., Wibisono Parikesit, D., Shine, R. and Natusch, D. 2023. Abundance, demography, and harvesting of water snakes from agricultural landscapes in West Java, Indonesia. *Wildlife Research* 50: 272–282.

Lynch, T.P., Alford, R.A. and Shine, R. 2021. Mistaken identity may explain why male seasnakes (*Aipysurus laevis*, Elapidae, Hydrophiinae) 'attack' scuba divers. *Scientific Reports* 11: 15267.

Madsen, T., Shine, R., Olsson, M. and Wittzell, H. 1999. Restoration of an inbred adder population. *Nature* 402: 34–35.

Mell, R. 1929. *Beitrage zur fauna sinica. IV. Grundzu¨ge einer ¨okologie der chinesischen reptilien und einer herpetologischen tiergeographie Chinas*. Walter de Gruyter, Germany.

Murphy, J.C. 2007. *Homalopsid snakes: evolution in the mud*. Krieger Publishing Company, Malabar.

Sergeev, A.M. 1940. Researches in the viviparity of reptiles. *Moscow Society of Naturalists* (Jubilee Issue): 1–34.

Shine, R. 1978. Sexual size dimorphism and male combat in snakes. *Oecologia* 33: 269–277.

Shine, R. and Bonnet, X. 2000. Snakes: a new 'model organism' in ecological research? *Trends in Ecology & Evolution* 15: 221–222.

Shine, R. and Elphick, M.J. 2023. When, where and why has research been conducted on snakes? *Journal of Herpetology* 57: 197–203.

Stradling, A. 1882. On the treatment of snakes in captivity. *The Zoologist* 6: 448–456.

Sumner, R. 1993. *A woman in the wilderness: the story of Amalie Dietrich in Australia*. University of NSW Press, Kensington.

Thomson, D.F. 1933. Notes on Australian snakes of the genera *Pseudechis* and *Oxyuranus*. *Proceedings of the Zoological Society of London* 1933: 855–860.

Uetz, P. 2016. The reptile database turns 20. *Herpetological Review* 47: 330–334.

Weekes, H.C. 1935. A review of placentation among reptiles with particular regard to the function and evolution of the placenta. *Proceedings of the Zoological Society of London* 105: 625–645.

Chapter 3. First, catch your snake

Aldrich, C. 1879. Mimicry in a snake. *American Naturalist* 13: 711–712.

Armstrong, G., Reid, J.R.W. and Hutchinson, M.N. 1993. Discovery of a population of the rare scincid lizard, *Tiliqua adelaidensis* (Peters). *Records of the South Australian Museum* 36: 153–155.

Broadley, D.G. 1962. *FitzSimons' snakes of southern Africa*. Delta Books, Johannesburg.

Cooper, J.G. 1876. A true 'snake story'. *American Naturalist* 10: 493.

Fayrer, J. 1872. *The thanatophidia of India: being a description of the venomous snakes of the Indian Peninsula, with an account of the influence of their poison on life; and a series of experiments*. J.A. Churchill, London.

Fitch, H.S. 1951. A simplified type of funnel trap for reptiles. *Herpetologica* 7: 77–80.

Freymiller, G.A., Whitford, M.D., Higham, T.E. and Clark, R.W. 2019. Escape dynamics of free-ranging desert kangaroo rats (Rodentia: Heteromyidae) evading rattlesnake strikes. *Biological Journal of the Linnean Society* 127: 164–172.

Greene, H.W. 1986. Natural history and evolutionary biology. In *Predator-prey relationships: perspectives and approaches from the study of lower vertebrates* (M.E. Feder and G.V. Lauder, editors), pp. 99–108. University of Chicago Press, Chicago.

Hattori, Z., Inoue, T. and Okonogi, T. 1974. In front of a pile of seasnake carcasses. *The Snake* 6: 94–98.

Imler, R.H. 1945. Bullsnakes and their control on a Nebraska wildlife refuge. *Journal of Wildlife Management* 9: 265–273.

Ionides, C.J.P. 1918. Notes on snakes in East Africa. *Journal of the East African and Ugandan Natural History Society* 13: 315–388.

Ionides, C.J.P. 1966. *Mambas and man-eaters: a hunter's story*. Holt, Rinehart and Winston, New York.

Jackley, A.M. 1939. Rattlesnake control and conservation. *South Dakota Conservation Digest* 6: 11.

Krefft, G. 1869. *The snakes of Australia: an illustrated and descriptive catalogue of all the known species*. Thomas Richards, Government Printer, Sydney.

Nicholson, E. 1874. *Indian snakes: an elementary treatise on ophiology with a descriptive catalogue of the snakes found in India and the adjoining countries*. Higginbotham and Co., Madras.

Parker, W.S. and Brown, W.S. 1980. Comparative ecology of two colubrid snakes, *Masticophis t. taeniatus* and *Pituophis melanoleucus deserticola,* in northern Utah. Issue 7 of publications in biology and geology, Milwaukee Public Museum, Milwauke.

Rodda, G.H. 1993. Where's Waldo (and the snakes)? *Herpetological Review* 24: 44–45.

Rodda, G.H., Sawai, Y., Chizsar, D. and Tamnaka H. 1999. *Problem snake management: the habu and brown treesnake*. Comstock Publishing Associates, Ithaca.

Shine, R. 2022. *So many snakes, so little time*. CRC Press, Boca Raton.

Shine, R. 2024. *Snakes without borders*. Reed New Holland Publishers, Sydney.

Stradling, A. 1882. Snakes and how to tame them. *The Boy's Own Paper* 5: 10–11.

Trecul, M.A. 1876. On the capture of rattlesnakes. *Annals and Magazine of Natural History Series* 4: 339–440.

Vasile, R.S. 1900. The Dude snake hunter: Howard K. Gloyd (1902–1978) and the Chicago Academy of Sciences. *Bulletin of the Chicago Herpetological Society* 25: 173–180.

Viitanen, P. 1967. Hibernation and seasonal movements of the viper, *Vipera berus berus* (L.), in southern Finland. *Annales Zoologici Fennici* 4: 472–546.

Whitford, M.D., Freymiller, G.A. and Clark, R.W. 2017. Avoiding the serpent's tooth: predator–prey interactions between free-ranging sidewinder rattlesnakes and desert kangaroo rats. *Animal Behaviour* 130: 73–78.

Willson, J.D., Winne, C.T. and Fedewa, L.A. 2005. Unveiling escape and capture rates of aquatic snakes and salamanders (*Siren* spp. and *Amphiuma means*) in commercial funnel traps. *Journal of Freshwater Ecology* 20: 397–403.

Woodbury, A.M. and Hansen, R.M. 1950. A snake den in Tintic Mountains Utah. *Herpetologica* 6: 66–70.

Woodbury, A.M. 1951. Introduction: a ten-year study. *Herpetologica* 7: 4–14.

Chapter 4. Obtaining data from a squirming reptile

Anonymous. 1786. Le serpent de la Martinique. *Nouvelles de la République des Lettres et des Arts* 7: 461–462.

Avolio, C., Shine, R. and Pile, A. 2006. Sexual dimorphism in scale rugosity in seasnakes (Hydrophiidae). *Biological Journal of the Linnean Society* 89: 343–354.

Bauwens, D., Claus, K. and Mergeay, J. 2018. Genotyping validates photo-identification by the head scale pattern in a large population of the European adder (*Vipera berus*). *Ecology and Evolution* 8: 2985–2992.

Bertram, N. and Larsen, K.W. 2004. Putting the squeeze on venomous snakes: accuracy and precision of length measurements taken with the 'squeeze box'. *Herpetological Review* 35: 235.

Blanchard, F.N. and Finster, E.B. 1933. A method of marking living snakes for future recognition, with a discussion of some problems and results. *Ecology* 14: 334–347.

Brown, W.S. and Parker, W.S. 1976. A ventral scale clipping system for permanently marking snakes (Reptilia, Serpentes). *Journal of Herpetology* 10: 247–249.

Bull, J.J. and Shine, R. 1979. Iteroparous animals that skip opportunities for reproduction. *American Naturalist* 114: 296–303.

Cope, E.D. 1895. The classification of the Ophidia. *Transactions of the American Philosophical Society* 18: 186–219.

Davis, V.A. 1888. Serpent myths. *The North American Review* 146: 161–171.

Durso, A.M. and Mullin, S.J. 2017. Ontogenetic shifts in the diet of plains hog-nosed snakes (*Heterodon nasicus*) revealed by stable isotope analysis. *Zoology* 120: 83–91.

Fitch, H.S. 1960. Autecology of the copperhead. *University of Kansas Publications, Museum of Natural History* 13: 85–288.

Fitch, H.S. 1987. Collecting and life-history techniques. In *Snakes. Ecology and evolutionary biology* (R.A. Seigel, J.T. Collins and S.S. Novak, editors), pp. 143–164. Macmillan, New York.

Folwell, M.J., Sanders, K.L., Brennan, P.L. and Crowe-Riddell, J.M. 2022. First evidence of hemiclitores in snakes. *Proceedings of the Royal Society B* 289: 20221702.

Flower, S.S. 1899. Notes on a second collection of reptiles made in the Malay Peninsula and Siam, from November 1896 to September 1898, with a list of species recorded from those countries. *Proceedings of the Zoological Society of London* 1899: 600–696.

Glissmeyer, H.R. 1951. Egg production of the Great Basin rattlesnake. *Herpetologica* 7: 24–27.

Gnudi, G., Volta, A., Di Ianni, F., Bonazzi, M., Manfredi, S. and Bertoni, G. 2009. Use of ultrasonography and contrast radiography for snake gender determination. *Veterinary Radiology & Ultrasound* 50: 309–311.

Goetz, S.M., Hileman, E.T., Nafus, M.G., Yackel Adams, A.A., Bryant, A.R., Reed, R.N. and Siers, S.R. 2021. Brown treesnake mortality after aerial application of toxic baits. *Journal of Wildlife Management* 85: 1507–1514.

Greene, H.W. 1983. Dietary correlates of the origin and radiation of snakes. *American Zoologist* 23: 431–441.

Heyrend, F.L. and Call, A. 1951. Growth and age in western striped racer and Great Basin rattlesnake. *Herpetologica* 7: 28–40.

Kane, D., Tapley, B., Guthrie, A., Sparrow, S., Tahas, S.A. and Michaels, C.J. 2022. A novel approach to sexing *Lachesis stenophrys* (Serpentes: Viperidae) using radiography. *Herpetological Review* 53: 54–57.

Khaire, A., Khaire, N. and Katdare, M. 1985. Observations on feeding, mating, egglaying and seasonal moulting of checkered keel back water snake (*Xenochrophis piscator*). *The Snake* 17: 25–30.

Langkilde, T. and Shine, R. 2006. How much stress do researchers inflict on their study animals? A case study using a scincid lizard, *Eulamprus heatwolei*. *Journal of Experimental Biology* 209: 1035–1043.

Laopichienpong, N., Tawichasri, P., Chanhome, L., Phatcharakullawarawat, R., Singchat, W., Kantachumpoo, A., Muangmai, N., Suntrarachun, S., Matsubara, K., Peyachoknagul, S. and Srikulnath, K. 2017. A novel method of caenophidian snake sex identification using molecular markers based on two gametologous genes. *Ecology and Evolution* 7: 4661–4669.

Meiri, S., Feldman, A., Schwarz, R. and Shine, R. 2020. Viviparity does not affect the numbers and sizes of reptile offspring. *Journal of Animal Ecology* 89: 360–369.

Mole, R.R. and Urich, F.W. 1894. A preliminary list of the reptiles and batrachians of the island of Trinidad. *Journal of the Trinidad Field Naturalists' Club* 1894: 77–90.

Moktadir, N.A. and Hasan, M.K. 2016. Unusual feeding behavior of the Checkered Keelback *Xenochrophis piscator* on Jahangirnagar University Campus, Savar, Dhaka, Bangladesh. *Reptile RAP* 18: 32–33.

Morton, T. 1634. *New English Canaan*. Jacob Stam, Amsterdam.

Pizzatto, L., Almeida-Santos, S.M. and Shine, R. 2007. Life-history adaptations to arboreality in snakes. *Ecology* 88: 359–366.

Prestt, I. 1971. An ecological study of the viper *Vipera berus* in southern Britain. *Journal of Zoology* 164: 373–418.

Rahn, H. 1942. The reproductive cycle of the prairie rattler. *Copeia* 1942: 233–240.

Saint Girons, H. 1996. Structure et évolution d'une petite population de *Vipera aspis* (L.) dans une région de bocage de l'ouest de la France. *Revue d'Ecologie, Terre et Vie* 51: 223–241.

Savage, T.A. 1844. Observations on the habits of *Python natalensis*. *Annals and Magazine of Natural History* 14: 148–150.

Schneck, J. 1882. General notes – zoology. *American Naturalist* 16: 1008.

Setser, K. 2007. Use of anesthesia increases precision of snake length measurements. *Herpetological Review* 38: 409.

Shine, C., Shine, N., Shine, R. and Slip, D. 1988. Use of subcaudal scale anomalies as an aid in recognising individual snakes. *Herpetological Review* 19: 79.

Shine, R. 1993. Sexual dimorphism in snakes. In *Snakes: ecology and behavior* (R.A. Seigel and J.T. Collins, editors), pp. 49–86. McGraw-Hill, New York.

Shine, R. 1994. Sexual size dimorphism in snakes revisited. *Copeia* 1994: 326–346.

Shine, R., Amiel, J., Munn, A., Stewart, M., Vyssotski, A. and Lesku, J. 2015. Is cooling then freezing a humane way to kill amphibians and reptiles? *Biology Open* 4: 760–763.

Young, H.C. 1887. Ovo-viviparous generation in *Tropidonotus*. *Proceedings of the Academy of Natural Sciences of Philadelphia* 39: 121.

Wilson, D., Heinsohn, R. and Wood, J. 2006. Life-history traits and ontogenetic colour change in an arboreal tropical python, *Morelia viridis*. *Journal of Zoology* 270: 399–407.

Chapter 5. A snake in the lab is worth two in the bush

Ayers, D.Y. and Shine, R. 1997. Thermal influences on foraging ability: body size, posture and cooling rate of an ambush predator, the python *Morelia spilota*. *Functional Ecology* 11: 342–347.

Baumann, F. 1929. Experimente über den Geruchssinn und den Beuteerwerb der Viper (*Vipera aspis* L.). *Zeitschrift für vergleichende Physiologie* 10: 36–119.

Bechstein, J.M. 1797. *Naturgeschichte; oder, Anleitung zur Kenntniss und Wartung der Säugethiere, Amphibien, Fische, Insecten und Würmer, welche man in der Stube halten kann {Natural History or Guide to Knowledge and Care of Mammals, Amphibians, Fishes, Insects and Worms which can be kept at Home}*. Carl Wilhelm Ettinger, Germany.

Bittner, T.D., King, R.B. and Kerfin, J.M. 2002. Effects of body size and melanism on the thermal biology of garter snakes (*Thamnophis sirtalis*). *Copeia* 2002: 477–482.

Burghardt, G.M. 1969. Comparative prey-attack studies in newborn snakes of the genus *Thamnophis*. *Behaviour* 33: 77–114.

Burghardt, G.M. 1970. Intraspecific geographical variation in chemical food cue preferences of newborn garter snakes (*Thamnophis sirtalis*). *Behaviour* 36: 246–257.

Burghardt, G.M. 1977. Learning processes in reptiles. In *Biology of the Reptilia. Ecology and behaviour A. Volume 7* (C. Gans and D.W. Tinkle, editors), pp. 555–681. Academic Press, Cambridge.

Gans, C. 1974. *Biomechanics: an approach to vertebrate biology*. Lippincott, Philadelphia.

Gibson, A.R. and Falls, J.B. 1979. Thermal biology of the common garter snake *Thamnophis sirtalis* (L.). II. The effects of melanism. *Oecologia* 43: 99–109.

Green, E.E. 1903. Notes on the habits of the green whip-snake. *Spolia Zeylanica* 1: 36–38.

Greenlees, M.J., Webb, J.K. and Shine, R. 2005. Led by the blind: bandy-bandy snakes *Vermicella annulata* (Elapidae) follow blindsnake chemical trails. *Copeia* 2005: 184–187.

Lourdais, O., Brischoux, F. and Barantin, L. 2005. How to assess musculature and performance in a constricting snake? A case study in the Colombian rainbow boa (*Epicrates cenchria maurus*). *Journal of Zoology* 265: 43–51.

Lourdais, O., Brischoux, F., Shine, R. and Bonnet, X. 2005. Adaptive maternal cannibalism in snakes (*Epicrates cenchria maurus*, Boidae). *Biological Journal of the Linnean Society* 84: 767–774.

Luiselli, L. 1996. Individual success in mating balls of the grass snake, *Natrix natrix*: size is important. *Journal of Zoology* 239: 731–740.

Madsen, T. and Shine, R. 1993. Male mating success and body size in European grass snakes. *Copeia* 1993: 561–564.

Mullin, S.J. and Cooper, R.J. 1998. The foraging ecology of the gray rat snake (*Elaphe obsoleta spiloides*)—visual stimuli facilitate location of arboreal prey. *American Midland Naturalist* 140: 397–401.

Mullin, S.J. and Cooper, R.J. 2002. Barking up the wrong tree: climbing performance of rat snakes and its implications for depredation of avian nests. *Canadian Journal of Zoology* 80: 591–595.

Natusch, D.J., Lyons, J.A. and Shine, R. 2017. Safety first: terrestrial predators drive selection of highly specific nesting sites in colonial-breeding birds. *Journal of Avian Biology* 48: 1104–1113.

Noble, G.K. and Clausen, H.J. 1936. The aggregation behavior of *Storeria dekayi* and other snakes, with especial reference to the sense organs involved. *Ecological Monographs* 6: 269–316.

Phillips, B. and Shine, R. 2007. When dinner is dangerous: toxic frogs elicit species-specific responses from a generalist snake predator. *American Naturalist* 170: 936–942.

Phipson, H.M. 1887. The poisonous snakes of the Bombay prefecture. *Journal of the Bombay Natural History Society* 1887: 244–250.

Pore, G. 1888. Correspondence. Can snakes hear? *Journal of the Bombay Natural History Society* 3: 65.

Rudolph, D.C., Kyle, H. and Conner, R.N. 1990. Red-cockaded woodpeckers vs rat snakes: the effectiveness of the resin barrier. *Wilson Bulletin* 102: 14–22.

Shine, R. 1991. Why do larger snakes eat larger prey items? *Functional Ecology* 5: 493–502.

Shine, R. and Shetty, S. 2001. The influence of natural selection and sexual selection on the tails of sea-snakes (*Laticauda colubrina*). *Biological Journal of the Linnean Society* 74: 121–129.

Shine, R., Langkilde, T. and Mason, R.T. 2003. The opportunistic serpent: male garter snakes adjust courtship tactics to mating opportunities. *Behaviour* 140: 1509–1526.

Shine, R., O'Connor, D. and Mason, R.T. 2000. Female mimicry in garter snakes: behavioural tactics of 'she-males' and the males that court them. *Canadian Journal of Zoology* 78: 1391–1396.

Shine, R., O'Connor, D., Lemaster, M.P. and Mason, R.T. 2001. Pick on someone your own size: ontogenetic shifts in mate choice by male garter snakes result in size-assortative mating. *Animal Behaviour* 61: 1133–1141.

Shine, R., Olsson, M.M., Moore, I.T., LeMaster, M.P. and Mason, R.T. 1999. Why do male snakes have longer tails than females? *Proceedings of the Royal Society of London B* 266: 2147–2151.

Shine, R., Olsson, M.M., Moore, I.T., LeMaster, M.P., Greene, M. and Mason, R.T. 2000. Body size enhances mating success in male garter snakes. *Animal Behaviour* 59: F4–F11.

Shine, R., Langkilde, T., Wall, M. and Mason, R.T. 2005. Alternative male mating tactics in garter snakes. *Animal Behaviour* 70: 387–396.

Tyler, Lieutenant. 1849. The serpents of St. Lucia. *Proceedings of the Zoological Society of London* 17: 100–104.

Chapter 6. Long-term experiments in the lab

Arnold, S.J. and Peterson, C.R. 2002. A model for optimal reaction norms: the case of the pregnant garter snake and her temperature-sensitive embryos. *American Naturalist* 160: 306–316.

Aubret, F. and Shine, R. 2008. Early experience influences both habitat choice and locomotor performance in Tigersnakes. *American Naturalist* 171: 524–531.

Aubret, F., Bignon, F., Kok, P.J. and Blanvillain, G. 2016. Only child syndrome in snakes: eggs incubated alone produce asocial individuals. *Scientific Reports* 6: 35752.

Bonnet, X., Shine, R., Naulleau, G. and Thiburce, C. 2001. Plastic vipers: influence of food intake on the size and shape of Gaboon Vipers (*Bitis gabonica*). *Journal of Zoology* 255: 341–351.

Booth, W. and Schuett, G.W. 2016. The emerging phylogenetic pattern of parthenogenesis in snakes. *Biological Journal of the Linnean Society* 118: 172–186.

Bronikowski, A.M. 2000. Experimental evidence for the adaptive evolution of growth rate in the garter snake *Thamnophis elegans*. *Evolution* 54: 1760–1767.

Brown, G.P. and Shine, R. 2005. Do changing moisture levels during incubation influence phenotypic traits of hatchling snakes (*Tropidonophis mairii*, Colubridae)? *Physiological and Biochemical Zoology* 78: 524–530.

Brown, G.P. and Shine, R. 2007. Rain, prey and predators: climatically driven shifts in frog abundance modify reproductive allometry in a tropical snake. *Oecologia* 154: 361–368.

Brown, G.P. and Shine, R. 2007. Like mother, like daughter: inheritance of nest-site location in snakes. *Biology Letters* 3: 131–133.

Brown, G.P., Madsen, T., Dubey, S. and Shine, R. 2017. The causes and ecological correlates of head scale asymmetry and fragmentation in a tropical snake. *Scientific Reports* 7: 11363.

Bull, C.M. 2000. Monogamy in lizards. *Behavioural Processes* 51:7–20.

Burger, J. 1991. Effects of incubation temperature on behavior of hatchling pine snakes: implications for reptilian distribution. *Behavioral Ecology and Sociobiology* 28: 297–303.

Burghardt, G.M., Partin, A.M., Pepper, H.E., Steele, J.M., Liske, S.M., Stokes, A.E., Lathan, A.N., Springer, C.M. and Jenkins, M.S. 2021. Chemically mediated self-recognition in sibling juvenile common gartersnakes (*Thamnophis sirtalis*) reared on same or different diets: evidence for a chemical mirror? *Behaviour* 158: 1169–1191.

Carpenter, C.C. 1977. Communication and displays of snakes. *American Zoologist* 17: 217–223.

Charnier, M. 1966. Action de la temperature sur la sex-ratio chez l'embryon d'*Agama agama* (Agamidae: Lacertilia). *C.R. Seances Societe Biologique L'Ouest Africain* 160: 620–622.

Clark, R.W. 2004. Kin recognition in rattlesnakes. *Proceedings of the Royal Society B* 271: S243–S245.

Noble, G.K. and Clausen, H.J. 1936. The aggregation behavior of *Storeria dekayi* and other snakes, with especial reference to the sense organs involved. *Ecological Monographs* 6: 269–316.

DeKay, J.E. 1842. *Zoology of New-York or the New-York fauna. Part III. Reptiles and amphibia.* W. & A. White & J. Visscher, Albany, New York.

De Haan, C.C. and Cluchier, A. 2006. Chemical marking behaviour in the psammophiine snakes *Malpolon monspessulanus* and *Psammophis phillipsi*. In *Proceedings of the 13th Congress of the Societas Europaea Herpetologica*, pp. 211–212.

Diller, L.V. and Wallace, R.L. 2002. Growth, reproduction, and survival in a population of *Crotalus viridis oreganus* in North Central Idaho. *Herpetological Monographs* 16: 26–45.

Dubach, J., Sajewicz, A. and Pawley, R. 1997. Parthenogenesis in the Arafuran filesnake (*Acrochordus arafurae*). *Herpetological Natural History* 5: 11–18.

Edgehouse, M., Latta IV, L.C., Brodie III, E.D. and Brodie Jr, E.D. 2014. Interspecific aggression and habitat partitioning in garter snakes. *PLoS One* 9: e86208.

Emer, S.A., Mora, C.V., Harvey, M.T. and Grace, M.S. 2015. Predators in training: operant conditioning of novel behavior in wild Burmese Pythons (*Python molurus bivitattus*). *Animal Cognition* 18: 269–278.

Flower, S. 1899. Notes on a second collection of reptiles made in the Malay Peninsula and Siam, from November 1896 to September 1898, with a list of the species recorded from those countries. *Proceedings of the Zoological Society of London* 1899: 600–697.

Ford, N.B. and Seigel, R.A. 1994. An experimental study of the trade-offs between age and size at maturity: effects of energy availability. *Functional Ecology* 8: 91–96.

Friesen, R.R. 2017. Spatial learning of shelter locations and associative learning of a foraging task in the cottonmouth (*Agkistrodon piscivorus*). Masters thesis, Missouri State University.

Glaudas, X., Winne, C.T. and Fedewa, L.A. 2006. Ontogeny of anti-predator behavioral habituation in cottonmouths (*Agkistrodon piscivorus*). *Ethology* 112: 608–615.

Goldberg, S.R. and Rosen, P.C. 2000. Reproduction in the Mojave Rattlesnake, *Crotalus scutulatus* (Serpentes: Viperidae). *Texas Journal of Science* 52: 101–109.

Günther, A.C. 1864. *The reptiles of British India*. Robert Hardwicke, London.

Hampton, R.E. and Gillingham, J.C. 1989. Habituation of the alarm reaction in neonatal eastern garter snakes, *Thamnophis sirtalis*. *Journal of Herpetology* 23: 433–435.

Herzog, H.A.J., Bowers, B.B. and Burghardt, G.M. 1989. Development of antipredator responses in snakes: IV. Interspecific and intraspecific differences in habituation of defensive behavior. *Developmental Psychobiology* 22: 489–508.

Holtzman, D.A., Harris, T.W., Aranguren, G. and Bostock, E. 1999. Spatial learning of an escape task by young corn snakes, *Elaphe guttata guttata*. *Animal Behaviour* 57: 51–60.

Huang, W.S., Greene, H.W., Chang, T.J. and Shine, R. 2011. Territorial behavior in Taiwanese kukrisnakes (*Oligodon formosanus*). *Proceedings of the National Academy of Sciences* 108: 7455–7459.

Li, H., Holleley, C.E., Elphick, M., Georges, A. and Shine, R. 2016. The behavioural consequences of sex reversal in dragons. *Proceedings of the Royal Society B* 283: 20160217.

Lourdais, O., Bonnet, X., Shine, R., DeNardo, D., Naulleau, G. and Guillon, M. 2002. Capital-breeding and reproductive effort in a variable environment: a longitudinal study of a viviparous snake. *Journal of Animal Ecology* 71: 470–479.

Lourdais, O., Brischoux, F., Denardo, D. and Shine, R. 2004. Protein catabolism in pregnant snakes (*Epicrates cenchria maurus* Boidae) compromises musculature and performance after reproduction. *Journal of Comparative Physiology B* 174: 383–391.

Loveridge, A. 1940. A serpent-seeking safari in Equatoria. I. *The Scientific Monthly* 50: 498–512.

Loveridge, A. 1944. *Many happy days I've squandered. Adventures of a naturalist whose life has been one long holiday*. Harper and Brothers, New York.

Löwenborg, K. and Hagman, M. 2017. Scale asymmetries and lateral rib duplication in snakes: correlates and effects on locomotor performance. *Biological Journal of the Linnean Society* 120: 189–194.

Löwenborg, K., Shine, R. and Hagman, M. 2011. Fitness disadvantages to disrupted embryogenesis impose selection against suboptimal nest-site choice by female grass snakes, *Natrix natrix* (Colubridae). *Journal of Evolutionary Biology* 24: 177–183.

Madsen, T. and Shine, R. 1993. Phenotypic plasticity in body sizes and sexual size dimorphism in European grass snakes. *Evolution* 47: 321–325.

Madsen, T. and Shine, R. 2000. Rain, fish and snakes: climatically driven population dynamics of Arafura filesnakes in tropical Australia. *Oecologia* 124: 208–215.

Madsen, T. and Shine, R. 2000. Silver spoons and snake body sizes: prey availability early in life influences long-term growth rates of free-ranging pythons. *Journal of Animal Ecology* 69: 952–958.

Madsen, T., Ujvari, B., Shine, R. and Olsson, M. 2006. Rain, rats and pythons: climate-driven population dynamics of predators and prey in tropical Australia. *Austral Ecology* 31: 30–37.

Massot, M. and Aragon, P. 2013. Phenotypic resonance from a single meal in an insectivorous lizard. *Current Biology* 23: 1320–1323.

McDowell, S.B. 1967. Osteology of the Typhlopidae and Leptotyphlopidae: a critical review. *Copeia* 1967: 686–692.

O'Connor, D.E. and Shine, R. 2004. Parental care protects against infanticide in the lizard *Egernia saxatilis* (Scincidae). *Animal Behaviour* 68: 1361–1369.

Pieau, C. 1971. Sur le proportion sexuelle chez les embryons de deux Chelonians (*Testudo graeca* L. et *Emys orbicularis* L.) issus d'ouefs incubes artificiellement. *Comptes Rendus Academie Sciences de Paris* 272: 3071–3074.

Place, A.J. and Abramson, C.I. 2008. Habituation of the rattle response in western diamondback rattlesnakes, *Crotalus atrox*. *Copeia* 2008: 835–843.

Quelch, J.J. 1888. The boa-constrictors of British Guiana. *Annals and Magazine of Natural History* 1888: 296–308.

Robb, J. 1960. The internal anatomy of *Typhlops schneider* (Reptilia). *Australian Journal of Zoology* 8: 181–216.

Rosen, P.C. and Goldberg, S.R. 2002. Female reproduction in the Western Diamond-backed Rattlesnake, *Crotalus atrox* (Serpentes: Viperidae), from Arizona. *Texas Journal of Science* 54: 347–356.

Roth, E.D. and Lutterschmidt, W.I. 2011. Experimental validation of sex differences in spatial behavior patterns of free-ranging snakes: implications for social interactions. *Ethology* 117: 852–858.

Seigel, R.A. and Ford, N.B. 1992. Effect of energy input on variation in clutch size and offspring size in a viviparous reptile. *Functional Ecology* 6: 382–385.

Sharma, S. 2004. Group hunting and mass feeding by checkered keel-back Water Snake (*Xenochrophis piscator*) in Shipra River. *Reptile RAP* 6: 10.

Shine, R. and Brown, G.P. 2002. Effects of seasonally varying hydric conditions on hatchling phenotypes of keelback snakes (*Tropidonophis mairii*, Colubridae) from the Australian wet-dry tropics. *Biological Journal of the Linnean Society* 76: 339–347.

Shine, R., Langkilde, T., Wall, M. and Mason, R.T. 2005. The fitness correlates of scalation asymmetry in garter snakes *Thamnophis sirtalis parietalis*. *Functional Ecology* 19: 306–314.

Shine, R., Shine, T., Shine, J.M. and Shine, B.G. 2005. Synchrony in capture dates suggests cryptic social organization in seasnakes (*Emydocephalus annulatus*, Hydrophiidae). *Austral Ecology* 30: 805–811.

Skinner, M., Hazell, M., Jameson, J. and Lougheed, S.C. 2023. Social networks reveal sex-and age-patterned social structure in Butler's gartersnakes (*Thamnophis butleri*). *Behavioral Ecology* 35: arad095.

Somaweera, R., Udyawer, V., Amarasinghe, A.T., de Fresnes, J., Catherall, J. and Molchanova, G. 2023. Apparent coordinated and communal hunting behaviours by Erabu sea krait *Laticauda semifactiata*. *Scientific Reports* 13: 21471.

Stone, A., Ford, N.B. and Holtzman, D.A. 2000. Spatial learning and shelter selection by juvenile spotted pythons, *Anteresia maculosus*. *Journal of Herpetology* 34: 575–587.

Webb, J.K., Scott, M.L., Whiting, M.J. and Shine, R. 2015. Territoriality in a snake. *Behavioral Ecology and Sociobiology* 69: 1657–1661.

Chapter 7. Using radio transmitters to pry into the snake's private life

Brischoux, F., Bonnet, X. and Shine, R. 2009. Kleptothermy: an additional category of thermoregulation, and a possible example in sea kraits (*Laticauda laticaudata*, Serpentes). *Biology Letters* 5: 729–731.

Corkery, I., Bell, B.D. and Nelson, N.J. 2014. Investigating kleptothermy: a reptile-seabird association with thermal benefits. *Physiological and Biochemical Zoology* 87: 216–221.

Duvall, D., Goode, M.J., Hayes, W.K., Leonhardt, J.K. and Brown, D.G. 1990. Prairie rattlesnake: field experimental analyses and survival value. *National Geographic Research* 6: 457–469.

Fitch, H.S. and Shirer, H.W. 1971. A radiotelemetric study of spatial relationships in some common snakes. *Copeia* 1971: 118–128.

Harlow, P. and Shine, R. 1988. Voluntary ingestion of radiotransmitters by snakes in the field. *Herpetological Review* 19: 57.

Heath, J.E. 1964. Reptilian thermoregulation: evaluation of field studies. *Science* 146: 784–785.

Hertz, P.E., Huey, R.B. and Stevenson, R.D. 1993. Evaluating temperature regulation by field-active ectotherms: the fallacy of the inappropriate question. *American Naturalist* 142: 796–818.

Holding, M.L., Frazier, J.A., Taylor, E.N. and Strand, C.R. 2012. Experimentally altered navigational demands induce changes in the cortical forebrain of free-ranging Northern Pacific Rattlesnakes (*Crotalus o. oreganus*). *Brain, Behavior and Evolution* 79: 144–154.

Houston, D. and Shine, R. 1994. Movements and activity patterns of Arafura filesnakes (Serpentes: Acrochordidae) in tropical Australia. *Herpetologica* 50: 349–357.

Huey, R.B., Peterson, C.R., Arnold, S.J. and Porter, W.P. 1989. Hot rocks and not-so-hot rocks: retreat-site selection by garter snakes and its thermal consequences. *Ecology* 70: 931–944.

Hyslop, N.L. 2009. Survival of radio-implanted Eastern Indigo Snakes (*Drymarchon couperi*) in relation to body size and sex. *Herpetologica* 65: 199–206.

Macartney, J.M., Gregory, P.T. and Larsen, K.W. 1988. A tabular survey of data on movements and home ranges of snakes. *Journal of Herpetology* 22: 61–73.

Madsen, T. and Shine, R. 1996. Seasonal migration of predators and prey – A study of pythons and rats in tropical Australia. *Ecology* 77: 149–156.

McGinnis, S.M. and Moore, R.G. 1969. Thermoregulation in the boa constrictor *Boa constrictor*. *Herpetologica* 25: 38–45.

Mosauer, W. 1933. Locomotion and diurnal range of *Sonora occipitalis*, *Crotalus cerastes*, and *Crotalus atrox* as seen from their tracks. *Copeia* 1933: 14–16.

Natusch, D., Lyons, J., Mears, L.A. and Shine, R. 2021. Biting off more than you can chew: attempted predation on a human by a giant snake (*Simalia amethistina*). *Austral Ecology* 46: 159–162.

Natusch, D.J.D., Lyons, J.A. and Shine, R. 2021. Rainforest pythons flexibly adjust foraging ecology to exploit seasonal concentrations of prey. *Journal of Zoology* 313: 114–123.

Osgood, D.W. 1970. Thermoregulation in water snakes studied by telemetry. *Copeia* 1970: 568–571.

Pearson, D.J. and Shine, R. 2002. Expulsion of interperitoneally-implanted radiotransmitters by Australian pythons. *Herpetological Review* 33: 261–263.

Reinert, H.K. and Cundall, D. 1982. An improved surgical implantation method for radio-tracking snakes. *Copeia* 1982: 702–705.

Reinert, H.K. 1984. Habitat separation between sympatric snake populations. *Ecology* 65: 478–486.

Reinert, H.K. 1984. Habitat variation within sympatric snake populations. *Ecology* 65: 1673–1682.

Schlegel, H. 1837. *Essai sur la physionomie des serpents. I. Partie générale. II. Partie descriptive*. Schonekat, Amsterdam.

Shine, R. 1979. Activity patterns in Australian elapid snakes (Squamata: Serpentes: Elapidae). *Herpetologica* 35: 1–11.

Shine, R. 1987. Intraspecific variation in thermoregulation, movements and habitat use by Australian blacksnakes, *Pseudechis porphyriacus* (Elapidae). *Journal of Herpetology* 21: 165–177.

Udyawer, V., Goiran, C. and Shine, R. 2021. Peaceful coexistence between people and deadly wildlife: why are recreational users of the ocean so rarely bitten by seasnakes? *People and Nature* 3: 335–346.

Udyawer, V., Goiran, C., Chateau, O. and Shine, R. 2020. Swim with the tide: tactics to maximize prey detection by a specialist predator, the greater seasnake (*Hydrophis major*). *PLoS One* 15: e0239920.

Újvári, B. and Korsós, Z. 2000. Use of radiotelemetry on snakes: a review. *Acta Zoologica Academiae Scientiarum Hungaricae* 46: 115–146.

Webb, J.K. and Shine, R. 1997. A field study of spatial ecology and movements of a threatened snake species, *Hoplocephalus bungaroides*. *Biological Conservation* 82: 203–217.

Whitaker, P.B. and Shine, R. 1999. Responses of free-ranging brownsnakes (*Pseudonaja textilis*: Elapidae) to encounters with humans. *Wildlife Research* 26: 689–704.

Whitaker, P.B. and Shine, R. 2003. A radiotelemetric study of movements and shelter-site selection by free-ranging brownsnakes (*Pseudonaja textilis*, Elapidae). *Herpetological Monographs* 17: 130–144.

Chapter 8. Testing hypotheses in the field

Aubret, F., Michniewicz, R.J. and Shine, R. 2011. Correlated geographic variation in predation risk and antipredator behaviour within a wide-ranging snake species (*Notechis scutatus*, Elapidae). *Austral Ecology* 36: 446–452.

Beck, D.D. 1996. Effects of feeding on body temperatures of rattlesnakes: a field experiment. *Physiological Zoology* 69: 1442–1455.

Beyer, G.E. 1898. Contributions on the life histories of certain snakes. *American Naturalist* 32: 17–24.

Bjelica, V. and Golubović, A. 2024. Synergistic effects of musking and autohaemorrhaging on the duration of death feigning in dice snakes (*Natrix tessellata*). *Biology Letters* 20: 20240058.

Blouin-Demers, G. and Weatherhead, P.J. 2001. An experimental test of the link between foraging, habitat selection and thermoregulation in black rat snakes *Elaphe obsoleta obsoleta*. *Journal of Animal Ecology* 70: 1006–1013.

Bonnet, X., Lecq, S., Lassay, J.L., Ballouard, J.M., Barbraud, C., Souchet, J., Mullin, S.J. and Provost, G. 2016. Forest management bolsters native snake populations in urban parks. *Biological Conservation* 193: 1–8.

Brown, G.P. and Shine, R. 2004. Effects of reproduction on the antipredator tactics of snakes (*Tropidonophis mairii*, Colubridae). *Behavioral Ecology and Sociobiology* 56: 257–262.

Brown, G.P. and Weatherhead, P.J. 2000. Thermal ecology and sexual size dimorphism in northern water snakes, *Nerodia sipedon*. *Ecological Monographs* 70: 311–330.

Capehart, G.D., Escallón, C., Vernasco, B.J., Moore, I.T. and Taylor, E.N. 2016. No drought about it: effects of supplemental hydration on the ecology, behavior, and physiology of free-ranging rattlesnakes. *Journal of Arid Environments* 134: 79–86.

Farrell, T.M., May, P.G. and Andreadis, P.T. 2011. Experimental manipulation of tail color does not affect foraging success in a caudal luring rattlesnake. *Journal of Herpetology* 45: 291–293.

Fernandes, I.Y., Koch, E.D. and Monico, A.T. 2023. First record of a snake call in South America: the unusual sounds of an Ornate Snail-eater *Dipsas catesbyi*. *Acta Amazonica* 53: 243–245.

Glaudas, X. and Alexander, G.J. 2017. Food supplementation affects the foraging ecology of a low-energy, ambush-foraging snake. *Behavioral Ecology and Sociobiology* 71: 5.

Huxley, T.H. 1887. The progress of science. In *The Reign of Queen Victoria: a survey of fifty years of progress* (T.H. Ward, editor), pp. 322–387. Smith, Elder, London.

Jojola-Elverum, S.M., Shivik, J.A. and Clark, L. 2001. Importance of bacterial decomposition, and carrion substrate to foraging, brown treesnakes. *Journal of Chemical Ecology* 27: 1315–1331.

Lemaster, M.P., Moore, I.T. and Mason, R.T. 2001. Conspecific trailing behaviour of red-sided garter snakes, *Thamnophis sirtalis parietalis*, in the natural environment. *Animal Behaviour* 61: 827–833.

MacGowan, B.J., Currylow, A.F. and MacNeil, J.E. 2017. Short-term responses of Timber Rattlesnakes (*Crotalus horridus*) to even-aged timber harvests in Indiana. *Forest Ecology and Management* 387: 30–36.

McCauley, D.J., Keesing, F., Young, T.P., Allan, B.F. and Pringle, R.M. 2006. Indirect effects of large herbivores on snakes in an African savanna. *Ecology* 87: 2657–2663.

Madsen, T., Shine, R., Loman, J. and Håkansson, T. 1992. Why do female adders copulate so frequently? *Nature* 355: 440–441.

Mao, J.J. 2004. Population ecology of genus *Sinonatrix* in Taiwan. PhD thesis, University of Trier, Germany.

Maritz, B. 2012. To run or hide? Escape behaviour in a cryptic African snake. *African Zoology* 47: 270–1274.

Mason, R.T., Fales, H.M., Jones, T.H., Pannell, L.K., Chinn, J.W. and Crews, D. 1989. Sex pheromones in snakes. *Science* 245: 290–293.

Murphy, J.B. 2015. Studies on non-venomous colubrid snakes and a few other families in zoos and aquariums. *Herpetological Review* 46: 119–134.

Parker, M.R. and Mason, R.T. 2016. Pheromones in snakes: history, patterns and future research directions. In *Reproductive Biology and Phylogeny of Snakes* (D.M. Sever and R.D. Aldridge, editors), pp. 551–572. CRC Press, Florida.

Parker, M.R. and Kardong, K.V. 2017. Airborne chemical information and context-dependent post-strike foraging behavior in Pacific Rattlesnakes (*Crotalus oreganus*). *Copeia* 105: 649–656.

Perez-Martinez, C. and Vallejos, J.G. 2023. Squeaks in the dark: vocalisations in the Claw-snouted Blind Snake, *Anilios unguirostris* (Peters, 1867). *Herpetology Notes* 16: 885–887.

Pike, D.A., Webb, J.K. and Shine, R. 2011. Removing forest canopy cover restores a reptile assemblage. *Ecological Applications* 21: 274–280.

Pope, C.H. 1958. *Snakes alive and how they live*. Viking Press, New York.

Reed, R.N., Hart, K.M., Rodda, G.H., Mazzotti, F.J., Snow, R.W., Cherkiss, M., Rozar, R. and Goetz, S. 2011. A field test of attractant traps for invasive Burmese Pythons (*Python molurus bivittatus*) in southern Florida. *Wildlife Research* 38: 114–121.

Rivas, J.A. and Burghardt, G.M. 2001. Understanding sexual size dimorphism in snakes: wearing the snake's shoes. *Animal Behaviour* 62: F1–F6.

Roe, J.H., Frank, M.R., Gibson, S.E., Attum, O. and Kingsbury, B.A. 2010. No place like home: an experimental comparison of reintroduction strategies using snakes. *Journal of Applied Ecology* 47: 1253–1261.

Roth, E.D., May, P.G. and Farrell, T.M. 1999. Pigmy Rattlesnakes use frog-derived chemical cues to select foraging sites. *Copeia* 1999: 772–774.

Shine, R. 2005. All at sea: aquatic life modifies mate-recognition modalities in seasnakes (*Emydocephalus annulatus*, Hydrophiidae). *Behavioral Ecology and Sociobiology* 57: 591–598.

Shine, R. 2012. Sex at the snake den: lust, deception and conflict in the mating system of red-sided gartersnakes. *Advances in the Study of Behaviour* 44: 1–51.

Shine, R. and Mason, R.T. 2012. An airborne sex pheromone in snakes. *Biology Letters* 8: 183–185.

Shine, R. and Sun, L.X. 2003. Attack strategy of an ambush predator: which attributes of the prey trigger a pit-viper's strike? *Functional Ecology* 17: 340–348.

Shine, R., Brown, G.P. and Elphick, M.J. 2004. Field experiments on foraging in free-ranging water snakes *Enhydris polylepis* (Homalopsinae). *Animal Behaviour* 68: 1313–1324.

Shine, R., Sun, L., Fitzgerald, M. and Kearney, M. 2002. Antipredator responses of free-ranging pitvipers (*Gloydius shedaoensis*, Viperidae). *Copeia* 2002: 843–850.

Shine, R., Olsson, M.M., Lemaster, M.P., Moore, I.T. and Mason, R.T. 2000. Effects of sex, body size, temperature and location on the antipredator tactics of free-ranging gartersnakes (*Thamnophis sirtalis*, Colubridae). *Behavioral Ecology* 11: 239–245.

Shine, R., Phillips, B., Waye, H., LeMaster, M. and Mason, R.T. 2003. Chemosensory cues allow courting male garter snakes to assess body length and body condition of potential mates. *Behavioral Ecology and Sociobiology* 54: 162–166.

Shine, R., Phillips, B., Waye, H. and Mason, R.T. 2003. Behavioral shifts associated with reproduction in garter snakes. *Behavioral Ecology* 14: 251–256.

Shine, R., Bonnet, X. and Cogger, H.G. 2003. Antipredator tactics of amphibious sea-snakes (Serpentes, Laticaudidae). *Ethology* 109: 533–542.

Shine, R., Wall, M., Langkilde, T. and Mason, R.T. 2005. Scaling the heights: thermally driven arboreality in garter snakes. *Journal of Thermal Biology* 30: 179–185.

Shine, R., Wall, M., Langkilde, T. and Mason, R.T. 2005. Do female garter snakes evade males to avoid harassment or to enhance mate quality? *American Naturalist* 165: 660–668.

Shivik, J.A. and Clark, L. 1997. Carrion seeking in brown tree snakes: importance of olfactory and visual cues. *Journal of Experimental Zoology* 279: 549–553.

Siers, S.R., Yackel Adams, A.A. and Reed, R.N. 2018. Behavioral differences following ingestion of large meals and consequences for management of a harmful invasive snake: a field experiment. *Ecology and Evolution* 8: 10075–10093.

Steen, D.A., Osborne, P.A., Dovciak, M., Patrick, D.A. and Gibbs, J.P. 2015. A preliminary investigation into the short-term effects of a prescribed fire on habitat quality for a snake assemblage. *Herpetological Conservation and Biology* 10: 263–272.

Taylor, E.N., Malawy, M.A., Browning, D.M., Lemar, S.V. and DeNardo, D.F. 2005. Effects of food supplementation on the physiological ecology of female western diamond-backed rattlesnakes (*Crotalus atrox*). *Oecologia* 144: 206–213.

Tsairi, H. and Bouskila, A. 2004. Ambush site selection of a desert snake (*Echis coloratus*) at an oasis. *Herpetologica* 60: 13–23.

Udyawer, V., Goiran, C., Chateau, O. and Shine, R. 2020. Swim with the tide: tactics to maximise prey detection by a specialist predator, the greater sea snake (*Hydrophis major*). *PLoS One* 15: e0239920.

Wasko, D.K. and Sasa, M. 2012. Food resources influence spatial ecology, habitat selection, and foraging behavior in an ambush-hunting snake (Viperidae: *Bothrops asper*): an experimental study. *Zoology* 115: 179–187.

Webb, J.K. and Shine, R. 2000. Paving the way for habitat restoration: can artificial rocks restore degraded habitats of endangered reptiles? *Biological Conservation* 92: 93–99.

Webb, J.K., Shine, R. and Pringle, R.M. 2005. Canopy removal restores habitat quality for an endangered snake in a fire suppressed landscape. *Copeia* 2005: 894–900.

Chapter 9. Studying snakes without studying snakes

Andren, C. and Nilson, G. 1981. Reproductive success and risk of predation in normal and melanistic colour morphs of the adder, *Vipera berus*. *Biological Journal of the Linnean Society* 15: 235–246.

Aubret, F. and Mangin, A. 2014. The snake hiss: potential acoustic mimicry in a Viper–Colubrid complex. *Biological Journal of the Linnean Society* 113: 1107–1114.

Bates, H.W. 1863. *The naturalist on the river Amazons: a record of adventures, habits of animals, sketches of Brazilian and Indian life, and aspects of nature under the Equator, during eleven years of travel*. J. Murray, London.

Beckmann, C. and Shine, R. 2012. Do drivers intentionally target wildlife on roads? *Austral Ecology* 37: 629–632.

Bouskila, A. 1995. Interactions between predation risk and competition: a field study of kangaroo rats and snakes. *Ecology* 76: 165–178.

Breviglieri, C.P.B. and Romero, G.Q. 2016. Snakes and forbidden fruits: non-consumptive effects of snakes on the behaviors of frugivorous birds. *Behavioral Ecology and Sociobiology* 70: 777–783.

Brischoux, F. and Lillywhite, H.B. 2011. Light-and flotsam-dependent 'float-and-wait' foraging by pelagic seasnakes (*Pelamis platurus*). *Marine Biology* 158: 2343–2347.

Brodie, E.D. 1993. Differential avoidance of coral snake banded patterns by free-ranging avian predators in Costa Rica. *Evolution* 47: 227–235.

Brodie III, E.D. and Janzen, F.J. 1995. Experimental studies of coral snake mimicry: generalized avoidance of ringed snake patterns by free-ranging avian predators. *Functional Ecology* 9: 186–190.

Collinson, W.J., Marneweck, C. and Davies-Mostert, H.T. 2019. Protecting the protected: reducing wildlife roadkill in protected areas. *Animal Conservation* 22: 396–403.

Cyriac, V.P. and Kodandaramaiah, U. 2019. Conspicuous colours reduce predation rates in fossorial uropeltid snakes. *PeerJ* 7: e7508.

De Solan, T., Renoult, J.P., Geniez, P., David, P. and Crochet, P.A. 2020. Looking for mimicry in a snake assemblage using deep learning. *American Naturalist* 196: 74–86.

Downes, S. and Shine, R. 1998. Sedentary snakes and gullible geckos: predator–prey coevolution in nocturnal rock-dwelling reptiles. *Animal Behaviour* 55: 1373–1385.

Downes, S.J. 2002. Does responsiveness to predator scents affect lizard survivorship? *Behavioral Ecology and Sociobiology* 52: 38–42.

Dutton, G. 1890. Mimicry in the animal world. *Victorian Naturalist* 7: 78–82.

Flower, S.S. 1899. Notes on a second collection of reptiles made in the Malay Peninsula and Siam, from November 1896 to September 1898, with a list of species recorded from those countries. *Proceedings of the Zoological Society of London* 1899: 600–696.

Glaudas, X. and Alexander, G.J. 2017. A lure at both ends: aggressive visual mimicry signals and prey-specific luring behaviour in an ambush-foraging snake. *Behavioral Ecology and Sociobiology* 71: 2.

Goiran, C., Shine, T. and Shine, R. 2022. The banded colour patterns of seasnakes discourage attack by predatory fishes, enabling Batesian mimicry by harmless species. *Proceedings of the Royal Society B* 289: 20221759.

Goode, G.B. 1873. Mimicry in snakes. *American Naturalist* 7: 747–748.

Griffiths, R.A., Schley, L., Sharp, P.E., Dennis, J.L. and Roman, A. 1998. Behavioural responses of Mallorcan midwife toad tadpoles to natural and unnatural snake predators. *Animal Behaviour* 55: 207–214.

Hagman, M., Phillips, B.L. and Shine, R. 2008. Tails of enticement: caudal luring by an ambush-foraging snake (*Acanthophis praelongus*, Elapidae). *Functional Ecology* 22: 1134–1139.

Kotler, B.P., Brown, J.S., Slotow, R.H., Goodfriend, W.L. and Strauss, M. 1993. The influence of snakes on the foraging behavior of gerbils. *Oikos* 67: 309–316.

Liu, J. and Liang, W. 2021. Snake slough in birds' nests acts as a nest predator deterrent. *Ethology Ecology & Evolution* 33: 591–602.

Madsen, T. 1987. Are juvenile grass snakes, *Natrix natrix*, aposematically coloured? *Oikos* 48: 265–267.

Madsen, T., Stille, B., Ujvari, B., Bauwens, D. and Endler, J.A. 2022. Negative frequency-dependent selection on polymorphic color morphs in adders. *Current Biology* 32: 3385–3388.

Mario-da-Rosa, C., Abegg, A.D., Malta-Borges, L., Righi, A.F., Bernarde, P.S., Cechin, S.Z. and Santos, T.G.D. 2020. A fisherman's tale: activity, habitat use and the first evidence of lingual lure behavior in a South American snake. *Salamandra* 56: 39–47.

Martínez-Freiría, F., Toyama, K.S., Freitas, I. and Kaliontzopoulou, A. 2020. Thermal melanism explains macroevolutionary variation of dorsal pigmentation in Eurasian vipers. *Scientific Reports* 10: 16122.

Medlin, E.C. and Risch, T.S. 2006. An experimental test of snake skin use to deter nest predation. *The Condor* 108: 963–965.

Miller, A.K. 2022. Scents and Scentability: An Investigation into the Chemical Crypsis of the Puff Adder (Bitis arietans). PhD thesis, University of the Witwatersrand, Johannesburg.

Moore, R.D., Griffiths, R.A., O'Brien, C.M., Murphy, A. and Jay, D. 2004. Induced defences in an endangered amphibian in response to an introduced snake predator. *Oecologia* 141: 139–147.

Mouy, H. 2024a. The function of red and banded patterns in snakes: a review of hypotheses and evidence. *Biological Journal of the Linnean Society* 142: 351–374.

Mouy, H. 2024b. The function of red and banded patterns in snakes: the eyes of the beholders – also, the function of bands in fish. *Biological Journal of the Linnean Society* 142: 452–467.

Niskanen, M. and Mappes, J. 2005. Significance of the dorsal zigzag pattern of *Vipera latastei gaditana* against avian predators. *Journal of Animal Ecology* 74: 1091–1101.

Preest, M.R., Ward, M.J., Poon, T. and Hermanson, J.W. 2016. Chemical prey luring in Jackson's chameleons. *Physiological and Biochemical Zoology* 89: 110–117.

Reiserer, R.S. 2002. Stimulus control of caudal luring and other feeding responses: a program for research on visual perception in vipers. In *Biology of the vipers* (G.W. Schuett, M. Höggren, M.E. Douglas and H.W. Greene editors), pp. 361–383. Eagle Mountain Publishing, Utah.

Rohwer, V.G., Houtz, J.L., Vitousek, M.N., Bailey, R.L. and Miller, E.T. 2025. The evolution of using shed snake skin in bird nests. *American Naturalist* in press. https://doi.org/10.1086/733208

Santos, X., Azor, J.S., Cortés, S., Rodríguez, E., Larios, J. and Pleguezuelos, J.M. 2018. Ecological significance of dorsal polymorphism in a Batesian mimic snake. *Current Zoology* 64: 745–753.

Sena, A.T. and Ruane, S. 2022. Concepts and contentions of coral snake resemblance: Batesian mimicry and its alternatives. *Biological Journal of the Linnean Society* 135: 631–644.

Shine, R. and Downes, S.J. 1999. Can pregnant lizards adjust their offspring phenotypes to environmental conditions? *Oecologia* 119: 1–8.

Smith, S. 1975. Innate recognition of coral snake pattern by a possible avian predator. *Science* 187: 759–760.

Stradling, A. 1890. Mistakes about snakes. Part I. *The Boy's Own Paper* 13: 58–59.

Stuart-Fox, D., Whiting, M.J. and Moussalli, A. 2006. Camouflage and colour change: antipredator responses to bird and snake predators across multiple populations in a dwarf chameleon. *Biological Journal of the Linnean Society* 88: 437–446.

Sullivan, A.M., Madison, D.M. and Maerz, J.C. 2005. Nocturnal shift in the antipredator response to predator-diet cues in laboratory and field trials. In *Chemical signals in vertebrates 10* (R.T. Mason, M.P. LeMaster and D. Müller-Schwarze, editors), pp. 349–356. Springer, Boston.

Sullivan, A.M., Maerz, J.C. and Madison, D.M. 2002. Anti-predator response of red-backed salamanders (*Plethodon cinereus*) to chemical cues from garter snakes (*Thamnophis sirtalis*): laboratory and field experiments. *Behavioral Ecology and Sociobiology* 51: 227–233.

Tooke, W.H. 1886. Mimicry in snakes. *Nature* 34: 547.

Valkonen, J.K. and Mappes, J. 2014. Resembling a viper: implications of mimicry for conservation of the endangered smooth snake. *Conservation Biology* 28: 1568–1574.

Waite, E.R. 1898. *A popular account of Australian snakes: with a complete list of the species and an introduction to their habits and organisation*. Thomas Shine, Sydney.

Wallace, A.R. 1879. The protective colours of animals. In *Science for all. Volume 2* (C.H. Smith, editor), pp. 128–137. Cassell, Petter, Galpin & Co., London.

Wallace, A.R. 1867. Mimicry, and other protective resemblances among animals. *Westminster Review. New Series*. 32: 1–43.

Wasko, D.K., Bonilla, F. and Sasa, M. 2014. Behavioral responses to snake cues by three species of Neotropical rodents. *Journal of Zoology* 292: 142–150.

Webb, J.K., Pike, D.A. and Shine, R. 2010. Olfactory recognition of predators by nocturnal lizards: safety outweighs thermal benefits. *Behavioral Ecology* 21: 72–77.

Werner, Y.L. and Frankenberg, E. 1982. Head triangulation in two colubrine snakes: probable behavioural reinforcement of Batesian mimicry. *Israel Journal of Zoology* 31: 137–150.

Wilson, D., Heinsohn, R. and Endler, J.A. 2007. The adaptive significance of ontogenetic colour change in a tropical python. *Biology Letters* 3: 40–43.

Wilson, L., Lonsdale, G., Curlis, J.D., Hunter, E.A. and Cox, C.L. 2022. Predator-based selection and the impact of edge sympatry on components of coral snake mimicry. *Evolutionary Ecology* 36: 135–149.

Wüster, W., Allum, C.S., Bjargardóttir, I.B., Bailey, K.L., Dawson, K.J., Guenioui, J., Lewis, J., McGurk, J., Moore, A.G., Niskanen, M. and Pollard, C.P. 2004. Do aposematism and Batesian mimicry require bright colours? A test, using European viper markings. *Proceedings of the Royal Society of London B* 271: 2495–2499.

Young, B.A. 1991. Morphological basis of 'growling' in the king cobra, *Ophiophagus hannah*. *Journal of Experimental Zoology* 260: 275–287.

Young, B.A. 1997. A review of sound production and hearing in snakes, with a discussion of intraspecific acoustic communication in snakes. *Journal of the Pennsylvania Academy of Science* 71: 39–46.

Young, B.A. 2003. Snake bioacoustics: toward a richer understanding of the behavioral ecology of snakes. *Quarterly Review of Biology* 78: 303–325.

Young, B.A., Solomon, J. and Abishahin, G.E.E. 1999. How many ways can a snake growl? The morphology of sound production in *Ptyas mucosus* and its potential mimicry of *Ophiophagus*. *Herpetological Journal* 9: 89–94.

Chapter 10. The pioneers: a ragtag assemblage of zealots

Beyer, G.E. 1898. Contributions on the life histories of certain snakes. *American Naturalist* 32: 17–24.

Blanchard, F.N. and Blanchard, F.C. 1940. Factors determining time of birth in the garter snake *Thamnophis sirtalis sirtalis* (Linnaeus). *Papers from the Michigan Academy of Science, Arts and Letters* 26: 161–176.

Blanchard, F.N. and Blanchard, F.C. 1940. The inheritance of melanism in the garter snake *Thamnophis sirtalis sirtalis* (Linnaeus), and some evidence of effective autumn mating. *Papers from the Michigan Academy of Science, Arts and Letters* 26: 177–193.

Bonnet, X., Ineich, I. and Shine, R. 2005. Terrestrial locomotion in seasnakes: the effects of sex and species on cliff-climbing ability in sea kraits (Serpentes, Elapidae, *Laticauda*). *Biological Journal of the Linnean Society* 85: 433–441.

Boulenger, G.A. 1885. XXXVI.—Remarks on Mr CW De Vis's recent contributions to the Herpetology of Australia. *Journal of Natural History* 16: 386–387.

Calmette, A. 1896. The treatment of animals poisoned with snake venom by the injection of antivenomous serum. *British Medical Journal* 2: 399.

Cushing, N. and Markwell, K. 2009. Balancing biography and institutional history: Eric Worrell's Australian Reptile Park. *Public History Review* 16: 78–91.

De Rooij, N. 1917. *The reptiles of the Indo-Australian archipelago: Ophidia* (Vol. 2). E.J. Brill, Netherlands.

Fitch, H.S. 1960. Autecology of the copperhead. *University of Kansas Museum of Natural History, Miscellaneous Publications* 52: 1–247.

Fitch, H.S. 1999. *A Kansas snake community: composition and changes over 50 years*. Kreiger Publishing, Florida.

Fitch, H.S. and Pisani, G.R. 2020. University of Kansas Field Station: cumulative field records of snake species collected by Dr Henry S. Fitch 1948–2003, with a few additional records collected 2004–2016. Records contain capture locations, measurements, notes on reproduction, recapture, and growth data. This data package contains individual files for 14 species. ver 1. Environmental Data Initiative. https://doi.org/10.6073/pasta/e7ef3cdfb1723f97cbb82ffc29ba2527.

Fitch, H.S. 1949. Study of snake populations in central California. *The American Midland Naturalist* 41: 513–579.

Fleay, D. 1943. The brown snake – a dangerous fellow. *Victorian Naturalist* 59: 147–152.

Fleay, D. 1981. *Living with animals*. Booralong Publications, Brisbane.

Fukada, H. 1992. *Snake life history in Kyoto*. Impact Shuppankai, Tokyo.

Gadow, H. 1901. *Amphibians and reptiles*. MacMillan, UK.

Gans, Carl. 1978. All animals are interesting! *American Zoologist* 1978: 3–9.

Gregory, P.T. and Stewart, K.W. 1975. Long-distance dispersal and feeding strategy of the red-sided garter snake (*Thamnophis sirtalis parietalis*) in the Interlake of Manitoba. *Canadian Journal of Zoology* 53: 238–245.

Hay, O.P. 1887. The massasauga and its habits. *American Naturalist* 21: 211–218.

Kopstein, F. 1932. The poisonous animals of Java, and their significance for mankind. *Mededeelingen van den Dienst der Volksgezondheid in Nederlandsch-Indie* 1932: 222–256.

Laker, L. 1998. David Fleay: Australian naturalist and educator [Paper presented to the Royal Historical Society of Queensland on 5 November 1997]. *Journal of the Royal Historical Society of Queensland*, 17: 515–524.

Lockwood, S. 1875. The pine snake of New Jersey. *American Naturalist* 9: 1–14.

Lourdais, O., Brischoux, F. and Barantin, L. 2005. How to assess musculature and performance in a constricting snake? A case study in the Colombian rainbow boa (*Epicrates cenchria maurus*). *Journal of Zoology* 265: 43–51.

Markwell, K. and Cushing, N. 2010. *Snake bitten: Eric Worrell and the Australian Reptile Park*. UNSW Press, Sydney.

Mell, R. 1929a. *Beitrage zur Fauna Sinica. IV. Grundzuge einer Okologie der Chinesischen Reptilien und einer*

Herpetologischen Tiergeographie Chinas. Walter de Gruyter, Berlin.

Mell, R. 1929b. 1931. Preliminary contributions to an ecology of East Asiatic reptiles, especially snakes. *Lingnan Science Journa*l 8: 187–197.

Mendyk, R.W. 2022. A peculiar case of ophiomania: the herpetological pursuits, contributions and advocacy of Arthur Stradling (1851–1902). *Bibliotheca Herpetologica* 16: 14–32.

Murphy, J.B. and Card, W. 1998. A glimpse into the life of a zoo herpetologist. *Herpetological Review* 29: 85–91.

Natusch, D.J., Lyons, J.A. and Shine, R. 2017. Safety first: terrestrial predators drive selection of highly specific nesting sites in colonial-breeding birds. *Journal of Avian Biology* 48: 1104–1113.

Naulleau, G. 1964. Première observations sur le comportement de chasse et de capture chez les vipères et les couleuvres. *Revue d'Écologie (La Terre et La Vie)* 18: 54–76.

Natusch, D., Aust, P.W., Caraguel, C., Taggart, P.L., Alexander, G.J., Shine, R. and Coulson, T. 2024. Python farming as a flexible and efficient form of agricultural food security. *Scientific Reports* 14: 5419.

Pope, C.H. 1935. *The reptiles of China*. American Museum of Natural History, New York.

Saint Girons, H. 1982. Reproductive cycles of male snakes and their relationships with climate and female reproductive cycles. *Herpetologica* 38: 5–16.

Saint Girons, H., Bradshaw, S.D. and Bradshaw, F.J. 1993. Sexual activity and plasma levels of sex steroids in the aspic viper *Vipera aspis* L.(Reptilia, Viperidae). *General and Comparative Endocrinology* 91: 287–297.

Shine, R. and Koenig, J. 2001. Snakes in the garden: an analysis of reptiles 'rescued' by community-based wildlife carers. *Biological Conservation* 102: 271–283.

Shine, R. and Spawls, S. 2020. An ecological analysis of snakes captured by CJP Ionides in eastern Africa in the mid–1900s. *Scientific Reports* 10: 5096.

Shine, R. 2002. Do dietary habits predict scale counts in snakes? *Journal of Herpetology* 36: 268–272.

Volsøe, H. 1944. Structure and seasonal variation of the male reproductive organs of *Vipera berus (L.) Spolia zoologica Musei Hauniensis* 5: 7–157.

Wall, F. 1921. *Ophidia Taprobanica or the snakes of Ceylon*. H.R. Cottle, Government Printer, Ceylon.

Worrell, E. 1963. *Reptiles of Australia: crocodiles, turtles, tortoises, lizards, snakes; describing all Australian species, their appearance, their haunts, their habits*. Angus & Robertson, Sydney.

Chapter 11. Fallen fighters: casualties of the revolution

Cann, J. 2014. *Historical snakeys*. ECO Herpetological Publishing & Distribution, New Mexico.

Coniff, R. 2023. https://strangebehaviors.wordpress.com/2011/01/14/the-wall-of-the-dead/

Gewolb, J. 2001. Venomous bite kills snake researcher. *Science* 294: 45.

Gow, G.F. 1983. *Snakes of Australia*. Harper Collins Publishers, Sydney.

Haast, W.E. and Winer, M.L. 1955. Complete and spontaneous recovery from the bite of a blue krait snake (*Bungarus caeruleiis*). *American Journal of Tropical Medicine and Hygiene* 4: 1135–1137.

Isbister, G.K. and Brown, S.G.A. 2012. Bites in Australian snake-handlers – Australian snakebite project (ASP–15). *Queensland Journal of Medicine* 105: 1089–1095.

Keyler, D.E. 2008. Famous snake bites: fatal mistakes of four American herpetologists. *Journal of Medical Toxicology* 4: 48.

Martin, W.H. 1993. Reproduction of the timber rattlesnake (*Crotalus horridus*) in the Appalachian Mountains. *Journal of Herpetology* 27: 133–143.

Mendyk, R.W. 2024. Just how common (or uncommon) are fatal snakebites in zoological parks and related facilities? *Herpetological Review* 54: 524–528.

Mirtschin, P. 2006. The pioneers of venom production for Australian antivenoms. *Toxicon* 48: 899–918.

Stradling, A. 1894. A bad five minutes with a python. Part 1. *The Boy's Own Paper* 17: 12.

Sutherland, S. 1998. *A venomous life*. Hyland House, South Melbourne.

Chapter 12. New methods, new challenges

Botelho, L.M., Da Silva, A.K., Machado, I.F., Sazima, I. and Muscat, E. 2023. A water snake uses the tail and body to scan for fish prey in tide pools. *Herpetological Bulletin* 165: 39–40.

Brons, H.A. 1882. Notes on the habits of some western snakes. *American Naturalist* 16: 564–567.

Camayo, R.A. and Zuniga-Baos, J.A. 2022. Skin secretions from the Velvet Swamp Snake *Erythrolampus typhlus*. *The Herpetological Bulletin* 162: 39–40.

Charas, M. 1673. *New experiments upon the vipers, with exquisite remedies that may be drawn from them, as well as for the cure of their bitings, as for that of other maladies*. J. Martyn, Printer to the Royal Society.

Clayton, J. 1694. On the beasts and serpents of Virginia. *Philosophical Transactions of the Royal Society of London* 18: 121–135.

Crowe-Riddell, J.M., Simões, B.F., Partridge, J.C., Hunt, D.M., Delean, S., Schwerdt, J.G., Breen, J., Ludington, A., Gower, D.J. and Sanders, K.L. 2019. Phototactic tails: evolution and molecular basis of a novel sensory trait in seasnakes. *Molecular Ecology* 28: 2013–2028.

Dubey, S., Brown, G.P., Madsen, T. and Shine, R. 2008. Male-biased dispersal in a tropical Australian snake (*Stegonotus cucullatus*, Colubridae). *Molecular Ecology* 17: 3506–3514.

Dubey, S., Brown, G.P., Madsen, T. and Shine, R. 2009. Sexual selection favours large body size in males of a tropical snake (*Stegonotus cucullatus*, Colubridae). *Animal Behaviour* 77: 177–182.

Durso, A.M. *et al*., 2021. Citizen science and online data: opportunities and challenges for snake ecology and action against snakebite. *Toxicon* 9–10: 100071

Glover, T. 1676. An account of Virginia, its situation, temperature, productions, inhabitants, and their manner of planting and ordering tobacco etc. communicated by Mr Thomas Glover, an ingenious chirurgion that hath lived some years in that country. *Philosophical Transactions of the Royal Society London* 11: 623–636.

Greene, H.W. and Burghardt, G.M. 1978. Behavior and phylogeny: constriction in ancient and modern snakes. *Science* 200: 74–77.

Hutchinson, D.A., Mori, A., Savitzky, A.H., Burghardt, G.M., Wu, X., Meinwald, J. and Schroeder, F.C. 2007. Dietary sequestration of defensive steroids in nuchal glands of the Asian snake *Rhabdophis tigrinus*. *Proceedings of the National Academy of Sciences USA* 104: 2265–2270.

Jones, T.R. 1845. *The natural history of animals (invertebrates only), being the substance of three courses of lectures as Fullerian Professor.* John Van Voorst, London.

Krefft, G. 1869. Descriptions of new Australian snakes. *Proceedings of the Zoological Society London* 1869: 318–322.

Lane, A. and Shine, A. 2011. Intraspecific variation in the direction and degree of sex-biased dispersal among sea-snake populations. *Molecular Ecology* 20: 1870–1876.

Linnaeus. 1735. *Systema Naturae*. Laurentii Salvii, Stockholm.

Maritz, R.A. and Maritz, B. 2020. Sharing for science: high-resolution trophic interactions revealed rapidly by social media. *PeerJ* 8: e9485.

Nankivell, J.H., Maryan, B., Bush, B.G. and Hutchinson, M.N. 2023. Whip it into shape: revision of the *Demansia psammophis* (Schlegel, 1837) complex (Squamata: Elapidae), with a description of a new species from central Australia. *Zootaxa* 5311: 301–339.

Phipson, H.M. 1887. The poisonous snakes of the Bombay prefecture. *Journal of the Bombay Natural History Society* 1887: 244–250.

Rasmussen, A.R. 2002. Phylogenetic analysis of the 'true' aquatic Elapid snakes Hydrophiinae (*sensu* Smith *et al*., 1977) indicates two independent radiations into water. *Steenstrupia* 27: 47–63.

Roll, U., Mittermeier, J.C., Diaz, G.I., Novosolov, M., Feldman, A., Itescu, Y., Meiri, S. and Grenyer, R. 2016. Using Wikipedia page views to explore the cultural importance of global reptiles. *Biological Conservation* 204: 42–50.

Scanlon, J.D. 1998. Prey-scaring by visual pursuit predators: a new use for tail-waving in snakes. *Herpetofauna* 28: 4–10.

Shine, R. 1991. *Australian snakes. A natural history*. Reed, Sydney.

Shine, R., Whiting, M. and Jolly, C. 2023. When legislation to protect wildlife becomes a problem. *Nature* 615: 394.

Udyawer, V., Goiran, C., Chateau, O., Coutures, E., Vigliola, L. and Shine, R. 2023. Long-distance movements of free-ranging seasnakes (*Hydrophis*, Elapidae). *Coral Reefs* 42: 987–996.

Ukuwela, K.D., de Silva, A., Fry, B.G., Lee, M.S. and Sanders, K.L. 2013. Molecular evidence that the deadliest seasnake *Enhydrina schistosa* (Elapidae: Hydrophiinae) consists of two convergent species. *Molecular Phylogenetics and Evolution* 66: 262–269.

Wall, F. and Evans, G. 1901. Notes on Ophidia collected in Burma from May to December 1899. *Journal of the Bombay Natural History Society* 13: 343–354.

Wallach, V., Wuester, W. and Broadley, D.G. 2009. In praise of subgenera: taxonomic status of cobras of the genus *Naja* Laurenti (Serpentes: Elapidae). *Zootaxa* 2236: 26–36.

Zimmerman, K. and Heatwole, H., 1990. Cutaneous photoreception: a new sensory mechanism for reptiles. *Copeia* 1990: 860–862.

Chapter 13. New combatants join the revolution

Baeckens, S., Blomberg, S. and Shine, R. 2020. Inclusive science: ditch archaic terms. *Nature* 580: 185.

Bell, R. and Prates, I. 2021. Bertha Maria Júlia Lutz. *Ichthyology & Herpetology* 109: 910–911.

Burger, J. and Zappalorti, R.T. 2011. *The Northern Pine Snake (*Pituophis melanoleucus*) in New Jersey: its life history, behavior and conservation*. Nova Science Publishers, New York.

Chuliver, M., Grosso, J., Fontanarrosa, G., Fratani, J., Paola Ferraro, D., Duport-Bru, A.S., Gabriela Schneider, R., Dolores Casagranda, M., Pereyra, L., Vicente, N. and José Salica, M. 2021. Gender inequities in herpetology:

the case of the Argentine community. *Cuadernos de Herpetología* 35: 195–205.

Cyriac, V.P., Dharwardkar, S., Mital, A. and Mohan, A.V. 2022. 70 years of herpetology in India: insights into shifts in focal research areas and gender ratios among authors. *Amphibia-Reptilia* 43: 141–153.

Davidson, J.P. 1997. *The bone sharp: the life of Edward Drinker Cope*. The Academy of Natural Sciences of Philadelphia, Philadelphia.

Georgiou, P., Zanos, P., Mou, T.C.M., An, X., Gerhard, D.M., Dryanovski, D.I., Potter, L.E., Highland, J.N., Jenne, C.E., Stewart, B.W. and Pultorak, K.J. 2022. Experimenters' sex modulates mouse behaviors and neural responses to ketamine via corticotropin releasing factor. *Nature Neuroscience* 25: 1191–1200.

Goiran, C. and Shine, R. 2019. Grandmothers and deadly snakes: an unusual project in 'citizen science'. *Ecosphere* 10: e02877.

Grosso, J., Fratani, J., Fontanarrosa, G., Chuliver, M., Duport-Bru, A.S., Schneider, R.G., Casagranda, M.D., Ferraro, D.P., Vicente, N., Salica, M.J. and Pereyra, L. 2021. Male homophily in South American herpetology: one of the major processes underlying the gender gap in publications. *Amphibia-Reptilia* 42: 407–418.

Hamidy, A., Arida, E., Maireda, N.L., Herlambang, A.E.N., Riyanto, A., Shine, R. and Natusch, D.J. 2024. Sexual dimorphism and reproductive biology of commercially harvested oriental rat snakes (*Ptyas mucosa*: Colubridae) from West Java. *Australian Journal of Zoology* 72: ZO23030.

Jackson, K. 2008. *Mean and lowly things: snakes, science, and survival in the Congo*. Harvard University Press, Massachusetts.

May, P.G., Farrell, T.M., Heulett, S.T., Pilgrim, M.A., Bishop, L.A., Spence, D.J., Rabatsky, A.M., Campbell, M.G., Aycrigg, A.D. and Richardson, W.E. 1996. Seasonal abundance and activity of a rattlesnake (*Sistrurus miliarius barbouri*) in central Florida. *Copeia* 1996: 389–401.

Mendelson III, J.R. 2022. What happens when a field biologist becomes disabled? *Herpetological Review* 53: 64–66.

Mervosh, S. 2018. Turtle researcher's award rescinded after he uses racy photos of women in presentation. *New York Times*, 16 July 2018. https://www.nytimes.com/2018/07/16/us/turtle-researcher-women-bikinis-richard-vogt.html, accessed 25 July 2020.

Nielsen, M.W., Alegria, S., Börjeson, L., Etzkowitz, H., Falk-Krzesinski, H.J., Joshi, A., Leahey, E., Smith-Doerr, L., Williams Woolley, A. and Schiebinger, L. 2017. Gender diversity leads to better science. *Proceedings of the National Academy of Sciences USA* 114: 1740–1742.

Parenti, L.R. and Wake, M.H. 2016. Evolution of the role of women in the American Society of Ichthyologists and Herpetologists. *Copeia* 104: 594–601.

Perry, G., Muths, E., Crump, M., Distel, C., Hansen, R., Harvey, M., Rowe, J., Walls, S. and Woodley, S. 2020. Increasing diversity and inclusivity in herpetology: small but critical steps from the editors of herpetological journals. *Herpetological Review* 51: 765–766.

Pope, C.H. 1961. *The giant snakes: the natural history of the boa constrictor, the anaconda, and the largest pythons, including comparative facts about other snakes and basic information on reptiles in general*. Knopf, New York.

Rivas, J.A. 2020. *Anaconda: the secret life of the world's largest snake*. Oxford University Press, USA.

Rock, K.N., Barnes, I.N., Deyski, M.S., Glynn, K.A., Milstead, B.N., Rottenborn, M.E., Andre, N.S., Dekhtyar, A., Dekhtyar, O. and Taylor, E.N. 2021. Quantifying the gender gap in authorship in herpetology. *Herpetologica* 77: 1–13.

Salerno, P.E., Páez-Vacas, M., Guayasamin, J.M. and Stynoski, J.L. 2019. Male principal investigators (almost) don't publish with women in ecology and zoology. *PLoS One* 14: e0218598.

Ward-Fear, G., Balanggarra Rangers, Pearson, D., Bruton, M. and Shine, R. 2019. Sharper eyes see shyer lizards: collaboration with indigenous peoples can alter the outcomes of conservation research. *Conservation Letters* 12: e12643.

Whitaker, R. 2019. Snakebite mitigation project of the Madras Crocodile Bank/Centre for Herpetology, India: background and a brief summary of activities. *Transactions of the Royal Society of Tropical Medicine and Hygiene* 113: 818–819.

Whitaker, R. and Andrews, H.V. 1996. Snake capture and venom extraction in Tamil Nadu, India. In *Assessing the sustainability of uses of wild species. Case studies and initial assessment procedure* (R. and C. Prescott-Allen, editors), pp. 40–46. Occasional Paper of the IUCN Species Survival Commission No. 12.

Wilson, D.S. 1998. Patterns in publishing in three north American herpetological journals: gender biases. *Herpetologica* 54: S35–S42.

Yang *et al.* 2022. Gender-diverse teams produce more novel and high-impact scientific ideas. *Proceedings of the National Academy of Sciences USA* 119: e2200841119.

Index

C

D

H

I

J

K

L

Q

R

S

T

U

V

W

Y

Z

OTHER NATURAL HISTORY TITLES BY REED NEW HOLLAND INCLUDE:

Snakes Without Borders
Rick Shine
ISBN 9781921073700

A Complete Guide to Reptiles of Australia Seventh Edition
Steve K Wilson and Gerry Swan
ISBN 9781760796457

A Field Guide to Reptiles of Queensland
Third Edition
Steve K Wilson
ISBN 9781925546842

A Field Guide to Reptiles of New South Wales
Fourth Edition
Gerry Swan
ISBN 9781925546835

A Field Guide to Reptiles and Frogs of the ACT
Brian La Rance, Wesley Read and Bridget Lunn
ISBN 9781760796181

A Field Guide to Reptiles and Frogs of the Red Centre
Chris Williams, Rex Neindorf and Brian Bush
ISBN 9781760796259

Reed Concise Guide: Snakes of Australia
Gerry Swan
ISBN 9781921517891

Reed Concise Guide: Lizards of Australia
Steve K Wilson
ISBN 9781925546576

What Snake Is That? Second Edition
Gerry Swan and Steve K Wilson
ISBN 9781760796433

What Lizard Is That? Second Edition
Steve K Wilson and Gerry Swan
ISBN 9781760796891

Tadpoles and Frogs of Australia Second Edition
Marion Anstis
ISBN 9781925546019

Urban Reptiles
Australian Herpetological Society
Chelsea Maier and Chris Williams
ISBN 9781925546934

Incredible Lizards
Steve K Wilson
ISBN 9781925546989

A Tribute to the Reptiles and Amphibians of Australia and New Zealand
Australian Herpetological Society
Edited by Chris Williams and Chelsea Maier
ISBN 9781925546590

Reptiles and Amphibians of Australia, New Zealand and New Guinea
Australian Herpetological Society
Edited by Chris Williams and Chelsea Maier
ISBN 9781925546736

Crocodiles of the World
Colin Stevenson
ISBN 9781925546811

For details of these books and hundreds of other Natural History titles see newhollandpublishers.com

and follow ReedNewHolland and NewHollandPublishers on Facebook

---

Published in 2025 by Reed New Holland Publishers

newhollandpublishers.com

A record of this book is held at the National Library of Australia.

ISBN 9781760796976

Managing Director: Fiona Schultz
General Manager: Olga Dementiev
Publisher and Project Editor: Simon Papps
Designer: Andrew Davies
Production Director: Arlene Gippert

Keep up with Reed New Holland and New Holland Publishers
NewHollandPublishers
@newhollandpublishers and @ReedNewHolland

Front cover: Green Pythons (*Morelia viridis*) are yellow or red when they hatch, but turn bright green as they age. PIXABAY

Page 1: A Red Diamond Rattlesnake (*Crotalus ruber*) warns the photographer to keep his distance. NICHOLAS HESS

Pages 2–3: Indonesian Pit Viper (*Trimeresurus insularis*), Komodo Island. PIXABAY